AIR QUALITY A TO Z:

A Directory of Air Quality data for the United Kingdom in the 1990s

Victoria Bertorelli and Richard Derwent
Atmospheric Processes Research Branch
Meteorological Office
Bracknell

June 1995

Compiled at the request of the Air Quality Division of the Department of the Environment under contract number PECD 7/12/182

Introduction

Air quality is all-pervading and exerts an important impact on human health, on ecosystems, on buildings and materials, and on the overall quality of life. In spite of the progress made in combating air pollution in recent decades and the promise of significant reductions in many pollutants over the medium and long term, much remains to be done to improve air quality further.

The Air Quality Division of the Department of the Environment has identified the public availability and dissemination of air quality data as a key priority task. They have set up air quality monitoring networks and arranged for the widespread dissemination of air quality data and bulletins to the media and general public and to local authorities and other agencies involved in air quality management. The vast majority of air quality data, however, are not amenable to these automatic data handling procedures but are nonetheless valuable in the assessment and management of air quality. Air quality data play an important role in local air quality appraisal, environmental impact assessment and the regulation of the emissions to the atmosphere from industrial plants. This data compilation has been prepared to assist those involved in planning, regulating or managing local air quality.

The compilation of the Air Quality A to Z has been commissioned by Air Quality Division to provide for widespread dissemination of air quality data on the widest possible range of substances in the air, in suspended particulate matter and in rain in the UK. All of the measurement programmes have been funded either fully or partially by the Department of the Environment. The patient help given by the department's research contractors is gratefully acknowledged.

The compilation contains air quality data for 249 pollutants. Entries are provided for all the main classes of trace gases and air pollutants including greenhouse gases, ozone-depleting chemicals, toxic and aggressive urban pollutants, volatile organic compounds, trace elements, toxic organic micropollutants and polycyclic aromatic hydrocarbons. Data are provided for rural, urban, kerbside and industrial locations where they are available. Both the IUPAC and common names are used for organic compounds and alternative names are given where appropriate.

Acknowledgements

This compilation of Air Quality data could not have been completed without the patient help of a number of individuals and institutions listed below. The support and encouragement of Air Quality Division, Department of the Environment through the Air Quality Research Programme (Contract number: PECD 7/12/182) is deeply appreciated.

Steve Baker at NETCEN for supplying trace element data.

Geoff Broughton and Jonathon Bower at NETCEN for supplying full calendar year statistical tables on O_3, SO_2, CO, NO_2 and NO.

Rachel Burgess of the School of Environmental Sciences, University of East Anglia for supplying hydrocarbon data collected at West Beckham and Great Dun Fell.

Glenn Campbell at NETCEN for his help in providing data from the Secondary Precipitation Network.

Peter Coleman and John Branson at NETCEN for their help in providing and interpreting data on TOMPS (Toxic Organic Micropollutants).

Geoff Dollard, Trevor Davies and Peter Dumitrean at NETCEN for providing data on hydrocarbons.

Robert Field at NETCEN for providing VOC and PAH data at Exhibition Road, London from the Imperial College roadside monitoring site.

Colin Gillham, formerly of Warren Spring Laboratory, for providing smoke and SO_2 data.

Professor Roy Harrison and Toby Smith for supplying PAH data.

Brian Jones at NETCEN, for providing three-month running means for hydrocarbons at the rural site near Harwell, Oxfordshire.

David Lee at NETCEN for supplying ammonia data from the Secondary Precipitation Chemistry diffusion tube network, aerosol data from the Review Group on Acid Rain and trace element data.

Professor Michael Pilling, Alastair Lewis and Suzanne Hassoun at the School of Chemistry, University of Leeds for their help in providing hydrocarbon, oxygenates and PAH data together with their structures.

Alison Loader at NETCEN for supplying smoke and SO_2 data.

Gordon McInnes, formerly of Warren Spring Laboratory, for supplying multi-element data and central London sulphate aerosol data.

Steve Moorcroft at TBV Science for supplying PM_{10} and EUN monitoring network site data.

David Oram of the School of Environmental Sciences, University of East Anglia for supplying methyl iodide data.

Peter Simmonds at INSCON for supplying data on the radiatively active and ozone-depleting gases.

Ken Stevenson at NETCEN for help with site information.

Keith Vincent at NETCEN for supplying rural SO_2 data.

Methods of measurement were taken from Askey et al. (1995), Bower et al. (1989), Bower et al. (1994), Broughton et al. (1993), Brown et al. (1995), Campbell et al. (1994b), Cawse et al.(1994), Cvitaš and Kley (1994), Derwent et al. (1994), Devenish (1986), DoE (1994a), DoE (1994b), Downing et al. (1994), Hall (1986), Lee et al. (1994), Smith and Harrison (1994), Solberg et al. (1994), Willis (1994).

Site descriptions were taken from Bower et al. (1994), Brown et al. (1995), Campbell et al. (1994), Cawse et al. (1994), Clayton et al. (1992), Cvitaš and Kley (1994), Davis (1993), Derwent et al. (1994), Derwent et al. (1995), Devenish (1986), Hall (1986), Pattenden (1974), PORG (1987), PORG (1993), Smith and Harrison (1994), Willis (1994).

Structures were created with the help of the CRC Handbook of Chemistry and Physics using ChemWindow 3 chemistry drawing software.

Synonyms and chemical formulae were taken from Chambers Science and Technology Dictionary and the CRC Handbook of Chemistry and Physics.

Tables were created using Microsoft Word for Windows version 6.0. Graphs were created using Microsoft Excel version 5.0 and Lotus 1-2-3 Release 4.

The patient help of the Publication Section of the Meteorological Office with the preparation of this compilation of data is acknowledged.

A copy of the A to Z on CD-ROM is available from the authors.

Bibliography

Atkins D.H.F., Lee D.S. (1992). The distribution of ammonia in the United Kingdom. Report number: AEA-EE-0330. Harwell Laboratory, Oxfordshire.

Baker S.J., Cawse P.A., Page R.A. (1988). Atmospheric measurements of lead and cadmium in Wales, 1984-1987. Report No: AERE R 13311. Harwell Laboratory, Oxfordshire.

Bartle K.D., Denha A., Hassoun S., Kupiszewska D., Lewis A.C., Pilling M.J. (1995). A catalogue of urban hydrocarbons, January to December 1994. Report number: PECD7/12/111. School of Chemistry, University of Leeds.

Booker J. (1993). UK rural air quality monitoring network:evaluation of network performance. Report number: TBV/AQ/757. TBV Science, Lansdowne Road, Croydon.

Bower J.S., Lampert J.E., Stevenson K.J., Atkins D.H.F., Law D.V. (1989). Results of a national survey of ambient nitrogen dioxide levels in urban areas of the United Kingdom. Report number: LR 726 (AP) M. Warren Spring Laboratory, Stevenage, Herts.

Bower J.S., Broughton G.F.J., Willis P.G., Clark H. (1995). Air pollution in the UK: 1993/94. Report number : AEA/CSR/1033/C, ISBN 0 85356 422 1. AEA Technology, National Environmental Technology Centre, Culham Laboratory, Oxfordshire.

Broughton G.F.J., Bower J.S., Stevenson K.J., Lampert J.E., Sweeney B.P., Wilken J., Eaton S.W., Clark A.G., Willis P.G., Stacey B.R.W., Driver G.S., Laight S.E., Berwick R., Jackson M.S. (1993). Air quality in the UK: a summary of results from instrumented air monitoring networks in 1991/92. Report number: LR 941 (AP). Warren Spring Laboratory, Stevenage, Herts.

Brown J.R., Field R.A., Goldstone M.E., Lester J.N., Perry R. (1995). Polycyclic aromatic hydrocarbons in central London air in recent years. Submitted for publication.

Campbell G.W., Stedman J.R., Downing C.E.H., Vincent K.J., Hasler S.E., Davies M. (1994a). Acid Deposition in the United Kingdom: Data Report 1993. Report number : AEA/CS/16419029/001. AEA Technology, National Environmental Technology Centre, Culham Laboratory, Oxfordshire.

Campbell G.W., Stedman J.R., Stevenson K. (1994b). A survey of nitrogen dioxide concentrations in the United Kingdom using diffusion tubes, July to December 1991. *Atmospheric Environment* **28**, 477-486.

Carroll J.D., McInnes G. (1988). Multi-element and sulphate in particulate surveys: Summary of the eighth year's results (1983/84). Report number: LR 655 (AP)M. Warren Spring Laboratory, Stevenage, Herts.

Cawse P.A., Baker S.J., Law D.V. (1994). A survey of atmospheric trace elements in Great Britain. 1972-1991. Report number: AEA/CS/18358008/REMA-039. AEA Technology, National Environmental Technology Centre, Culham Laboratory, Oxfordshire.

Chambers Science and Technology Dictionary. (1988). General editor: Professor Peter M. B. Walker.

Clayton P., Davis B.J., Jones K., Jones P. (1992). Toxic organic micropollutants in urban air. Report number: LR 904 (AP). Warren Spring Laboratory, Stevenage, Herts.

CRC Handbook of Chemistry and Physics. (1969). Editor-in-chief: Dr Robert C. Weast.

Cunnold D.M., Fraser P.J., Weiss R.F., Prinn R.G., Simmonds P.G., Miller B.R., Alyea F.N., Crawford A.J. (1994). Global trends and annual releases of CCl_3F and CCl_2F_2 estimated from ALE/GAGE and other measurements from July 1978 to June 1991. *Journal of Geophysical Research*, **99**, 1107-1126.

Cvitaš T., Kley D. (1994). The TOR Network : A Description of TOR Measurement Stations. EUROTRAC, International Scientific Secretariat, Garmisch-Partenkirchen, Germany.

Davis B.J. (1993). Toxic organic micropollutants in the atmosphere and in deposition at certain sites in the UK. Report number: LR 997. Warren Spring Laboratory, Stevenage, Herts.

Derwent J., Dumitrean P., Chandler J., Davies T.J., Derwent R.G., Dollard G.J., Delaney M., Jones B.M.R., Nason P.D. (1994). A preliminary analysis of hydrocarbon monitoring data from an urban site. AEA report number: AEA/CS/18358030/005/ Issue 2. AEA Technology, National Environmental Technology Centre, Culham Laboratory, Oxfordshire.

Derwent R.G., Middleton D.R., Field R.A., Goldstone M.E., Lester J.N., Perry R. (1995). Analysis and interpretation of air quality data from an urban roadside location in Central London over the period from July 1991 to July 1992. *Atmospheric Environment* **29**, 923-946.

Derwent R.G., Simmonds P.G., Collins W.J. (1994). Ozone and carbon monoxide measurements at a remote maritime location, Mace Head, Ireland, from 1990 to 1992. *Atmospheric Environment* **28**, 2623-2637.

Devenish M. (1986). The United Kingdom precipitation composition monitoring networks. Warren Spring report: LR 584 (AP) M. Warren Spring Laboratory, Stevenage, Herts.

DoE. (1992). Digest of environmental and water statistics no.15. HMSO, London.

DoE. (1994a). Expert panel on air quality standards: carbon monoxide. HMSO, London.

DoE. (1994b). Expert panel on air quality standards: ozone. HMSO, London.

DoE. (1995). Air Quality: Meeting the Challenge. Department of the Environment, London.

Dollard G.J., Jones B.M.R., Nason P., Chandler J., Davies T., Dumitrean P. and Delaney M. (1993). The UK urban hydrocarbon monitoring network. AEA Report number: AEA-CS-18358030-01. AEA Technology, Harwell Laboratory, Oxfordshire.

Dollard G.J. (1994). UK hydrocarbon monitoring network : provisional data summaries. AEA report number: AEA-CS-118358030/06. AEA Technology, National Environmental Technology Centre, Culham Laboratory, Oxfordshire.

Dollard G., Broughton G., Dumitrean P., Stedman J., Campbell G., Davies T. (1995). Quality of urban air review group meeting-provisional hydrocarbon data summaries. AEA report number: AEA-CS-18358030/07. AEA Technology, National Environmental Technology Centre, Culham Laboratory, Oxfordshire.

Downing C.E.H., Campbell G.W., Bailey J.C. (1994). A survey of sulphur dioxide, ammonia and hydrocarbon concentrations in the United Kingdom, using diffusion tubes : July to December 1992. Report number: LR 964. Warren Spring Laboratory, Stevenage, Herts.

Hall D.J. (1986). The precipitation collector for use in the Secondary National Acid Deposition Network. Warren Spring report number: LR 561 (AP) M. Warren Spring Laboratory, Stevenage, Herts.

HMSO (1990). This Common Inheritance. Cmn 1200. H M Stationery Office, London.

Lee D.S., Garland J.A., Fox A.A. (1994). Atmospheric concentrations of trace elements in urban areas of the United Kingdom. *Atmospheric Environment* **28**, 2691-2713.

Lewis A. C., Bartle K. D., Pilling M. J. (1995). Monitoring the formation of derivative polycyclic aromatic compounds via transient pollution episodes. Submitted to *Environ. Sci. Technol.*

Oram D.E., Penkett S.A. (1993). Observations in Eastern England of elevated methyl iodide concentrations in air of Atlantic origin. *Atmospheric Environment* **28**, 1159-1174.

Pattenden N.J. (1974). Atmospheric concentrations and deposition rates of some trace elements measured in the Swansea-Neath-Port Talbot area. AERE Harwell report number: R-7729. HMSO, London.

PORG report (1987). Interim report : Ozone in the United Kingdom. United Kingdom Photochemical Oxidants Review Group, UKAEA, Harwell Laboratory, Oxfordshire.

PORG report (1993). Ozone in the United Kingdom. United Kingdom Photochemical Oxidants Review Group, UKAEA, Harwell Laboratory, Oxfordshire.

Schaug J., Pederson U., Skjelmoen J.E., Arnesen K. (1994). Data report 1992. Part 2: Monthly and seasonal summaries. Report number : EMEP/CCC-Report 5/94. Norwegian Institute for Air Research, Postboks 100, N-2007 Kjeller, Norway.

Simmonds P.G., Cunnold D.M., Dollard G.J., Davies T.J., McCulloch A., Derwent R.G. (1993). Evidence of the phase-out of CFC use in Europe over the period 1987-1990. *Atmospheric Environment*, **27A**, 1397-1407.

Smith D.J.T., Harrison R.M. (1994). Measurements of airborne concentrations of polynuclear aromatic hydrocarbons collected in Birmingham, UK. Institute of Public and Environmental Health, University of Birmingham.

Solberg S., Dye C., Schmidbauer N. (1994). VOC measurements 1993. Report number : EMEP/CCC-Report 3/94. Norwegian Institute for Air Research, Postboks 100, N-2007 Kjeller, Norway.

Willis P.G. (1994). The UK National Air Monitoring Networks, 1994. AEA report number: LR 1004 (AP). NETCEN, Culham Laboratory, Oxfordshire.

Contents

Contents

Contents

Contents

Contents

Contents

Contents

Contents

Contents

Contents

Contents

Contents

Site Information

Location	OS Grid Reference	Sample Height (m)	Description
Achanarras	ND 151550	1.75	Open moorland, farm pastures. Altitude 210 m.
Altrincham	SJ 7588	6.0	GPO depot, Altrincham, Greater Manchester. Urban residential.
Aston Hill	SO 298901	3.0	Rural, Mid-Wales. On the summit of a hill with clear views of surrounding arable farmland. Altitude 370 m.
Balquhidder	NN 521206	1.75	Open sheep pasture at loch-side. Altitude 135 m.
Bannisdale	NY 515043	1.75	Open moorland, sheep grazing. Altitude 265 m.
Barcombe Mills	TQ 437149	1.75	Water pumping site. Altitude 10 m.
Barnsley	SE 342067	10.0	Barnsley, S. Yorkshire. Urban background. Municipal building on the edge of a coal mining town.
Beddgelert	SH 556518	1.75	Upland hill farming in very open moorland. Altitude 358 m.
Bedwas	-	-	Urban site in Mid Glamorgan, Wales.
Belfast A	J 357740 (N.Ireland)	4.0	Belfast East. Urban background. Situated in a first floor room of a recreation centre in a residential district.
Belfast B	-	3.5	Belfast centre. Urban city centre. Pedestrianised street (Lombard Street), 25 m from major road.
Belfast C	J 333726 (N.Ireland)	3.0	Queen's university. Urban residential. Address : Rear of No.7 College Gardens (Garage, access via Elmwood Avenue and Elmwood Mews), Belfast.
Bexley	TQ 518763	3.5	Whitehall Lane, Bexley. Suburban.
Billingham	NZ 470237	5.0	Cleveland. Urban industrial. Residential area. A council depot with a large complex of chemical / manufacturing plants 1-3 km to the south.
Bircotes	SK 629922	-	A residential area 1 km north of a colliery and 2 km west of the A1(M).
Birmingham A	SP 064868	3.5	Birmingham centre. Urban city centre. Pedestrianised area (Centenary Square), 100 m from major road, 10 m from small car park.
Birmingham B	SP 115888	3.5	Birmingham East. Urban residential. Located in the playground of a junior school (Wardend School) approx. 20 m from the nearest building and 5 km north east of the city centre.
Birmingham C	-	-	Kerbside site.

Location	OS Grid Reference	Sample Height (m)	Description
Bloomsbury	TQ 302820	3.5	Bloomsbury, London. Urban city centre. Land at Russell Square Gardens (south east quadrant). 35 m from kerbside.
Bottesford	SK 797376	3.5	Rural, Nottinghamshire. 1km from Bottesford village on open rural pasture. 1km south of A52. Altitude 32 m.
Bowland	SD 493578	1.5	Bowland Fells, close to Lancaster University, Lancashire. Established September 1992. Used as rural site in TOMPs network. Also known as Hazelrigg. Altitude 92 m.
Brent	TQ 213866	2.5	Neasden public library, London. Urban residential.
Bridge Place	TQ 289788	8.0	Urban background, London. Second floor office overlooking backstreet near Victoria station. Altitude 20 m. Moved from Central London Laboratories, Minster House, 1990 which in turn moved there from Endell Street in 1976.
Bristol A	ST 599729	3.0	Bristol East. Urban residential. Address: Hannah More C of E School, Jubilee Street, Bristol.
Bristol B	-	3.5	Bristol city centre.
Bush	NT 245635	3.0	Rural, South Scotland. On a flat plain between hills. Site surrounded by open and forested land. ITE buildings nearby. Altitude 180 m.
Cambridge	-	-	Bridge Street, Cambridge. Monitoring equipment stored in a shop basement with inlets at kerbside street level.
Canvey	TQ 782847	3.0	Rural, 2 km from oil refinery. Altitude 3 m.
Cardiff A	ST 184765	3.5	Cardiff centre. Urban city centre. Pedestrianised street (Frederick Street), 190 m from major road.
Cardiff B	ST 193773	4.0	Cardiff East. Urban residential. Address: City Analysts Laboratory, City of Cardiff Environmental Services, Croft Street, Cardiff. CF2 3DY
Cardiff C	ST 184772	30.0	Cardiff university, TOMPs site. Altitude 10 m.
Cardiff D	ST 148773	-	Kerbside site on Queen's Street, Cardiff, outside Burton's tailors.
Central London	TQ 291790	-	Central London Laboratories, Minster House, Vauxhall Bridge Road. Moved to Bridge Place 1990. Altitude 20 m.
Chilton	SU 474863	3.0	Identical to Harwell site but implies measurements taken under a different contract.
Chilworth	SU 405183	-	Rural site in Hampshire. Research institute buildings nearby.

Location	OS Grid Reference	Sample Height (m)	Description
Compton	SU 512804	1.75	Rough meadow, near pumping station. Altitude 105 m.
Cottered	TL 322283	-	Rural site at Cottered Warren Farm, Hertfordshire.
Cow Green Reservoir	NY 817298	1.75	Very open moorland. Altitude 510 m.
Cromwell Road	TQ 264789	2.5	London kerbside. Located at the kerbside of a busy arterial road in Central London. Traffic density approx 60,000 vehicles per day. Altitude 20 m.
Driby	TF 386744	1.75	Sheep pasture. Altitude 47 m.
East Kilbride	NS 638534	-	Open area in new town.
Edgbaston	SP 050836	16.0	Urban sampling site on the roof of the three storey Radiation Centre Building at the north side of the Birmingham University campus, Edgbaston. The height of the building is approximately 15 m, located about 300 m from the Bristol Road, one of Birmingham's busiest spine roadways.
Edinburgh A	NT 257730	4.0	Edinburgh Medical School. Urban residential. Address: New Medical Extension, Medical School, University of Edinburgh, Teviot Place, Edinburgh.
Edinburgh B	-	3.5	Edinburgh city centre. Urban parkland (East Princes Street Gardens), 35 m from major road
Eltham	TQ 440747	5.0	Eltham, London. Urban residential. Address: The Environmental Curriculum Centre, 77 Bexley Road, Eltham, London. SE9 2PE.
Eskdalemuir	NT 235028	3.0	Rural, South Scotland. Situated on open moorland adjacent (500 m) to Met. Office Observatory. Altitude 259 m.
Exhibition Road	-	5.0	Main arterial road in South Kensington, Central London, 5 m from kerbside. Road runs north-south and is lined by buildings to a height of about 15 m. Traffic density moderate, reaching 1500-1750 vehicles per hour at peak times. Site located halfway between junctions with Cromwell Road and Kensington Gore, both significantly busier roads.
Featherstone	SE 429195	-	A residential area 1 km south of a colliery.
Flatford Mill	TM 077333	1.75	Open meadow, near River Stour. Altitude 5 m.
Flixton	SJ 746945	6.0	Flixton House, Flixton Road, Trafford, Greater Manchester. Urban residential.

Location	OS Grid Reference	Sample Height (m)	Description
Glasgow A	NS 595653	8.0	Urban background. Central city near-kerbside location (8 m from road). Partially residential area, but with large traffic volumes in surrounding areas.
Glasgow B	-	-	Hope St., Glasgow.
Glasgow C	-	-	St. Mungo's Academy, Glasgow.
Glazebury	SJ 690959	3.0	Cheshire. Suburban. On open flat, ground in horticultural area between conurbations.
Glen Dye	NO 642864	1.75	Open moorland. Altitude 85 m.
Goonhilly	SW 723214	1.75	Open moorland, satellite tracking station. Altitude 108 m.
Great Dun Fell	NY 711322	4.0	Rural mountain peak, Cumbria. Near mountain summit and often above the cloud base. Altitude 847 m.
Harrow	TQ 43874	-	Outer London, residential area, light industry.
Harwell (Chilton)	SU 474863	3.0	Altitude 137 m. In central southern England, about 90 km from the English Channel.The sampling apparatus is situated on the Western perimeter of the Atomic Energy Research Establishment, where a meteorological station and monitoring for radioactive fallout has been established for some years. The surroundings are predominantly rural, with large areas devoted to cereal cultivation. The busy A34 is nearby.
High Muffles	SE 776939	3.0	Rural, North Yorkshire Moors. Hilly moorland and forestry plantation. Altitude 267 m.
Hillsborough Forest	J 243577 (N.Ireland)	-	Open arable, cows graze in summer.
Hull	SE 105293	3.5	Queen's Gardens, Guildhall Road, Hull city centre.
Islington	TQ 321831	-	Commercial, inner city area.
Jenny Hurn	SK 816986	1.75	Open arable land. Altitude 4 m.
Ladybower	SK 164892	3.0	Rural, Derbyshire. Adjacent to forested area overlooking reservoir in Peak National Park.
Lambeth	TQ 320727	-	Thurlow Park School, Elcourt Road, Lambeth, London. Urban residential.
Leicester	SK 587040	3.5	New Walk centre, Welford Road, Leicester city centre.
Leeds	SE 299343	-	Leeds market, Market Buildings, Vicar Lane, West Yorkshire. Urban city centre.
Liverpool	SJ 349908	3.5	St.John's Gardens, Liverpool urban city centre, Merseyside.
Llyn Brianne	SN 822507	1.75	Open moorland, upland hill farming. Altitude 420 m.

Location	OS Grid Reference	Sample Height (m)	Description
Loch Dee	NX 468779	1.75	Open moorland. Altitude 230 m.
London	TQ 301792	35.0	TOMPs site, roof of Romney House (Department of the Environment). Altitude 5 m.
Lough Navar	H 065545 (N.Ireland)	2.0	Rural, Northern Ireland. Clearing within a forestry plantation near Forestry Offices. Altitude 130 m.
Lullington Heath	TQ 538016	3.0	Rural, East Sussex. On a high plateau 5 km from the south coast. Immediate area is a NCC heathland. Altitude 120 m
Mace Head	IL740320 (Irish grid)	20.0	County Galway. Sited on the west coast of Ireland, immediately adjacent to beach/cliff. Altitude 10m.
Manchester A	SJ 838980	25.0	Urban background. City centre but elevated location. 20 m from nearest road, 150 m from large thoroughfare (St. Peter's Square).
Manchester B	SJ 834982	30.0	On roof of law courts, TOMPs site. Altitude 30 m.
Manchester C	SJ 817876	-	Kerbside site.
Manchester City North	SJ 876985	2.5	Site in Bradford, Greater Manchester. Ashton New Road, Clayton. Industrial/residential.
Manchester City South	SJ 849961	4.5	Chest clinic, Denmark Road, Rusholme, Greater Manchester. Urban residential.
Middlesbrough	NZ 505194	4.0	Longlands College, TOMPs site, established late April 1992. Urban background. Residential area away from the immediate influence of motor traffic. Address: Longlands College of Further Education, Douglas Street, Middlesbrough, Cleveland. Altitude 8m.
Motherwell	-	-	Civic centre, Motherwell.
Newcastle A	NZ 251649	3.5	Newcastle centre. Urban city centre. Land at Princess Square (north-side), 40 m from road.
Newcastle B	NZ 241688	-	Site at Gosforth High School, Newcastle.
North Petherton	ST 292329	-	Rural site in Somerset, close to the M5.
North Tyneside	NZ 309677	-	Urban site at Holy Cross School, Wallsend.
Plynlimon	SN 823854	1.75	Open moorland, upland hill farming. Altitude 410 m.
Polloch	NM 792689	1.75	Open moorland, in forest area.
Port Talbot	-	-	Urban site at Velindre, near Port Talbot, West Galamorgan, Wales.
Preston Montford	SJ 432143	1.75	Field adjacent to study centre. Altitude 70 m.
Queensferry	-	-	Urban site in Clwyd, Wales.
Redesdale	NY 833954	1.75	Open moorland, very open sheep farming land. Altitude 240m.
River Mharcaidh	NH 876052	1.75	Moorland, in forestry SW Cairngorms. Altitude 366m.

Location	OS Grid Reference	Sample Height (m)	Description
Rugeley	SK 043173	-	Urban. Sited at a municipal building on the edge of a small town.
Sheffield	SK 403905	3.0	Sheffield, South Yorkshire. Urban industrial. Near community centre in a mixed residential / industrial area 200 m from the M1.
Sibton	TM 364719	3.0	Rural, Suffolk. Open flat cereal farmland. Woodland to the north west. Altitude 46 m.
Southampton	SU 429121	3.5	Northam Road, Southampton city centre.
Stevenage	TL 237225	8.0	Warren Spring Laboratory, Stevenage. Suburban. Sited on the edge of a residential new town near a light industrial estate. 100 m east of A1(M) motorway. Topography flat. Location equipment moved to Middlesbrough after 9/4/92. Altitude 90 m.
Stoke Ferry	TL 700988	1.75	Grassed land at water treatment works. Alt. 15 m.
Strath Vaich	NH 347750	3.0	North Scotland. Remote hilly moorland used for sheep grazing, sited at a dam. Altitude 270 m.
Styrrup	SK 606898 moved to SK 561906	-	Altitude 15 m. Situated in the East Midlands, 2 km to the south-west of Bircotes colliery and 9 km to the north-east of Dinnington colliery. The sampling station is placed in a rural area, but industrial influences are very strong and 25 km to the west lies Sheffield industrial complex with steelworks and coal mining. Until 1982, the station was accomodated at the Institute of Geological Sciences groundwater research compound which was then closed. Consequently the station was moved to Sandbeck Park which is 4.5 km to the west of Styrrup.
Sunderland	-	14.0	Urban background site. John Street, Sunderland. Commercial and residential with river and port industries from north west and east.
Swansea	SS 651937	-	Mount Pleasant site, hospital grounds, Swansea city centre.
Thorganby	SE 676428	-	Open meadow and arable land.
Trebanos	SN 712023	-	Altitude 23 m. In the grounds of a sewage works in the River Tawe valley, 11 km inland from Swansea Bay, West Glamorgan. The site is just on the outer limit of the industrial zone, which has major activities of oil refining at Llandarcy and steelworks at Port Talbot. Smelting of nickel takes place at Clydach, only 2 km to the south-west of Trebanos sampling station.

Location	OS Grid Reference	Sample Height (m)	Description
Tycanol Wood	SN 093364	1.75	Open moorland. Altitude 205 m.
UCL	TQ 299822	4.0	University College, London. Kerbside. Address: Department of Geography, University College London, 26 Bedford Way. London. WC1H 0AP
Walsall	SO 995985	10.0	Walsall, West Midlands. Urban industrial. Alumwell Comprehensive School, Primley Avenue. 200 m to the west of the M6 (traffic flow approx 70,000 vehicles per day). Residential area with metal smelting plant 500 m to the south.
Wardlow Hay Cop	SK177739	1.75	Open moorland. Altitude 350 m.
Wasthills	SP 038762	10.0	Rural sampling site on the roof of Wasthills House, which stands in large grounds and is surrounded by farmland. It is located 2 km beyond the southernmost boundary of the Birmingham conurbation, in the county of Hereford and Worcester.
West Beckham	-	-	Flat agricultural land, with both livestock and arable farming. 5 km from North Sea, alt. 87 m.
West London	TQ 251788	7.0	Earls Court, London. Urban background. Located in a municipal depot in a partially residential area bounded on all sides by major roads. 90 m from Warwick Road.
Wharley Croft	NY 698247	3.0	Rural, Cumbria. Within valley at the base of Great Dun Fell. Altitude 206 m.
Whiteadder	NT 664633	1.75	Open moorland. Altitude 250 m.
Woburn	SP 964361	-	Pasture site in Bedfordshire.
Wray	SD 619678	-	Rural site in Cumbria. Altitude 100 m.
Wraymires	SD 362974	1.5	Altitude 84 m. A rural site by the side of Esthwaite Water, near Lake Windermere in Cumbria, about 25 km from the Irish Sea and 32 km to the north-east of Barrow-in-Furness, where there is shipbuilding industry. At 40 km to the south of Wraymires is the Heysham oil refinery. The station is considered to be fairly clean with moderate maritime influence and a high annual rainfall; there is hardly any arable farming in the area which might give rise to local soil dust.
Wrexham	-	-	Urban site in Clwyd, Wales.
WSL	TL 237225	8.0	Warren Spring Laboratory, Stevenage.
Yarner Wood	SX 867890	3.0	Devon. Remote. Undulating moorland with semi-natural broadleaved woodland. Sited in a nature reserve. Altitude 119 m.

Acenaphthene in air

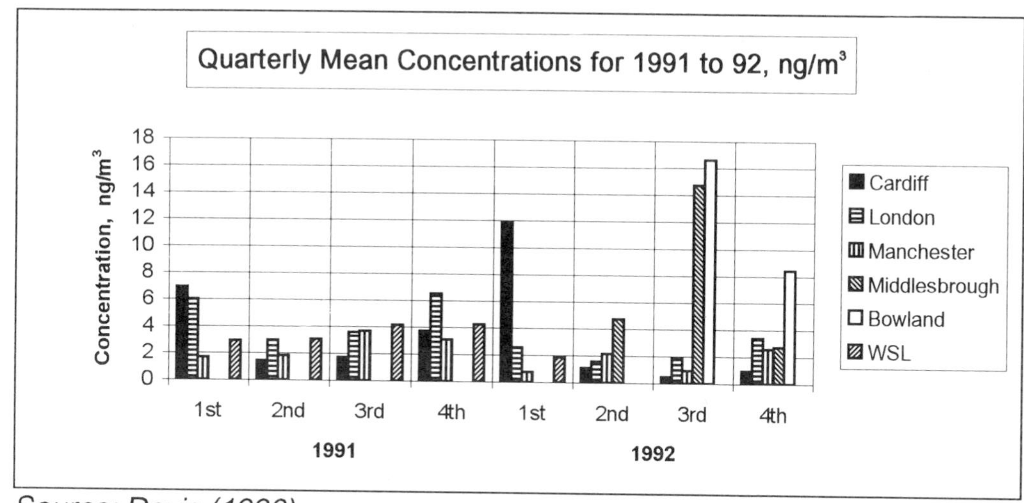

Source: Davis (1993)

Acenaphthene in deposition 1

Chemical formula : $C_{12}H_{10}$

Alternative names : Naphthyleneethylene, PAH EPA no.1

Type of pollutant : Polynuclear Aromatic Hydrocarbon (PAH)

Structure :

CH_2-CH_2

Air quality data summary :

Location	Annual Mean ng/m^2/day		
	1991	1992	1993
Bowland	*	*	*
Cardiff C	362.87	229.57	*
London	60.10	81.00	*
Manchester B	205.33	165.77	*
Middlesborough	*	*	793.32
WSL	63.73	*	*

Source: Davis (1993)

Notes: * signifies no data available

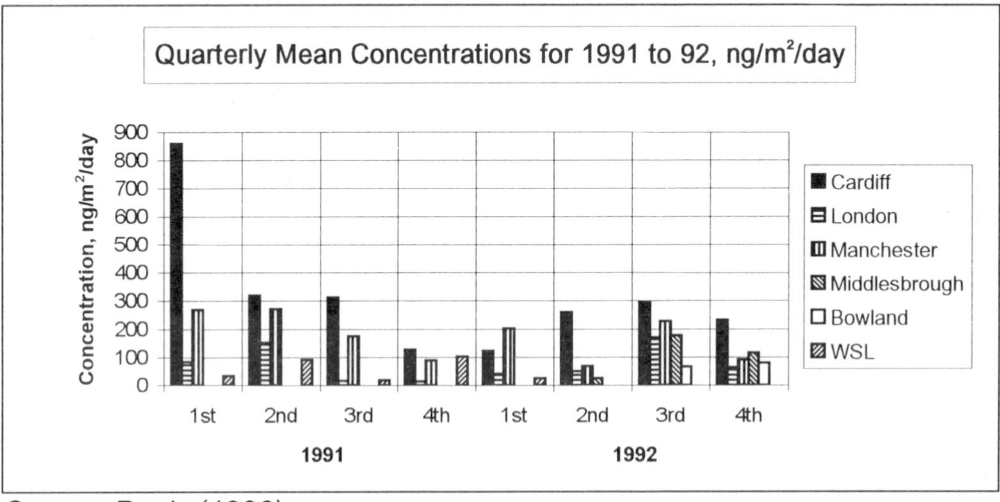

Source: Davis (1993)

Acenaphthylene in air

Chemical formula : $C_{12}H_8$

Alternative names : PAH EPA no.77

Type of pollutant : Polynuclear Aromatic Hydrocarbon (PAH)

Structure :

Air quality data summary :

Location	Annual Mean ng/m^3		
	1991	1992	1993
Bowland	*	*	*
Cardiff C	*	*	*
London	11.20	5.16	1.89
Manchester B	*	*	*
Middlesbrough	*	*	1.58
WSL	6.05	*	*

Source: Davis (1993)

Notes: * signifies no data available

Location	Season 1992	Total Concentration in Air ng/m^3
Edgbaston	Winter (February)	15.40
Edgbaston	Summer (August)	2.72
Wasthills	Summer (August)	0.66

Source: Smith and Harrison (1994)

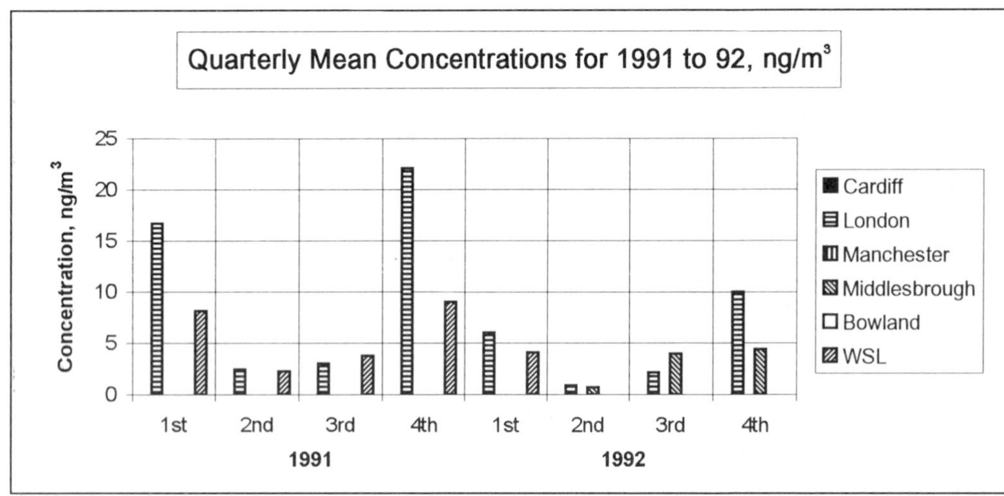

Source: Davis (1993)

Acenaphthylene in deposition 2

Chemical formula : $C_{12}H_8$

Alternative names : PAH EPA no.77

Type of pollutant : Polynuclear Aromatic Hydrocarbon (PAH)

Structure :

Air quality data summary :

Location	Annual Mean $ng/m^2/day$		
	1991	1992	1993
Bowland	*	*	*
Cardiff C	*	*	*
London	27.20	35.40	*
Manchester B	*	*	*
Middlesbrough	*	*	*
WSL	28.88	*	*

Source: Davis (1993)

Notes: * signifies no data available

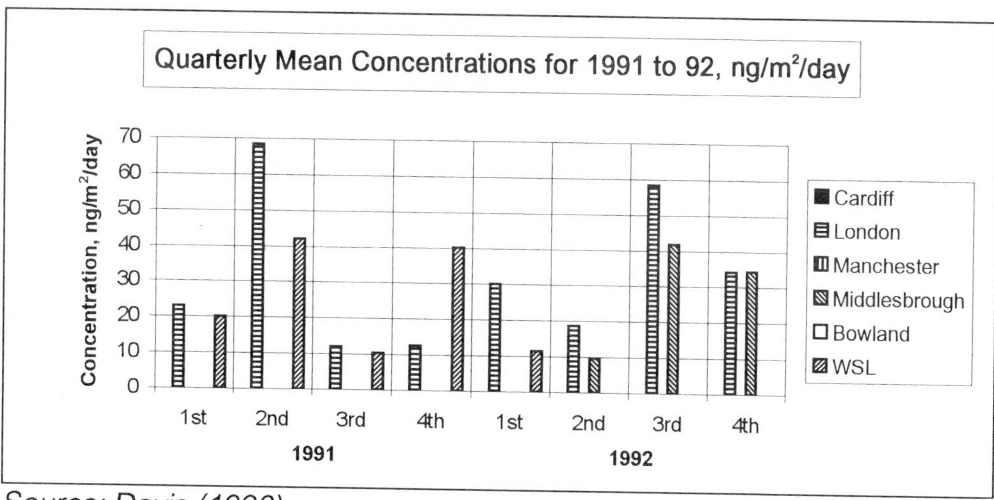

Source: Davis (1993)

Acetophenone

Chemical formula : C_8H_8O

Alternative names : Acetyl benzene, phenyl methyl ketone

Type of pollutant : (Volatile) organic compound (VOC), hydrocarbon, oxygenate.

Structure :

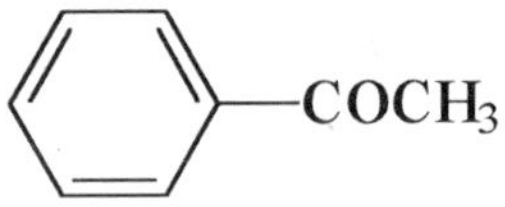

Air quality data summary :

Rural Concentrations

Month 1993	Air Concentration at Harwell site, ppb
	Monthly Mean
August	0.016
September	0.008

Source: Solberg et al. (1994)

Acetylene 4

Chemical formula : C_2H_2

Alternative names : Ethyne

Type of pollutant : (Volatile) Organic Compound (VOC), hydrocarbon

Structure :

HC≡CH

Air quality data summary :

Remote rural concentrations:

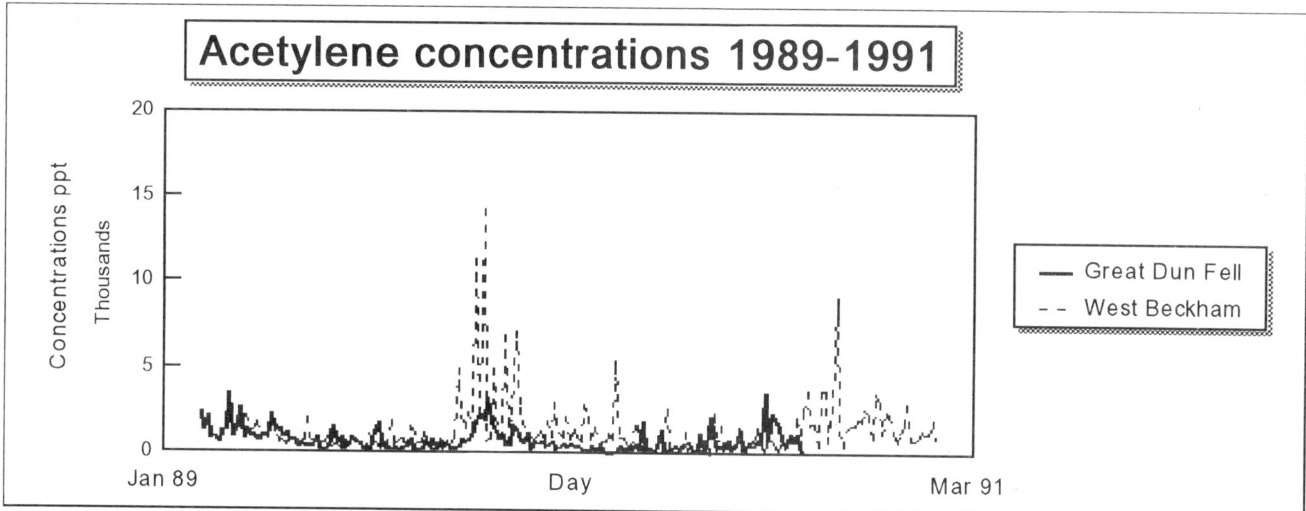

Source: PORG (1993)

Urban concentrations:

	1994-95 Monthly Means, ppb								
	Belfast C	Birmingham B	Bristol A	Cardiff B	Edinburgh A	Eltham	Harwell	Middlesbrough	UCL
Jan 94	5.13	9.90	-	5.53	-	2.14	-	12.02	7.28
Feb 94	6.85	9.39	-	5.88	3.41	2.27	-	16.29	11.43
Mar 94	2.91	5.90	-	2.89	1.50	1.46	-	2.07	5.51
Apr 94	2.92	5.61	11.62	2.56	3.15	2.88	-	28.51	4.32
May 94	3.12	5.18	5.10	2.96	2.98	4.04	-	3.57	5.85
Jun 94	2.20	3.57	2.23	1.81	1.49	1.92	-	2.21	4.83
Jul 94	2.20	4.85	2.69	2.14	1.79	1.98	-	4.53	5.81
Aug 94	2.41	4.06	2.87	2.60	1.92	1.81	-	5.24	5.24
Sep 94	4.24	4.02	2.67	2.61	2.27	1.74	-	11.99	6.50
Oct 94	6.57	7.24	3.92	5.86	5.02	4.02	-	6.77	11.13
Nov 94	5.96	7.47	5.44	7.00	4.52	3.54	-	5.81	11.74
Dec 94	5.23	8.11	6.55	4.60	3.03	4.58	-	3.54	8.83
Jan 95	4.20	8.38	3.66	4.15	3.69	4.81	0.24	3.20	5.40
Feb 95	3.18	8.72	3.33	3.55	1.60	3.47	0.14	3.26	4.49

Source: Dollard (1995)

Rural concentrations:

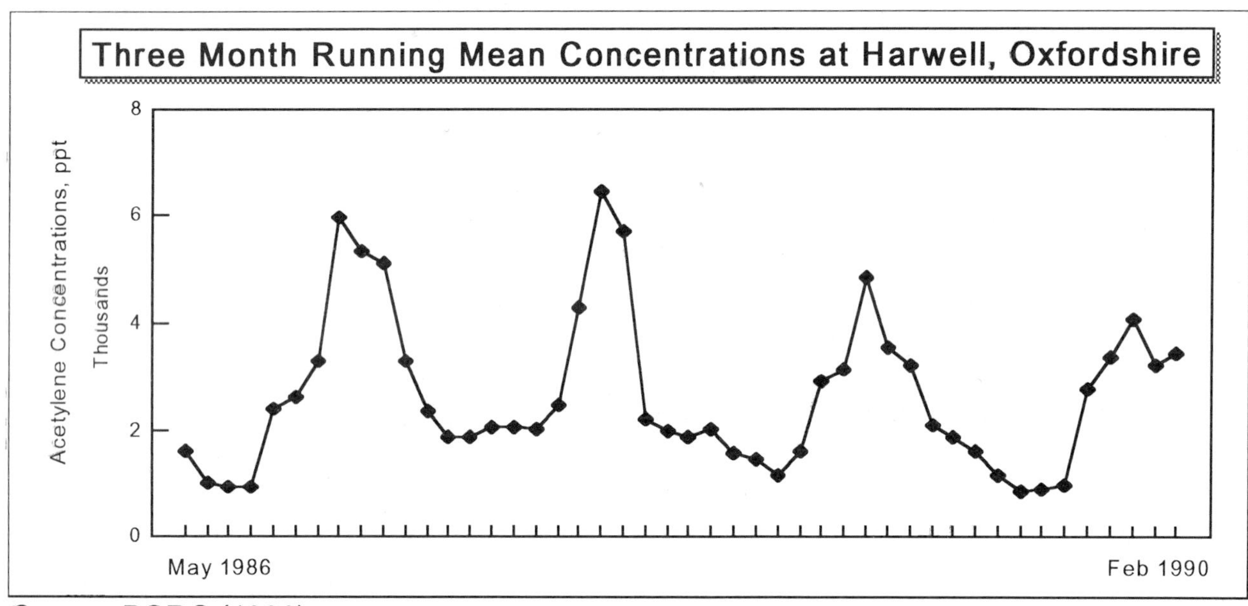

Source: PORG (1993)

Chemical formula : H_2SO_4

Alternative names : Sulphuric acid aerosol, acid particulate

Type of pollutant : Suspended particulate matter

Structure :

H_2SO_4

Air quality data summary :

Rural Concentrations

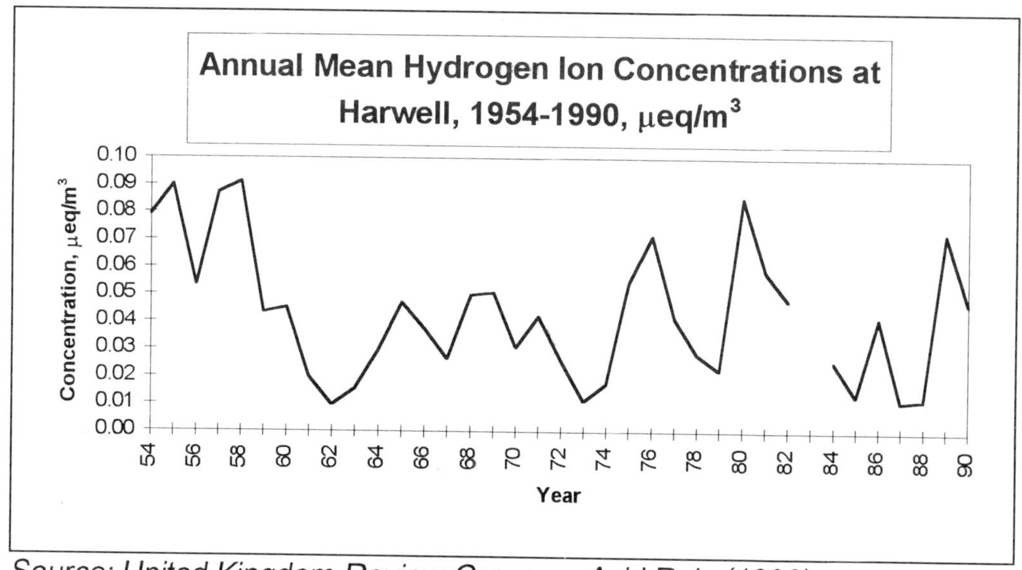

Source: United Kingdom Review Group on Acid Rain (1990)

Aluminium aerosol

Chemical formula : Al

Alternative names : Particulate aluminium

Type of pollutant : Suspended particulate matter, trace element

Air quality data summary :

Rural Concentrations

Location	Average Annual Concentration, ng/m^3			
	Mean	Trend	Mean	Trend
	1972-1981	%/yr	1982-1991	%/yr
Harwell, Oxfordshire.	242	-7.3	140	3.9
Styrrup, Nottinghamshire.	508	-8.9	355	-4.2
Trebanos, Glamorgan.	260	-	-	-
Wraymires, Cumbria.	192	nst	109	nst

Source: Cawse et al. (1994)

Note: nst=no significant trend

Location	Nature of site	Measurement period	Mean concentration ng/m^3
Altrincham	Residential	1978-1989	563
Brent	Residential	1975-1989	489
Chilton	Rural	1971-1989	222
Flixton	Residential	1975-1989	694
Lambeth	Residential	1976-1982	636
Manchester City North	Industrial/ Residential	1975-1988	616
Manchester City South	Residential	1975-1989	545
Swansea	Urban	1972-1981	459
Walsall	Industrial	1976-1989	838
Wraymires	Rural	1970-1989	142

Source: Lee et al. (1994)

Aluminium in rain

Chemical formula : Al

Alternative names : Precipitation aluminium

Type of pollutant : Trace contaminant of rain, trace element

Air quality data summary :

Rural Concentrations

Location	Average Annual Rainfall Concentration, μg per litre	
	1972-1981	1982-1991 *
Harwell, Oxfordshire.	582	70
Styrrup, Nottinghamshire.	2586	101
Wraymires, Cumbria.	133	35

Source: Cawse et al. (1994)

Note: total deposition expressed as apparent rainfall concentration.

* based on soluble fraction only.

Ammonia

Chemical formula : NH_3

Alternative names : Ammonia gas or vapour

Type of pollutant : Trace gas of NH_x family

Structure :

NH_3

Air quality data summary :

Rural Concentrations

Ammonia data from the diffusion tube network for 1987 (scaled by 0.45):

Site	OS Grid Reference	NH_3 concentration, ppb
Achanarras	ND 151550	1.7
Altnaheglish Reservoir	C 698041	1.2
Balqhuidder	NN 521206	2.0
Baltasound	HP 609090	0.6
Bannisdale	NY 515043	1.4
Barcombe Mills	TQ 437149	3.3
Beddgelert	SH 556518	1.2
Beinn Eigh	NH 025629	0.7
Birds Hill	ST 056363	2.1
Bottesford	SK 797376	2.2
Bowood House	ST 953699	4.1
Broadford	NG 652230	0.7
Brooms Barn	TL 753656	2.1
Compton	SU 512804	3.8
Cow Green reservoir	NY 817298	1.2
Devoke Water	SD 163973	0.9
Driby	TF 386744	3.7
East Ruston	TG 341279	2.4
Eskdalemuir	NT 235030	0.9
Flatford Mill	TM 077333	3.2
Fort Augustus	NH 366091	1.3
Gisla	NB 129258	0.7
Glen Dye	ND 642864	0.9
Goonhilly	SW 723214	1.4
Hartland Moor	SY 942845	2.2
Hebden Bridge	SE 011327	1.5
High Muffles	SE 776939	1.4
Hill of Shurton	HU 444400	1.1
Isle of Man	SC 367861	1.3

Site	OS Grid reference	NH_3 concentration, ppb
Jenny Hurn	SK 816986	2.3
Kershope Forest	NY 492792	1.4
Liphook	SU 859297	1.8
Llyn Brianne	SN 822507	0.8
Loch Ard	NS 470987	0.9
Loch Dee	NX 468779	0.9
Loch Levan	NT 158993	2.4
Lough Navar	H 065545	1.4
Ludlow	SO 570741	3.5
Malham Tarn	SD 894672	1.5
Myres Hill	NS 569465	1.8
Pitsford	SP 763686	2.3
Plaxtol	TQ 618521	2.2
Plynlimon	SN 822841	1.4
Preston Montford	SJ 432143	4.8
Ridgehill	SO 508353	4.4
River Mharcaidh	NH 876052	1.7
Rothamsted	TL 132133	1.6
Silent Valley	J 306243	1.3
Stoke Ferry	TL 700988	3.2
Strathvaich Dam	NH 347750	0.7
Tycanol Wood	SN 093364	1.7
Wardlow Hay Cop	SK 177739	2.7
Woburn	SP 964361	2.6
Yarner Wood	SX 786789	1.6

Source: Atkins and Lee (1992)

Urban Concentrations:

Six monthly mean concentrations for ammonia from July to December 1992, (ppb):

Location	Mean Concentration, ppb	Location	Mean Concentration, ppb
ACTON 13	4.5	BELFAST 14	6.4
ADDLESTONE 1	8.5	BELFAST 40	7.5
BARKING 15	4.3	BRADFORD 22	3.1
BARNSLEY 9	4.4	BRIERLEY HILL 15	6.7
BATH 6	3.5	BRISTOL 26	4.7
BEDFORD 10	5.8	BURHAM 1	5.4
BELFAST 13	8.0	CAMPHILL 11	1.7

Location	Mean Concentration, ppb	Location	Mean Concentration, ppb
CARLISLE 13	9.5	LONDONDERRY 11	10.7
CHEADLE & GATLEY 6	4.4	MAIDSTONE 7	4.5
COALVILLE 5	8.1	MANCHESTER 11	9.0
COVENTRY 13	8.0	MANCHESTER 15	8.9
CRAWLEY 3	3.1	MIDDLESBROUGH 29	7.2
CREWE 9	11.6	MIDDLETON 3	9.9
CROSBY 3	6.8	MOTHERWELL 14	3.4
DARTFORD 9	3.9	NORWICH 7	9.5
DIBDEN PURLIEU 1	5.6	NOTTINGHAM 19	5.8
EALING 3	3.2	NOTTINGHAM 20	4.7
EDINBURGH 14	4.6	OLDHAM 3	5.5
ELLESMERE PORT 12	9.0	ORRELL 1	7.6
ELLESMERE PORT 9	13.4	OTLEY 3	8.3
ESTON 9	14.2	PETERHEAD 1	8.6
GARFORTH 1	10.4	PETERHEAD 2	5.8
GLASGOW 86	4.5	PLYMOUTH 11	3.8
GLASGOW 92	6.2	PONTYPOOL 7	5.3
GLASGOW 96	3.7	PORT TALBOT 14	5.6
GLOUCESTER 6	4.0	PORTADOWN 4	7.7
GRANGEMOUTH 2	2.8	RHYDARGEAU 1	4.2
HAMMERSMITH 6	10.2	SELBY 4	11.6
HASLINGDEN 4	7.3	SHEFFIELD 83	4.6
HEANOR 7	8.7	SHEFFIELD 86	3.6
ILFORD 6	6.2	SMETHWICK 9	5.8
ILKESTON 7	5.5	SOUTH KIRKBY 1	4.6
ILKESTON 8	5.3	ST ALBANS 3	8.7
IMMINGHAM 5	8.9	STAINFORTH 1	8.5
INCE-IN-MAKERFIELD 1	6.6	STEPNEY 5	4.4
IPSWICH 14	7.3	STEVENAGE 4	4.0
ISLINGTON 9	4.5	ST HELENS 29	10.2
KENSINGTON 11	9.3	ST HELENS 38	11.5
KENSINGTON 12	7.6	SUNDERLAND 12	6.9
KETTERING 5	5.4	SUNDERLAND 8	5.0
KILMARNOCK 2	5.6	TEDDINGTON 3	4.6
KNOTTINGLEY 1	6.5	TRAFFORD 1	6.6
LEEDS 37	1.9	WALSALL 15	10.6
LEEDS 4	6.5	WALTHAMSTOW 8	5.2
LINCOLN 5	7.0	WIDNES 9	12.9
LIVERPOOL 116	9.1	WOLVERHAMPTON 7	4.4
LIVERPOOL 16	9.4	WREXHAM 7	11.3
LIVERPOOL 19	8.4	YORK 7	8.7

Source: Downing et al. (1994)

Ammonium aerosol

Chemical formula : NH_4

Alternative names : Particulate ammonium

Type of pollutant : Suspended particulate matter

Structure :

NH_4

Air quality data summary :

Rural Concentrations

Location	1992 Monthly Mean Concentration in Air*, µg/m³											
	Jan	Feb	Mar	Apr	May	Jun	Jul	Aug	Sep	Oct	Nov	Dec
Eskdalemuir	2.18	1.20	0.59	1.07	2.48	1.38	1.07	0.50	0.97	0.36	0.29	1.06
High Muffles	-	-	-	-	-	3.28	1.72	1.51	2.23	1.04	0.88	2.17

Source: Schaug et al. (1994)

Note: * These data represent results for a mixture of ammonia and ammonium aerosols

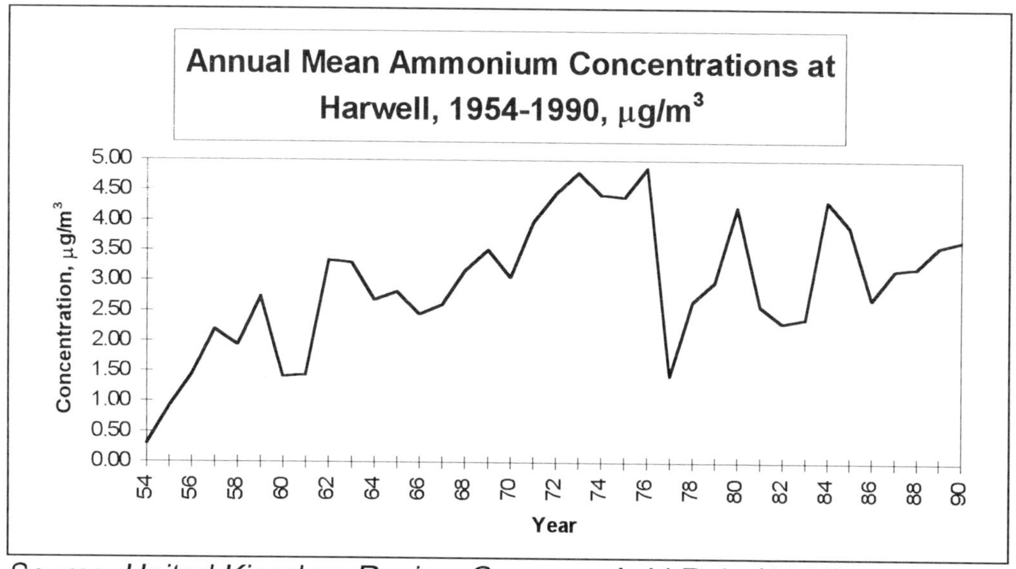

Source: United Kingdom Review Group on Acid Rain (1990)

Ammonium in rain

Chemical formula : NH_4

Alternative names : Precipitation ammonium

Type of pollutant : Trace contaminant of rain

Structure : NH_4

Air quality data summary :

Rural Concentrations:

Site	Precipitation-weighted Annual Mean Ammonium Concentration, 1986-93, (μ eql^{-1})								
	OS Ref	1986	1987	1988	1989	1990	1991	1992	1993
Achanarras	ND 152552	11	35	21	18	15	26	9	8
Balquhidder	NN 521206	14	15	12	14	11	16	16	15
Bannisdale	NY 515043	35	27	30	30	32	34	27	31
Barcombe Mills	TQ 437149	38	41	38	39	35	50	31	16
Beddgelert	SH 556518	14	11	12	15	14	13	15	14
Bottesford	SK 797376	56	45	49	68	54	48	40	33
Compton	SU 512804	70	73	46	56	55	63	57	40
Cow Green Reservoir	NY 817298	20	19	25	23	24	26	25	28
Driby	TF 386744	53	60	64	53	67	76	55	42
Eskdalemuir	NT 234028	20	16	19	22	18	26	17	18
Flatford Mill	TM 077333	-	50	49	66	44	59	40	31
Glen Dye	NO 642864	-	26	29	28	25	32	22	28
Goonhilly	SW 723214	17	22	12	18	16	24	15	30
High Muffles	SE 776939	40	46	54	53	48	64	44	40
Hillsborough Forest	J 243577	-	-	-	60	45	48	40	43
Jenny Hurn	SK 816986	64	51	53	64	64	65	45	28
Llyn Brianne	SN 822507	12	13	14	16	16	20	18	15
Loch Dee	NX 468779	21	34	21	20	21	24	28	21
Lough Navar	H 065545	11	9	8	11	8	9	12	11
Plynlimon	SN 822841	-	-	-	13	13	17	20	14
Polloch	NM 792689	-	-	-	-	-	8	8	5
Preston Montford	SJ 432143	47	57	49	53	44	57	57	36
Redesdale	NY 833954	41	15	23	34	24	32	30	21
River Mharcaidh	NH 882045	6	10	3	7	5	5	4	4
Stoke Ferry	TL 700988	65	60	56	75	69	74	54	43
Strathvaich Dam	NH 347750	-	4	3	4	3	5	5	4
Thorganby	SE 676428	59	56	61	65	80	124	82	-
Tycanol Wood	SN 093364	13	15	13	15	14	19	13	11
Wardlow Hay Cop	SK 177739	34	40	39	39	40	57	45	39
Whiteadder	NT 664633	30	20	35	32	17	30	27	22
Woburn	SP 964361	54	50	52	56	43	52	41	35
Yarner Wood	SX 786789	15	28	14	19	13	22	17	23

Source: Campbell et al. (1994a)

Rural Concentrations:

Location	1992 Monthly Weighted Mean Concentration in Precipitation, mg/l											
	Jan	Feb	Mar	Apr	May	Jun	Jul	Aug	Sep	Oct	Nov	Dec
Eskdalemuir	0.47	0.40	0.38	0.35	0.34	2.07	0.33	0.13	0.13	0.15	0.17	0.14
High Muffles	0.38	0.69	0.72	0.35	1.00	0.88	0.33	0.56	0.38	0.34	0.50	0.32
Lough Navar	0.17	0.18	0.13	0.18	0.25	1.23	0.29	0.08	0.12	0.11	0.07	0.09
Strath Vaich	0.18	0.06	0.06	0.04	0.47	0.91	0.14	0.06	0.09	0.03	0.04	0.02
Yarner Wood	0.25	0.31	0.24	0.14	0.91	0.51	0.26	0.11	0.35	0.21	0.10	0.12

Source: Schaug et al. (1994)

Anthanthrene

Chemical formula : $C_{22}H_{12}$

Alternative names :

Type of pollutant : Polynuclear Aromatic Hydrocarbon (PAH)

Structure :

Air quality data summary :

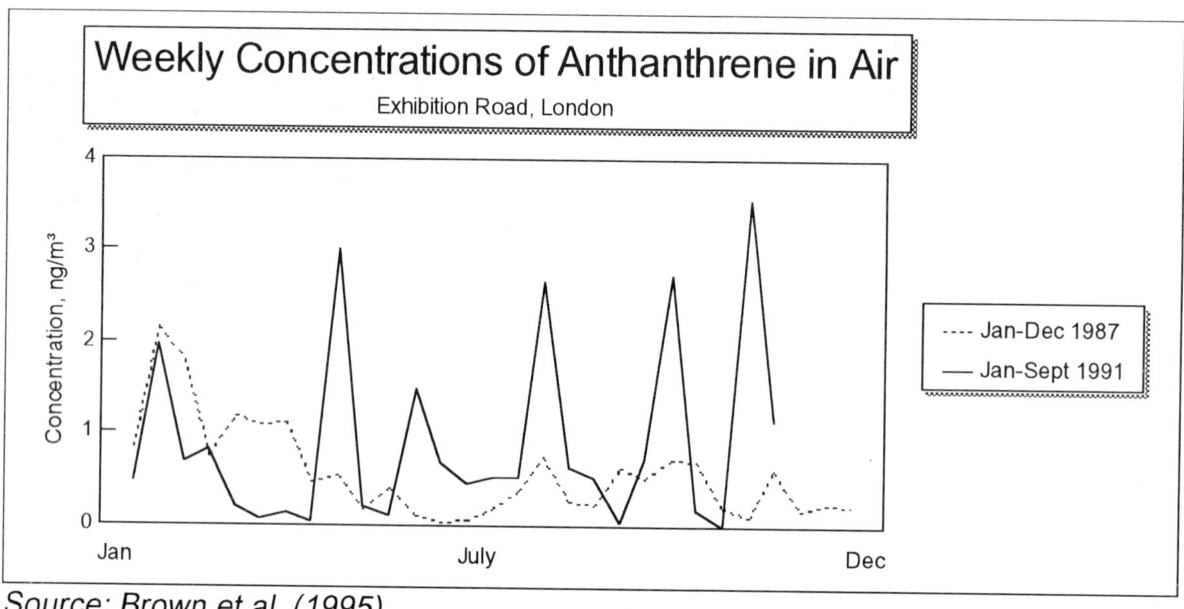

Source: Brown et al. (1995)

Anthracene in air

Chemical formula : $C_{14}H_{10}$

Alternative names : PAH EPA no.78

Type of pollutant : Polynuclear Aromatic Hydrocarbon, (PAH)

Structure :

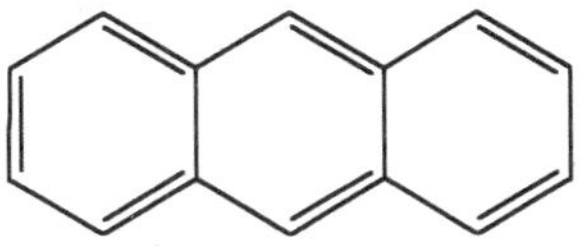

Air quality data summary :

Location	Annual Mean ng/m^3		
	1991	1992	1993
Bowland	*	*	7.54
Cardiff C	3.90	1.95	*
London	6.92	5.24	7.93
Manchester B	4.28	2.14	3.02
Middlesbrough	*	*	9.63
WSL	3.70	*	*

Source: Davis (1993)

Notes: * signifies no data available

Location	Season 1992	Total Concentration in Air ng/m^3
Edgbaston	Winter (February)	4.49
Edgbaston	Summer (August)	0.61
Wasthills	Summer (August)	0.17

Source: Smith and Harrison (1994)

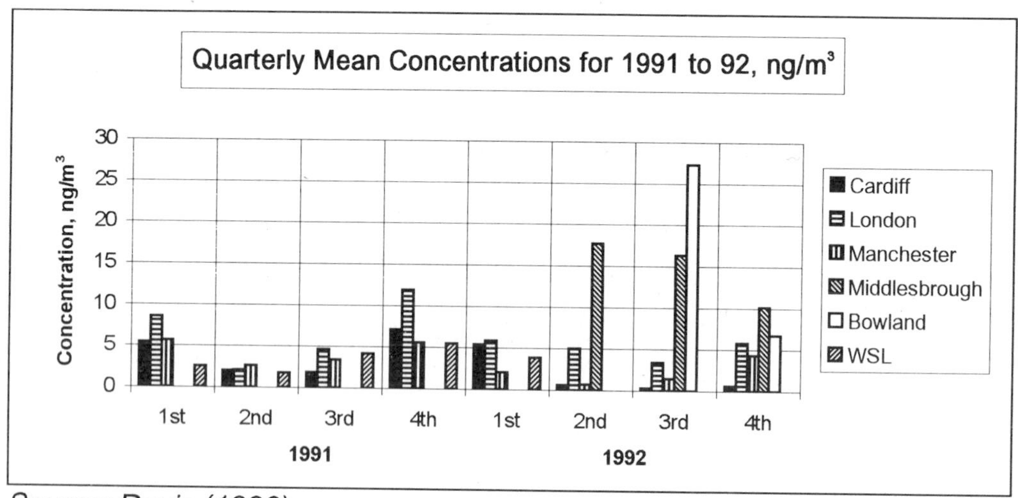

Source: Davis (1993)

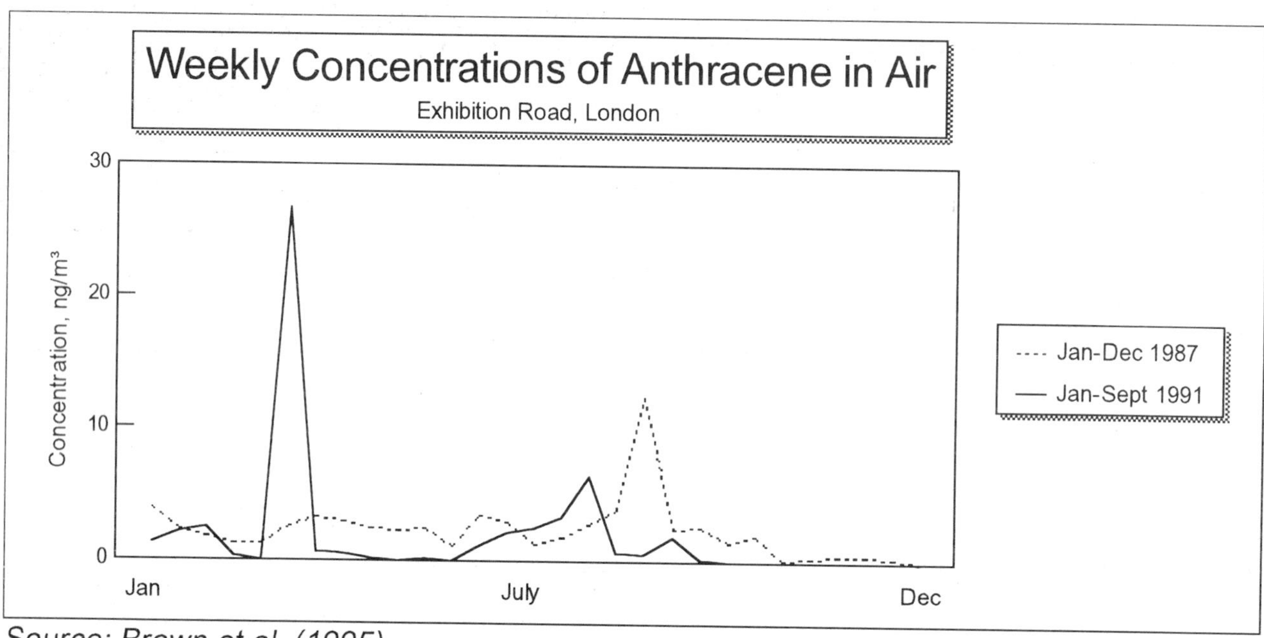

Source: Brown et al. (1995)

Chemical formula : $C_{14}H_{10}$

Alternative names : PAH EPA no.78

Type of pollutant : Polynuclear Aromatic Hydrocarbon, (PAH)

Structure :

Air quality data summary :

Location	Annual Mean $ng/m^2/day$		
	1991	1992	1993
Bowland	*	*	1.56
Cardiff C	63.09	22.09	*
London	211.40	2045.00	*
Manchester B	137.04	24.14	*
Middlesbrough	*	*	*
WSL	153.56	*	*

Source: Davis (1993)

Notes: * signifies no data available

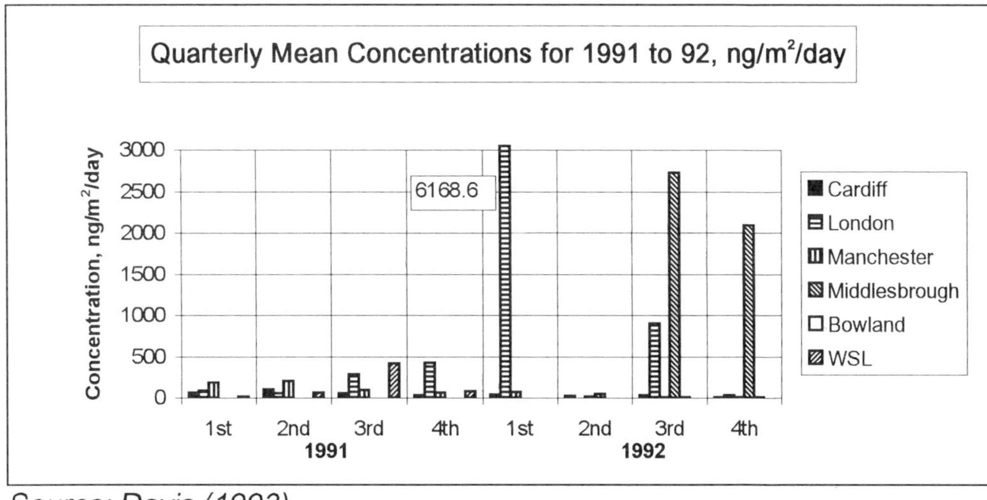

Source: Davis (1993)

Anthraquinone 11

Chemical formula	:	$C_6H_4(CO)_2C_6H_4$
Alternative names	:	Diphenylene diketone
Type of pollutant	:	Oxygenated Polynuclear Aromatic Compound, (PAC)
Structure	:	

Air quality data summary :

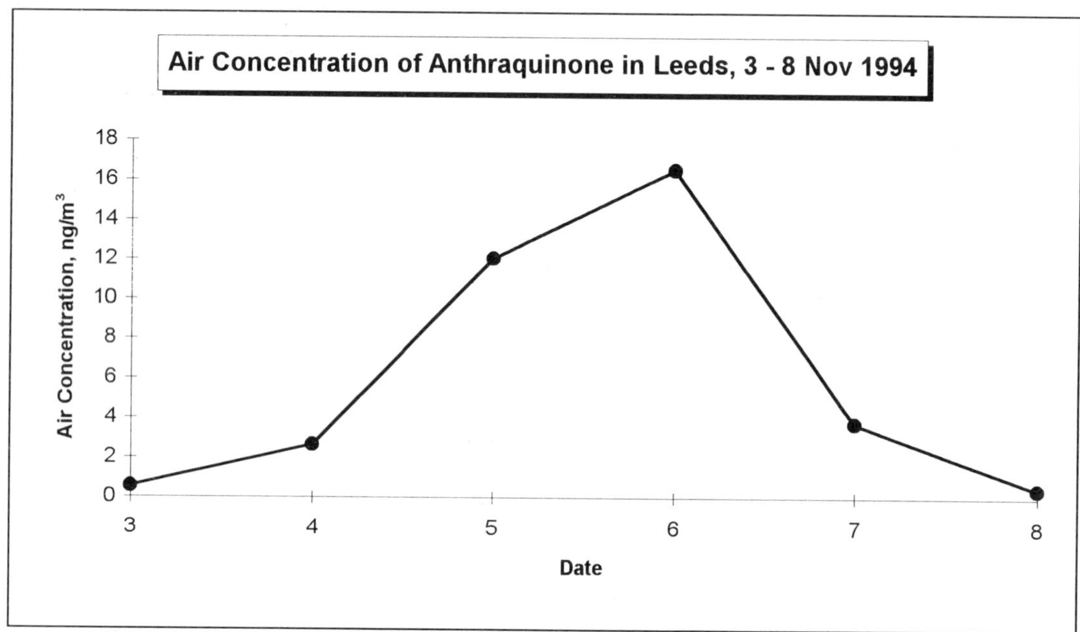

Source: Lewis et al. (1995)

Antimony aerosol

Chemical formula : Sb

Alternative names : Particulate antimony

Type of pollutant : Suspended particulate matter, trace element

Air quality data summary :

Location	Concentrations, ng/m^3			
	Mean	Trend	Mean	Trend
	1972-1981	%/yr	1982-1991	%/yr
Harwell, Oxfordshire.	2	nst	1.5	nst
Styrrup, Nottinghamshire.	5	-4.7	4.7	-6.5
Swansea.	5	nst	-	-
Trebanos, Glamorgan.	3	-	2.5	-
Wraymires, Cumbria.	2	-6.2	0.8	-7.4

Source: Cawse et al. (1994), Pattenden (1974).

Note: nst=no significant trend

Chemical formula : Sb

Alternative names : Precipitation antimony

Type of pollutant : Trace contaminant of rain, trace element

Air quality data summary :

Rural Concentrations:

Location	Average Annual Rainfall Concentration µg per litre	
	1972-1981	1982-1991 *
Harwell, Oxfordshire.	0.5	1.9
Styrrup, Nottinghamshire.	1.4	2.2
Wraymires, Cumbria.	0.2	1.6

Source: Cawse et al. (1994)

Note: total deposition expressed as apparent rainfall concentration.
* based on soluble fraction only.

Chemical formula : As

Alternative names : Particulate arsenic

Type of pollutant : Suspended particulate matter, trace element

Air quality data summary :

Rural Concentrations:

Location	Concentration, ng/m^3				
	Mean	Trend	Mean		Trend
	1972-1981	%/yr	1982-1991		%/yr
Harwell, Oxfordshire.	4	-10.0	1.7		-7.8
Styrrup, Nottinghamshire.	15	-14.3	4.4		-5.2
Trebanos, Glamorgan.	7	-6.0	3.5		-
Wraymires, Cumbria.	3	nst	0.82	*	-7.3

Source: Cawse et al. (1994)

Note: nst=no significant trend
* only 68% of measurements were positive.

Location	Nature of site	Measurement period	Mean concentration ng/m^3
Altrincham	Residential	1978-1989	4.7
Brent	Residential	1975-1989	6.1
Chilton	Rural	1971-1989	2.7
Flixton	Residential	1975-1989	7.1
Lambeth	Residential	1976-1982	7.2
Manchester City North	Industrial/ Residential	1975-1988	7.6
Manchester City South	Residential	1975-1989	6.5
Swansea	Urban	1972-1981	19.0
Walsall	Industrial	1976-1989	93.9
Wraymires	Rural	1970-1989	1.8

Source: Lee et al. (1994)

Arsenic in rain

Chemical formula : As

Alternative names : Precipitation arsenic

Type of pollutant : Trace contaminant of rain, trace element

Air quality data summary :

Rural Concentrations:

Location	Average Annual Rainfall Concentration, μg per litre	
	1972-1981	1982-1991*
Harwell, Oxfordshire.	1.9	<1
Styrrup, Nottinghamshire.	6.9	<1
Wraymires, Cumbria.	1.1	<1

Source: Cawse et al. (1994)

Note: total deposition expressed as apparent rainfall concentration.
* based on soluble fraction only.

Benz(a)anthracene in air

Chemical formula : $C_{18}H_{12}$

Alternative names : 1,2-benzanthracene, PAH EPA no.72

Type of pollutant : Polynuclear Aromatic Hydrocarbon, (PAH)

Structure :

Air quality data summary :

Location	Annual Mean ng/m³		
	1991	1992	1993
Bowland	*	*	0.49
Cardiff C	2.49	1.27	*
London	1.91	0.87	0.38
Manchester B	2.51	1.08	0.56
Middlesbrough	*	*	0.57
WSL	1.18	*	*

Source: Davis (1993)

Notes: * signifies no data available

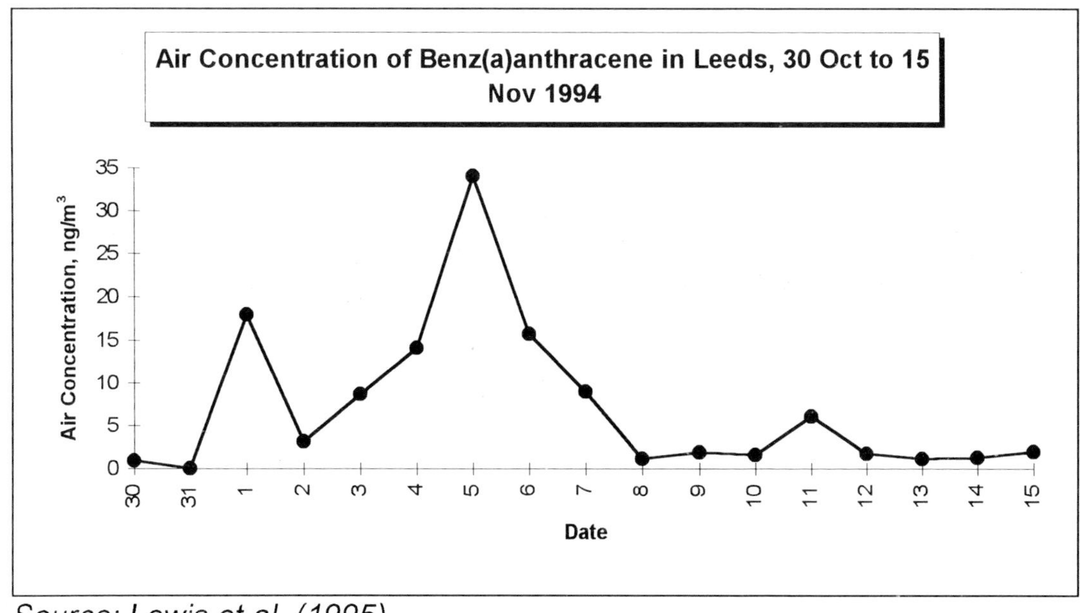

Source: Lewis et al. (1995)

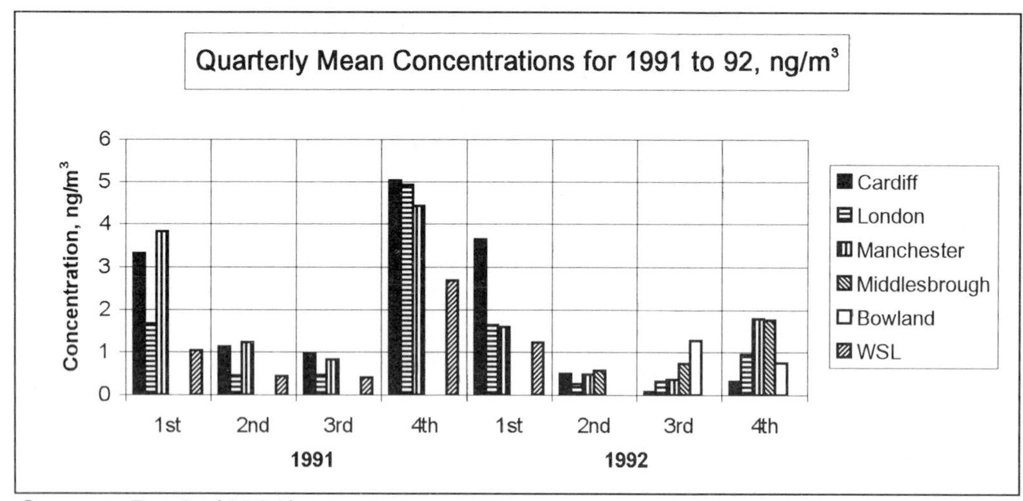

Source: Davis (1993)

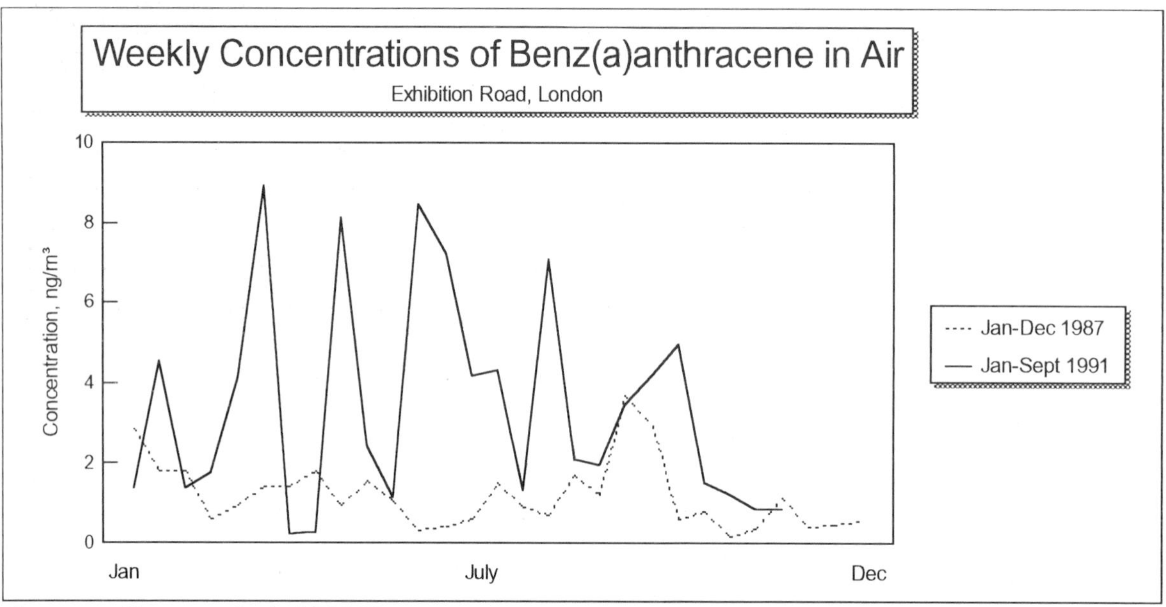

Source: Brown et al. (1995)

Location	Season 1992	Total Concentration in Air ng/m^3
Edgbaston	Winter (February)	5.59
Edgbaston	Summer (August)	0.34
Wasthills	Summer (August)	0.08

Source: Smith and Harrison (1994)

Benz(a)anthracene in deposition

Chemical formula : $C_{18}H_{12}$

Alternative names : 1,2-benzanthracene, PAH EPA no.72

Type of pollutant : Polynuclear Aromatic Hydrocarbon, (PAH)

Structure :

Air quality data summary :

Location	Annual Mean ng/m²/day		
	1991	1992	1993
Bowland	*	*	18.72
Cardiff C	447.75	124.02	*
London	263.30	321.20	*
Manchester B	675.75	131.89	*
Middlesbrough	*	*	*
WSL	140.73	*	*

Source: Davis (1993)

Notes: * signifies no data available

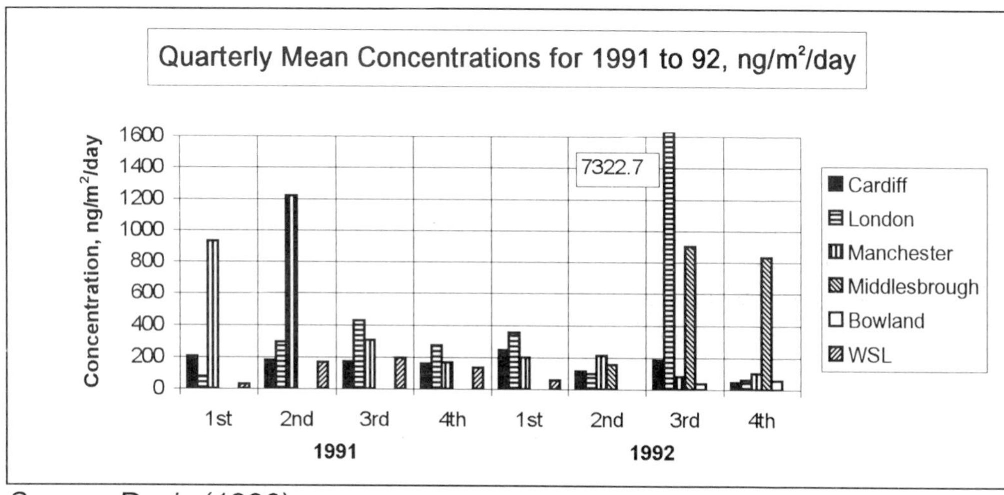

Source: Davis (1993)

Benzene

Chemical formula : C_6H_6

Alternative names :

Type of pollutant : (Volatile) organic compound (VOC), hydrocarbon, air toxic

Structure :

Air quality data summary :

Remote rural concentrations

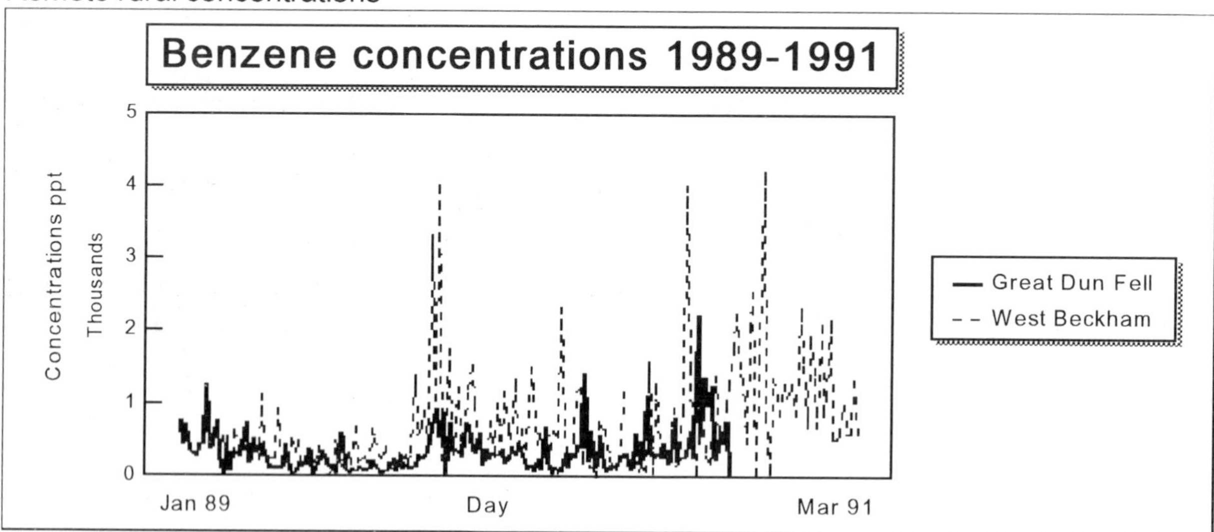

Source: PORG (1993)

Rural Concentrations

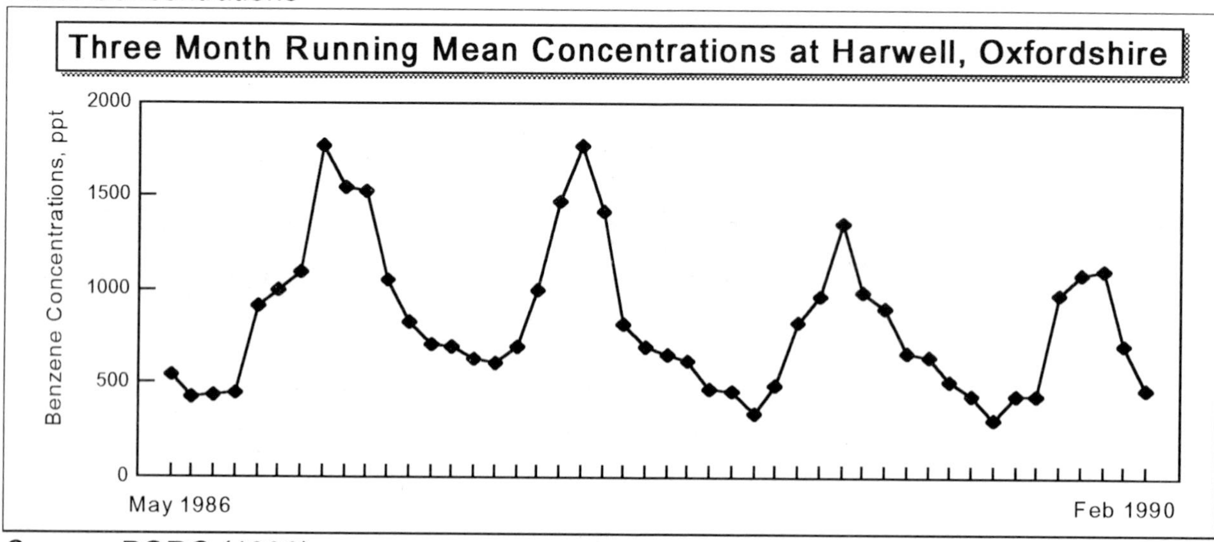

Source: PORG (1993)

Urban Concentrations

	1994-95 Monthly Means, ppb								
	Belfast C	Birmingham B	Bristol A	Cardiff B	Edinburgh A	Eltham	Harwell	Middlesbrough	UCL
Jan 94	1.26	2.15	-	1.82	0.15	0.71	-	1.01	1.50
Feb 94	1.68	2.41	-	2.09	0.84	0.95	-	1.28	2.42
Mar 94	0.72	1.09	-	0.96	0.49	0.44	-	0.77	1.13
Apr 94	0.77	1.03	0.43	0.80	0.62	0.47	-	0.62	1.15
May 94	0.93	1.08	0.68	1.20	0.63	0.50	-	0.35	2.00
Jun 94	0.61	0.80	0.48	0.70	0.46	0.54	-	0.42	1.19
Jul 94	0.61	0.77	0.59	0.89	0.57	0.64	-	1.84	1.48
Aug 94	0.67	0.75	0.69	0.90	0.57	0.62	-	1.06	1.28
Sep 94	1.08	0.88	0.84	1.03	0.65	0.74	-	2.68	1.59
Oct 94	1.53	1.62	1.74	2.15	0.88	1.07	-	1.53	2.30
Nov 94	1.42	1.68	1.21	2.15	0.84	1.71	-	1.65	2.20
Dec 94	1.60	1.80	1.38	1.97	0.84	1.93	-	0.81	1.92
Jan 95	1.09	0.86	1.02	1.37	0.72	1.19	0.30	0.82	1.23
Feb 95	0.86	0.66	1.09	1.16	0.60	0.96	0.25	0.71	1.11

Source: Dollard (1995)

Mean Air Concentration in Leeds, 19/8/94 to 8/9/94	
Location	21 day mean, $\mu g/m^3$
Albion Street	0.853
Cliff Lane	0.692
EUN monitoring site	1.058
Kerbside site	1.230
Kirkstall Road	1.145
Park site	0.935
Queen Street	0.984
Vicar Lane	3.086

Source: Bartle et al. (1995)

Six monthly mean concentrations of benzene from July to December 1992, (ppb):

Location	Mean Concentration, ppb	Location	Mean Concentration, ppb
ADDLESTONE 1	1.2	BURHAM 1	0.6
BARKING 15	1.1	CAMPHILL 11	0.4
BATH 6	1.3	CARLISLE 13	0.6
BELFAST 13	0.9	CRAWLEY 3	0.9
BIRMINGHAM 26	0.7	DARTFORD 9	1.2
BRADFORD 22	1.1	DIBDEN PURLIEU 1	1.1
BRISTOL 26	1.2	EALING 3	1.5

Location	Mean Concentration, ppb	Location	Mean Concentration, ppb
EDINBURGH 14	0.7	MANCHESTER AIRPORT	1.0
ELLESMERE PORT 9	2.0	MIDDLESBROUGH 35	0.9
ESTON 9	1.3	NORWICH 7	1.1
GLASGOW 86	0.8	NOTTINGHAM 20	1.0
GLASGOW 92	0.7	PETERHEAD 2	0.6
GLASGOW 96	0.7	PLYMOUTH 11	1.0
GRANGEMOUTH 2	0.8	PONTYPOOL 7	2.0
HAMMERSMITH 6	4.6	SELBY 4	0.8
ILFORD 6	2.2	SHEFFIELD 86	0.8
ILKESTON 8	1.0	ST ALBANS 3	1.5
IMMINGHAM 5	0.8	STAINFORTH 1	0.8
IPSWICH 14	0.9	STEPNEY 5	0.8
ISLINGTON 9	1.2	STEVENAGE 4	1.2
KENSINGTON 11	1.3	ST HELENS 29	0.7
KENSINGTON 14	3.3	SUNDERLAND 8	1.0
KNOTTINGLEY 1	0.9	TEDDINGTON 3	1.1
LEEDS 37	1.1	WALSALL 15	1.2
LIVERPOOL 16	1.1	WALTHAMSTOW 8	1.4
LIVERPOOL 19	0.8	WIDNES 9	0.5
LONDONDERRY 11	1.3	WOLVERHAMPTON 7	0.7
MAIDSTONE 7	1.9	WREXHAM 7	1.0
MANCHESTER 11	1.5	YORK 7	0.8
MANCHESTER 15	1.0		

Source: Downing et al. (1994)

Benzene-carbanaldehyde

Chemical formula : C_7H_6O

Alternative names : Benzaldehyde, oil of bitter almonds

Type of pollutant : (Volatile) organic compound (VOC), hydrocarbon, oxygenate

Structure :

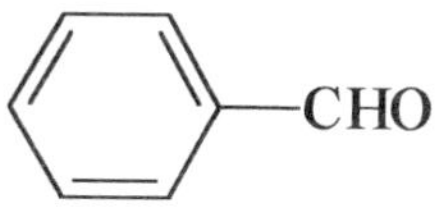

CHO

Air quality data summary :

Rural Concentrations

Month 1993	Air Concentration at Harwell site, ppb
	Monthly Mean
August	0.018
September	0.009
October	*
November	0.025

Source: Solberg et al. (1994)

Note: * signifies no data available

Benzo(e)acenaphthylene

Chemical formula : $C_{16}H_{12}$

Alternative names :

Type of pollutant : Polynuclear Aromatic Hydrocarbon (PAH)

Structure :

Air quality data summary :

Urban Concentrations

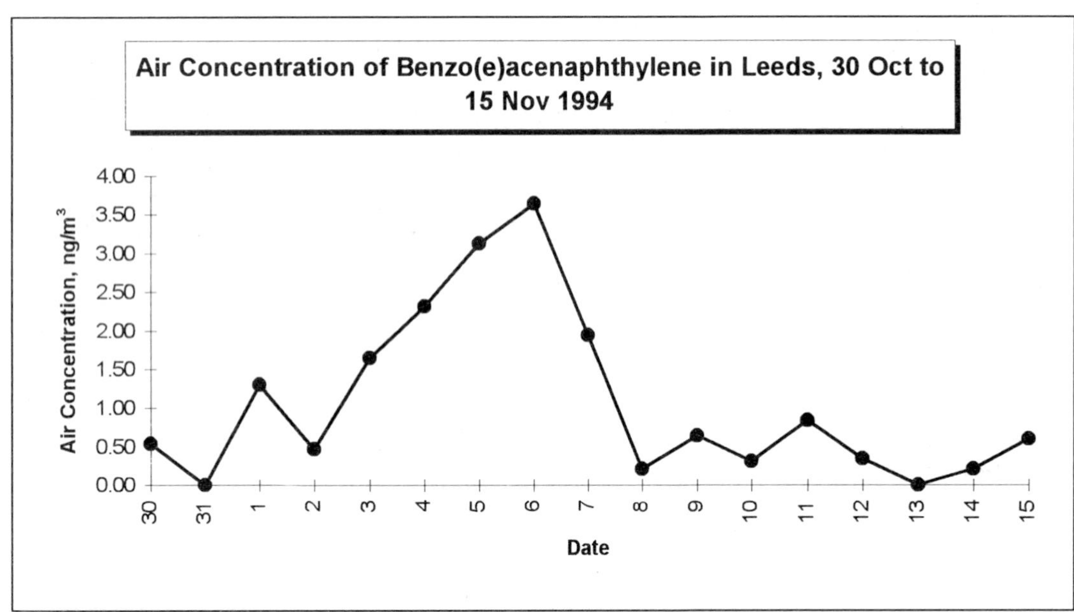

Source: Lewis et al. (1995)

Benzo(b)fluoranthene in air

Chemical formula : $C_{20}H_{12}$

Alternative names : PAH EPA no.74

Type of pollutant : Polynuclear Aromatic Hydrocarbon, (PAH)

Structure :

Air quality data summary :

Location	Annual Mean ng/m^3		
	1991	1992	1993
Bowland	*	*	0.48
Cardiff C	2.26	1.93	*
London	1.72	1.25	2.92
Manchester B	1.52	1.42	1.00
Middlesbrough	*	*	1.52
WSL	1.28	*	*

Source: Davis et al. (1993)

Notes: * signifies no data available

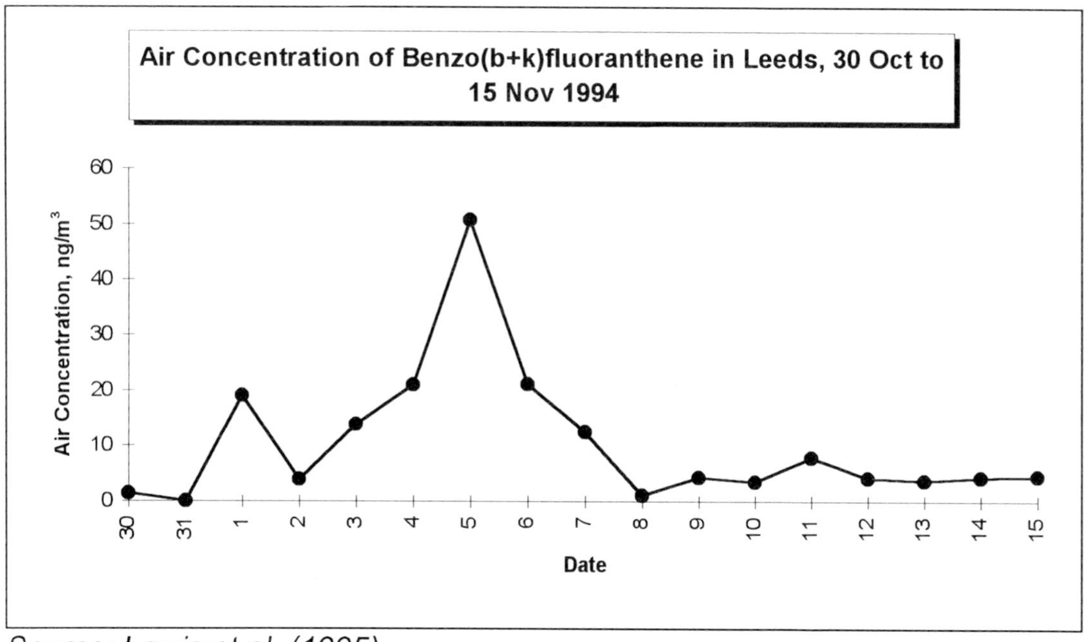

Source: Lewis et al. (1995)

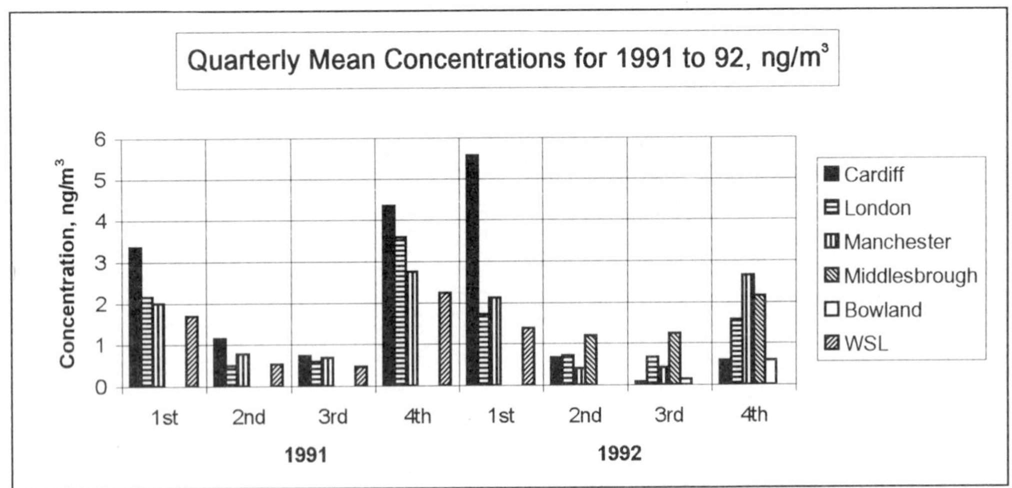

Source: Davis (1993)

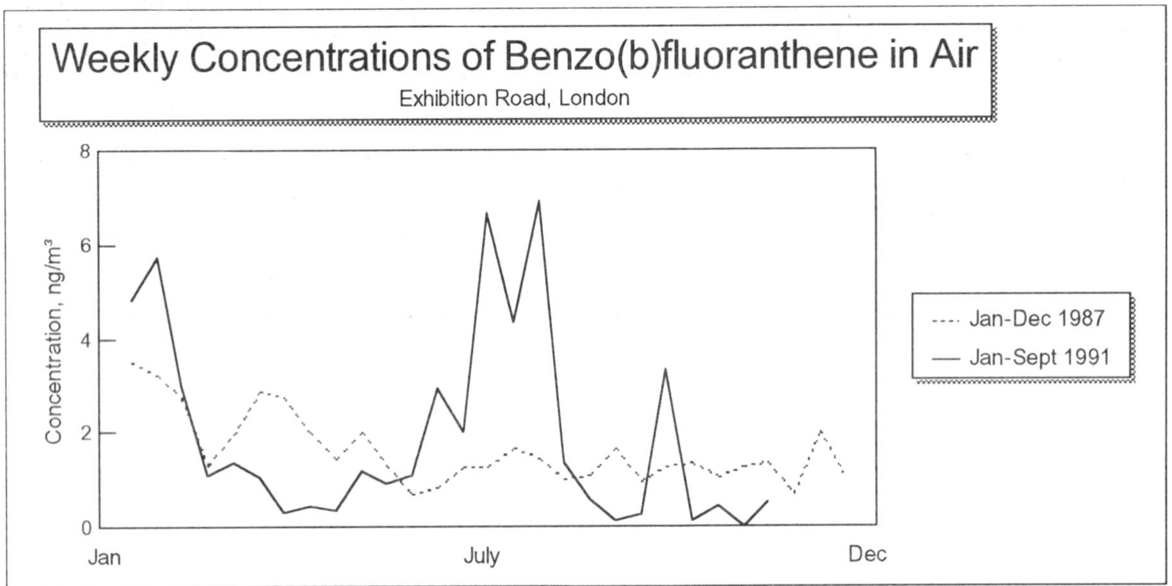

Source: Brown et al. (1995)

Location	Season 1992	Total Concentration in Air ng/m^3
Edgbaston	Winter (February)	2.15
Edgbaston	Summer (August)	0.38
Wasthills	Summer (August)	0.14

Source: Smith and Harrison (1994)

Benzo(b)fluoranthene in deposition

Chemical formula : $C_{20}H_{12}$

Alternative names : PAH EPA no.74

Type of pollutant : Polynuclear Aromatic Hydrocarbon, (PAH)

Structure :

Air quality data summary :

Location	Annual Mean ng/m²/day		
	1991	1992	1993
Bowland	*	*	53.76
Cardiff C	365.61	148.69	*
London	235.50	354.60	*
Manchester B	662.97	237.88	*
Middlesbrough	*	*	*
WSL	144.69	*	*

Source: Davis (1993)

Notes: * signifies no data available

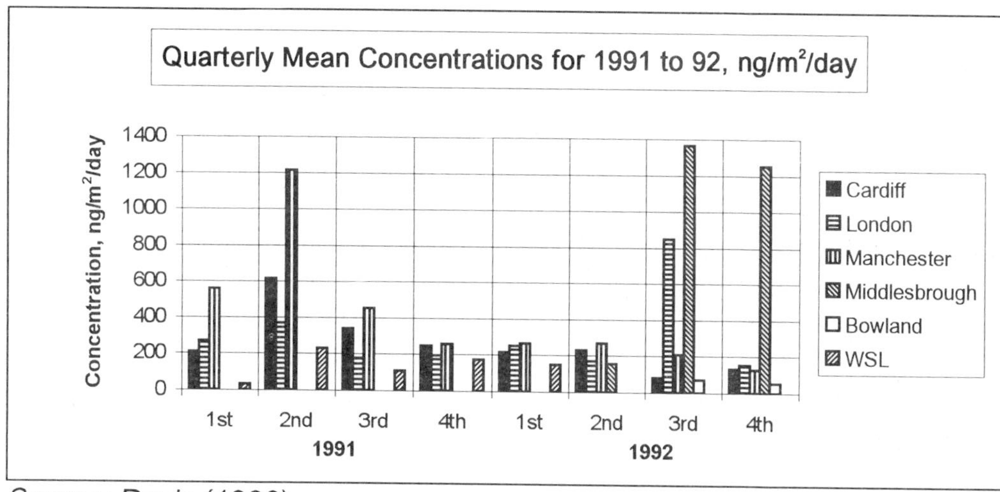

Source: Davis (1993)

Benzo(ghi)fluoranthene

Chemical formula : $C_{18}H_{10}$

Alternative names :

Type of pollutant : Polynuclear Aromatic Hydrocarbon, (PAH)

Structure :

Air quality data summary :

Urban Concentrations:

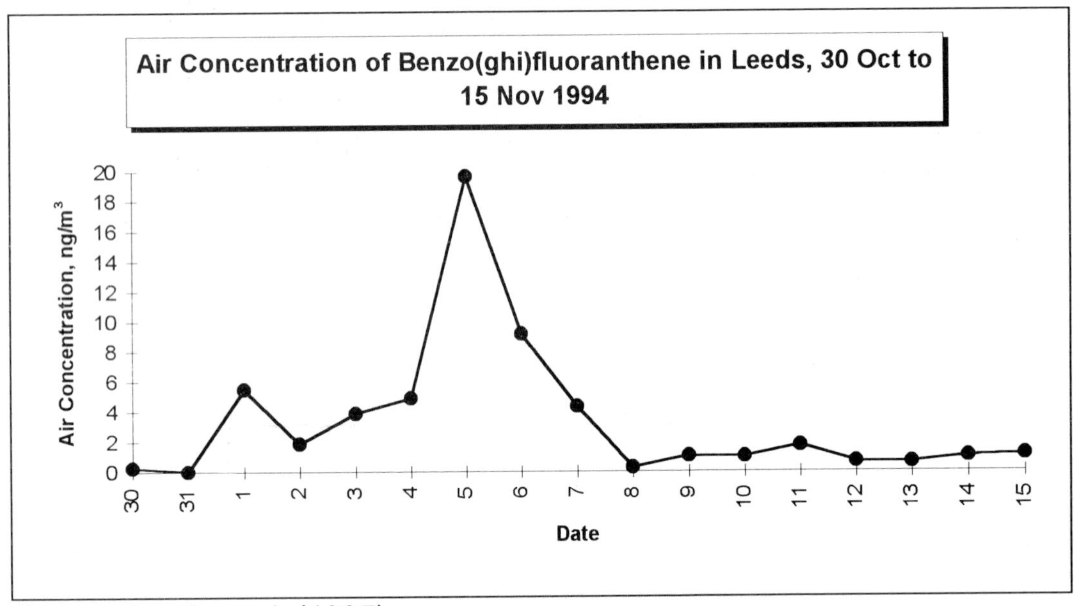

Source: Lewis et al. (1995)

Benzo(k)fluoranthene in air

Chemical formula : $C_{20}H_{12}$

Alternative names : PAH EPA no.75

Type of pollutant : Polynuclear Aromatic Hydrocarbon, (PAH)

Structure :

Air quality data summary :

Location	Annual Mean ng/m^3		
	1991	1992	1993
Bowland	*	*	0.38
Cardiff C	*	*	*
London	1.87	1.12	2.39
Manchester B	1.89	1.57	0.73
Middlesbrough	*	*	1.33
WSL	1.37	*	*

Source: Davis (1993)

Notes: * signifies no data available

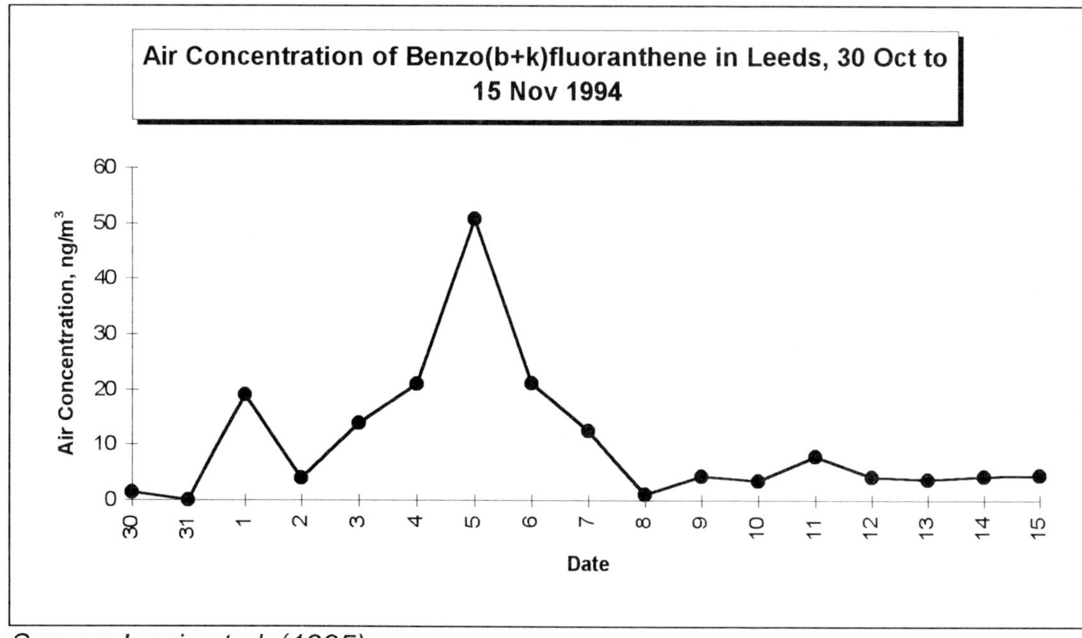

Source: Lewis et al. (1995)

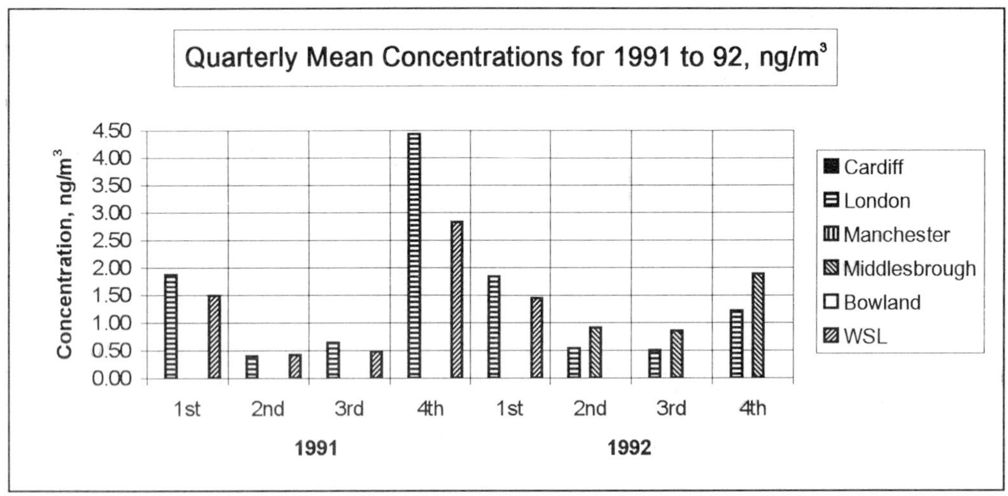

Source: Davis (1993)

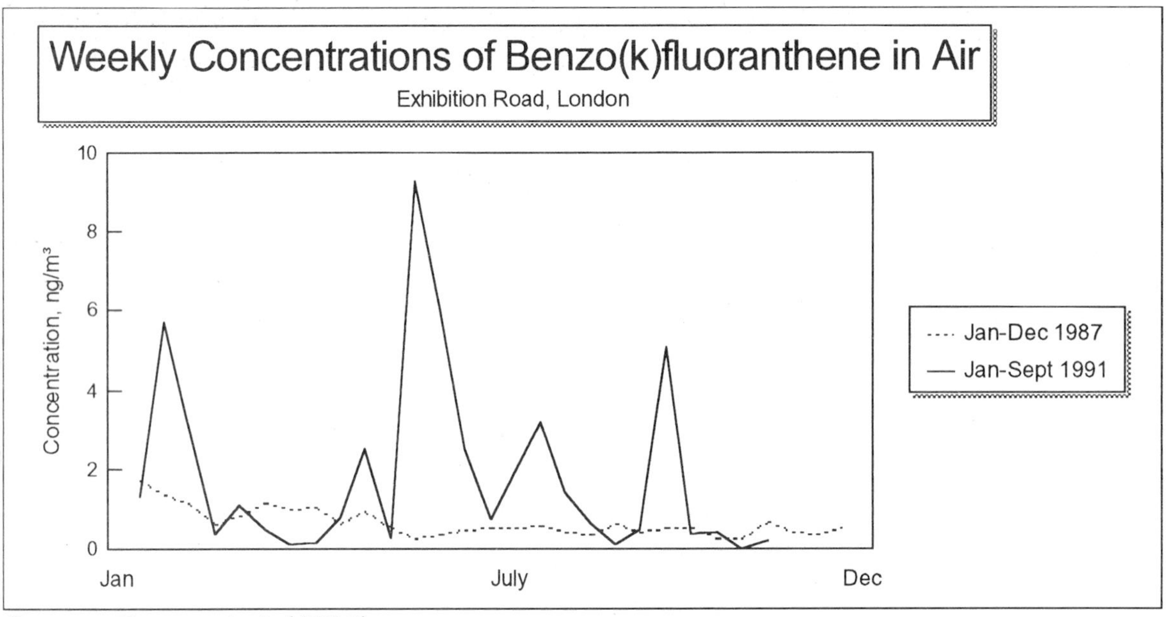

Source: Brown et al. (1995)

Location	Season 1992	Total Concentration in Air ng/m^3
Edgbaston	Winter (February)	1.20
Edgbaston	Summer (August)	0.16
Wasthills	Summer (August)	0.07

Source: Smith and Harrison (1994)

Benzo(k)fluoranthene in deposition

Chemical formula : $C_{20}H_{12}$

Alternative names : PAH EPA no.75

Type of pollutant : Polynuclear Aromatic Hydrocarbon, (PAH)

Structure :

Air quality data summary :

Location	Annual Mean ng/m²/day		
	1991	1992	1993
Bowland	*	*	32.44
Cardiff C	*	*	*
London	238.40	301.90	*
Manchester B	*	*	*
Middlesbrough	*	*	*
WSL	133.48	*	*

Source: Davis (1993)

Notes: * signifies no data available

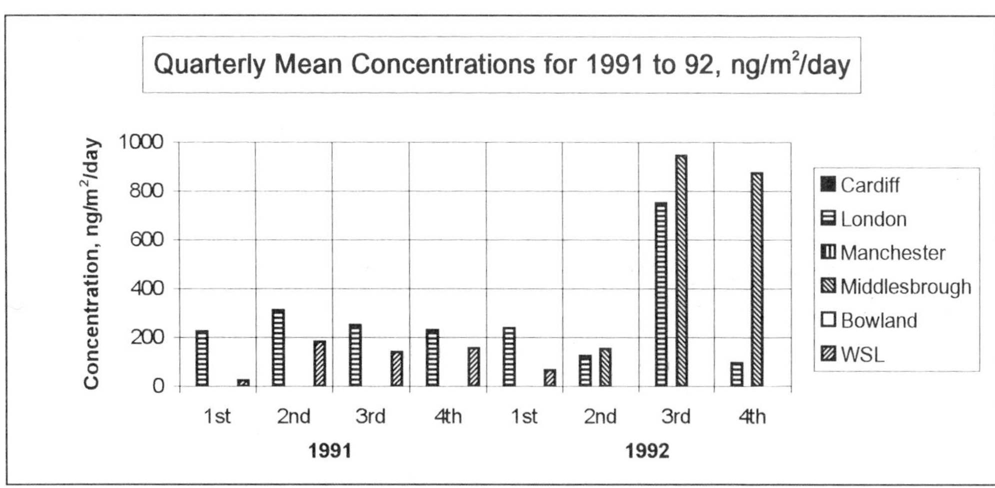

Source: Davis (1993)

Benzo(a)fluorene

Chemical formula	:	$C_{17}H_{12}$
Alternative names	:	Chrysofluorene
Type of pollutant	:	Polynuclear Aromatic Hydrocarbon, (PAH)
Structure	:	

Air quality data summary :

Urban Concentrations:

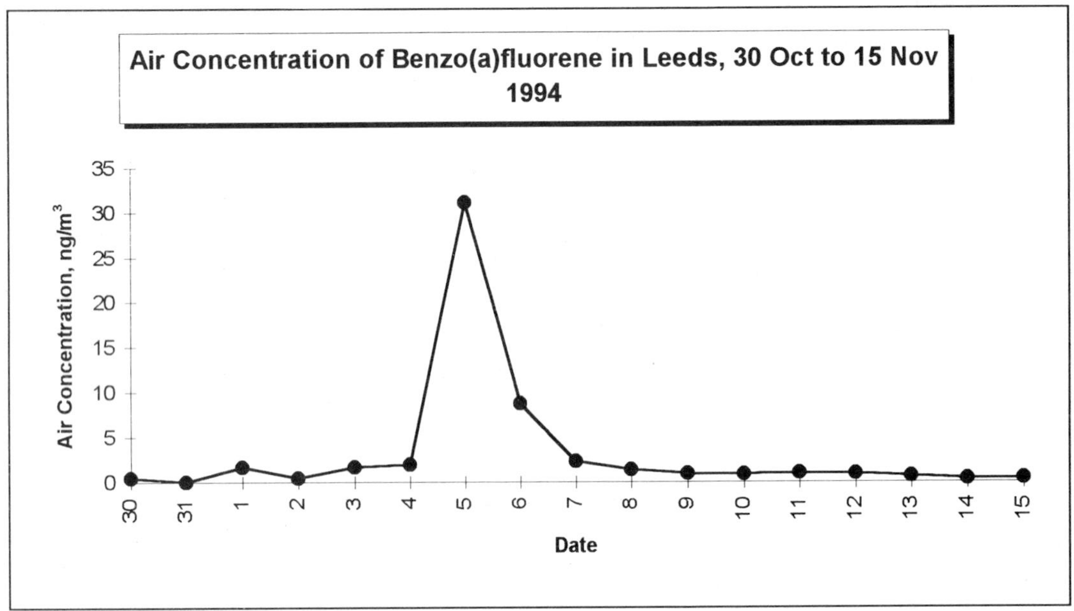

Source: Lewis et al. (1995)

Benzo(b)fluorene

Chemical formula : $C_{17}H_{12}$

Alternative names :

Type of pollutant : Polynuclear Aromatic Hydrocarbon, (PAH)

Structure :

Air quality data summary :

Urban Concentrations:

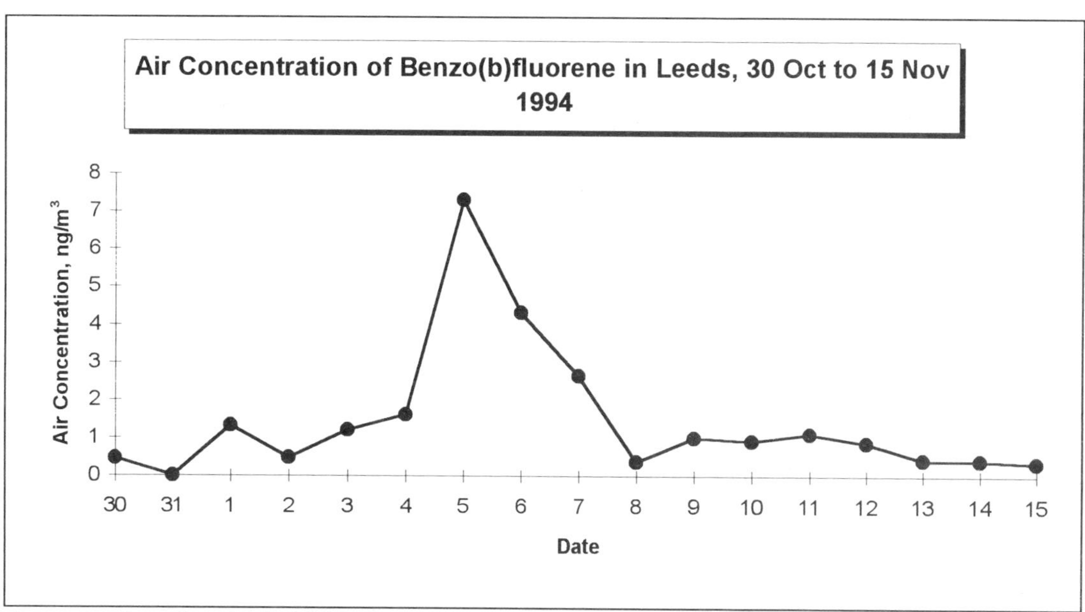

Source: Lewis et al. (1995)

Chemical formula : $C_{16}H_{10}S$

Alternative names :

Type of pollutant : Polynuclear Aromatic Hydrocarbon, (PAH)

Structure :

Air quality data summary :

Urban Concentrations:

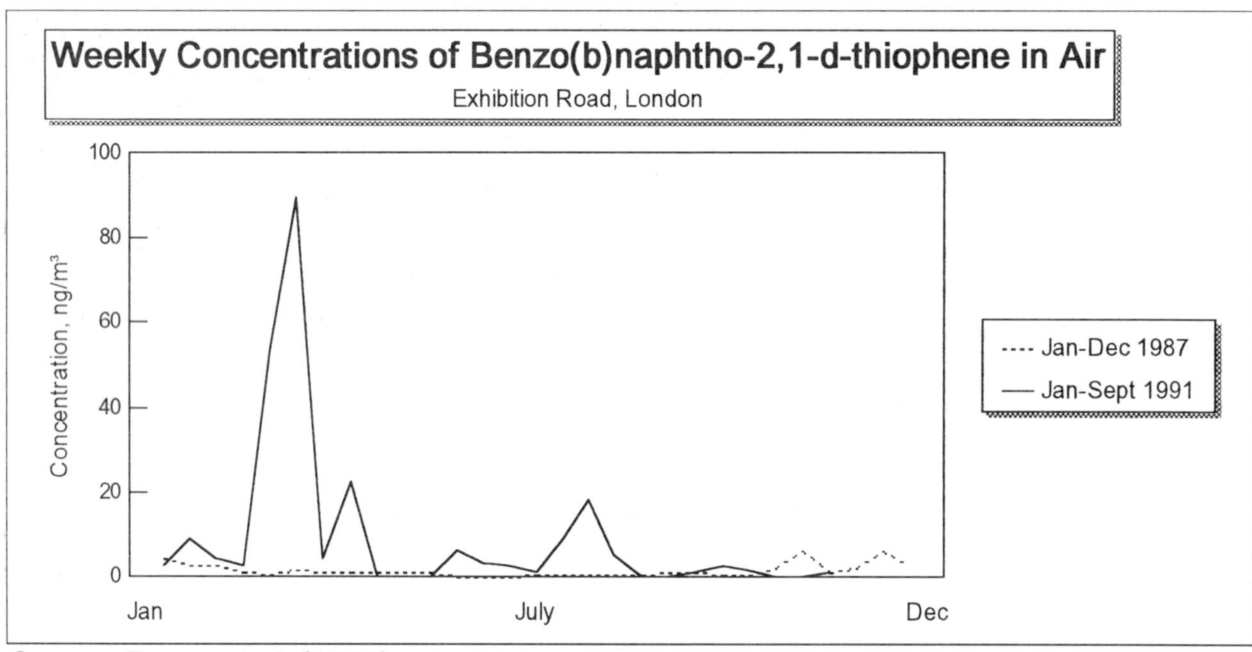

Source: Brown et al. (1995)

Location	Season 1992	Total Concentration in Air ng/m^3
Edgbaston	Winter (February)	1.32
Edgbaston	Summer (August)	0.33
Wasthills	Summer (August)	0.12

Source: Smith and Harrison (1994)

Chemical formula : $C_{22}H_{12}$

Alternative names : PAH EPA no.79

Type of pollutant : Polynuclear Aromatic Hydrocarbon, (PAH)

Structure :

Air quality data summary :

Location	Annual Mean ng/m^3		
	1991	1992	1993
Bowland	*	*	0.49
Cardiff C	2.38	1.37	*
London	5.61	4.79	1.15
Manchester B	2.47	2.00	1.38
Middlesbrough	*	*	1.22
WSL	3.51	*	*

Source: Davis (1993)

Notes: * signifies no data available

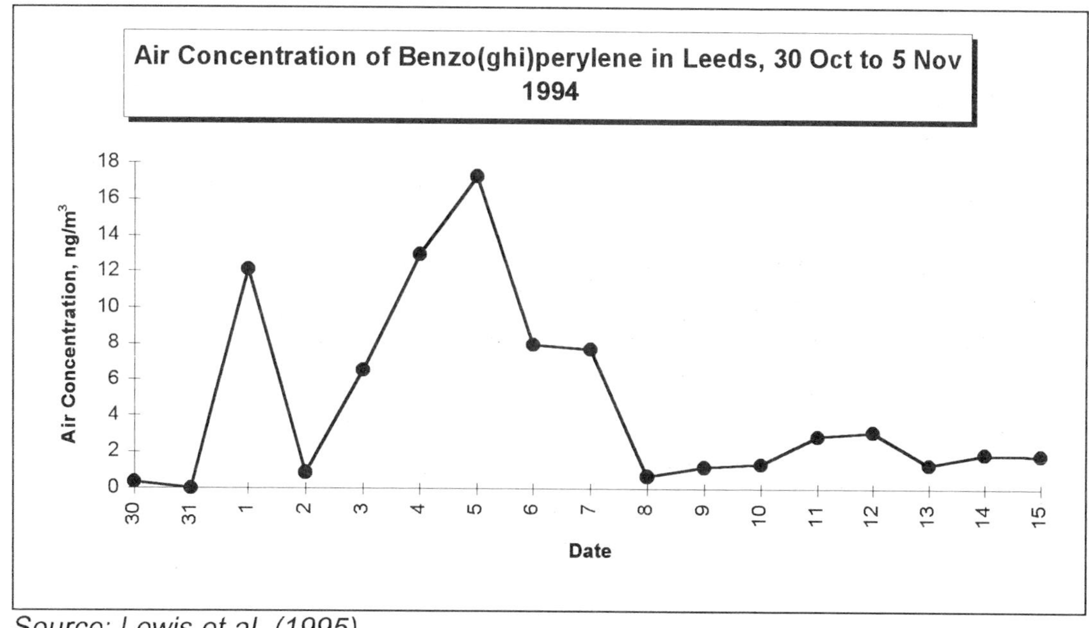

Source: Lewis et al. (1995)

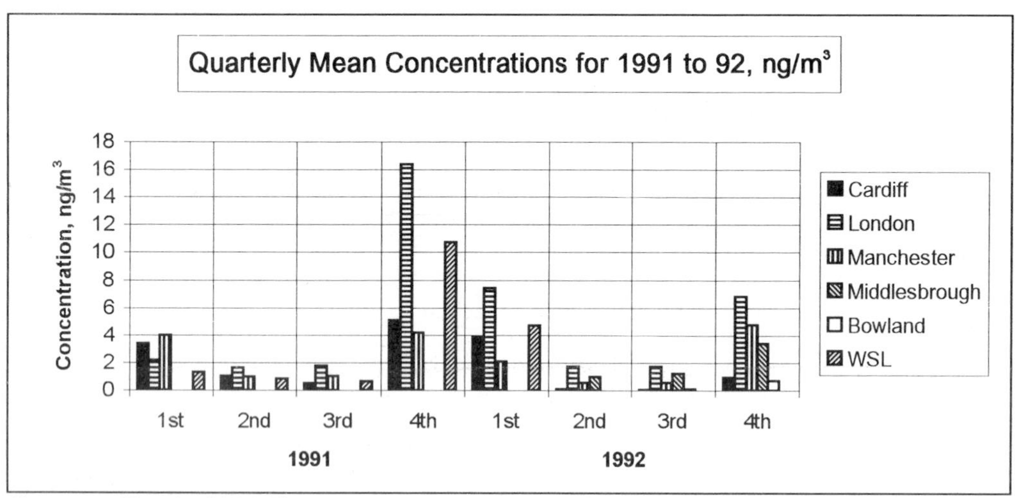

Source: Davis (1993)

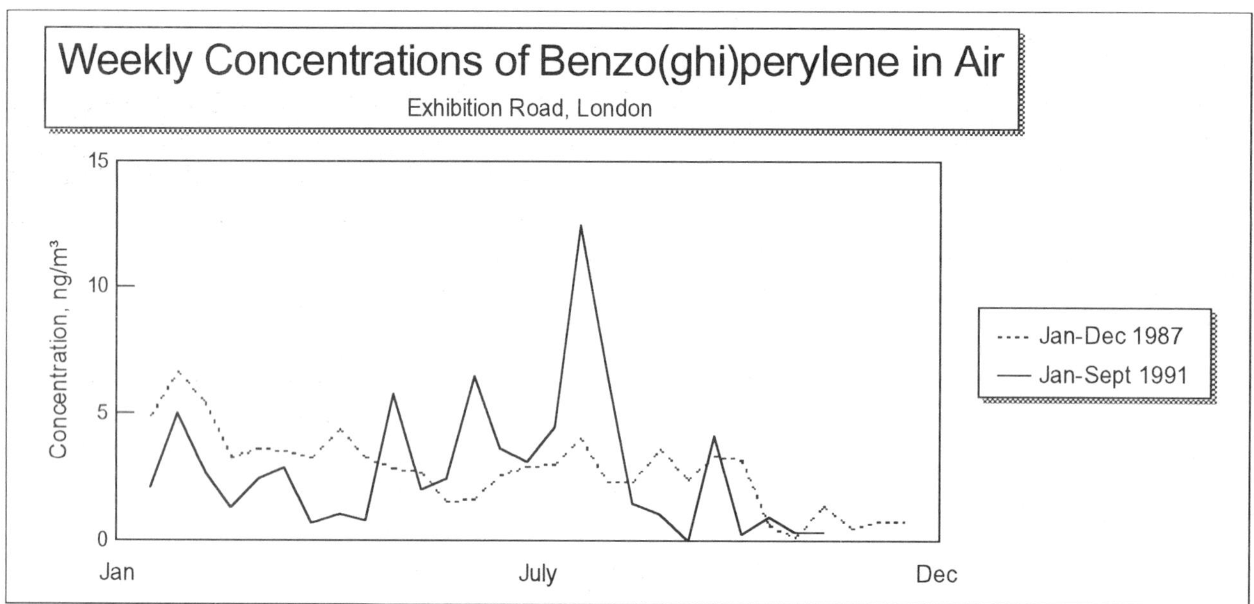

Source: Brown et al. (1995)

Location	Season 1992	Total Concentration in Air ng/m^3
Edgbaston	Winter (February)	1.97
Edgbaston	Summer (August)	0.76
Wasthills	Summer (August)	0.21

Source: Smith and Harrison (1994)

Chemical formula : $C_{20}H_{12}$

Alternative names : PAH EPA no.79

Type of pollutant : Polynuclear Aromatic Hydrocarbon, (PAH)

Structure :

Air quality data summary :

Location	Annual Mean ng/m²/day		
	1991	1992	1993
Bowland	*	*	62.85
Cardiff C	419.98	149.89	*
London	198.60	310.60	*
Manchester B	709.11	191.72	*
Middlesbrough	*	*	*
WSL	64.13	*	*

Source: Davis (1993)

Notes: * signifies no data available

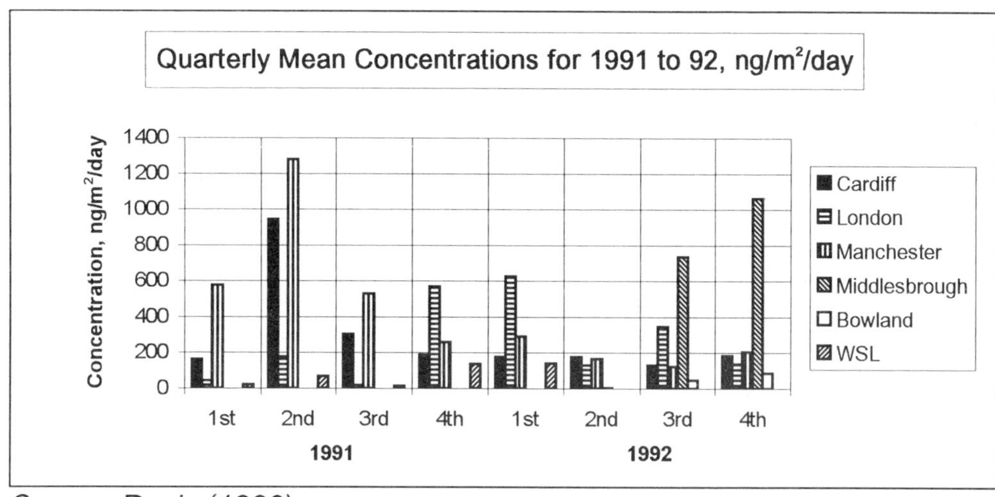

Source: Davis (1993)

Benzo(c)phenanthrene 25

Chemical formula : $C_{18}H_{12}$

Alternative names :

Type of pollutant : Polynuclear Aromatic Hydrocarbon, (PAH)

Structure :

Air quality data summary :

Urban Concentrations

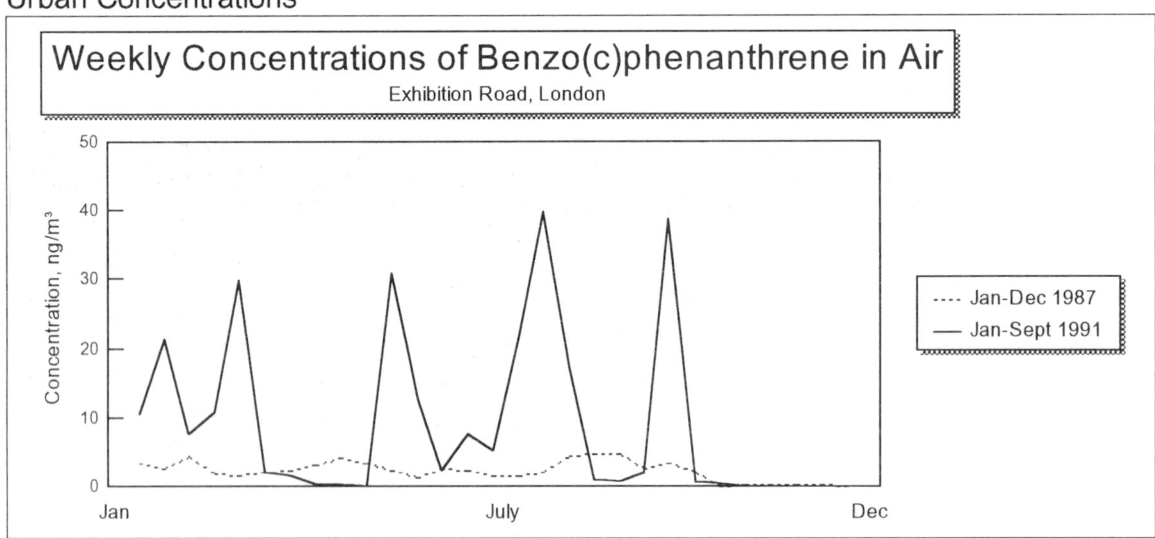

Source: Brown et al. (1995)

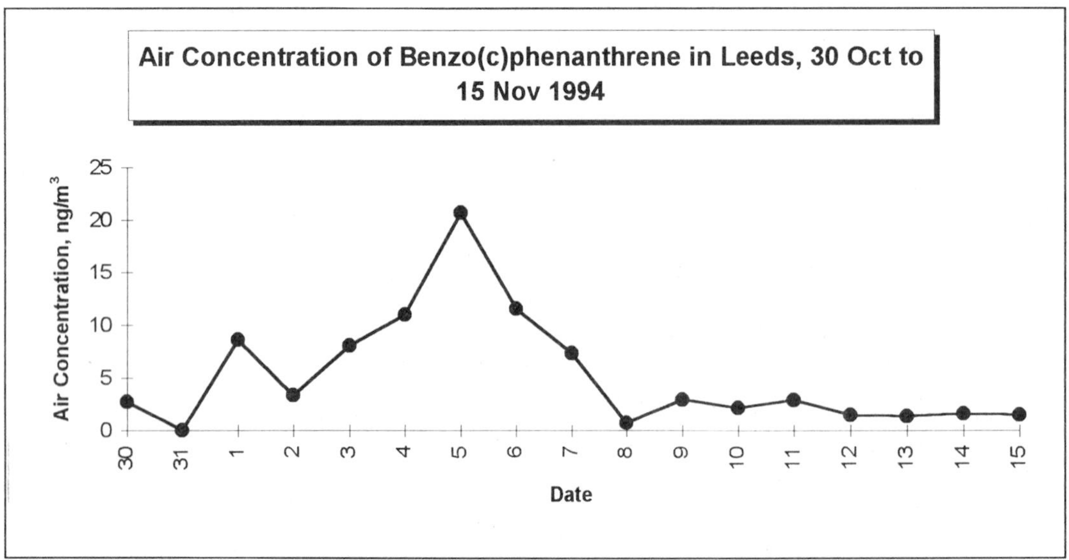

Source: Lewis et al. (1995)

Benzo(a)pyrene in air 26

Chemical formula : $C_{20}H_{12}$

Alternative names : 1,2-benzopyrene, PAH EPA no.73

Type of pollutant : Polynuclear Aromatic Hydrocarbon, (PAH)

Structure :

Air quality data summary :

Location	Annual Mean ng/m³		
	1991	1992	1993
Bowland	*	*	0.37
Cardiff C	2.18	1.01	*
London	1.11	0.63	0.85
Manchester B	1.85	1.56	0.70
Middlesbrough	*	*	0.57
WSL	0.67	*	*

Source: Davis (1993)

Notes: * signifies no data available

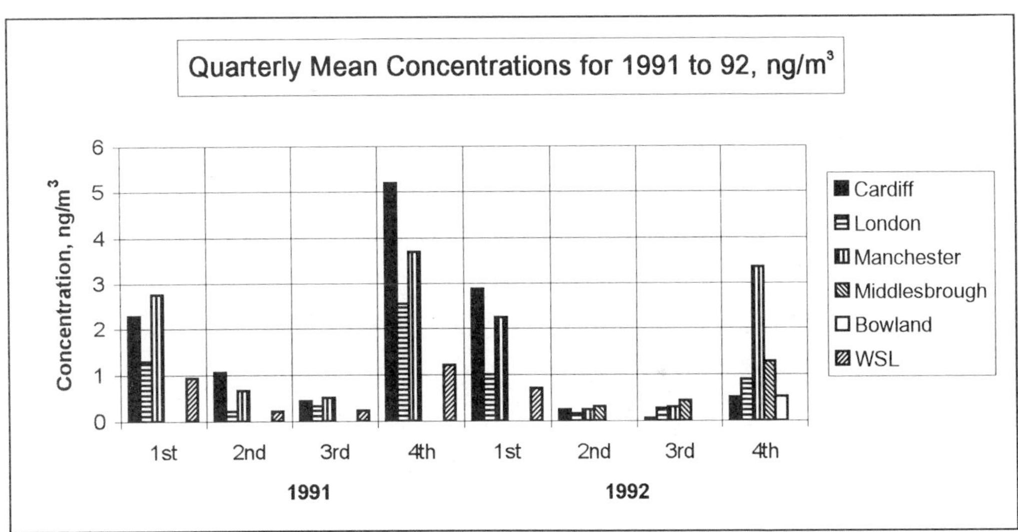

Source: Davis (1993)

Urban Concentrations:

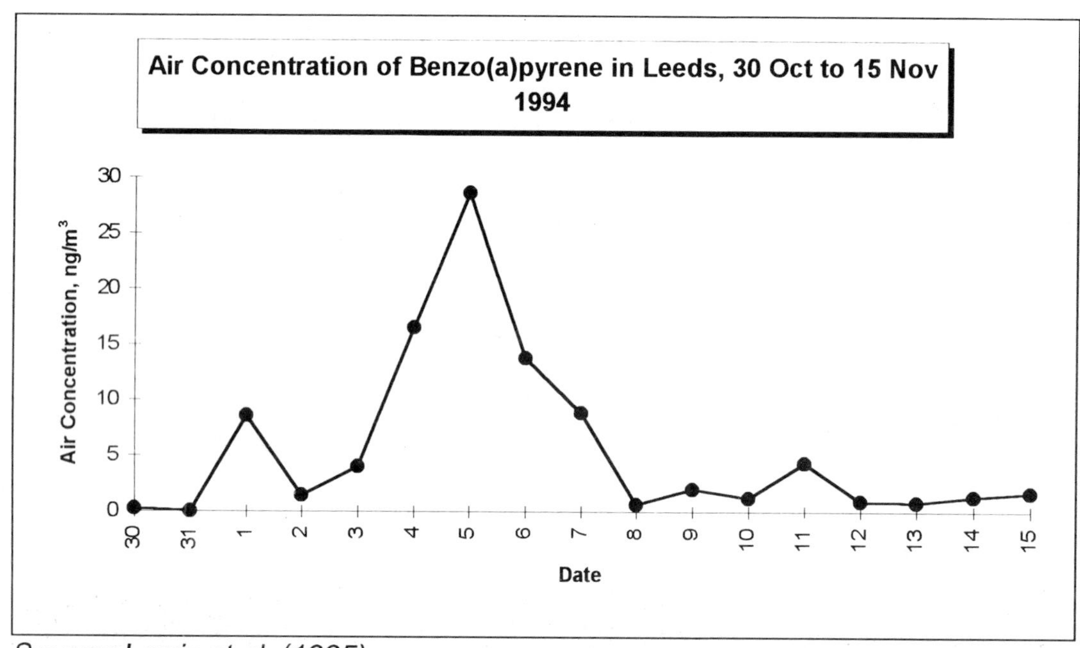

Source: Lewis et al. (1995)

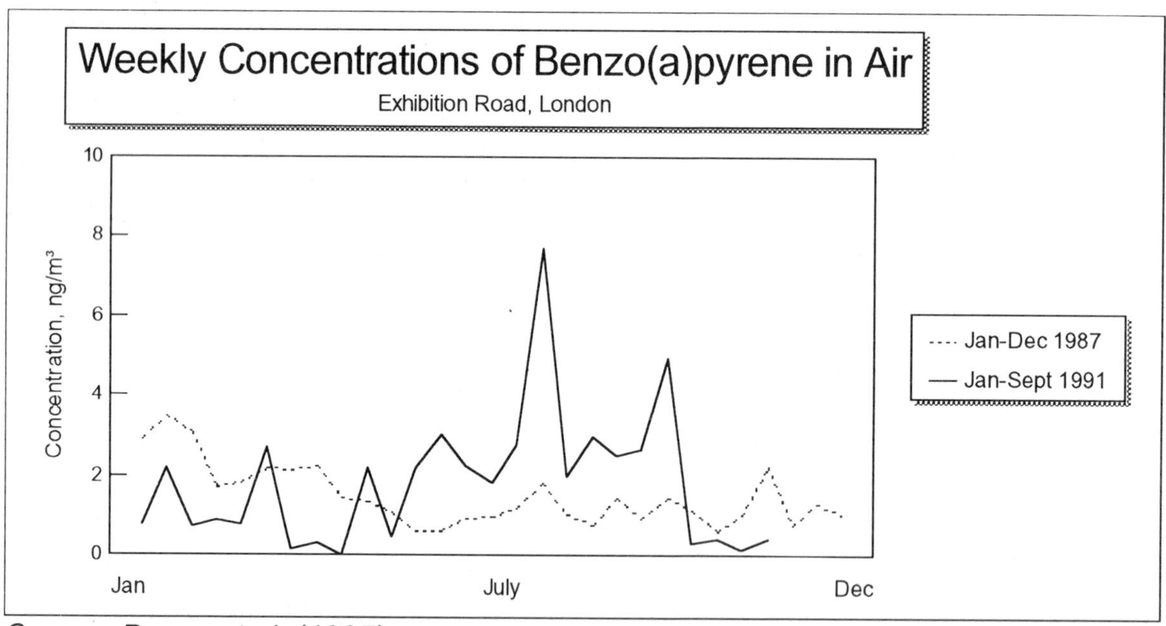

Source: Brown et al. (1995)

Location	Season 1992	Total Concentration in Air ng/m^3
Edgbaston	Winter (February)	0.81
Edgbaston	Summer (August)	0.25
Wasthills	Summer (August)	0.06

Source: Smith and Harrison (1994)

Benzo(a)pyrene in deposition 26

Chemical formula : $C_{20}H_{12}$

Alternative names : 1,2-benzopyrene, PAH EPA no.73

Type of pollutant : Polynuclear Aromatic Hydrocarbon, (PAH)

Structure :

Air quality data summary :

Location	Annual Mean ng/m²/day		
	1991	1992	1993
Bowland	*	*	48.38
Cardiff C	487.50	174.01	*
London	38.90	44.40	*
Manchester B	808.74	233.95	*
Middlesbrough	*	*	*
WSL	27.02	*	*

Source: Davis (1993)

Notes: * signifies no data available

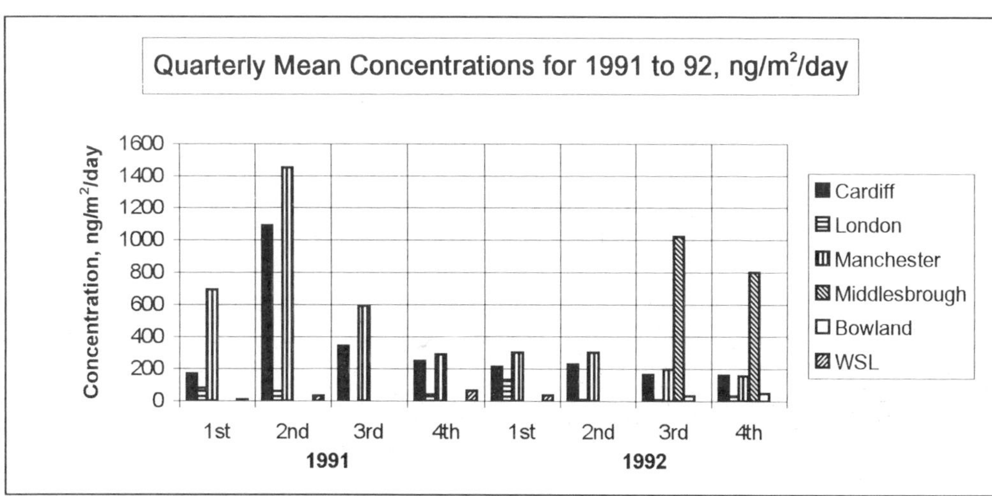

Source: Davis (1993)

Benzo(e)pyrene 27

Chemical formula : $C_{20}H_{12}$

Alternative names : 5,6-benzopyrene

Type of pollutant : Polynuclear Aromatic Hydrocarbon, (PAH)

Structure :

Air quality data summary :

Urban Concentrations

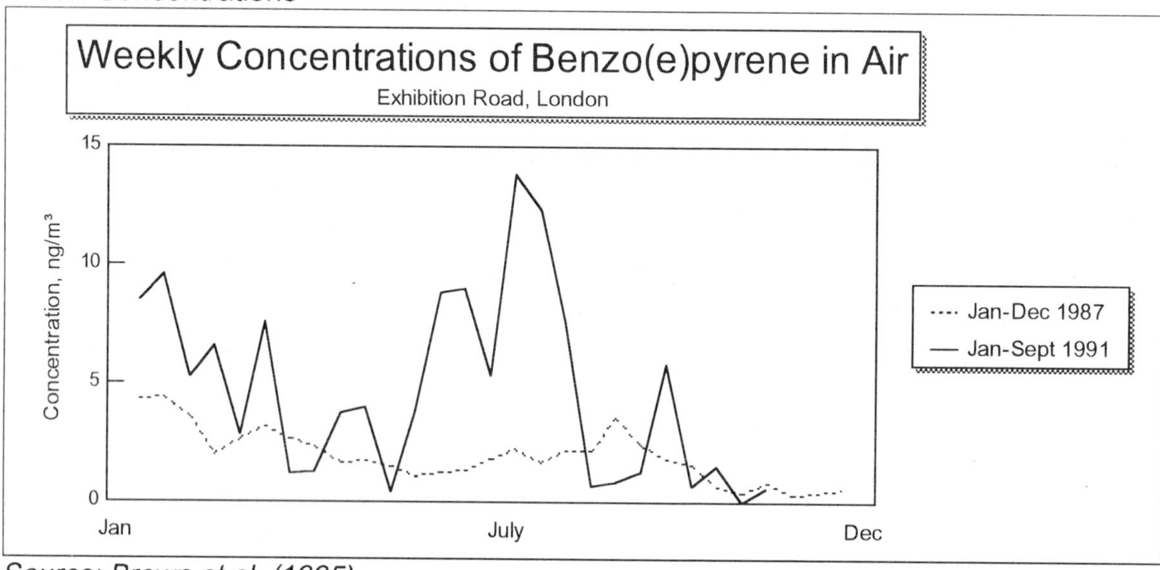

Source: Brown et al. (1995)

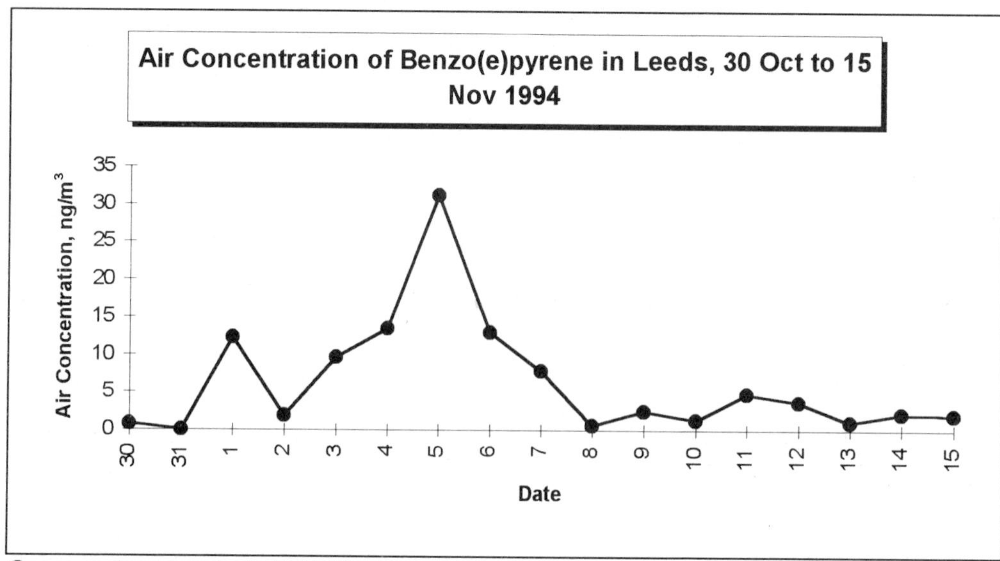

Source: Lewis et al. (1995)

7,8 Benzoquinoline 28

Chemical formula : $C_{13}H_9N$

Alternative names : α-Naphthoquinoline, benzo(h)quinoline

Type of pollutant : Polynuclear Aromatic Hydrocarbon, (PAH)

Structure :

Air quality data summary :

Urban Concentrations:

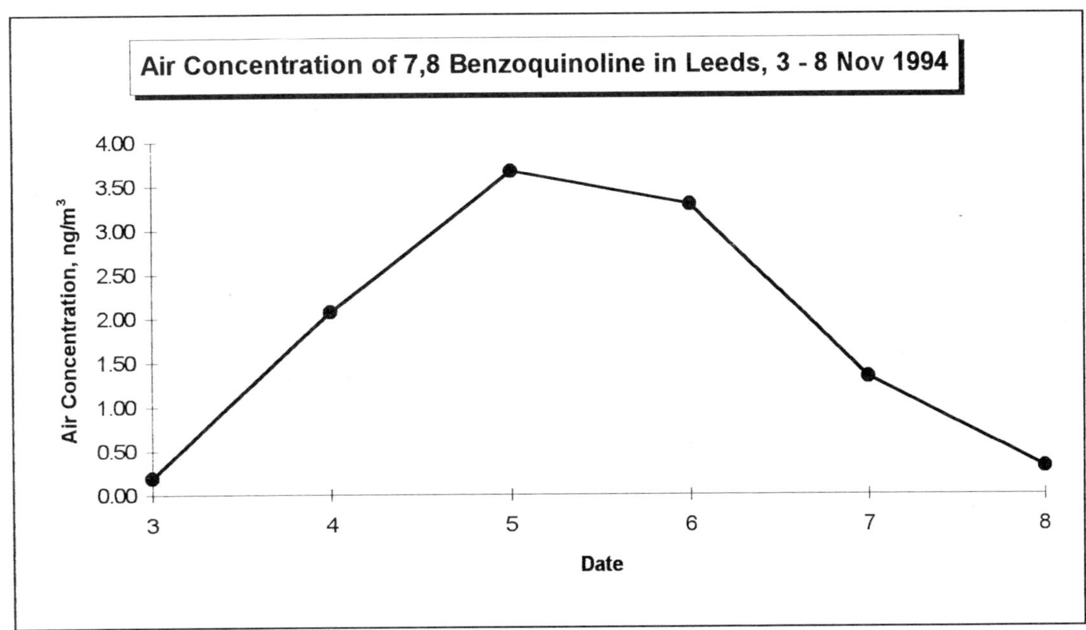

Source: Lewis et al. (1995)

Chemical formula : Br

Alternative names : Particulate bromide

Type of pollutant : Suspended particulate matter, trace element

Air quality data summary :

Rural Concentrations:

Location	Concentrations, ng/m^3			
	Mean	Trend	Mean	Trend
	1972-1981	%/yr	1982-1991	%/yr
Harwell, Oxfordshire.	45	-10.0	21.6	-4.7
Styrrup, Nottinghamshire.	108	-14.4	48.9	-4.7
Trebanos, Glamorgan.	48	-7.4	27.3	-
Wraymires, Cumbria.	29	-5.1	16.7	-9.6

Source: Cawse et al. (1994)

Urban Concentrations:

Location	Annual Mean Concentration, ng/m^3				
	1986	1987	1988	1989	1990
Brent	103.7	93.4	98.0	42.8	64.3
Motherwell	87.8	44.0	36.2	37.3	39.3
Glasgow C	62.6	104.0	99.8	99.1	83.2
Leeds	68.6	69.3	41.3	30.1	46.6

Source: DoE (1992)

Location	Nature of site	Measurement period	Mean concentration ng/m^3
Altrincham	Residential	1978-1989	108
Brent	Residential	1975-1989	232
Chilton	Rural	1971-1989	32
Flixton	Residential	1975-1989	177
Lambeth	Residential	1976-1982	182
Manchester City North	Industrial/ Residential	1975-1988	124
Manchester City South	Residential	1975-1989	121
Swansea	Urban	1972-1981	397
Walsall	Industrial	1976-1989	155
Wraymires	Rural	1970-1989	23

Source: Lee et al. (1994), Pattenden (1974).

Chemical formula : Br

Alternative names : Precipitation bromide

Type of pollutant : Trace contaminant of rain, trace element

Air quality data summary :

Rural Concentrations:

Location	Average Annual Rainfall Concentration, µg per litre	
	1972-1981	1982-1989 *
Harwell, Oxfordshire.	30	23
Styrrup, Nottinghamshire.	50	26
Wraymires, Cumbria.	26	19

Source: Cawse et al. (1994)

Note: total deposition expressed as apparent rainfall concentration.
* based on soluble fraction only.

Bromine not analysed in rainwater in 1990 and 1991.

1,3-Butadiene

Chemical formula : C_4H_6

Alternative names : buta-1,3-diene

Type of pollutant : (Volatile) organic compound (VOC), hydrocarbon, air toxic

Structure :

$CH_2=CHCH=CH_2$

Air quality data summary :

Remote rural concentrations

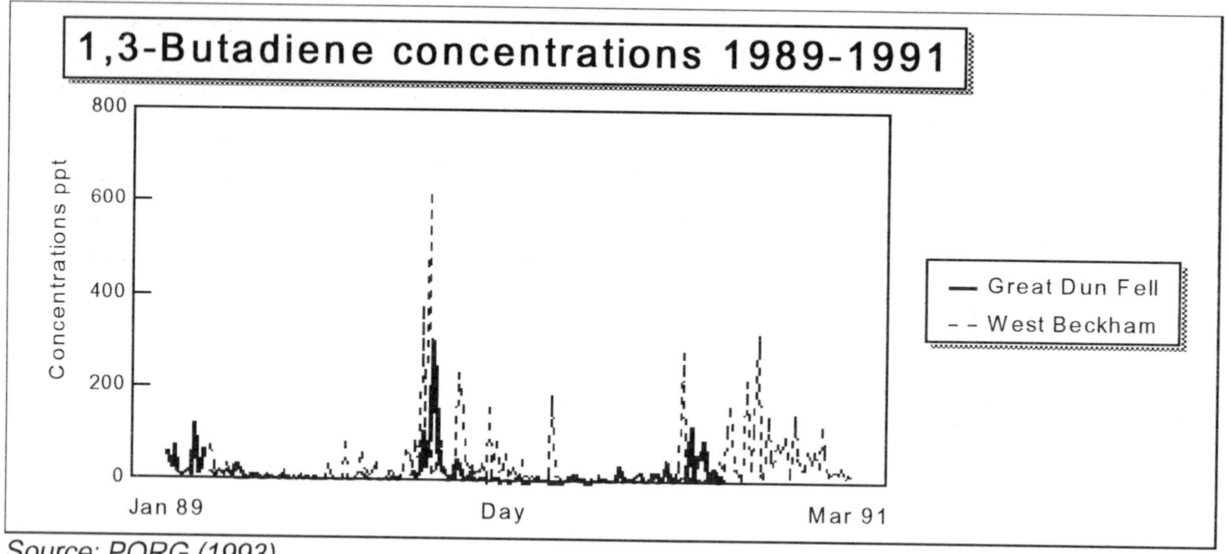

Source: PORG (1993)

Urban concentrations

	1994-95 Monthly Means, ppb								
	Belfast C	Birmingham B	Bristol A	Cardiff B	Edinburgh A	Eltham	Harwell	Middlesbrough	UCL
Jan 94	0.46	0.53	-	0.73	-	0.17	-	0.42	0.90
Feb 94	0.56	0.34	-	0.50	0.30	0.18	-	0.65	1.14
Mar 94	0.23	0.15	-	0.31	0.19	0.23	-	1.79	1.14
Apr 94	0.25	0.15	1.96	0.17	0.25	0.23	-	3.41	0.81
May 94	0.26	0.17	3.50	0.19	0.28	0.17	-	0.48	1.17
Jun 94	0.20	0.15	0.53	0.14	0.14	4.86	-	0.43	1.28
Jul 94	0.21	0.20	1.30	0.15	0.19	0.17	-	0.19	1.38
Aug 94	0.25	0.52	0.48	0.25	0.21	0.19	-	0.19	0.16
Sep 94	0.44	0.22	0.48	0.17	0.23	0.24	-	0.78	0.77
Oct 94	0.61	0.41	1.09	0.27	0.32	0.35	-	0.24	0.87
Nov 94	0.59	0.46	1.31	0.30	0.30	0.43	-	0.36	0.83
Dec 94	0.46	0.42	0.16	0.28	0.30	0.56	-	0.18	0.53
Jan 95	0.21	0.20	-	0.21	0.12	0.30	0.04	0.15	0.29
Feb 95	0.15	0.16	0.24	0.22	0.08	0.22	0.05	0.13	0.26

Source: Dollard (1995)

Chemical formula : C_4H_8O

Alternative names : Butyraldehyde

Types of pollutant : (Volatile) organic compound (VOC), hydrocarbon, oxygenate

Structure :

$CH_3CH_2CH_2CHO$

Air quality data summary :

Month 1993	Air Concentration at Harwell site, ppb
	Monthly Mean
August	0.053
September	0.033
October	0.026
November	0.043

Source: Solberg et al. (1994)

Chemical formula : $i\text{-}C_4H_{10}$

Alternative names : 2-methylpropane

Types of pollutant : (Volatile) organic compound (VOC), hydrocarbon

Structure :

$$CH_3\underset{\displaystyle CH_3}{\underset{|}{C}}HCH_3$$

Air quality data summary :

Remote rural concentrations

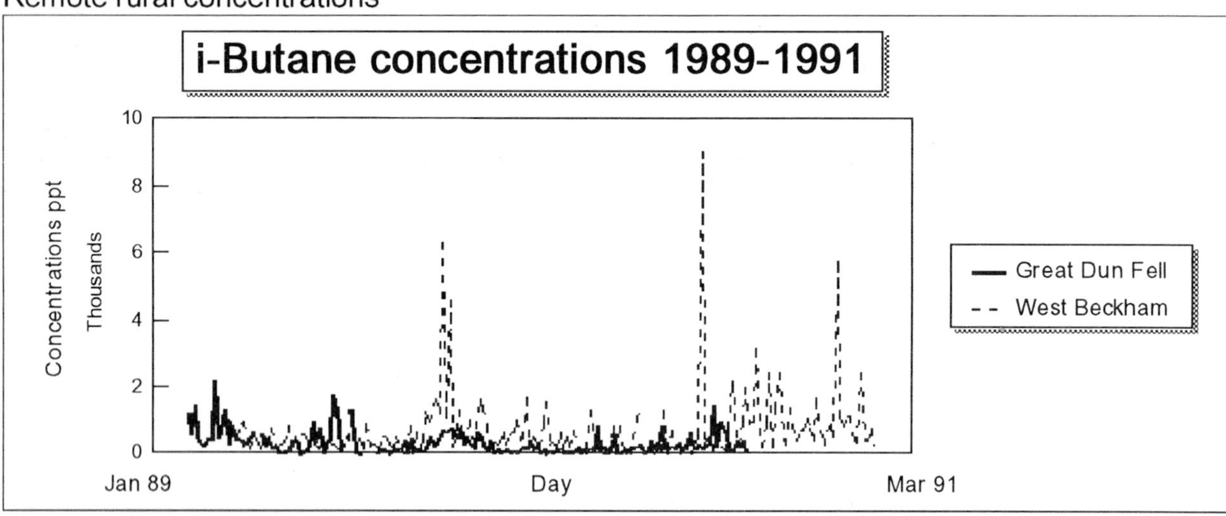

Source: PORG (1993)

Rural concentrations

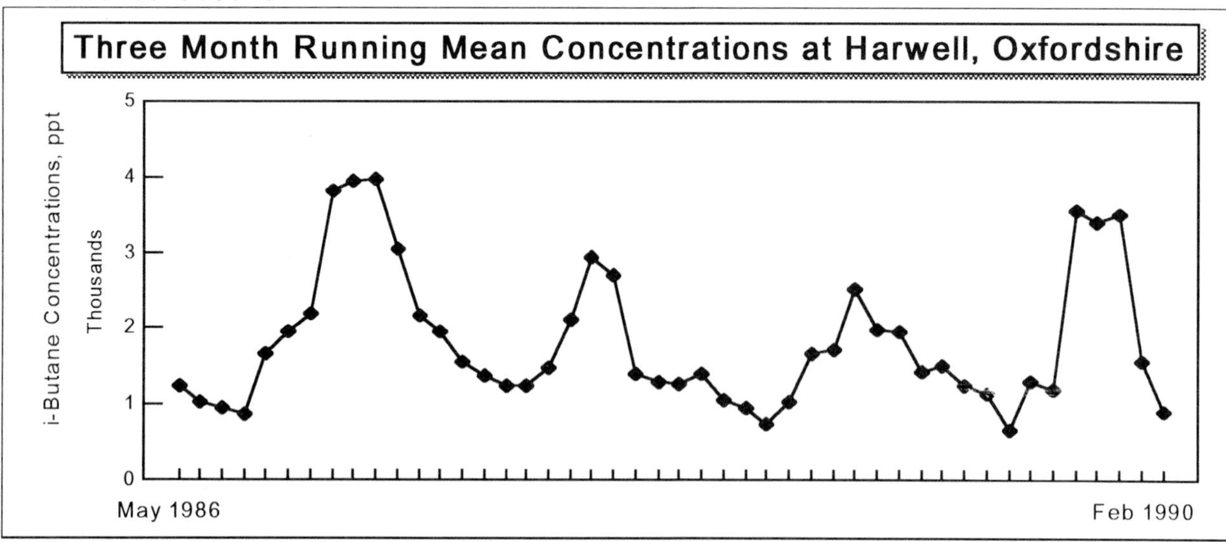

Source: PORG (1993)

Urban concentrations

	1994-95 Monthly Means, ppb								
	Belfast C	Birmingham B	Bristol A	Cardiff B	Edinburgh A	Eltham	Harwell	Middlesbrough	UCL
Jan 94	1.51	2.69	-	3.01	-	1.12	-	65.08	0.13
Feb 94	2.02	1.04	-	1.41	2.10	1.21	-	10.17	4.16
Mar 94	1.14	1.74	-	0.47	0.97	1.18	-	1.91	2.54
Apr 94	1.26	1.96	1.20	1.44	0.34	1.15	-	21.37	3.21
May 94	1.49	1.99	1.66	2.98	0.12	2.22	-	0.67	4.76
Jun 94	1.21	1.33	0.85	2.70	0.98	1.51	-	0.78	2.85
Jul 94	1.12	2.91	1.20	1.92	2.01	1.91	-	2.98	2.06
Aug 94	1.14	1.50	1.17	1.37	1.63	0.05	-	1.52	3.91
Sep 94	1.79	1.49	1.37	1.83	2.13	1.60	-	7.08	3.53
Oct 94	2.27	1.22	2.73	2.21	1.32	2.29	-	4.82	3.61
Nov 94	2.34	2.07	2.33	4.70	1.28	2.33	-	4.39	3.95
Dec 94	2.43	2.12	2.23	3.39	2.30	1.93	-	1.67	3.03
Jan 95	2.05	3.62	1.94	2.65	1.80	2.42	-	2.41	3.18
Feb 95	1.49	-	1.45	2.31	1.31	1.94	-	1.52	3.07

Source: Dollard (1995)

Chemical formula : $n\text{-}C_4H_{10}$

Alternative names :

Type of pollutant : (Volatile) organic compound (VOC), hydrocarbon

Structure :

$CH_3CH_2CH_2CH_3$

Air quality data summary :

Remote rural concentrations

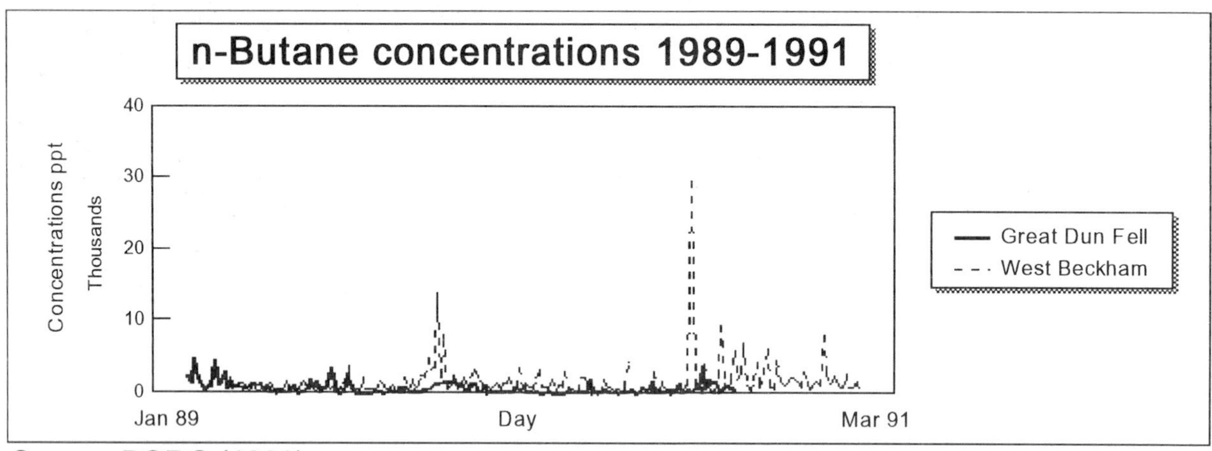

Source: PORG (1993)

Rural concentrations

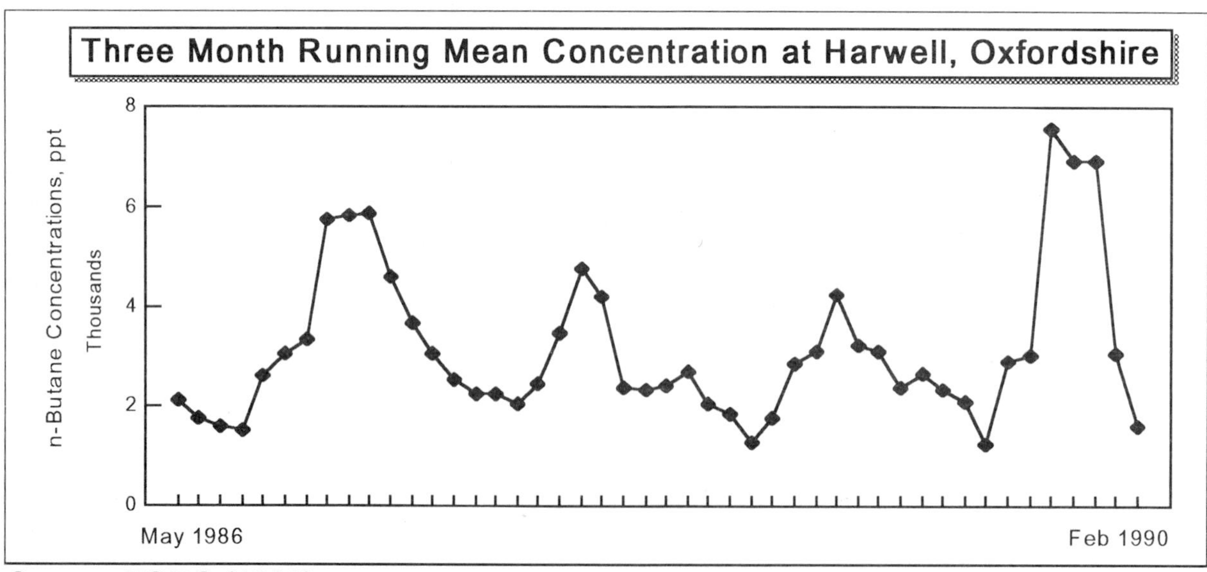

Source: PORG (1993)

Urban concentrations

	1994-95 Monthly Means, ppb								
	Belfast C	Birmingham B	Bristol A	Cardiff B	Edinburgh A	Eltham	Harwell	Middlesbrough	UCL
Jan 94	3.18	3.15	-	5.67	-	1.76	-	5.30	1.54
Feb 94	4.09	0.94	-	4.93	0.06	1.77	-	13.88	8.46
Mar 94	2.01	2.56	-	2.32	0.28	1.02	-	2.30	4.03
Apr 94	2.13	2.76	1.06	3.09	3.09	1.82	-	18.44	4.23
May 94	2.72	3.26	2.57	4.68	2.66	1.86	-	2.76	6.66
Jun 94	2.26	2.63	1.62	0.71	2.03	2.39	-	2.53	5.59
Jul 94	2.27	4.20	1.54	3.52	3.48	2.99	-	7.67	6.96
Aug 94	2.37	4.52	1.78	2.37	2.96	2.20	-	5.87	4.02
Sep 94	4.04	3.77	2.04	2.95	3.56	2.94	-	10.51	6.16
Oct 94	5.11	5.08	3.94	4.85	3.05	4.38	-	10.62	8.02
Nov 94	5.07	7.51	3.29	5.42	1.76	5.11	-	10.16	7.67
Dec 94	4.58	6.47	3.41	4.82	3.38	3.96	-	3.37	6.66
Jan 95	3.74	3.00	3.14	0.06	0.04	3.83	0.80	7.87	4.59
Feb 95	2.83	2.85	2.42	3.29	1.93	3.19	0.61	3.50	4.43

Source: Dollard (1995)

Chemical formula : C_4H_8O

Alternative names : Methyl ethyl ketone, MEK

Types of pollutant : (Volatile) organic compound (VOC), hydrocarbon, oxygenate

Structure :

$$CH_3\underset{\underset{O}{\|}}{C}CH_2CH_3$$

Air quality data summary :

Month 1993	Air Concentration at Harwell site, ppb
	Monthly Mean
August	0.173
September	0.203
October	0.097
November	0.347
December	0.060

Source: Solberg et al. (1994)

Chemical formula	:	C_4H_6O
Alternative names	:	Crotonaldehyde
Types of pollutant	:	(Volatile) organic compound (VOC), hydrocarbon, oxygenate
Structure	:	$CH_3CH{=}CHCHO$
Air quality data summary	:	

Month 1993	Air Concentration at Harwell site, ppb
	Monthly Mean
August	0.014
September	0.007

Source: Solberg et al. (1994)

Chemical formula : C_4H_8

Alternative names : but-1-ene

Type of pollutant : (Volatile) organic compound (VOC), hydrocarbon

Structure :

$CH_2{=}CHCH_2CH_3$

Air quality data summary :

Remote rural concentrations

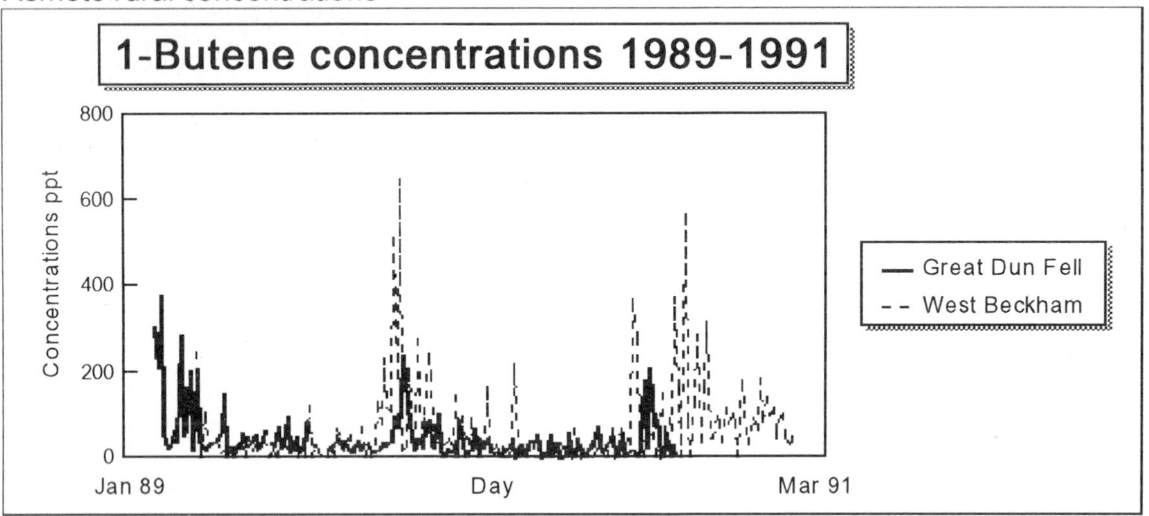

Source: PORG (1993)

Urban concentrations

1994-95 Monthly Means, ppb									
	Belfast C	Birmingham B	Bristol A	Cardiff B	Edinburgh A	Eltham	Harwell	Middlesbrough	UCL
Jan 94	0.21	0.84	-	0.49	-	0.11	-	0.94	0.73
Feb 94	0.25	0.19	-	0.39	0.18	0.11	-	1.12	0.66
Mar 94	0.12	0.14	-	0.56	0.10	0.21	-	3.02	0.33
Apr 94	0.14	0.16	0.26	0.17	0.46	0.51	-	3.05	0.58
May 94	0.15	0.16	0.38	0.20	0.41	0.26	-	0.49	0.44
Jun 94	0.13	0.15	0.21	0.62	0.12	0.10	-	0.33	0.29
Jul 94	0.12	0.30	0.39	0.20	0.13	0.13	-	0.28	0.36
Aug 94	0.17	0.42	0.19	0.36	0.15	0.11	-	0.29	0.79
Sep 94	0.28	0.19	0.17	0.15	0.15	0.16	-	0.81	0.38
Oct 94	0.33	0.34	0.54	0.30	0.21	0.26	-	0.60	0.56
Nov 94	0.27	0.40	0.26	0.19	0.19	0.31	-	0.46	0.53
Dec 94	0.35	0.45	0.24	0.24	0.19	0.36	-	0.20	0.65
Jan 95	0.22	0.18	0.24	0.19	0.11	0.31	0.05	0.19	0.27
Feb 95	0.14	0.16	0.19	0.18	0.08	0.21	0.04	0.15	0.25

Source: Dollard (1995)

3-Buten-2-one

Chemical formula : C_4H_6O

Alternative names : Methyl vinyl ketone

Type of pollutant : (Volatile) organic compound (VOC), hydrocarbon, oxygenate

Structure :

$$CH_3\underset{\underset{O}{\|}}{C}CH{=}CH_2$$

Air quality data summary :

Month 1993	Air Concentration at Harwell site, ppb
	Monthly Mean
August	0.014
September	0.007

Source: Solberg et al. (1994)

Chemical formula : $C_{10}H_{14}$

Alternative names :

Type of pollutant : (Volatile) organic compound (VOC), hydrocarbon

Structure :

$CH_2CH_2CH_2CH_3$

Air quality data summary :

Mean Air Concentration in Leeds, 19/8/94 to 8/9/94	
Location	21 day mean, μg/m^3
Albion Street	0.100
Cliff Lane	0.055
EUN monitoring site	0.568
Kirkstall Road	0.192
Park site	0.088
Queen Street	0.122
Kerbside site	0.320
Vicar Lane	0.382

Source: Bartle et al. (1995)

Note: It should be noted that 2 other compounds may also contribute to the peak attributed to n-butylbenzene

Chemical formula : C_4H_8

Alternative name : 2-methylpropene, i-butene

Type of pollutant : (Volatile) organic compound (VOC), hydrocarbon

Structure :

$CH_2=C(CH_3)_2$

Air quality data summary :

Remote rural concentrations

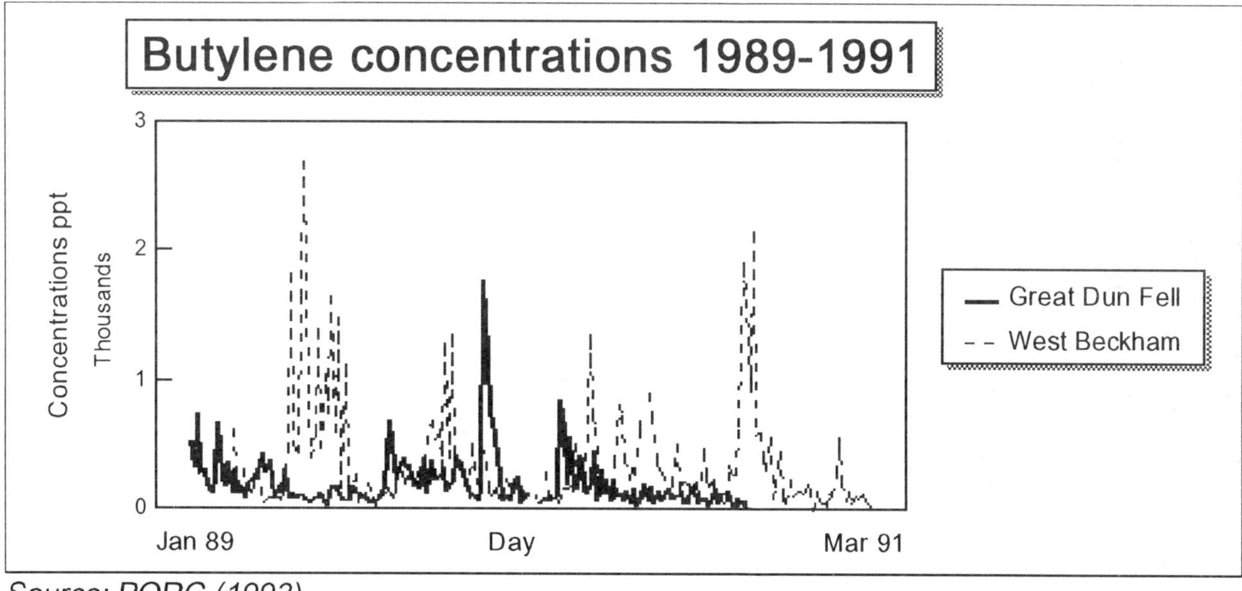

Source: PORG (1993)

Chemical formula : Cd

Alternative names : Particulate cadmium

Type of pollutant : Suspended particulate matter, trace element

Air quality data summary :

Rural Concentrations

Location	Concentrations, ng/m^3	
	Mean	Mean
	1975-1981	1982-1991
Harwell, Oxfordshire.	<2	<3
Styrrup, Nottinghamshire.	<4	<4
Trebanos, Glamorgan.	4	
Wraymires, Cumbria.	<2	<1

Source: Cawse (1994)

Urban Concentrations

Location	Concentrations, ng/m^3				
	Mean	Mean	Mean	Mean	Mean
	1985	1986	1987	1988	1989
Central London	3.6	2.7	7.2	10.0	1.4
Brent	1.4	0.9	1.7	2.2	5.6
Motherwell	2.5	1.1	3.6	2.1	8.5
Glasgow C	2.6	1.3	1.9	1.8	5.0
Leeds	2.0	1.4	1.9	1.4	6.1

Source: DoE(1992)

Location		Average annual concentration, ng/m^3			
		1984	1985	1986	1987
Plynlimon, Powys.	Rural	0.37	0.31	0.12	0.25
Trebanos, West Glamorgan.	Rural	0.44	0.86	0.31	0.70
Queensferry, Clwyd.	Urban	0.60	1.30	0.63	0.89
Wrexham, Clwyd.	Urban	0.75	1.10	0.49	0.84
Bedwas, Mid Glamorgan.	Urban	2.40	5.30	3.40	3.90
Port Talbot, West Glamorgan.	Urban	0.64	0.97	0.43	0.64

Source: Baker et al. (1988)

Location	Nature of site	Measurement period	Mean concentration ng/m^3
Altrincham	Residential	1978-1989	3.6
Brent	Residential	1975-1989	9.2
Chilton	Rural	1971-1989	3.1
Flixton	Residential	1975-1989	4.8
Lambeth	Residential	1976-1982	4.9
Manchester City North	Industrial/ Residential	1975-1988	6.5
Manchester City South	Residential	1975-1989	5.8
Walsall	Industrial	1976-1989	28.3
Wraymires	Rural	1970-1989	2.0

Source: Lee et al. (1994)

Cadmium in rain

Chemical formula : Cd

Alternative names : Precipitation cadmium

Type of pollutant : Trace contaminant of rain, trace element

Air quality data summary :

Rural Concentrations

Location	Average Annual Rainfall Concentration µg per litre	
	1972-1981	1982-1991 *
Harwell, Oxfordshire.	<3	0.65
Styrrup, Nottinghamshire.	<5	1.2
Wraymires, Cumbria.	<2	<0.5

Source: Cawse et al. (1994)

Note: total deposition expressed as apparent rainfall concentration.
* based on soluble fraction only.

Chemical formula : Cs

Alternative names : Particulate caesium

Type of pollutant : Suspended particulate matter, trace element

Air quality data summary :

Rural concentrations

Location	Concentrations, ng/m^3			
	Mean	Trend	Mean	Trend
	1972-1981	%/yr	1982-1991	%/yr
Harwell, Oxfordshire.	0.19	-12.4	0.093	nst
Styrrup, Nottinghamshire.	0.35	-18.8	0.110	-10.8
Swansea.	0.33	nst	-	-
Trebanos, Glamorgan.	0.19	-19.7	0.130	-
Wraymires, Cumbria.	0.12	-14.1	0.050	nst

Source: Cawse et al. (1994), Pattenden (1974).

Note: nst=no significant trend

Caesium in rain

Chemical formula : Cs

Alternative names : Precipitation caesium

Type of pollutant : Trace contaminant of rain, trace element

Air quality data summary :

Rural Concentrations

Location	Average Annual Rainfall Concentration µg per litre	
	1972-1981	1982-1989 *
Harwell, Oxfordshire.	0.09	<0.02
Styrrup, Nottinghamshire.	0.21	<0.03
Wraymires, Cumbria.	0.04	<0.02

Source: Cawse et al. (1994)

Note: total deposition expressed as apparent rainfall concentration.
* based on soluble fraction only.

Caesium not analysed in rainwater in 1990 and 1991.

Chemical formula : Ca

Alternative names : Particulate calcium

Type of pollutant : Suspended particulate matter, trace element

Air quality data summary :

Rural Concentrations

Location	Concentrations, ng/m^3				
	Mean	Trend	Mean		Trend
	1975-1981	%/yr	1982-1991		%/yr
Harwell, Oxfordshire.	917	nst	336	*	-19.0
Styrrup, Nottinghamshire.	1673	-8.6	454	**	nst
Trebanos, Glamorgan.	1054				
Wraymires, Cumbria.	719	nst	190	***	-12.5

Source: Cawse et al. (1994)

Note: * only 20% of measurements were positive (these positive data were obtained in 1990 and 1991 only).
** only 20% of measurements were positive (these positive data were obtained in 1990 and 1991 only).
*** only 15% of measurements were positive (these positive data were obtained in 1990 and 1991 only).

nst=no significant trend

Calcium in rain 42

Chemical formula : Ca

Alternative names : Precipitation calcium

Type of pollutant : Trace contaminant of rain, trace element

Air quality data summary :

Rural Concentrations

Location	Average Annual Rainfall Concentration, μg per litre	
	1972 - 1981	1982-1991*
Harwell, Oxfordshire	2239	<12000
Styrrup, Nottinghamshire	3017	<9300
Wraymires, Cumbria	1056	<4900

Source: Cawse et al. (1994)

Note: total deposition expressed as apparent rainfall concentration
* represents results from soluble fraction only

Site	Precipitation-weighted Annual Mean Calcium Concentration, 1986-93, (μ eql^{-1})							
	1986	1987	1988	1989	1990	1991	1992	1993
Achanarras	16	15	20	20	21	17	17	18
Balquhidder	8	5	6	9	8	11	8	11
Bannisdale	13	12	14	13	15	16	15	14
Barcombe Mills	20	29	22	30	33	32	22	20
Beddgelert	9	10	13	9	12	11	11	11
Bottesford	36	33	50	33	23	29	19	17
Compton	23	51	33	22	32	30	23	20
Cow Green Reservoir	7	8	12	12	13	11	13	12
Driby	18	19	27	34	33	27	18	19
Eskdalemuir	7	5	8	21	8	10	8	9
Flatford Mill	33	21	27	37	29	24	18	21
Glen Dye	-	7	10	11	9	9	10	10
Goonhilly	16	15	14	18	31	22	18	18
High Muffles	13	21	23	27	20	23	21	19
Hillsborough Forest	-	-	-	13	14	17	16	15
Jenny Hurn	56	45	73	48	50	39	27	26
Llyn Brianne	7	8	9	10	15	10	10	10
Loch Dee	10	9	11	9	11	10	11	9
Lough Navar	17	10	21	12	18	25	19	24

Site	Precipitation-weighted Annual Mean Calcium Concentration, 1986-93, (μ eql^{-1})							
	1986	1987	1988	1989	1990	1991	1992	1993
Plynlimon	-	-	-	7	11	11	9	7
Polloch	-	-	-	-	-	16	13	13
Preston Montford	14	19	19	14	14	37	18	17
Redesdale	12	10	20	18	11	14	13	10
River Mharcaidh	10	8	7	8	7	6	9	11
Stoke Ferry	31	22	24	28	45	33	32	25
Strathvaich Dam	-	7	7	8	13	9	10	13
Thorganby	25	25	30	37	35	67	27	24
Tycanol Wood	12	9	9	31	17	13	11	10
Wardlow Hay Cop	47	59	56	55	75	57	55	52
Whiteadder	14	14	20	16	11	13	12	12
Woburn	23	30	38	28	32	24	19	18
Yarner Wood	11	15	12	13	17	15	12	13

Source: Campbell et al. (1994a)

Location	1992 Monthly Weighted Mean Concentration in Precipitation, mg/l											
	Jan	Feb	Mar	Apr	May	Jun	Jul	Aug	Sep	Oct	Nov	Dec
Eskdalemuir	0.3	0.2	0.2	0.2	0.5	1.0	0.2	0.2	0.2	0.2	0.2	0.1
High Muffles	0.2	0.2	0.2	0.2	0.9	0.5	0.2	0.3	0.1	0.3	0.1	0.1
Lough Navar	0.1	0.3	0.3	0.2	0.3	0.4	0.2	0.1	0.2	0.3	0.2	0.2
Strath Vaich	0.3	0.2	0.2	0.1	0.1	0.3	0.1	0.1	0.1	0.2	0.2	0.1
Yarner Wood	0.2	0.2	0.2	0.2	1.0	0.2	0.1	0.2	0.3	0.4	0.1	0.1

Source: Schaug et al. (1994)

Carbon dioxide

Chemical formula : CO_2

Alternative names :

Type of pollutant : Radiatively-active trace gas, greenhouse gas

Structure :

CO_2

Air quality data summary :

Remote rural concentrations:

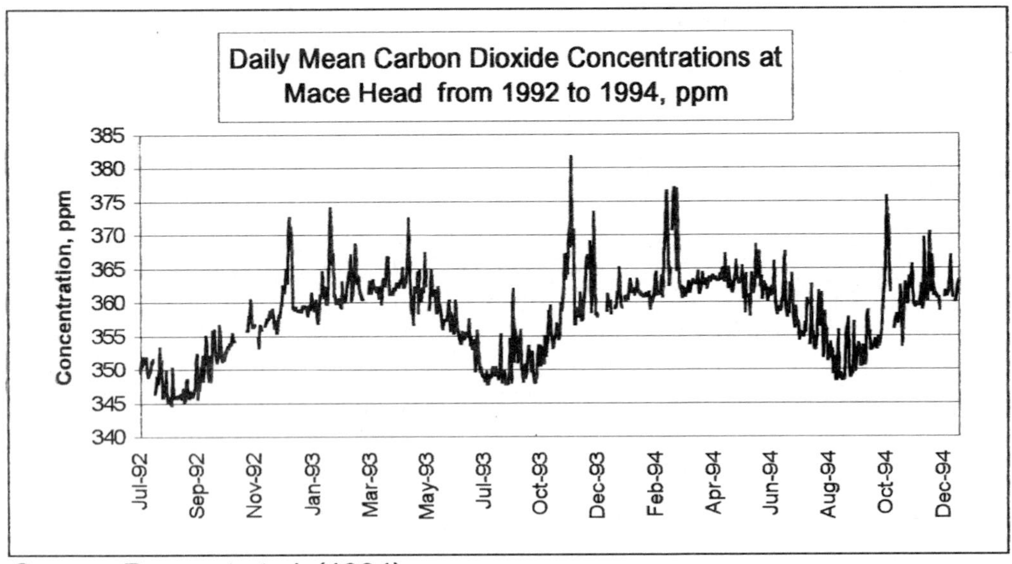

Source: Derwent et al. (1994)

Chemical formula : CO

Alternative names :

Type of pollutant : Trace gas, indirect greenhouse gas

Structure : CO

Air quality data summary :

Remote rural concentrations:

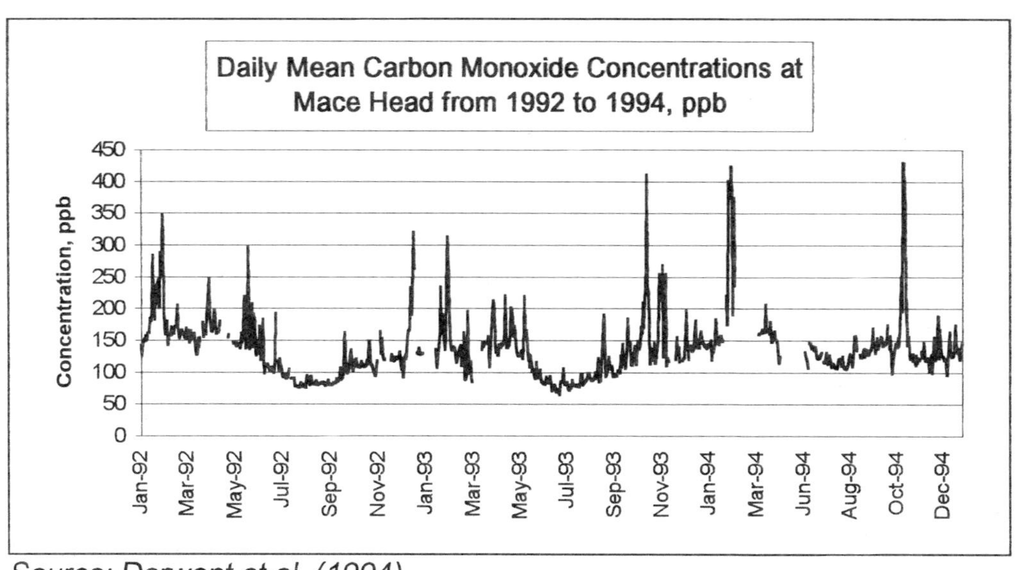

Source: Derwent et al. (1994)

Urban Concentrations

Location	Year	Mean ppm	Maximum 1 Hour ppm	Maximum 8 Hour ppm	Number 8 Hours ≥10 ppm
Central London	1990	0.9	4.2	2.2	0
	1989	1.2	20.9	16.2	1
	1988	1.1	15.1	6.0	1
	1987	1.9	8.0	5.3	0
Cromwell Road	1990	3.1	18.4	11.2	3
	1989	3.2	24.8	18.1	8
Glasgow A	1990	1.2	17.0	7.8	0
	1989	1.3	19.2	11.6	1

Location	Year	Mean ppm	Maximum 1 Hour ppm	Maximum 8 Hour ppm	Number 8 Hours ≥10 ppm
Stevenage	1990	0.7	5.7	2.1	0
	1989	0.6	6.4	3.3	0
West London	1990	1.6	13.2	8.8	1
	1989	1.5	18.5	14.4	2

Source: DoE (1994a)

Carbon Monoxide Calendar Year Statistics

Site	Year	Annual mean (ppm)	Max. run. 8 hour (ppm)		Site	Year	Annual mean (ppm)	Max. run. 8 hour (ppm)
Belfast B	92	0.7	10.3		Cambridge (cont.)	77	5.6	19.6
	93	0.7	10.6					
	94	0.7	13.4		Canvey	78	0.9	6.1
						79	0.7	3.6
Birmingham C	74	5.5	17.9					
	75	5.9	24.4		Cardiff D	73	8.2	28.8
	76	6.4	28.0			74	5.7	27.0
	77	5.9	16.9			75	6.2	26.9
						76	2.7	10.2
Birmingham A	92	0.6	10.8					
	93	0.6	3.8		Cardiff A	92	0.7	4.9
	94	0.7	9.7			93	0.6	5.9
						94	0.8	5.7
Birmingham B	94	0.5	11.4					
					Central London A	72	1.9	10.4
Bloomsbury	92	0.8	4.5			73	2.8	9.6
	93	0.6	3.5			74	3.4	10.8
	94	0.8	7.1			75	2.8	17.4
						76	3.4	13.6
Bridge Place	90	1.3	10.2			77	2.7	9.9
	91	1.4	11.2			78	2.2	9.4
	92	1.0	6.6			79	3.1	11.6
	93	0.9	7.5			80	1.0	5.5
	94	0.8	9.0			81	1.1	10.0
						82	0.9	3.3
Bristol B	93	0.8	4.2			83	0.8	9.2
	94	1.0	5.8			84	0.8	8.8
						85	0.7	5.4
Cambridge	75	5.0	18.9			86	0.7	4.3
	76	5.3	36.3			88	1.1	11.6

Carbon Monoxide Calendar Year Statistics								
Site	Year	Annual Mean (ppm)	Max.run. 8 hour (ppm)		Site	Year	Annual Mean (ppm)	Max.run. 8 hour (ppm)
Central London A	89	1.3	17.1		Harrow (cont.)	80	0.6	4.4
(cont.)	90	0.9	7.6					
					Hull	94	0.8	5.3
Cromwell Road	73	6.1	29.0					
	74	4.6	16.3		Leeds	93	0.8	8.9
	75	5.9	39.1			94	0.6	9.0
	76	6.9	27.3					
	77	5.1	23.0		Leicester	94	0.6	5.9
	78	6.1	25.4					
	79	4.7	16.9		Liverpool	93	0.5	3.4
	82	3.1	11.5			94	0.8	3.3
	83	2.4	15.3					
	84	2.5	10.7		Manchester A	91	0.9	5.7
	89	3.6	21.3			92	0.9	12.5
	90	2.9	15.5			93	0.6	3.6
	91	3.3	13.9			94	0.7	10.1
	92	2.8	8.7					
	93	2.2	9.1		Newcastle A	92	0.8	4.0
	94	2.0	10.5			93	0.7	6.1
						94	0.6	3.1
Edinburgh B	93	0.6	4.8					
	94	0.6	3.5		Sheffield	91	0.9	6.3
						92	0.7	7.4
Glasgow B	73	3.8	20.2			93	0.4	4.5
	74	3.8	18.2			94	0.4	4.5
	75	4.3	17.4					
	76	5.6	29.3		Southampton	94	0.8	8.6
	77	4.5	19.7					
	78	4.1	19.9		Stevenage	80	0.4	2.9
	79	3.8	24.9			81	0.4	3.4
	80	3.5	17.0			82	0.6	6.0
	81	3.8	16.5			83	0.4	2.6
	82	2.8	13.1			89	0.6	4.2
						90	0.7	3.5
Glasgow A	89	1.6	14.4			91	0.7	4.9
	90	1.1	11.6			92	0.6	3.0
	91	1.4	12.5					
	92	1.2	8.7		West London	90	1.5	10.2
	93	0.9	6.0			91	1.7	15.8
	94	0.8	5.4			92	1.1	6.3
						93	0.9	8.7
Harrow	79	0.9	5.0			94	1.4	9.0

Source: Bower et al. (1995)

Data displayed for data captures ≥ 25 %

Chemical formula : CCl_4

Alternative names : CFC 10

Type of pollutant : Ozone depleting halocarbon, radiatively active trace gas, greenhouse gas

Structure :

CCl_4

Air quality data summary :

Remote rural concentrations

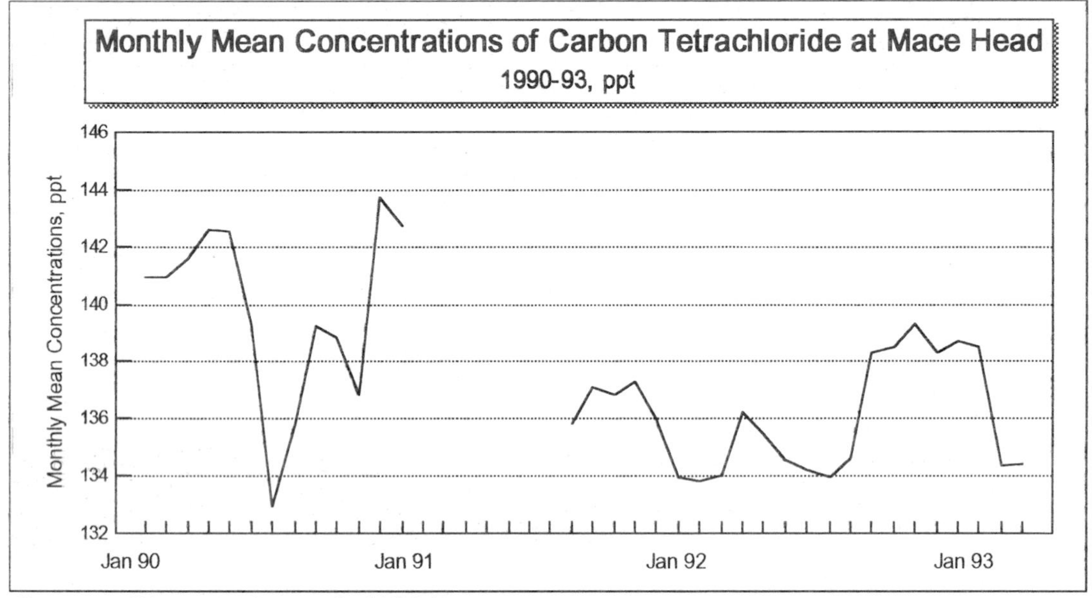

Source: Simmonds et al. (1994)

Chemical formula	:	Ce
Alternative names	:	Particulate cerium
Type of pollutant	:	Suspended particulate matter, trace element

Air quality data summary :

Rural concentrations

Location	Concentrations, ng/m^3			
	Mean	Trend	Mean	Trend
	1972-1981	%/yr	1982-1991	%/yr
Harwell, Oxfordshire.	0.43	nst	0.33	nst
Styrrup, Nottinghamshire.	0.68	-4.4	0.71	-3.9
Trebanos, Glamorgan.	0.51	-	0.46	-11.5
Wraymires, Cumbria.	0.27	nst	0.20	-5.8

Source: Cawse et al. (1994)

Note: nst=no significant trend

Location	Nature of site	Measurement period	Mean concentration ng/m^3
Altrincham	Residential	1978-1989	0.75
Brent	Residential	1975-1989	0.95
Chilton	Rural	1971-1989	0.38
Flixton	Residential	1975-1989	1.06
Lambeth	Residential	1976-1982	1.31
Manchester City North	Industrial/ Residential	1975-1988	0.92
Manchester City South	Residential	1975-1989	0.95
Swansea	Urban	1972-1981	0.99
Walsall	Industrial	1976-1989	1.07
Wraymires	Rural	1970-1989	0.21

Source: Lee et al. (1994), Pattenden (1974).

Cerium in rain 46

Chemical formula : Ce

Alternative names : Precipitation cerium

Type of pollutant : Trace contaminant of rain, trace element

Air quality data summary :

Rural Concentrations

Location	Average Annual Rainfall Concentration, µg per litre	
	1972-1981	1982-1989 *
Harwell, Oxfordshire.	0.60	0.48
Styrrup, Nottinghamshire.	1.24	0.16
Wraymires, Cumbria.	0.13	0.09

Source: Cawse et al. (1994)

Note: total deposition expressed as apparent rainfall concentration.
* based on soluble fraction only.

Cerium not analysed in rainwater in 1990 and 1991.

Chemical formula : CCl_3F

Alternative names : Trichlorofluoromethane

Type of pollutant : Ozone depleting halocarbon, radiatively-active trace gas, greenhouse gas

Structure :

CCl_3F

Air quality data summary :

Remote rural concentrations

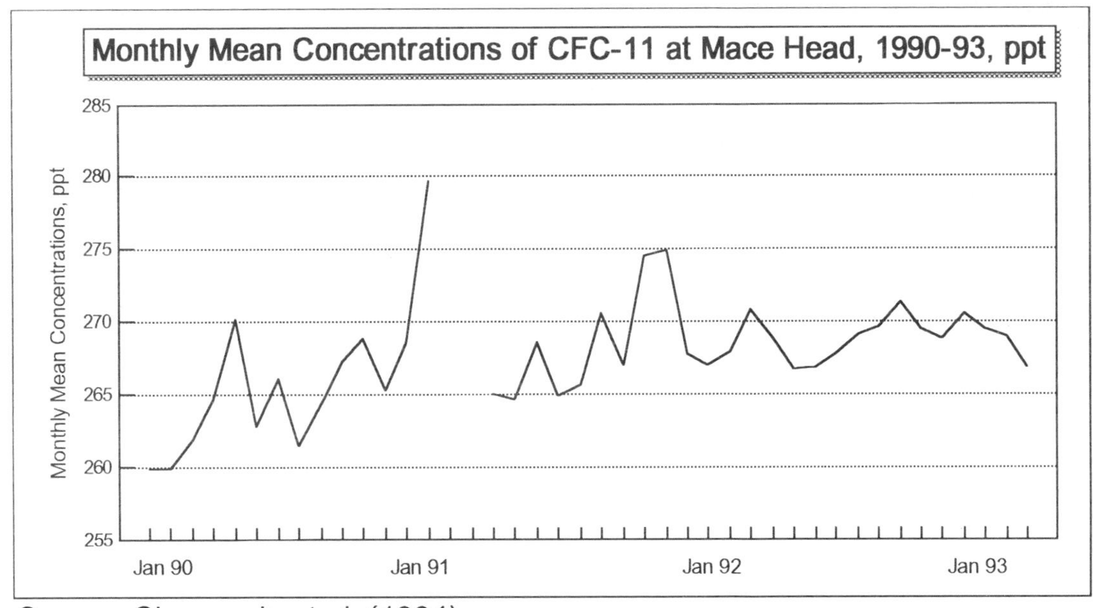

Source: Simmonds et al. (1994)

Chemical formula : CCl_2F_2

Alternative names : Dichlorodifluoromethane

Type of pollutant : Ozone depleting halocarbon, radiatively active trace gas, greenhouse gas

Structure :

CCl_2F_2

Air quality data summary :

Remote rural concentrations

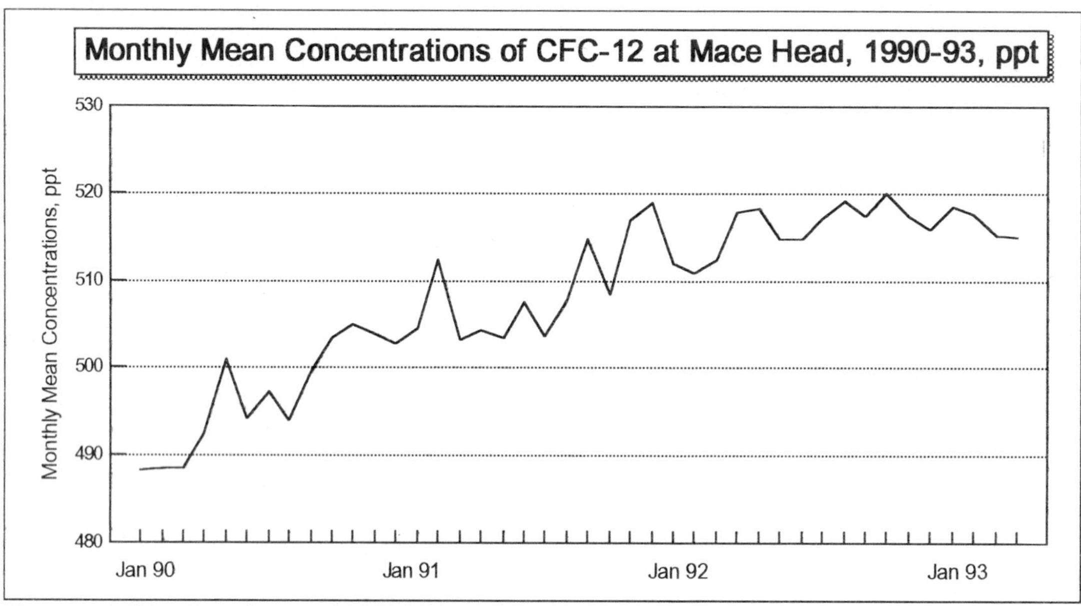

Source: Simmonds et al. (1994)

CFC-113

Chemical formula : $CCl_2F\ CClF_2$

Alternative names : 1,1,2-trichloro-1,2,2-trifluoroethane

Type of pollutant : Ozone depleting halocarbon, radiatively active trace gas, greenhouse gas

Structure :

CCl_2FCClF_2

Air quality data summary :

Remote rural concentrations

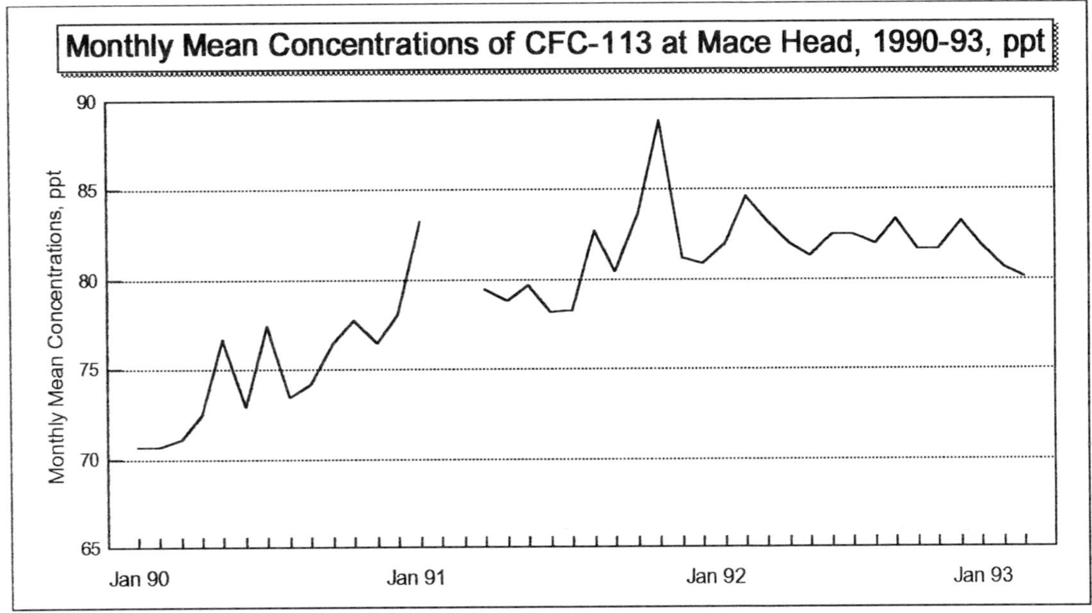

Source: Simmonds et al. (1994)

Chemical formula : Cl

Alternative names : Particulate chloride

Type of pollutant : Suspended particulate matter, trace element

Air quality data summary :

Rural Concentrations

Location	Average Annual Concentrations, ng/m^3			
	Mean	Trend	Mean	Trend
	1972-1981	%/yr	1982-1991	%/yr
Harwell, Oxfordshire.	2169	nst	1751	4.5
Styrrup, Nottinghamshire.	4462	-4.4	3508	nst
Trebanos, Glamorgan.	2603	-	-	-
Wraymires, Cumbria.	2169	nst	2038	nst

Source: Cawse et al. (1994)

Note: nst=no significant trend

Location	Nature of site	Measurement period	Mean concentration ng/m^3
Altrincham	Residential	1978-1989	4478
Brent	Residential	1975-1989	3401
Chilton	Rural	1971-1989	1939
Flixton	Residential	1975-1989	4554
Lambeth	Residential	1976-1982	4278
Manchester City North	Industrial/ Residential	1975-1988	5629
Manchester City South	Residential	1975-1989	4388
Swansea	Urban	1972-1981	5702
Walsall	Industrial	1976-1989	6216
Wraymires	Rural	1970-1989	2178

Source: Lee et al. (1994)

Chemical formula : Cl

Alternative names : Precipitation chloride

Type of pollutant : Trace contaminant of rain, trace element

Air quality data summary :

Rural Concentrations

Location	Average Annual Rainfall Concentration, μg per litre	
	1972 - 1981	1982-1991*
Harwell, Oxfordshire	6269	5900
Styrrup, Nottinghamshire	7931	4700
Wraymires, Cumbria	4111	5070

Source: Cawse et al. (1994)

Note: total deposition expressed as apparent rainfall concentration
* represents results based on soluble fraction only

Site	Precipitation-weighted Annual Mean Chloride Concentration, 1986-93, (μ eql^{-1})							
	1986	1987	1988	1989	1990	1991	1992	1993
Achanarras	280	174	253	317	251	272	209	255
Balquhidder	146	58	70	131	125	104	70	166
Bannisdale	148	75	168	141	193	213	107	124
Barcombe Mills	226	310	186	252	427	161	156	115
Beddgelert	154	83	137	156	225	185	107	128
Bottesford	115	58	100	78	97	85	62	63
Compton	54	92	94	110	159	89	54	73
Cow Green Reservoir	91	52	85	91	107	98	86	84
Driby	128	76	90	126	135	123	88	84
Eskdalemuir	105	47	76	97	103	118	65	71
Flatford Mill	109	80	70	99	95	88	71	67
Glen Dye	-	64	86	98	98	91	78	102
Goonhilly	311	242	253	322	595	373	265	255
High Muffles	89	96	106	131	146	140	110	139
Hillsborough Forest	-	-	-	106	165	123	84	102
Jenny Hurn	169	99	151	123	170	124	86	84
Llyn Brianne	107	83	99	131	178	129	81	109
Loch Dee	152	66	159	159	173	144	96	89
Lough Navar	293	125	409	166	298	222	153	215
Plynlimon	-	-	-	124	165	118	83	76

Site	Precipitation-weighted Annual Mean Chloride Concentration, 1986-93, (μ eql[-1])							
	1986	1987	1988	1989	1990	1991	1992	1993
Polloch	-	-	-	-	-	249	135	226
Preston Montford	109	56	114	59	123	203	50	83
Redesdale	133	54	84	112	83	97	72	92
River Mharcaidh	104	39	52	104	72	53	65	158
Stoke Ferry	95	65	66	73	101	90	72	63
Strathvaich Dam	-	101	129	148	207	168	138	227
Thorganby	140	102	121	139	166	180	123	106
Tycanol Wood	141	109	123	266	268	190	135	135
Wardlow Hay Cop	99	85	131	84	183	163	78	121
Whiteadder	129	64	100	110	93	69	93	117
Woburn	82	82	61	75	109	69	38	50
Yarner Wood	118	152	180	190	291	160	122	116

Source: Campbell et al. (1994a)

Location	1992 Monthly Weighted Mean Concentration in Precipitation, mg/l											
	Jan	Feb	Mar	Apr	May	Jun	Jul	Aug	Sep	Oct	Nov	Dec
Eskdalemuir	3.7	2.3	2.0	2.0	2.3	2.0	1.7	1.3	1.3	1.2	3.5	1.3
High Muffles	2.9	4.4	3.8	4.4	0.9	2.8	2.0	1.5	1.0	4.2	2.6	1.9
Lough Navar	2.1	6.9	11.5	5.4	6.8	0.5	1.9	3.2	5.0	6.7	7.7	3.8
Strath Vaich	6.4	2.7	3.3	4.2	3.0	0.8	3.1	0.7	2.3	6.7	5.9	2.0
Yarner Wood	2.6	2.6	5.3	3.4	2.3	0.4	1.4	3.5	2.1	14.6	4.1	3.8

Source: Schaug et al. (1994)

Chemical formula	:	Cr
Alternative names	:	Particulate chromium
Type of pollutant	:	Suspended particulate matter, trace element
Air quality data summary	:	

Rural Concentrations

Location	Average Annual Concentrations, ng/m^3			
	Mean	Trend	Mean	Trend
	1972-1981	%/yr	1982-1991	%/yr
Harwell, Oxfordshire.	3	-7.6	1.2	-7.4
Styrrup, Nottinghamshire.	12	-11.9	8.6	-4.9
Trebanos, Glamorgan.	11	-6.8	4.6	-
Wraymires, Cumbria.	2	-4.8	0.9	-10.2

Source: Cawse et al. (1994)

Urban Concentrations:

Location	Mean Annual Concentrations, ng/m^3						
	1972-1981	1985	1986	1987	1988	1989	1990
Swansea	8.0						
Central London		5.4	9.9	13.7	14.9	11.6	4.3
Brent		5.6	5.0	6.5	5.7	3.0	3.4
Motherwell		10.2	9.3	6.7	7.3	6.8	3.9
Glasgow C		4.7	5.6	3.6	5.0	3.8	1.9
Leeds		6.4	8.2	5.0	6.1	4.6	4.7

Source: DoE (1992), Pattenden (1974).

Location	Nature of site	Measurement period	Mean concentration ng/m^3
Altrincham	Residential	1978-1989	17.2
Brent	Residential	1975-1989	4.4
Chilton	Rural	1971-1989	2.2
Flixton	Residential	1975-1989	6.0
Lambeth	Residential	1976-1982	4.9
Manchester City North	Industrial/ Residential	1975-1988	8.1
Manchester City South	Residential	1975-1989	5.8
Walsall	Industrial	1976-1989	24.9
Wraymires	Rural	1970-1989	1.5

Source: Lee et al. (1994)

Chromium in rain

Chemical formula : Cr

Alternative names : Precipitation chromium

Type of pollutant : Trace contaminant of rain, trace element

Air quality data summary :

Rural Concentrations

Location	Average Annual Rainfall Concentration, µg per litre	
	1972-1981	1982-1991 *
Harwell, Oxfordshire.	2.84	<0.4
Styrrup, Nottinghamshire.	10.52	<0.8
Wraymires, Cumbria.	1.56	<0.9

Source: Cawse et al. (1994)

Note: total deposition expressed as apparent rainfall concentration.
* based on soluble fraction only.

Chrysene in air 52

Chemical formula : $C_{18}H_{12}$

Alternative names : PAH EPA no.76

Type of pollutant : Polynuclear Aromatic Hydrocarbon (PAH)

Structure :

Air quality data summary :

Location	Annual Mean ng/m³		
	1991	1992	1993
Bowland	*	*	1.02
Cardiff C	3.59	1.97	*
London	3.17	1.54	0.89
Manchester B	2.87	1.65	0.49
Middlesbrough	*	*	1.23
WSL	2.21	*	*

Source: Davis (1993)

Notes: * signifies no data available

Urban Concentrations

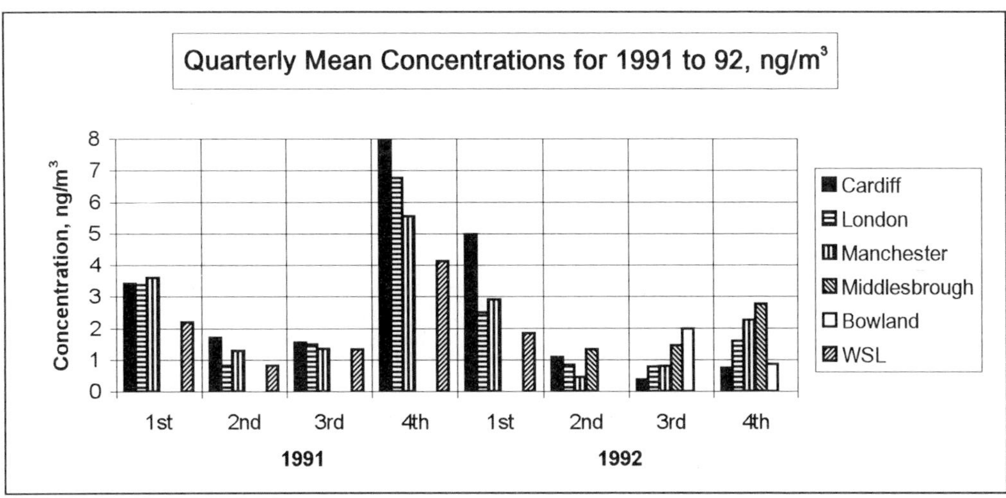

Source: Davis (1993)

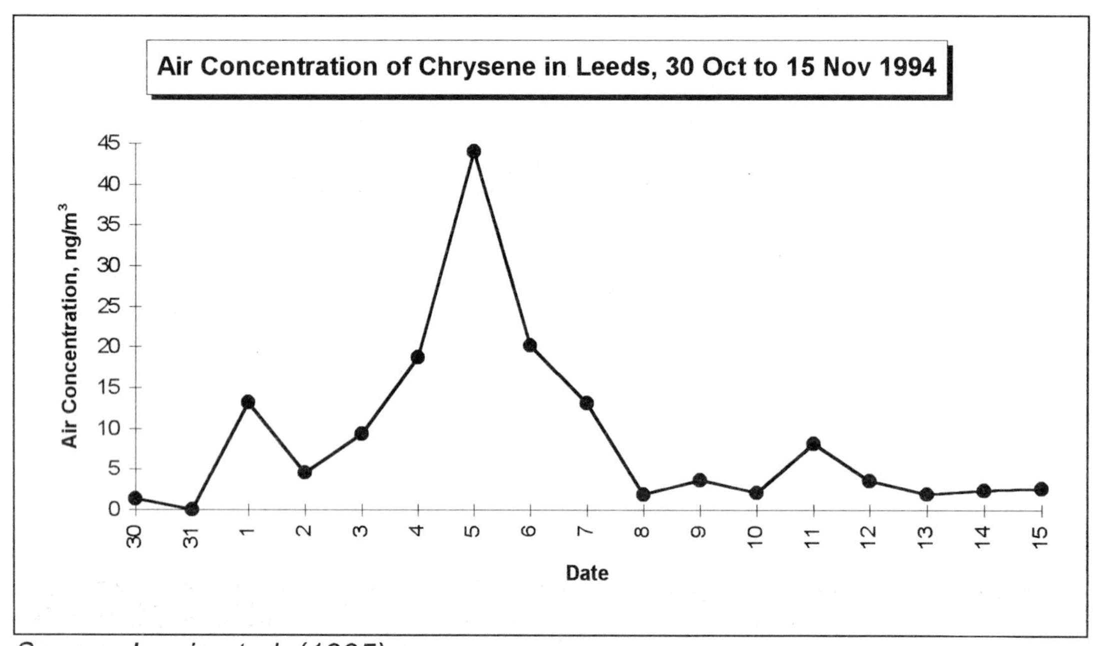

Source: Lewis et al. (1995)

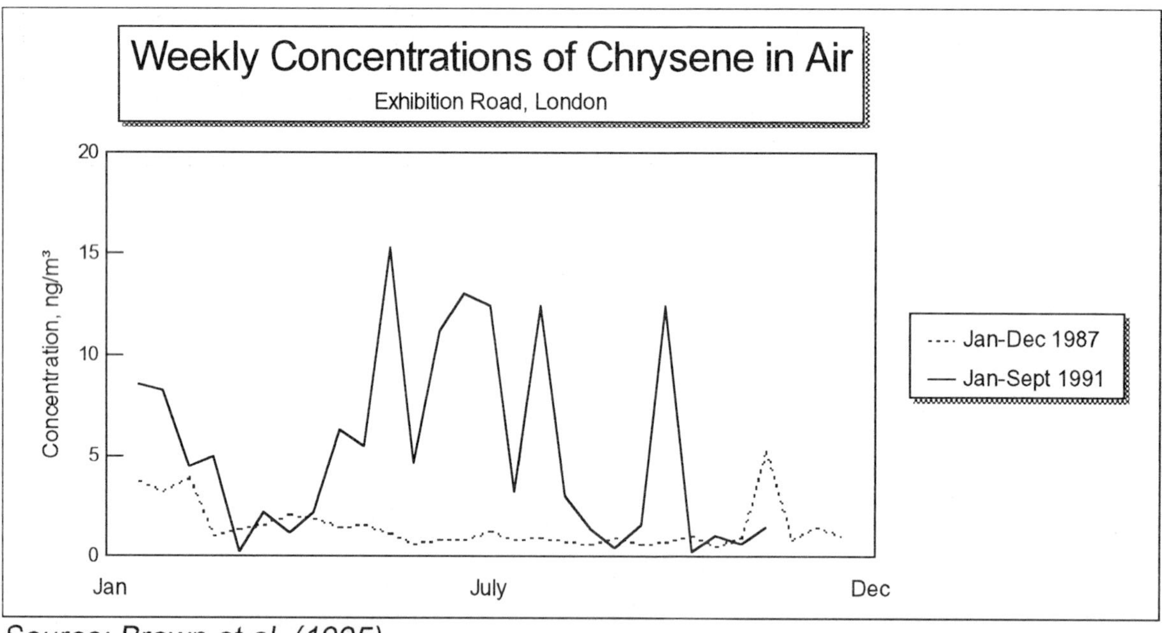

Source: Brown et al. (1995)

Location	Season 1992	Total Concentration in Air ng/m^3
Edgbaston	Winter (February)	6.49
Edgbaston	Summer (August)	0.61
Wasthills	Summer (August)	0.15

Source: Smith and Harrison (1994)

Chrysene in deposition

Chemical formula : $C_{18}H_{12}$

Alternative names : PAH EPA no.76

Type of pollutant : Polynuclear Aromatic Hydrocarbon (PAH)

Structure :

Air quality data summary :

Location	Annual Mean ng/m²/day		
	1991	1992	1993
Bowland	*	*	25.79
Cardiff C	612.15	162.20	*
London	598.00	585.30	*
Manchester B	803.00	138.04	*
Middlesbrough	*	*	*
WSL	321.97	*	*

Source: Davis (1993)

Notes: * signifies no data available

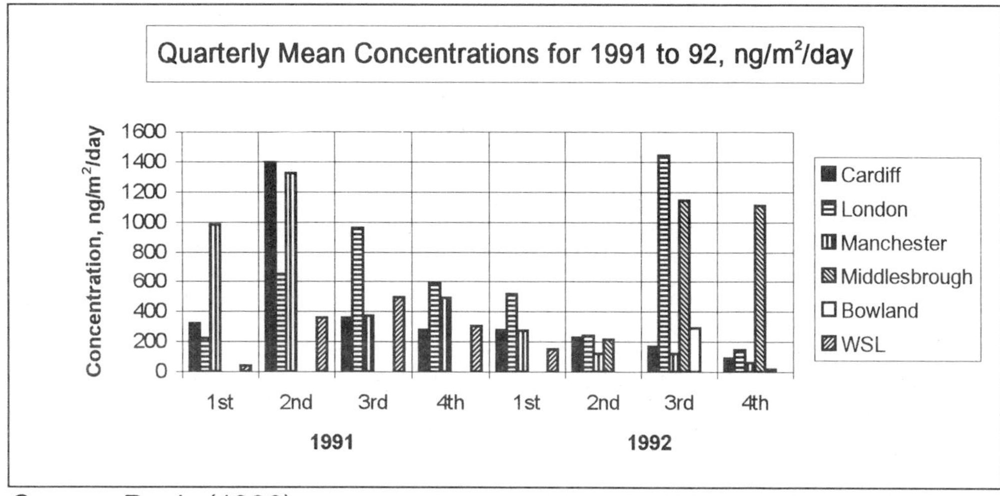

Source: Davis (1993)

Chemical formula : C_4H_8

Alternative names : Cis but-2-ene

Type of pollutant : (Volatile) organic compound (VOC), hydrocarbon

Structure :

$$\begin{matrix} H & & & & H \\ & \diagdown & & \diagup & \\ & & C{=}C & & \\ & \diagup & & \diagdown & \\ H_3C & & & & CH_3 \end{matrix}$$

Air quality data summary :

Urban concentrations

1994-95 Monthly Means, ppb									
	Belfast C	Birmingham B	Bristol A	Cardiff B	Edinburgh A	Eltham	Harwell	Middlesbrough	UCL
Jan 94	0.12	0.52	-	0.70	-	0.07	-	0.27	0.06
Feb 94	0.15	0.27	-	0.45	0.12	0.07	-	0.65	0.39
Mar 94	0.09	0.16	-	0.39	0.09	0.16	-	8.01	0.13
Apr 94	0.12	0.17	0.42	0.26	0.10	0.14	-	1.66	0.38
May 94	0.13	0.17	0.41	0.30	0.11	0.06	-	0.51	0.31
Jun 94	0.12	0.15	0.12	0.29	0.08	0.08	-	0.35	0.26
Jul 94	0.11	0.21	0.36	0.35	0.12	0.10	-	1.75	0.25
Aug 94	0.11	1.01	0.22	0.33	0.12	0.09	-	0.33	0.05
Sep 94	0.16	0.19	0.14	0.19	0.12	0.11	-	1.18	0.24
Oct 94	0.18	0.32	0.49	0.26	0.14	0.18	-	0.66	0.33
Nov 94	0.14	0.33	0.17	0.21	0.10	0.18	-	0.45	0.30
Dec 94	0.16	0.34	0.17	0.17	0.11	0.22	-	0.16	0.22
Jan 95	0.11	0.38	0.17	0.17	0.07	0.20	-	0.15	0.17
Feb 95	0.08	0.14	0.18	0.17	0.05	0.12	0.03	0.12	0.15

Source: Dollard (1995)

Remote rural concentrations

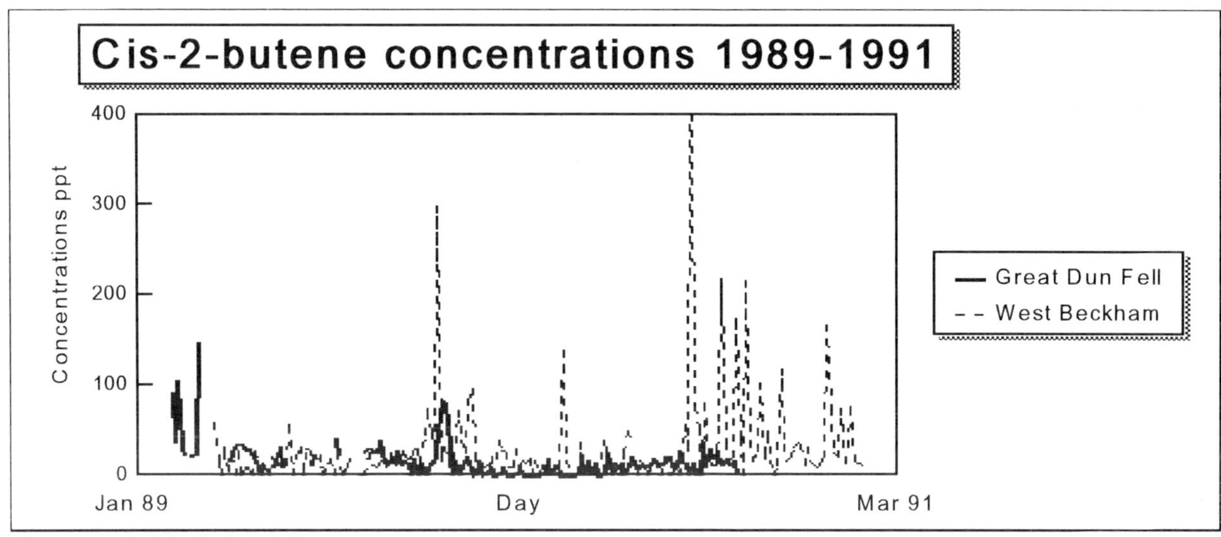

Source: PORG (1993)

Cis-1,3-dimethylcyclohexane

Chemical formula : C_8H_{16}

Alternative names :

Type of pollutant : (Volatile) organic compound (VOC), hydrocarbon

Structure :

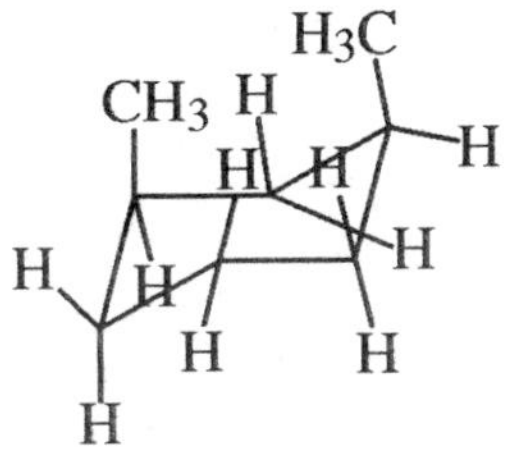

Air quality data summary :

Mean Air Concentration in Leeds, 19/8/94 to 8/9/94	
Location	21 day mean, $\mu g/m^3$
Albion Street	0.029
Cliff Lane	0.036
EUN monitoring site	0.036
Kerbside site	0.043
Kirkstall Road	0.041
Park site	0.030
Queen Street	0.036
Vicar Lane	0.104

Source: Bartle et al. (1995)

Cis-1,3-dimethylcyclopentane

Chemical formula : C_7H_{14}

Alternative names :

Type of pollutant : (Volatile) organic compound (VOC), hydrocarbon

Structure :

H_3C, CH—CH_2, CH_3, CH_2—CH, CH_2

Air quality data summary :

Mean Air Concentration in Leeds, 19/8/94 to 8/9/94	
Location	21 day mean, µg/m^3
Albion Street	0.032
Cliff Lane	0.034
EUN monitoring site	0.031
Kerbside site	0.046
Kirkstall Road	0.056
Park site	0.043
Queen Street	0.043
Vicar Lane	0.118

Source: Bartle et al. (1995)

Cis-2-pentene

Chemical formula : C_5H_{10}

Alternative names : Cis pent-2-ene

Type of pollutant : (Volatile) organic compound(VOC), hydrocarbon

Structure :

$$\begin{array}{ccc} H & & H \\ & C=C & \\ H_3C & & CH_2CH_3 \end{array}$$

Air quality data summary :

Urban concentrations

	1994-95 Monthly Means, ppb								
	Belfast C	Birmingham B	Bristol A	Cardiff B	Edinburgh A	Eltham	Harwell	Middlesbrough	UCL
Jan 94	0.07	0.12	-	0.38	-	0.05	-	0.20	0.18
Feb 94	0.10	0.13	-	0.30	0.07	0.05	-	0.74	0.31
Mar 94	0.04	0.05	-	0.08	0.07	0.14	-	1.44	0.12
Apr 94	0.05	0.05	0.09	0.07	0.09	0.17	-	1.26	0.39
May 94	0.05	0.06	0.43	0.09	0.09	0.09	-	0.25	0.44
Jun 94	0.05	0.06	0.05	0.08	0.04	0.09	-	0.06	0.24
Jul 94	0.05	0.10	0.16	0.11	0.06	0.05	-	0.29	0.14
Aug 94	0.06	0.23	0.13	0.18	0.07	0.07	-	0.20	0.07
Sep 94	0.09	0.10	0.10	0.09	0.07	0.08	-	1.77	0.15
Oct 94	0.12	0.20	0.54	0.31	0.09	0.12	-	0.37	0.24
Nov 94	0.10	0.19	0.13	0.12	0.07	0.13	-	0.26	0.23
Dec 94	0.09	0.21	0.12	0.09	0.08	0.15	-	0.08	0.18
Jan 95	0.07	0.09	0.11	0.08	0.05	0.18	-	0.08	0.10
Feb 95	0.05	0.08	0.09	0.08	0.04	0.08	-	0.09	0.09

Source: Dollard (1995)

Cobalt aerosol

Chemical formula : Co

Alternative names : Particulate cobalt

Type of pollutant : Suspended particulate matter, trace matter

Air quality data summary :

Rural Concentrations

Location	Concentrations, ng/m^3			
	Mean	Trend	Mean	Trend
	1972-1981	%/yr	1982-1991	%/yr
Harwell, Oxfordshire.	0.3	-7.0	0.21	4.0
Styrrup, Nottinghamshire.	0.6	-9.5	0.50	-5.1
Trebanos, Glamorgan.	9.7	-5.2	1.80	-
Wraymires, Cumbria.	0.2	nst	0.13	nst

Source: Cawse et al. (1994)

Note: nst=no significant trend

Urban Concentrations

Location	Mean Annual Concentrations, ng/m^3						
	1972-1981	1985	1986	1987	1988	1989	1990
Swansea	5.6						
Central London		0.8	0.9	1.4	2.2	0.7	0.8

Source: Pattenden (1974), DoE (1992)

Chemical formula : Co

Alternative names : Precipitation cobalt

Type of pollutant : Trace contaminant of rain, trace element

Air quality data summary :

Rural Concentrations

Location	Average Annual Rainfall Concentration µg per litre	
	1972-1981	1982-1991 *
Harwell, Oxfordshire.	0.36	0.25
Styrrup, Nottinghamshire.	1.03	0.29
Wraymires, Cumbria.	0.09	0.17

Source: Cawse et al. (1994)

Note: total deposition expressed as apparent rainfall concentration.
* based on soluble fraction only.

Chemical formula : Cu

Alternative names : Particulate copper

Type of pollutant : Suspended particulate matter, trace element

Air quality data summary :

Rural Concentrations

Location	Concentrations, ng/m^3				
	Mean	Trend	Mean		Trend
	1972-1981	%/yr	1982-1991		%/yr
Harwell, Oxfordshire.	19	nst	12	*	-13.0
Styrrup, Nottinghamshire.	32	nst	27	**	-19.1
Trebanos, Glamorgan.	30	-7.0	13	*	-
Wraymires, Cumbria.	17	nst	11	***	-16.9

Source: Cawse et al. (1994)

Note:
* only 38% of measurements were positive.
** only 45% of measurements were positive.
*** only 43% of measurements were positive.
nst=no significant trend

Urban Concentrations

Location	Mean Annual Concentrations, ng/m^3						
	1972-1981	1985	1986	1987	1988	1989	1990
Swansea	71.0	-	-	-	-	-	-
Central London	-	25.9	27.3	32.1	34.2	24.7	27.7
Brent	-	26.2	32.5	37.4	26.0	14.2	22.7
Motherwell	-	38.5	65.6	32.3	12.1	43.5	64.4
Glasgow C	-	28.4	43.3	44.1	30.4	15.3	26.9
Leeds	-	24.5	59.5	36.5	10.9	10.1	21.3

Source: Pattenden (1974), DoE (1992)

Copper in rain

Chemical formula : Cu

Alternative names : Precipitation copper

Type of pollutant : Trace contaminant of rain, trace element

Air quality data summary :

Rural Concentrations

Location	Average Annual Rainfall Concentration, μg per litre	
	1972-1981	1982-1990 *
Harwell, Oxfordshire.	25	12.5
Styrrup, Nottinghamshire.	41	10.7
Wraymires, Cumbria.	14	5.6

Source: Cawse et al. (1994)

Note: total deposition expressed as apparent rainfall concentration.
* based on soluble fraction only.

Results for 1991 are not available.

Coronene in air

Chemical formula : $C_{24}H_{12}$

Alternative names :

Type of pollutant : Polynuclear Aromatic Hydrocarbon (PAH)

Structure :

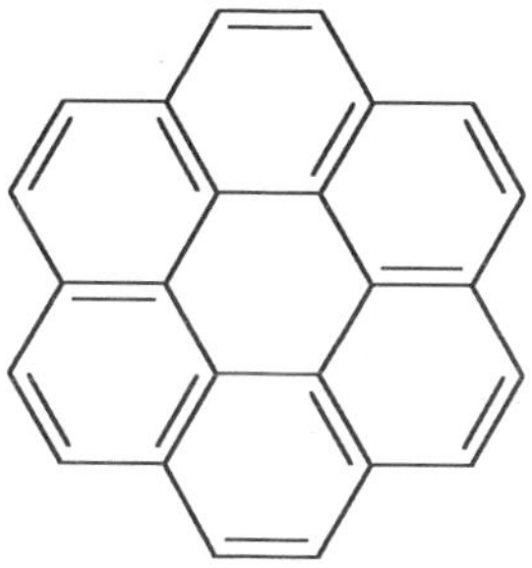

Air quality data summary :

Location	Annual Mean ng/m^3		
	1991	1992	1993
Bowland	*	*	0.16
Cardiff C	0.94	0.46	*
London	*	*	*
Manchester B	1.15	0.88	0.59
Middlesbrough	*	*	*
WSL	*	*	*

Source: Davis (1993)

Notes: * signifies no data available

Location	Season 1992	Total Concentration in Air ng/m^3
Edgbaston	Winter (February)	1.03
Edgbaston	Summer (August)	0.27
Wasthills	Summer (August)	0.06

Source: Smith and Harrison (1994)

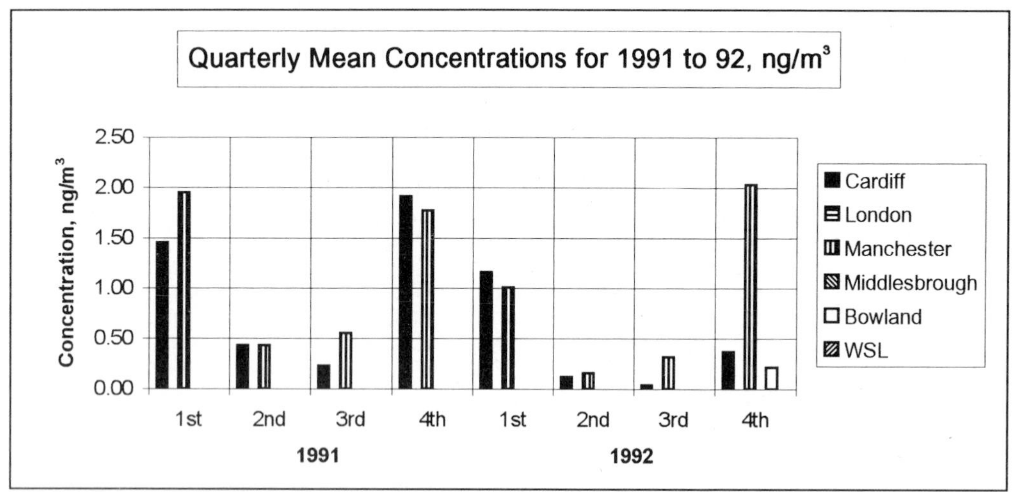

Source: Davis (1993)

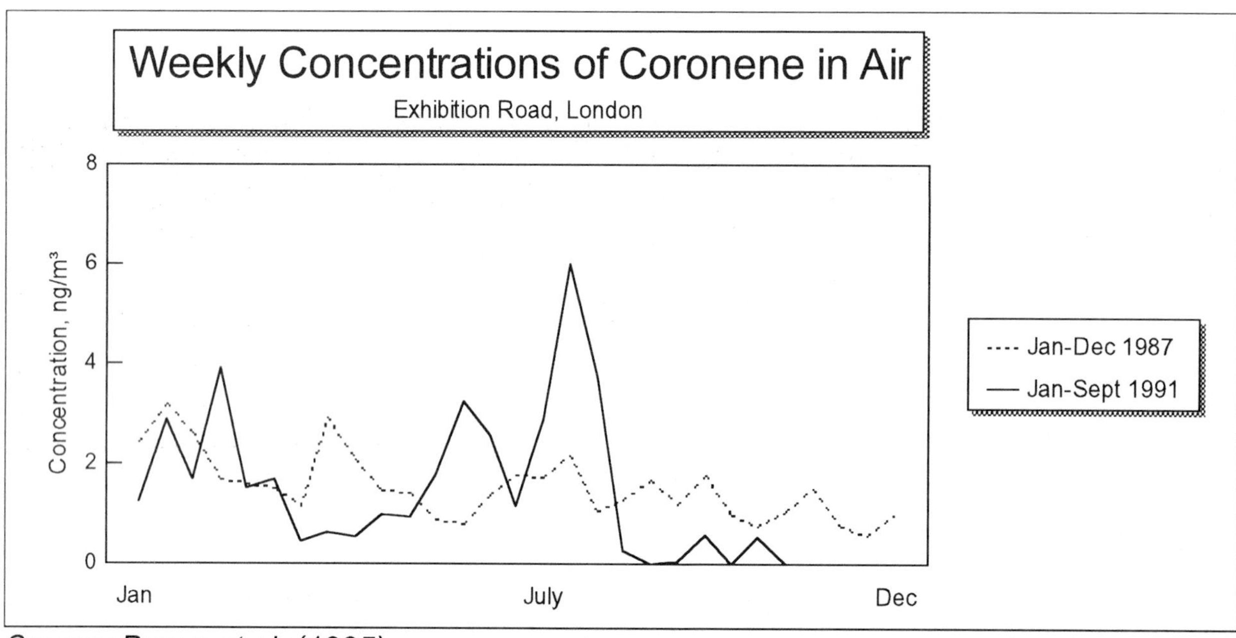

Source: Brown et al. (1995)

Coronene in deposition

Chemical formula : $C_{24}H_{12}$

Alternative names :

Type of pollutant : Polynuclear Aromatic Hydrocarbon (PAH)

Structure :

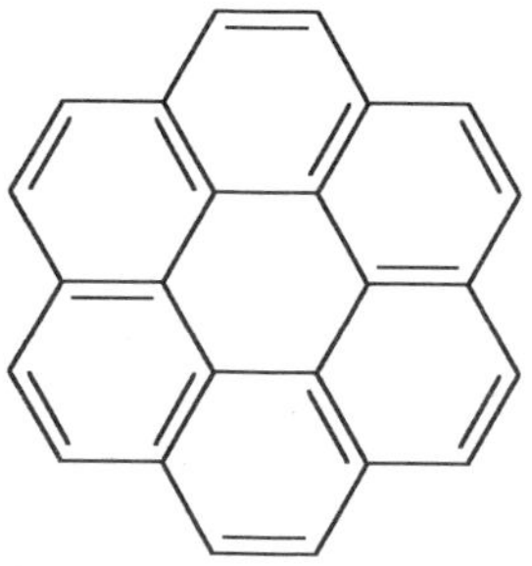

Air quality data summary :

Location	Annual Mean ng/m²/day		
	1991	1992	1993
Bowland	*	*	23.35
Cardiff C	164.20	50.26	*
London	*	*	*
Manchester B	283.10	63.61	*
Middlesbrough	*	*	*
WSL	*	*	*

Source: Davis (1993)

Notes: * signifies no data available

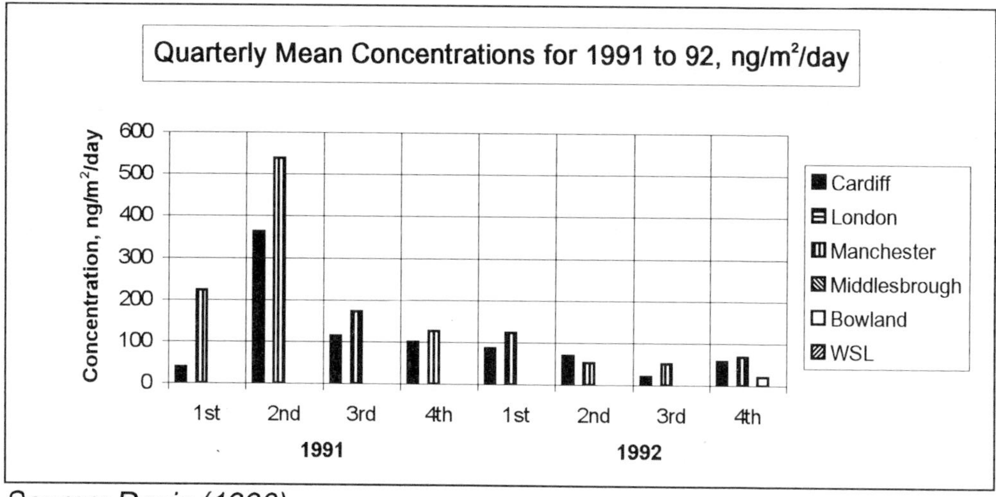

Source: Davis (1993)

Chemical formula : C_6H_{12}

Alternative names :

Type of pollutant : (Volatile) organic compound (VOC), hydrocarbon

Structure : $(CH_2)_6$

Air quality data summary :

Rural concentrations

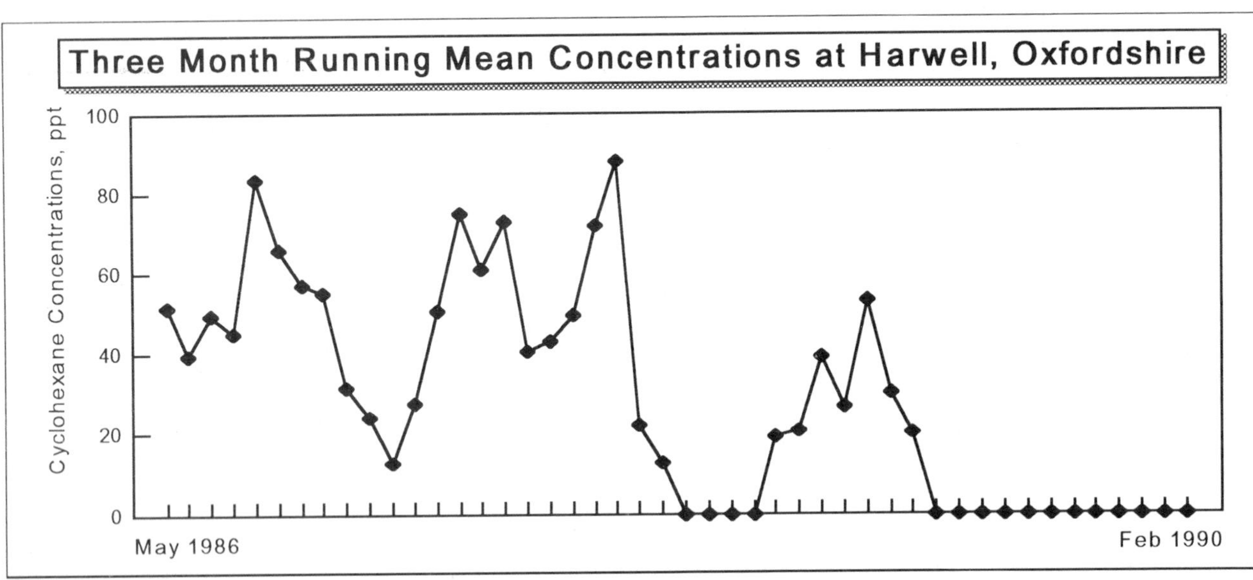

Source: PORG (1993)

Urban Concentrations

Mean Air Concentration in Leeds, 19/8/94 to 8/9/94	
Location	**21 day mean, μg/m^3**
Albion Street	0.043
Cliff Lane	0.039
EUN monitoring site	0.043
Kerbside site	0.049
Kirkstall Road	0.053
Park site	0.039
Queen Street	0.047
Vicar Lane	0.100

Source: Bartle et al. (1995)

Cyclopenta-(cd)-pyrene

Chemical formula : $C_{18}H_{10}$

Alternative names :

Type of pollutant : Polynuclear Aromatic Hydrocarbon (PAH)

Structure :

Air quality data summary :

Urban Concentrations

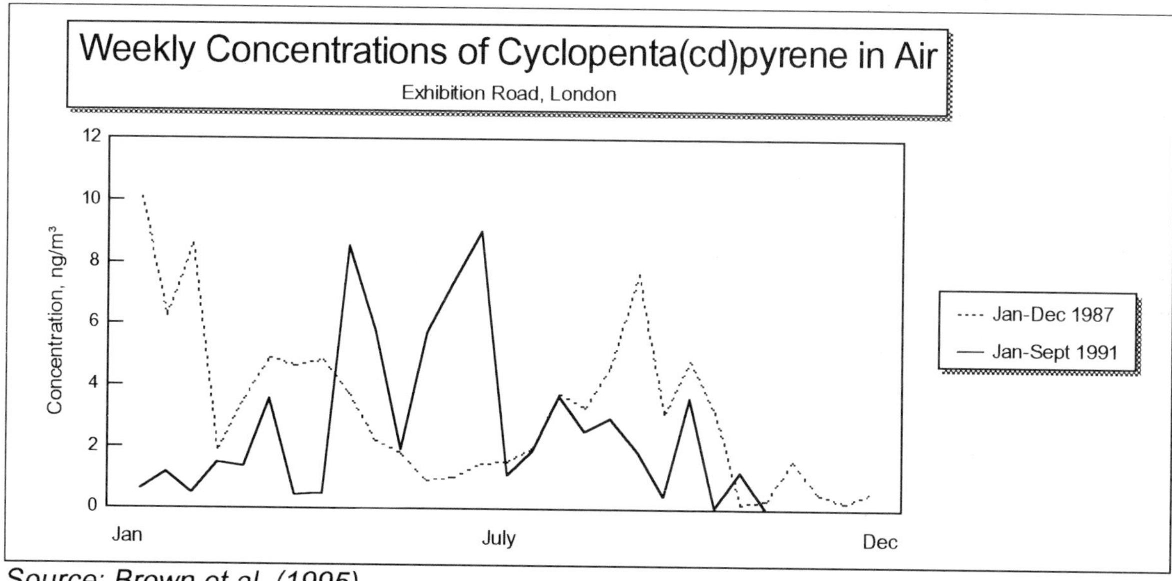

Source: Brown et al. (1995)

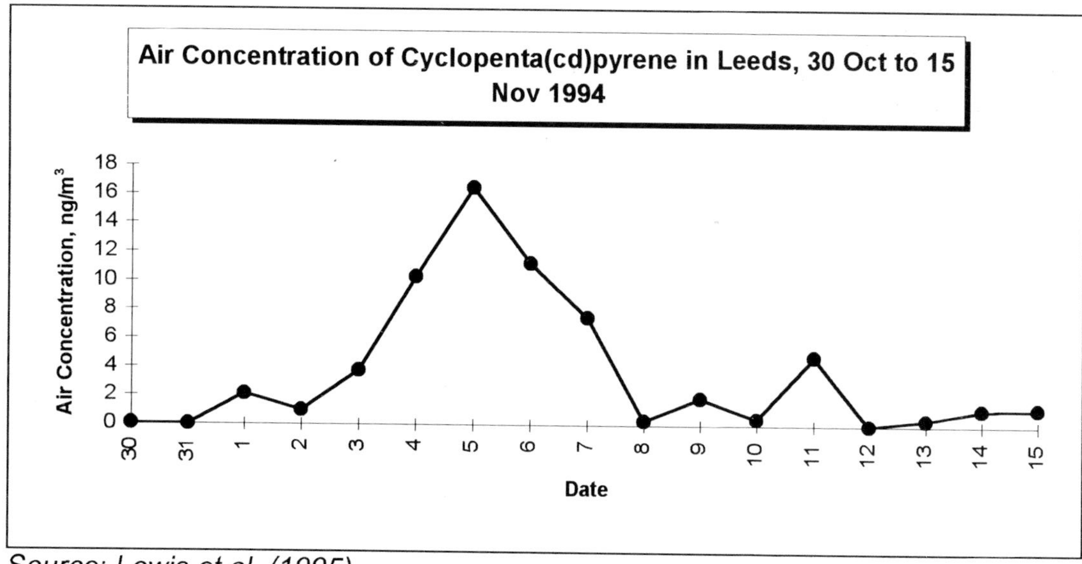

Source: Lewis et al. (1995)

Chemical formula : $C_{10}H_{22}$

Alternative names :

Type of pollutant : (Volatile) organic compound (VOC), hydrocarbon

Structure :

$CH_3—(CH_2)_8—CH_3$

Air quality data summary :

Mean Air Concentration in Leeds, 19/8/94 to 8/9/94	
Location	21 day mean, µg/m^3
Albion Street	0.430
Cliff Lane	0.260
EUN monitoring site	0.339
Kerbside site	0.477
Kirkstall Road	0.730
Park site	0.630
Queen Street	0.370
Vicar Lane	0.557

Source: Bartle et al. (1995)

Dibenzo-(ac/ah)-anthracene in air

Chemical formula : $C_{22}H_{14}$

Alternative names : PAH EPA no.82

Type of pollutant : Polynuclear Aromatic Hydrocarbon (PAH)

Structure :

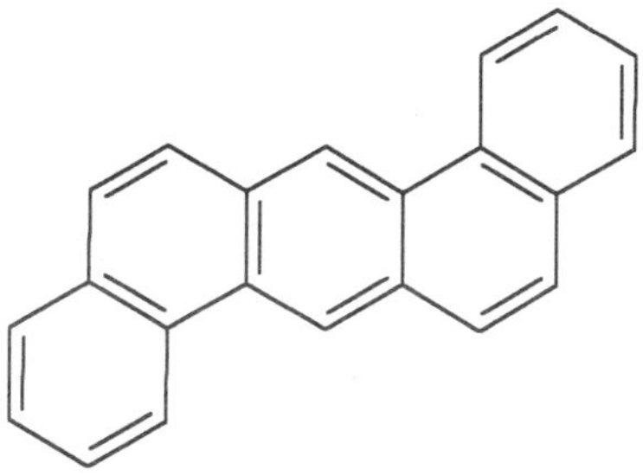

Air quality data summary :

Location	Annual Mean ng/m^3		
	1991	1992	1993
Bowland	*	*	0.38
Cardiff C	*	*	*
London	0.37	0.36	0.23
Manchester B	*	*	0.73
Middlesbrough	*	*	0.34
WSL	0.34	*	*

Source: Davis (1993)

Notes: * signifies no data available

Location	Season 1992	Total Concentration in Air ng/m^3
Edgbaston	Winter (February)	0.83
Edgbaston	Summer (August)	0.07
Wasthills	Summer (August)	0.03

Source: Smith and Harrison (1994)

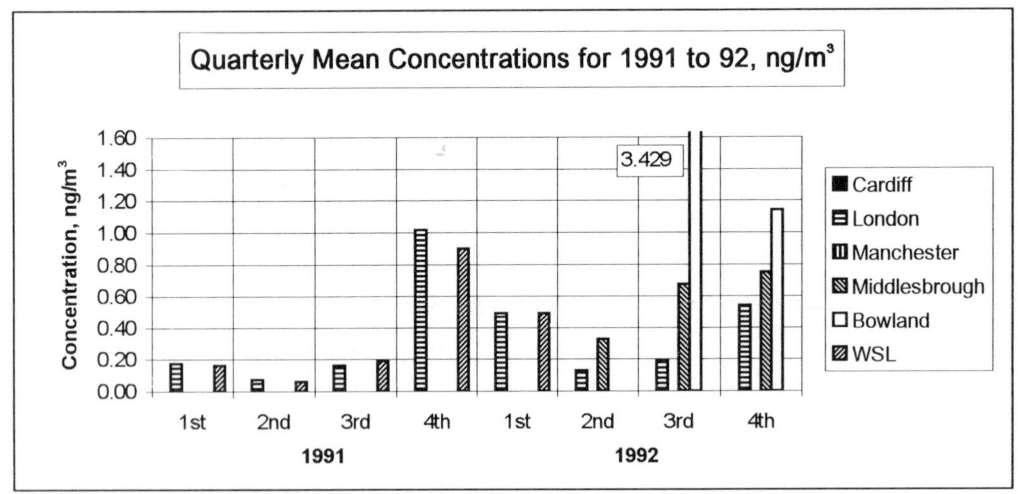

Source: Davis (1993)

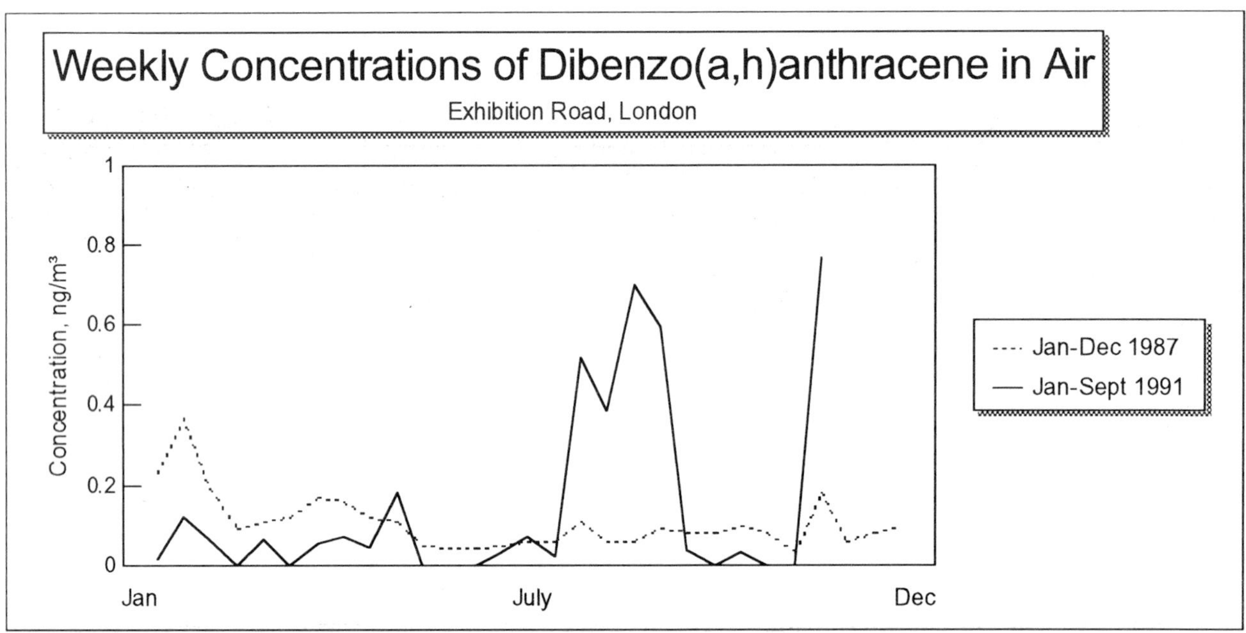

Source: Brown et al. (1995)

Chemical formula : $C_{22}H_{14}$

Alternative names : PAH EPA no.82

Type of pollutant : Polynuclear Aromatic Hydrocarbon (PAH)

Structure :

Air quality data summary :

Location	Annual Mean ng/m^2/day		
	1991	1992	1993
Bowland	*	*	32.44
Cardiff C	*	*	*
London	33.60	163.70	*
Manchester B	*	*	*
Middlesbrough	*	*	*
WSL	12.13	*	*

Source: Davis (1993)

Notes: * signifies no data available

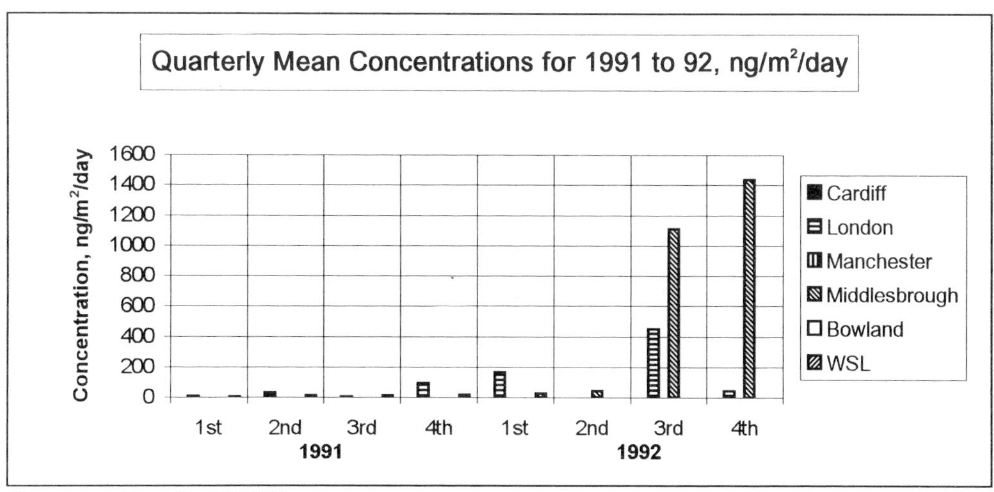

Source: Davis (1993)

Chemical formula : $C_{10}H_{14}$

Alternative names : m-diethylbenzene

Type of pollutant : (Volatile) organic compound (VOC), hydrocarbon

Structure :

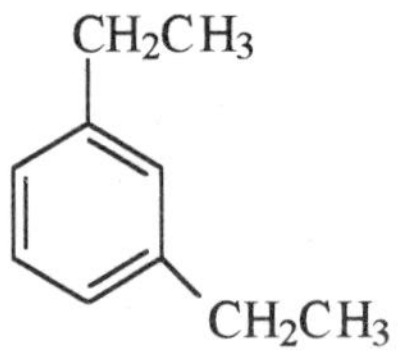

CH_2CH_3

CH_2CH_3

Air quality data summary :

Mean Air Concentration in Leeds, 19/8/94 to 8/9/94	
Location	21 day mean, $\mu g/m^3$
Albion Street	0.029
Cliff Lane	0.024
EUN monitoring site	0.037
Kerbside site	0.056
Kirkstall Road	0.058
Park site	0.029
Queen Street	0.039
Vicar Lane	0.126

Source: Bartle et al. (1995)

Chemical formula : C_8H_{16}

Alternative names :

Type of pollutant : (Volatile) organic compound (VOC), hydrocarbon

Air quality data summary :

Mean Air Concentration in Leeds, 19/8/94 to 8/9/94	
Location	21 day mean, $\mu g/m^3$
Albion Street	0.035
Cliff Lane	0.024
EUN monitoring site	0.033
Kerbside site	0.045
Kirkstall Road	0.037
Park site	0.029
Queen Street	0.024
Vicar Lane	0.074

Source: Bartle et al. (1995)

Note: These data represent results for an isomer of dimethylcyclohexane.

1,1-Dimethylcyclohexane

Chemical formula : C_8H_{16}

Alternative names :

Type of pollutant : (Volatile) organic compound (VOC), hydrocarbon

Structure :

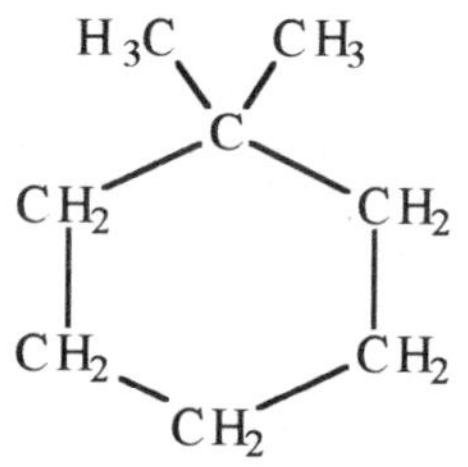

$$\text{1,1-dimethylcyclohexane: ring of } C(CH_3)_2 \text{ and five } CH_2 \text{ groups}$$

Air quality data summary :

Mean Air Concentration in Leeds, 19/8/94 to 8/9/94	
Location	21 day mean, $\mu g/m^3$
Albion Street	0.039
Cliff Lane	0.024
EUN monitoring site	0.040
Kerbside site	0.030
Kirkstall Road	0.037
Park site	0.038
Queen Street	0.030
Vicar Lane	0.039

Source: Bartle et al. (1995)

1,4-Dimethylcyclohexane

Chemical formula : C_8H_{16}

Alternative names :

Type of pollutant : (Volatile) organic compound (VOC), hydrocarbon

Structure :

CH_3
CH
CH_2 CH_2
CH_2 CH_2
CH_2
CH_3

Air quality data summary :

Mean Air Concentration in Leeds, 19/8/94 to 8/9/94	
Location	21 day mean, $\mu g/m^3$
Albion Street	0.036
Cliff Lane	0.041
EUN monitoring site	0.032
Kerbside site	0.034
Kirkstall Road	0.038
Park site	0.027
Queen Street	0.036
Vicar Lane	0.087

Source: Bartle et al. (1995)

1,2-Dimethyl-4-ethylbenzene

Chemical formula : $C_{10}H_{14}$

Alternative names :

Type of pollutant : (Volatile) organic compound (VOC), hydrocarbon

Structure :

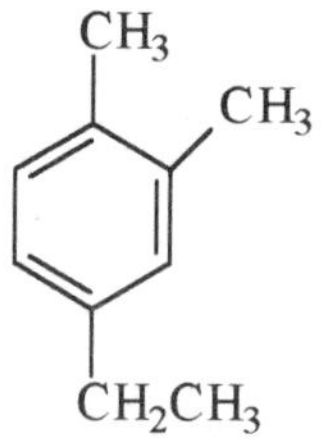

CH_3 CH_3 CH_2CH_3

Air quality data summary :

Mean Air Concentration in Leeds, 19/8/94 to 8/9/94	
Location	21 day mean, µg/m^3
Albion Street	0.071
Cliff Lane	0.041
EUN monitoring site	0.061
Kerbside site	0.103
Kirkstall Road	0.116
Park site	0.045
Queen Street	0.082
Vicar Lane	0.280

Source: Bartle et al. (1995)

1,3-Dimethyl-4-ethylbenzene

Chemical formula : $C_{10}H_{14}$

Alternative names :

Type of pollutant : (Volatile) organic compound (VOC), hydrocarbon

Structure :

CH_3

CH_3

CH_2CH_3

Air quality data summary :

Mean Air Concentration in Leeds, 19/8/94 to 8/9/94	
Location	21 day mean, $\mu g/m^3$
Albion Street	0.051
Cliff Lane	0.029
EUN monitoring site	0.048
Kerbside site	0.092
Kirkstall Road	0.091
Park site	0.038
Queen Street	0.066
Vicar Lane	0.222

Source: Bartle et al. (1995)

Chemical formula : $C_{10}H_{14}$

Alternative names :

Type of pollutant : (Volatile) organic compound (VOC), hydrocarbon

Structure :

CH_3 CH_2CH_3 CH_3

Air quality data summary :

Mean Air Concentration in Leeds, 19/8/94 to 8/9/94	
Location	21 day mean, µg/m^3
Albion Street	0.076
Cliff Lane	0.042
EUN monitoring site	0.067
Kerbside site	0.104
Kirkstall Road	0.131
Park site	0.065
Queen Street	0.086
Vicar Lane	0.255

Source: Bartle et al. (1995)

Chemical formula : C_9H_{20}

Alternative names :

Type of pollutant : (Volatile) organic compounds (VOC), hydrocarbons

Air quality data summary :

Mean Air Concentration in Leeds, 19/8/94 to 8/9/94	
Location	21 day mean, µg/m^3
Albion Street	0.040
Cliff Lane	0.028
EUN monitoring site	0.036
Kerbside site	0.088
Kirkstall Road	0.028
Park site	0.111
Queen Street	0.033
Vicar Lane	0.041

Source: Bartle et al. (1995)

Mean Air Concentration in Leeds, 19/8/94 to 8/9/94	
Location	21 day mean, µg/m^3
Albion Street	0.036
Cliff Lane	0.042
EUN monitoring site	0.043
Kerbside site	0.025
Kirkstall Road	0.035
Park site	0.026
Queen Street	0.032
Vicar Lane	0.063

Source: Bartle et al. (1995)

Note: These results represent two different isomers of dimethylheptane; each table representing a different isomer.

2,3-Dimethylhexane

Chemical formula : C_8H_{18}

Alternative names :

Type of pollutant : (Volatile) organic compound (VOC), hydrocarbon

Structure :

$$CH_3-\underset{\displaystyle CH_3}{\underset{|}{C}}H-\underset{\displaystyle CH_3}{\underset{|}{C}}H-CH_2-CH_2-CH_3$$

Air quality data summary :

Mean Air Concentration in Leeds, 19/8/94 to 8/9/94	
Location	21 day mean, µg/m^3
Albion Street	0.118
Cliff Lane	0.087
EUN monitoring site	0.136
Kerbside site	0.167
Kirkstall Road	0.191
Park site	0.062
Queen Street	0.169
Vicar Lane	0.511

Source: Bartle et al. (1995)

Chemical formula : C_8H_{18}

Alternative names :

Type of pollutant : (Volatile) organic compound (VOC), hydrocarbon

Structure :

$$CH_3-\underset{\displaystyle CH_3}{\underset{|}{CH}}-CH_2-\underset{\displaystyle CH_3}{\underset{|}{CH}}-CH_2-CH_3$$

Air quality data summary :

Mean Air Concentration in Leeds, 19/8/94 to 8/9/94	
Location	21 day mean, $\mu g/m^3$
Albion Street	0.083
Cliff Lane	0.056
EUN monitoring site	0.084
Kerbside site	0.121
Kirkstall Road	0.125
Park site	0.036
Queen Street	0.116
Vicar Lane	0.364

Source: Bartle et al. (1995)

Chemical formula : C_8H_{18}

Alternative names :

Type of pollutant : (Volatile) organic compound (VOC), hydrocarbon

Structure :

$$CH_3-\underset{\displaystyle CH_3}{\underset{|}{CH}}-CH_2-CH_2-\underset{\displaystyle CH_3}{\underset{|}{CH}}-CH_3$$

Air quality data summary :

Mean Air Concentration in Leeds, 19/8/94 to 8/9/94	
Location	21 day mean, $\mu g/m^3$
Albion Street	0.072
Cliff Lane	0.048
EUN monitoring site	0.073
Kerbside site	0.106
Kirkstall Road	0.111
Park site	0.034
Queen Street	0.097
Vicar Lane	0.299

Source: Bartle et al. (1995)

Chemical formula : $C_{10}H_{22}$

Alternative names :

Type of pollutant : (Volatile) organic compounds (VOC), hydrocarbons

Air quality data summary :

Mean Air Concentration in Leeds, 19/8/94 to 8/9/94	
Location	21 day mean, µg/m^3
Albion Street	0.060
Cliff Lane	0.039
EUN monitoring site	0.042
Kerbside site	0.073
Kirkstall Road	0.110
Park site	0.098
Queen Street	0.053
Vicar Lane	0.085

Source: Bartle et al. (1995)

Note: These data represent results for a mixture of different isomers.

2,3-Dimethylpentane

Chemical formula : C_7H_{16}

Alternative names :

Type of pollutant : (Volatile) organic compound (VOC), hydrocarbon

Structure :

$$CH_3-CH(CH_3)-CH(CH_3)-CH_2-CH_3$$

Air quality data summary :

Mean Air Concentration in Leeds, 19/8/94 to 8/9/94	
Location	21 day mean, $\mu g/m^3$
Albion Street	0.088
Cliff Lane	0.058
EUN monitoring site	0.086
Kerbside site	0.117
Kirkstall Road	0.141
Park site	0.039
Queen Street	0.107
Vicar Lane	0.348

Source: Bartle et al. (1995)

Chemical formula : C_7H_{16}

Alternative names :

Type of pollutant : (Volatile) organic compound (VOC), hydrocarbon

Structure :

$$CH_3-\underset{\displaystyle CH_3}{\underset{|}{C}H}-CH_2-\underset{\displaystyle CH_3}{\underset{|}{C}H}-CH_3$$

Air quality data summary :

Mean Air Concentration in Leeds, 19/8/94 to 8/9/94	
Location	21 day mean, µg/m^3
Albion Street	0.053
Cliff Lane	0.037
EUN monitoring site	0.047
Kerbside site	0.124
Kirkstall Road	0.094
Park site	0.042
Queen Street	0.065
Vicar Lane	0.214

Source: Bartle et al. (1995)

Chemical formula : $C_{12}H_{26}$

Alternative names :

Type of pollutant : (Volatile) organic compound (VOC), hydrocarbon

Structure :

$CH_3—(CH_2)_{10}—CH_3$

Air quality data summary :

Mean Air Concentration in Leeds, 19/8/94 to 8/9/94	
Location	21 day mean, μg/m³
Albion Street	0.081
Cliff Lane	0.044
EUN monitoring site	0.085
Kerbside site	0.090
Kirkstall Road	0.160
Park site	0.052
Queen Street	0.085
Vicar Lane	0.236

Source: Bartle et al. (1995)

Chemical formula : C_2H_4O

Alternative names : Acetaldehyde, acetic aldeyde

Type of pollutant : (Volatile) organic compound (VOC), hydrocarbon

Structure :

CH_3CHO

Air quality data summary :

Month 1993	Air Concentration at Harwell site, ppb
	Monthly Mean
August	0.63
September	0.44
October	0.40
November	0.74
December	0.23

Source: Solberg et al. (1994)

Chemical formula : C_2H_6

Alternative names :

Type of pollutant : (Volatile) organic compound (VOC), hydrocarbon

Structure :

CH_3CH_3

Air quality data summary :

Remote rural concentrations

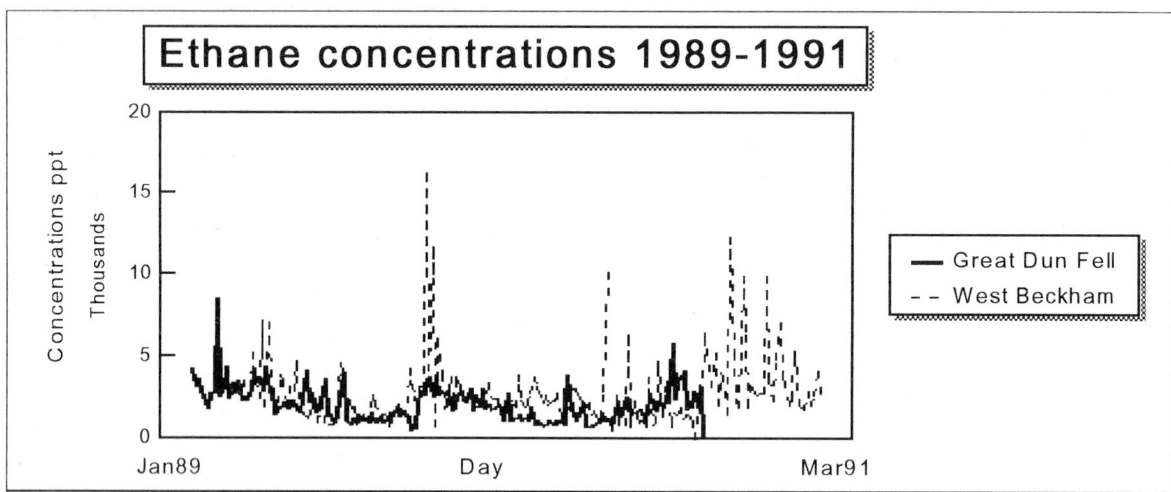

Source: PORG (1993)

Rural concentrations

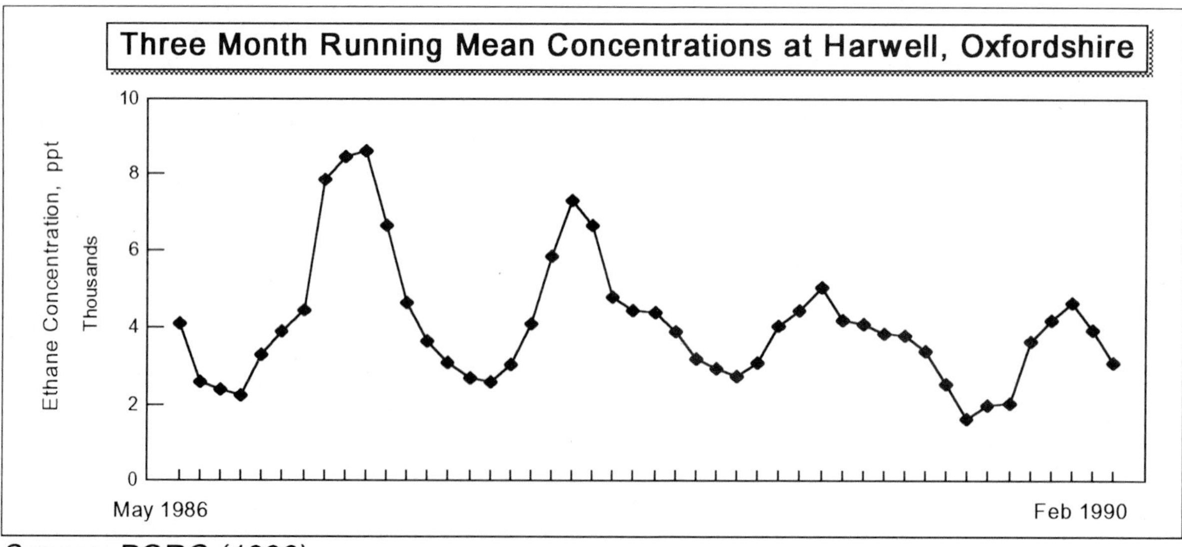

Source: PORG (1993)

Urban concentrations

	1994-95 Monthly Means, ppb								
	Belfast C	Birmingham B	Bristol A	Cardiff B	Edinburgh A	Eltham	Harwell	Middlesbrough	UCL
Jan 94	1.95	7.92	-	7.70	-	2.67	-	2.63	2.69
Feb 94	2.68	8.53	-	7.47	5.35	3.61	-	2.03	2.97
Mar 94	1.53	5.23	-	7.80	3.29	1.39	-	2.24	2.09
Apr 94	1.40	5.27	0.93	4.72	3.62	0.91	-	2.91	2.03
May 94	1.25	5.77	1.60	15.01	0.93	2.77	-	3.54	1.95
Jun 94	0.74	5.39	0.53	4.54	2.34	2.43	-	2.81	1.69
Jul 94	0.76	5.32	0.61	6.04	3.23	2.19	-	1.67	1.59
Aug 94	0.71	3.56	0.69	5.88	3.20	2.38	-	0.90	1.28
Sep 94	1.03	4.51	0.75	4.84	3.68	2.72	-	2.18	1.70
Oct 94	1.59	7.34	1.23	7.86	5.02	3.33	-	1.84	2.17
Nov 94	1.66	7.12	1.14	8.63	4.34	3.67	-	1.76	2.26
Dec 94	1.88	6.86	0.97	7.58	4.92	4.77	-	1.26	1.93
Jan 95	1.65	4.46	1.35	6.76	4.53	4.26	1.09	0.47	1.54
Feb 95	1.58	4.05	0.74	6.65	3.44	3.52	1.05	1.24	1.32

Source: Dollard (1995)

Ethylbenzene

Chemical formula : C_8H_{10}

Alternative names :

Type of pollutant : (Volatile) organic compound (VOC), hydrocarbon

Structure :

CH_2CH_3 (benzene ring)

Air quality data summary :

Remote rural concentrations

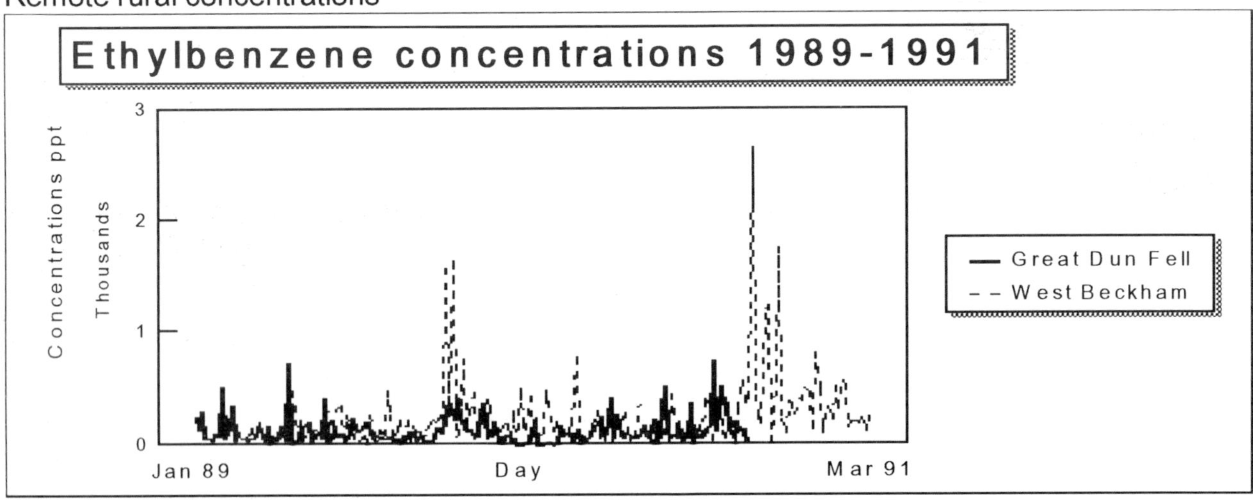

Source: PORG (1993)

Rural concentrations

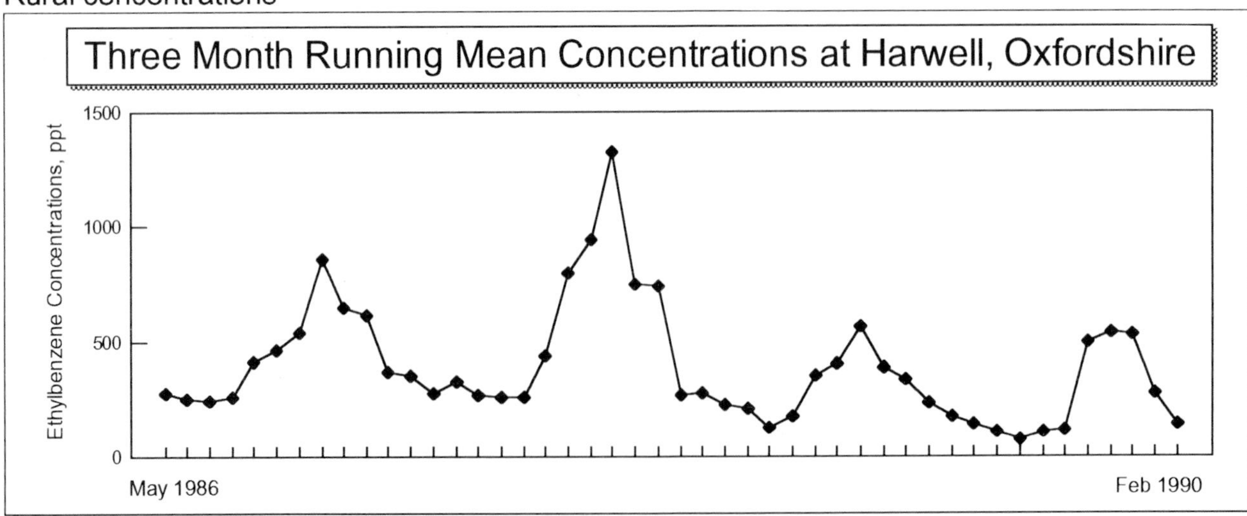

Source: PORG (1993)

Urban concentrations

	1994-95 Monthly Means, ppb								
	Belfast C	Birmingham B	Bristol A	Cardiff B	Edinburgh A	Eltham	Harwell	Middlesbrough	UCL
Jan 94	0.40	1.67	-	0.57	0.06	0.06	-	0.46	1.97
Feb 94	0.55	1.74	-	0.71	0.56	0.17	-	1.63	1.67
Mar 94	0.23	1.57	-	0.29	0.39	0.35	-	1.50	0.88
Apr 94	0.38	0.89	0.37	0.63	0.85	0.55	-	2.62	1.02
May 94	0.46	0.85	0.60	1.02	0.76	0.30	-	0.30	1.29
Jun 94	0.33	1.09	1.70	0.59	0.56	0.57	-	1.10	0.96
Jul 94	0.36	0.56	1.34	0.28	0.27	0.31	-	0.60	2.15
Aug 94	0.42	0.54	0.67	0.31	0.24	0.27	-	1.15	0.27
Sep 94	0.72	1.45	0.74	0.57	0.23	0.35	-	11.18	1.22
Oct 94	0.92	2.96	1.23	1.00	0.93	0.45	-	1.50	1.86
Nov 94	0.82	1.24	1.36	1.55	1.20	1.64	-	1.17	1.56
Dec 94	0.84	1.92	0.94	0.52	0.73	0.46	-	0.46	2.52
Jan 95	0.43	0.56	0.79	0.47	0.35	0.53	0.11	0.32	0.52
Feb 95	0.33	0.48	0.34	0.36	0.24	0.40	-	0.27	0.46

Source: Dollard (1995)

Mean Air Concentration in Leeds, 19/8/94 to 8/9/94	
Location	21 day mean, $\mu g/m^3$
Albion Street	0.327
Cliff Lane	0.216
EUN monitoring site	0.385
Kerbside site	0.564
Kirkstall Road	0.581
Park site	0.257
Queen Street	0.430
Vicar Lane	1.306

Source: Bartle et al. (1995)

Chemical formula : C_2H_4

Alternative names : Ethene

Type of pollutant : (Volatile) organic compound (VOC), hydrocarbon

Structure :

$CH_2{=}CH_2$

Air quality data summary :

Remote rural concentrations

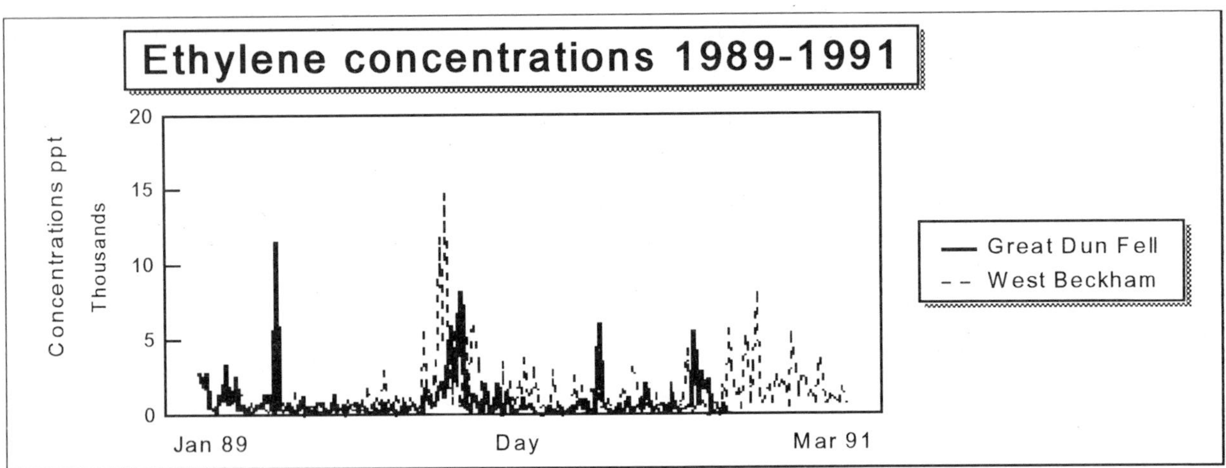

Source: PORG (1993)

Rural concentrations

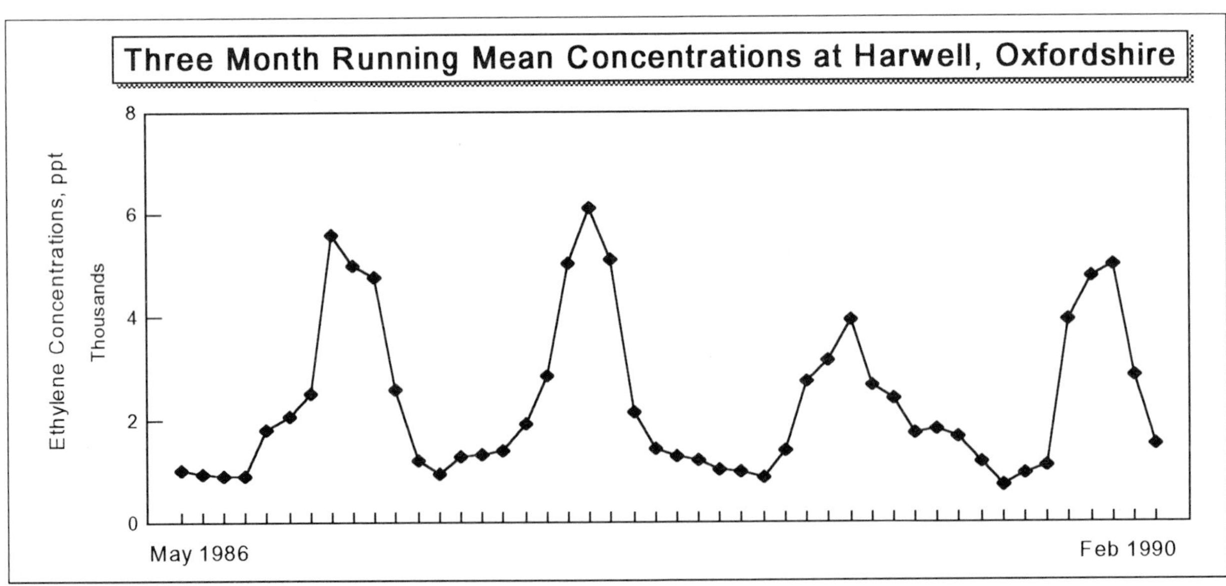

Source: PORG (1993)

Urban concentrations

	1994-95 Monthly Means, ppb								
	Belfast C	Birmingham B	Bristol A	Cardiff B	Edinburgh A	Eltham	Harwell	Middlesbrough	UCL
Jan 94	2.17	2.78	-	4.78	-	2.69	-	1.13	3.21
Feb 94	2.92	3.67	-	5.55	2.96	2.97	-	1.43	4.39
Mar 94	1.03	1.56	-	2.22	1.07	1.26	-	0.74	1.76
Apr 94	1.02	1.43	1.62	2.17	1.29	1.19	-	12.96	1.87
May 94	1.16	1.54	1.89	2.58	0.28	1.98	-	5.91	3.04
Jun 94	0.85	1.47	0.47	1.86	1.11	2.03	-	1.15	1.66
Jul 94	0.90	1.83	0.41	2.40	1.55	2.07	-	1.69	1.82
Aug 94	1.04	2.01	0.46	2.39	1.63	2.13	-	0.74	1.49
Sep 94	1.80	2.47	0.64	2.79	1.88	2.71	-	1.27	2.28
Oct 94	2.79	4.89	1.12	4.61	2.63	3.65	-	1.12	3.03
Nov 94	2.69	5.29	1.07	5.16	2.41	4.56	-	1.36	2.82
Dec 94	3.17	5.14	1.20	4.57	2.60	5.67	-	0.82	2.30
Jan 95	2.10	2.43	1.19	3.67	1.87	3.93	0.44	1.01	1.54
Feb 95	1.47	2.24	0.58	3.02	1.28	3.09	0.33	0.92	1.29

Source: Dollard (1995)

Chemical formula : C_9H_{12}

Alternative names :

Type of pollutant : (Volatile) organic compound (VOC), hydrocarbon

Structure :

CH_3 / C_2H_5

Air quality data summary :

Mean Air Concentration in Leeds, 19/8/94 to 8/9/94	
Location	21 day mean, μg/m^3
Albion Street	0.261
Cliff Lane	0.182
EUN monitoring site	0.294
Kerbside site	0.489
Kirkstall Road	0.684
Park site	0.163
Queen Street	0.412
Vicar Lane	1.238

Source: Bartle et al. (1995)

o-Ethyltoluene

Chemical formula : C_9H_{12}

Alternative names :

Type of pollutant : (Volatile) organic compound (VOC), hydrocarbon

Structure :

CH_3 C_2H_5

Air quality data summary :

Mean Air Concentration in Leeds, 19/8/94 to 8/9/94	
Location	21 day mean, µg/m^3
Albion Street	0.143
Cliff Lane	0.091
EUN monitoring site	0.149
Kerbside site	0.254
Kirkstall Road	0.378
Park site	0.105
Queen Street	0.218
Vicar Lane	0.625

Source: Bartle et al. (1995)

Chemical formula : C_9H_{12}

Alternative names :

Type of pollutant : (Volatile) organic compound (VOC), hydrocarbon

Structure :

CH_3 / C_2H_5

Air quality data summary :

Mean Air Concentration in Leeds, 19/8/94 to 8/9/94	
Location	21 day mean, $\mu g/m^3$
Albion Street	0.183
Cliff Lane	0.127
EUN monitoring site	0.192
Kerbside site	0.318
Kirkstall Road	0.453
Park site	0.156
Queen Street	0.269
Vicar Lane	0.730

Source: Bartle et al. (1995)

Europium aerosol

Chemical formula : Eu

Alternative names : Particulate europium

Type of pollutant : Suspended particulate matter, trace element

Air quality data summary :

Rural concentrations

Location	Concentrations, ng/m^3			
	Mean	Trend	Mean	Trend
	1972-1981	%/yr	1982-1991	%/yr
Harwell, Oxfordshire.	0.010	-	0.011	-
Styrrup, Nottinghamshire.	0.011	-	0.020	-9.4
Trebanos, Glamorgan.	0.009	-	0.013	-
Wraymires, Cumbria.	0.005	-	0.007	-

Source: Cawse et al. (1994)

Europium in rain

Chemical formula : Eu

Alternative names : Precipitation europium

Type of pollutant : Trace contaminant of rain, trace element

Air quality data summary :

Rural Concentrations

Location	Average Annual Rainfall Concentration, µg per litre	
	1972-1981	1982-1989 *
Harwell, Oxfordshire.	0.01	0.0039
Styrrup, Nottinghamshire.	0.02	0.0064
Wraymires, Cumbria.	<0.003	<0.002

Source: Cawse et al. (1994)

Note: total deposition expressed as apparent rainfall concentration.
* based on soluble fraction only.

Europium not analysed in rainwater in 1990 and 1991.

Chemical formula : $C_{14}H_{10}O$

Alternative names : 2-Fluorenecarboxaldehyde

Type of pollutant : Oxygenated polynuclear aromatic compound (PAC)

Structure :

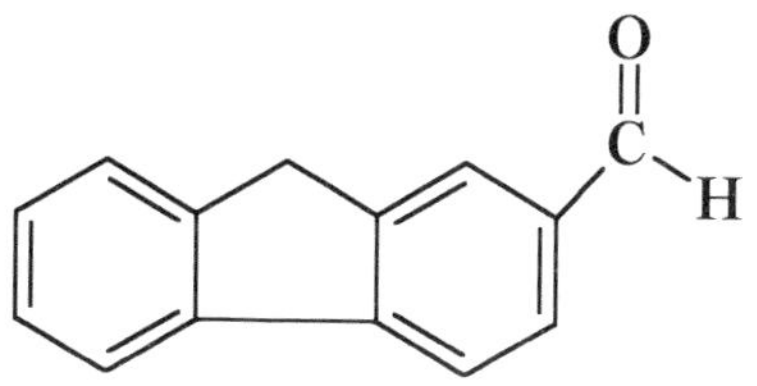

Air Quality Data Summary :

Urban Concentrations:

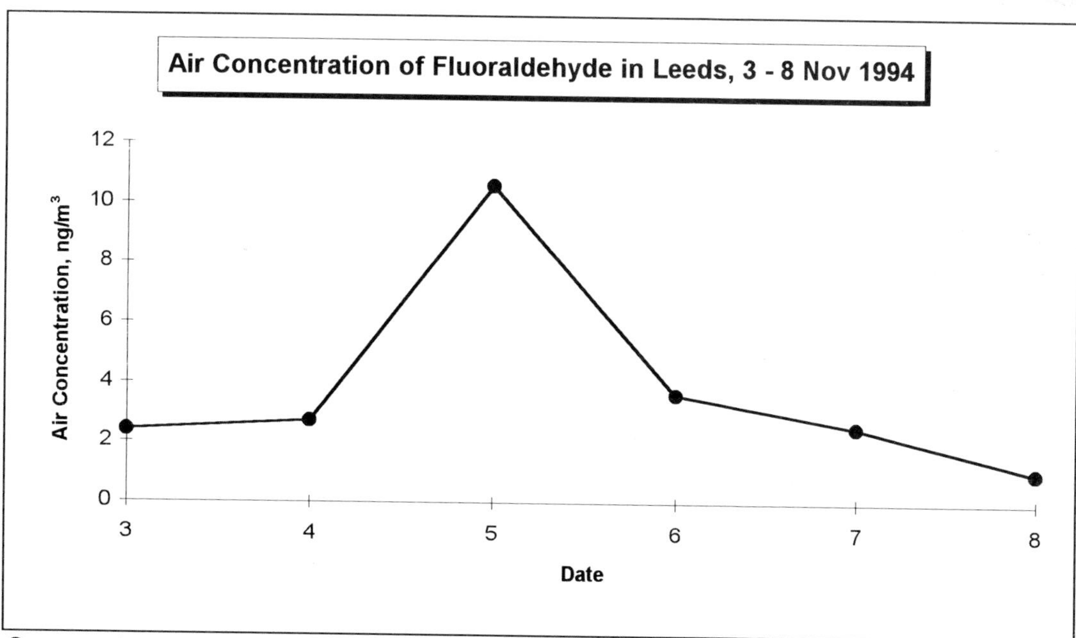

Source: Lewis et al. (1995)

Fluoranthene in air 88

Chemical formula : $C_{16}H_{10}$

Alternative names : PAH EPA no.39, 1,2-benzacenaphthene, Idryl.

Type of pollutant : Polynuclear Aromatic Hydrocarbon (PAH)

Structure :

Air quality data summary :

Location	Annual Mean ng/m^3		
	1991	1992	1993
Bowland	*	*	6.63
Cardiff C	*	*	*
London	13.62	8.06	6.14
Manchester B	*	*	12.98
Middlesbrough	*	*	8.51
WSL	7.93	*	*

Source: Davis (1993)

Notes: * signifies no data available

Urban Concentrations

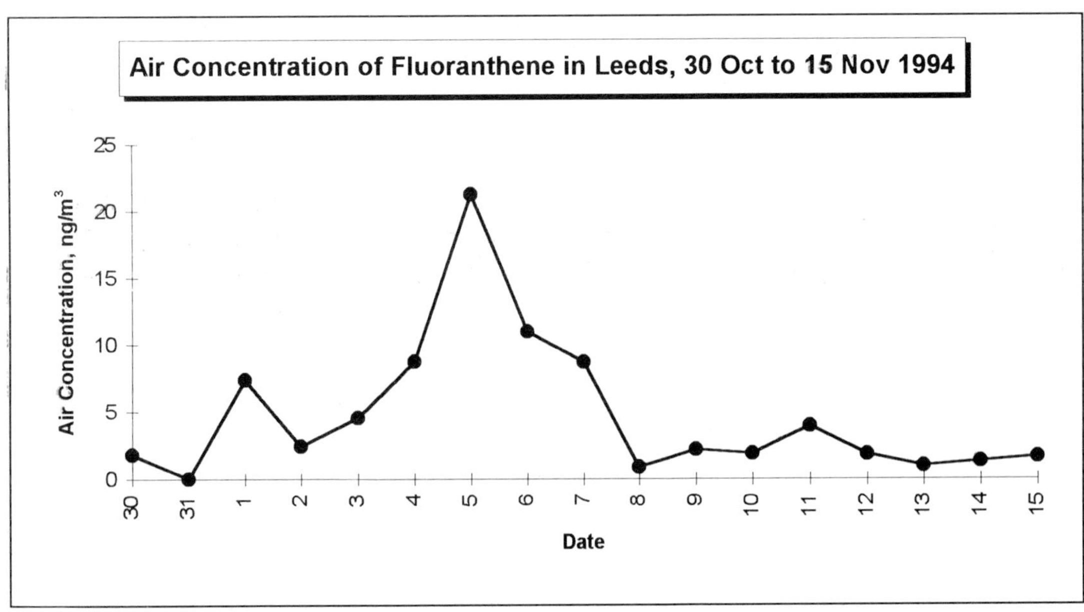

Source: Lewis et al. (1995)

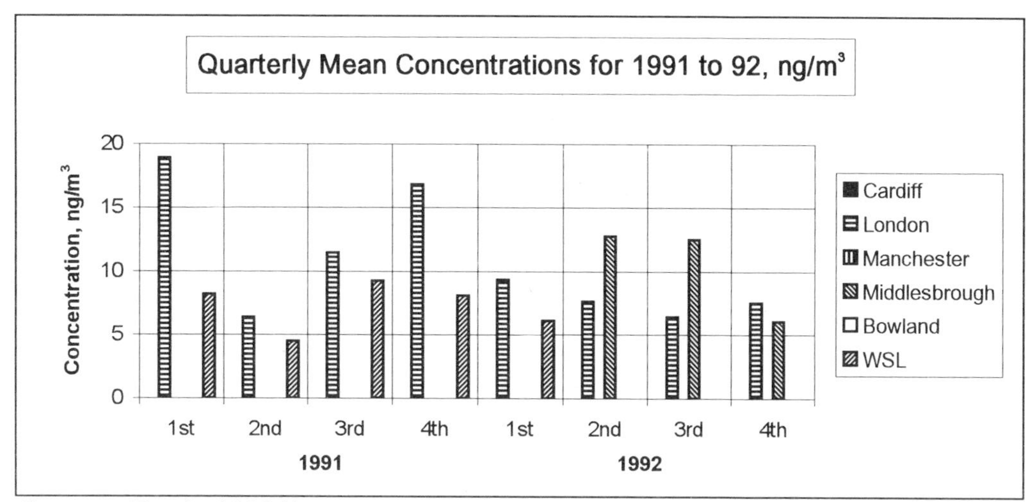

Source: Davis (1993)

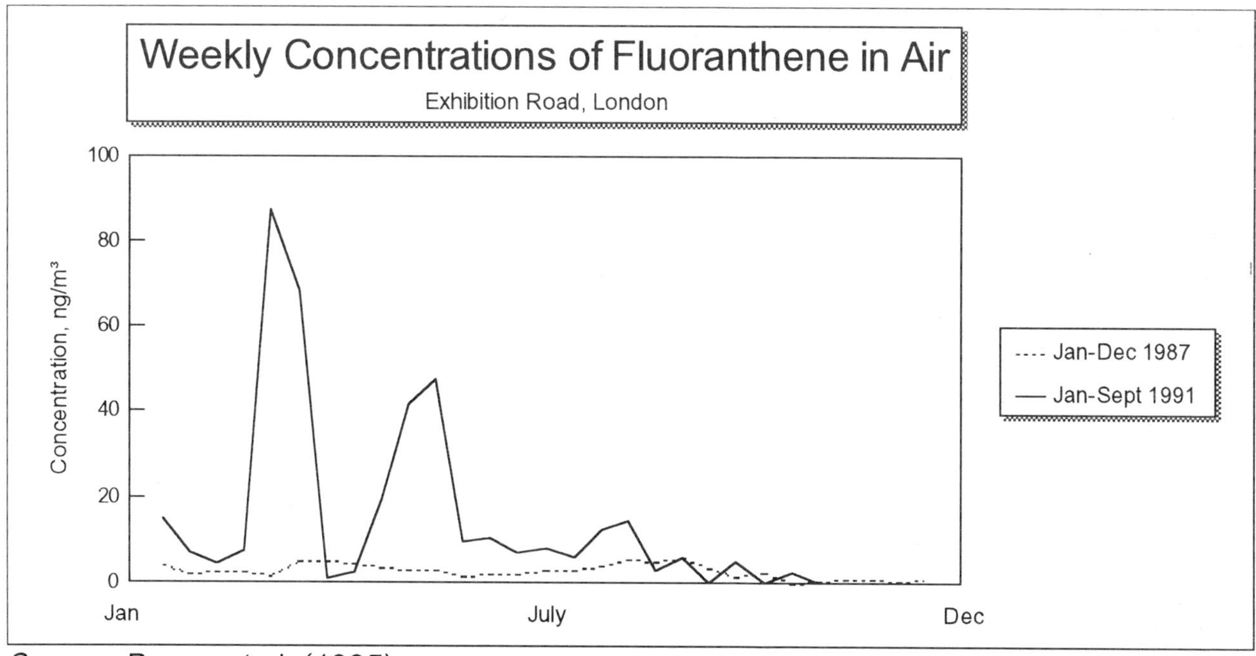

Source: Brown et al. (1995)

Location	Season 1992	Total Concentration in Air ng/m³
Edgbaston	Winter (February)	12.36
Edgbaston	Summer (August)	2.11
Wasthills	Summer (August)	0.41

Source: Smith and Harrison (1994)

Chemical formula : $C_{16}H_{10}$

Alternative names : PAH EPA no.39, 1,2-benzacenaphthene, Idryl.

Type of pollutant : Polynuclear Aromatic Hydrocarbon (PAH)

Structure :

Air quality data summary :

Location	Annual Mean ng/m²/day		
	1991	1992	1993
Bowland	*	*	242.99
Cardiff C	*	*	*
London	767.20	3832.50	*
Manchester B	*	*	*
Middlesbrough	*	*	*
WSL	504.89	*	*

Source: Davis (1993)

Notes: * signifies no data available

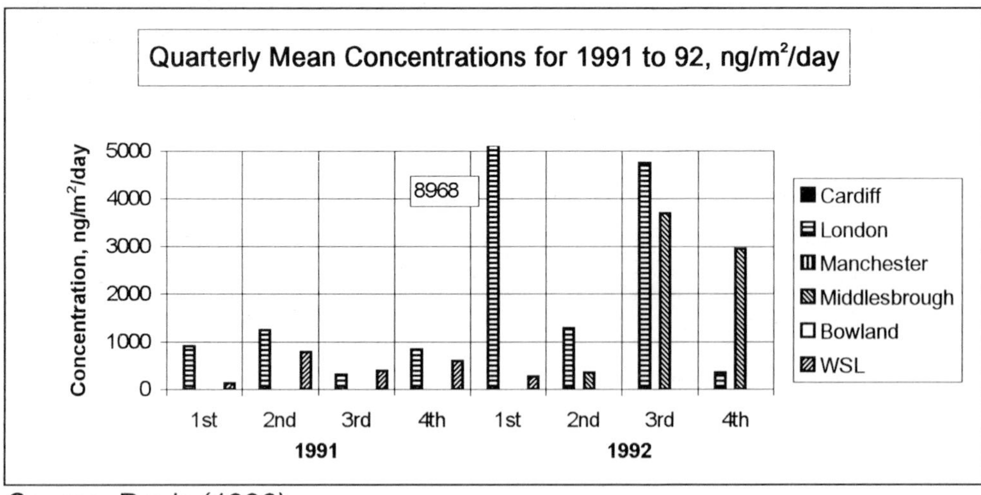

Source: Davis (1993)

Chemical formula	:	$C_{13}H_{10}$
Alternative names	:	Diphenylenemethane, PAH EPA no.80, 2,3-benzindene.
Type of pollutant	:	Polynuclear Aromatic Hydrocarbon (PAH)
Structure	:	

CH_2

Air quality data summary :

Location	Annual Mean ng/m^3		
	1991	1992	1993
Bowland	*	*	48.16
Cardiff C	21.34	8.77	*
London	32.51	14.68	7.17
Manchester B	20.93	16.43	20.22
Middlesbrough	*	*	22.61
WSL	21.21	*	*

Source: Davis (1993)

Notes: * signifies no data available

Location	Season 1992	Total Concentration in Air ng/m^3
Edgbaston	Winter (February)	13.65
Edgbaston	Summer (August)	7.00
Wasthills	Summer (August)	2.02

Source: Smith and Harrison (1994)

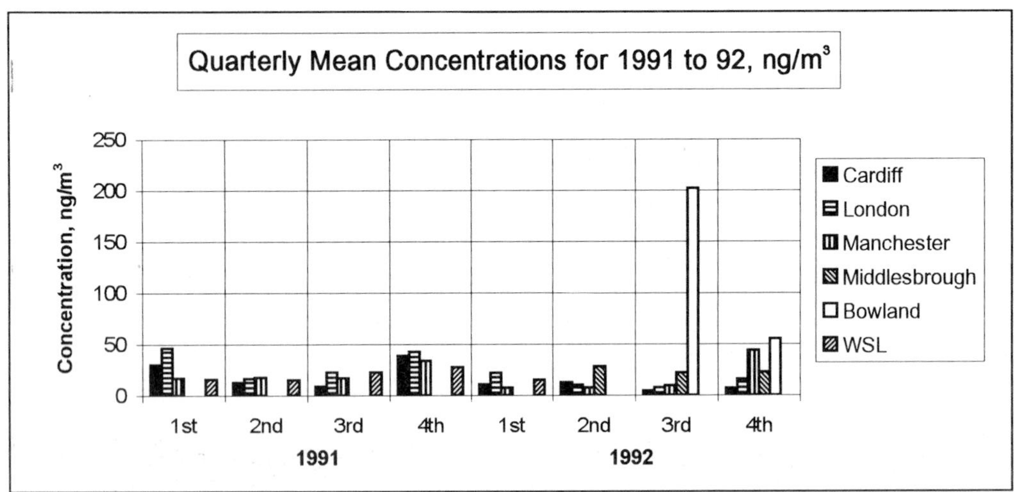

Source: Davis (1993)

Fluorene in deposition

Chemical formula : $C_{13}H_{10}$

Alternative names : Diphenylenemethane, PAH EPA no.80, 2,3-benzindene.

Type of pollutant : Polynuclear Aromatic Hydrocarbon (PAH)

Structure :

CH2

Air quality data summary :

Location	Annual Mean ng/m²/day		
	1991	1992	1993
Bowland	*	*	414.90
Cardiff C	355.05	282.77	*
London	116.10	125.20	*
Manchester B	436.52	95.55	*
Middlesbrough	*	*	*
WSL	120.68	*	*

Source: Davis (1993)

Notes: * signifies no data available

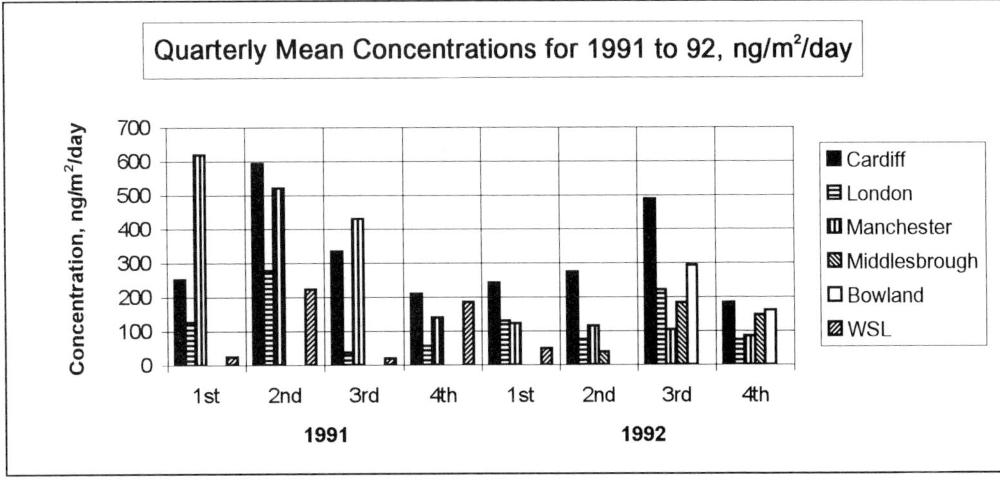

Source: Davis (1993)

Fluorenone 90

Chemical formula : $C_{13}H_8O$

Alternative names : Diphenylene ketone, 9-oxo-fluorene

Type of pollutant : Oxygenated polynuclear aromatic compound (PAC)

Structure :

Air quality data summary :

Urban Concentrations

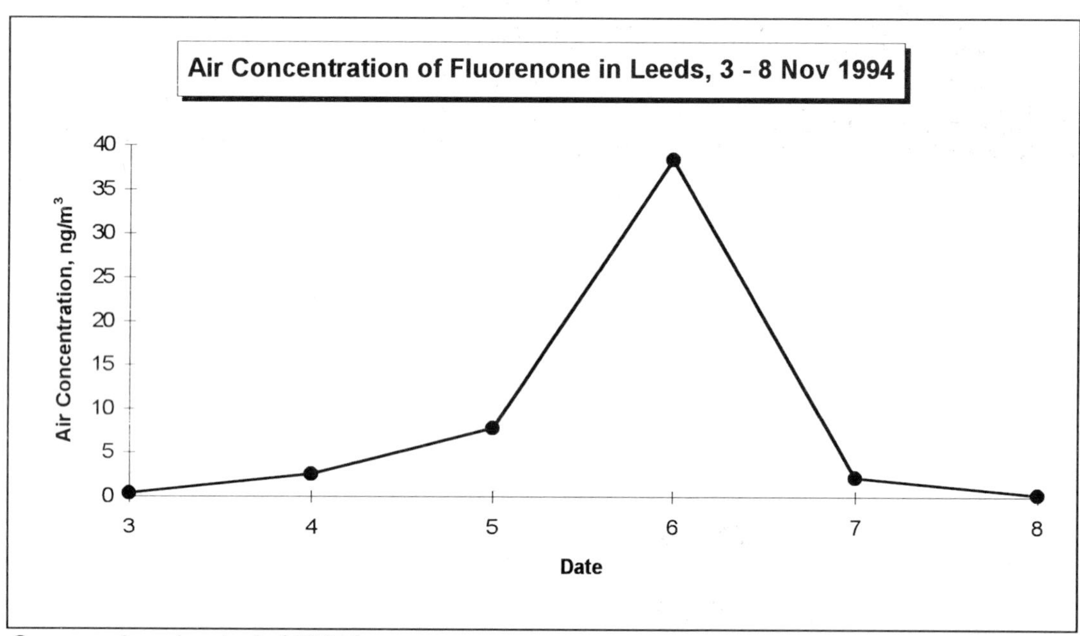

Source: Lewis et al. (1995)

Chemical formula : HCHO

Alternative names : Methanal

Type of pollutant : (Volatile) organic compound (VOC), oxygenated hydrocarbon

Structure :

HCHO

Air quality data summary :

Rural Concentrations

Month 1993	Air Concentration at Harwell site, ppb
	Monthly Mean
August	2.18
September	1.05
October	0.71
November	1.18
December	0.41

Source: Solberg et al. (1994)

Chemical formula : CHO.CHO

Alternative names : Ethan-1,2-dial

Type of pollutant : (Volatile) organic compound (VOC), oxygenated hydrocarbon

Structure :

CHO—CHO

Air quality data summary :

Rural Concentrations

Month 1993	Air Concentration at Harwell site, ppb
	Monthly Mean
August	0.012
September	0.012
October	*
November	0.054
December	0.025

Source: Solberg et al. (1994)

Note: * signifies no data available

Chemical formula : Au

Alternative names : Particulate gold

Type of pollutant : Suspended particulate matter, trace element

Air quality data summary :

Rural Concentrations

Location	Average Annual Concentration in Air, ng/m^3	
	1975-1981	1982-1991
Harwell, Oxfordshire.	0.011	<0.01
Styrrup, Nottinghamshire.	0.006	<0.004
Trebanos, Glamorgan.	0.006	-
Wraymires, Cumbria.	0.005	<0.002

Source: Cawse et al. (1994)

Gold in rain

Chemical formula : Au

Alternative names : Precipitation gold

Type of pollutant : Trace contaminant of rain, trace element

Air quality data summary :

Rural Concentrations

Location	Average Annual Rainfall Concentrations µg per litre	
	1972-1981	1982-1991 *
Harwell, Oxfordshire.	<0.02	<0.07
Styrrup, Nottinghamshire.	<0.01	<0.08
Wraymires, Cumbria.	<0.01	<0.10

Source: Cawse et al. (1994)

Note: total deposition expressed as apparent rainfall concentration.
* based on soluble fraction only.

2,2',3,3',4,4',5-Heptachlorobiphenyl in air

Chemical formula : $C_{12}H_3Cl_7$

Alternative names : PCB-170

Type of pollutant : (PCB) polychlorinated biphenyl, air toxic

Structure :

Cl Cl Cl Cl Cl Cl Cl

Air quality data summary :

Location	Annual Mean pg/m³		
	1991	1992	1993
Bowland	*	*	1.02
Cardiff C	5.55	4.39	*
London	*	*	*
Manchester B	6.78	5.48	1.10
Middlesbrough	*	*	*
WSL	*	*	*

Source: Davis (1993)

Notes: * signifies no data available

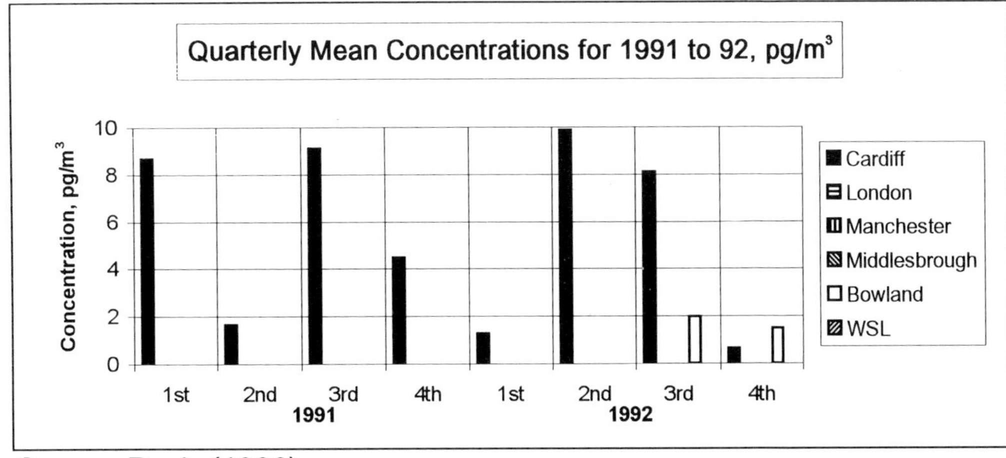

Source: Davis (1993)

Chemical formula : $C_{12}H_3Cl_7$

Alternative names : PCB-170

Type of pollutant : (PCB) polychlorinated biphenyl, air toxic

Structure :

Air quality data summary :

Location	Annual Mean ng/m²/day		
	1991	1992	1993
Bowland	*	*	2.64
Cardiff C	23.34	27.66	*
London	*	*	*
Manchester B	8.76	12.39	*
Middlesbrough	*	*	*
WSL	*	*	*

Source: Davis (1993)

Notes: * signifies no data available

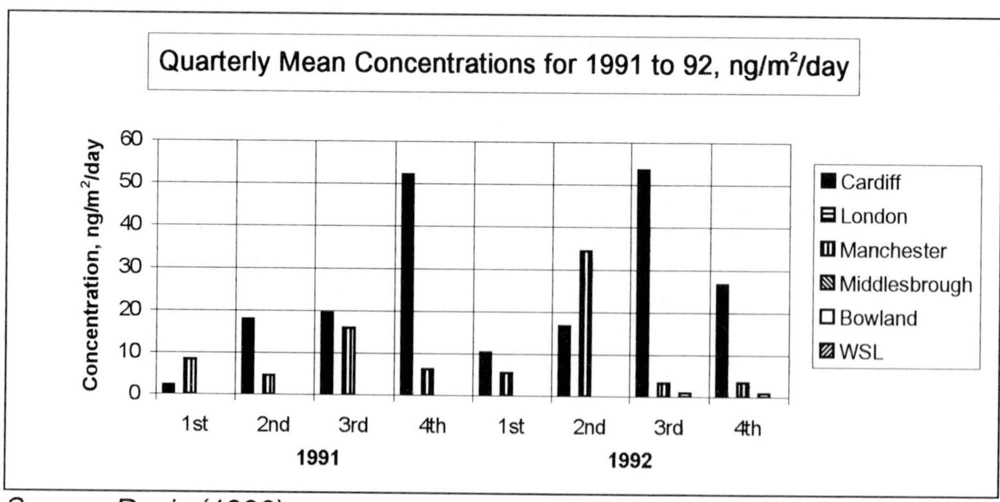

Source: Davis (1993)

2,2',3,4,4',5,5'-Heptachlorobiphenyl in air 95

Chemical formula : $C_{12}H_3Cl_7$

Alternative names : PCB-180

Type of pollutant : (PCB) polychlorinated biphenyl, air toxic

Structure :

Air quality data summary :

Location	Annual Mean pg/m^3		
	1991	1992	1993
Bowland	*	*	7.33
Cardiff C	16.31	18.17	*
London	11.34	12.83	11.02
Manchester B	22.38	24.47	21.32
Middlesbrough	*	*	7.41
WSL	7.51	*	*

Source: Davis (1993)

Notes: * signifies no data available

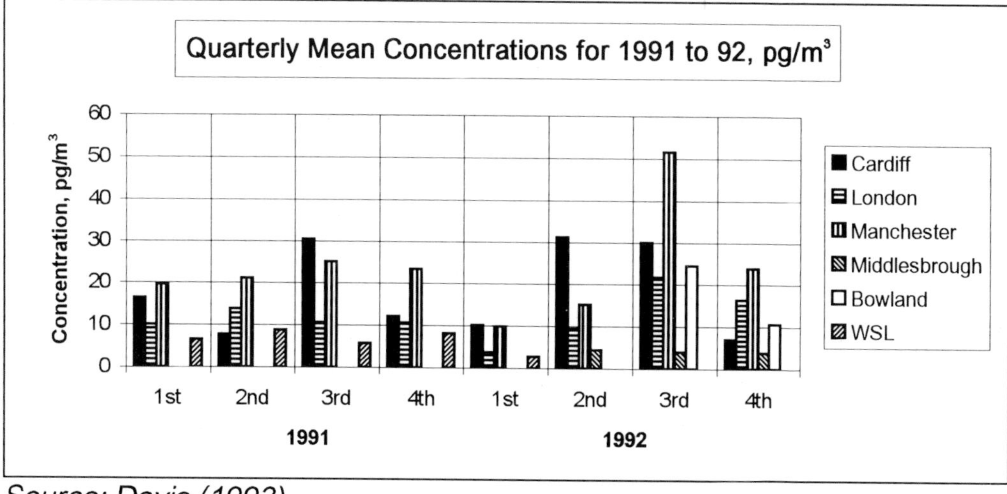

Source: Davis (1993)

2,2',3,4,4',5,5'-Heptachlorobiphenyl in deposition

Chemical formula : $C_{12}H_3Cl_7$

Alternative names : PCB-180

Type of pollutant : (PCB) polychlorinated biphenyl, air toxic

Structure :

Cl Cl Cl Cl Cl Cl Cl

Air quality data summary :

Location	Annual Mean ng/m²/day		
	1991	1992	1993
Bowland	*	*	9.39
Cardiff C	48.23	52.56	*
London	12.80	7.38	*
Manchester B	23.82	29.67	*
Middlesbrough	*	*	*
WSL	8.47	*	*

Source: Davis (1993)

Notes: * signifies no data available

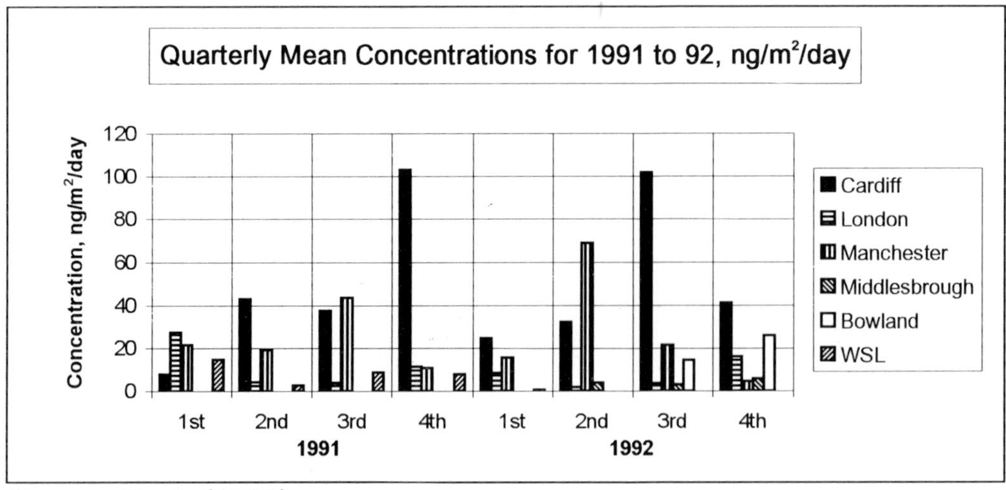

Source: Davis (1993)

2,2',3,4,4',5',6-Heptachlorobiphenyl in air

Chemical formula : $C_{12}H_3Cl_7$

Alternative names : PCB-183

Type of pollutant : (PCB) polychlorinated biphenyl, air toxic

Structure :

Cl Cl Cl Cl Cl Cl Cl

Air quality data summary :

Location	Annual Mean pg/m³		
	1991	1992	1993
Bowland	*	*	0.60
Cardiff C	6.37	4.59	*
London	*	*	*
Manchester B	7.58	8.55	4.64
Middlesbrough	*	*	*
WSL	*	*	*

Source: Davis (1993)

Notes: * signifies no data available

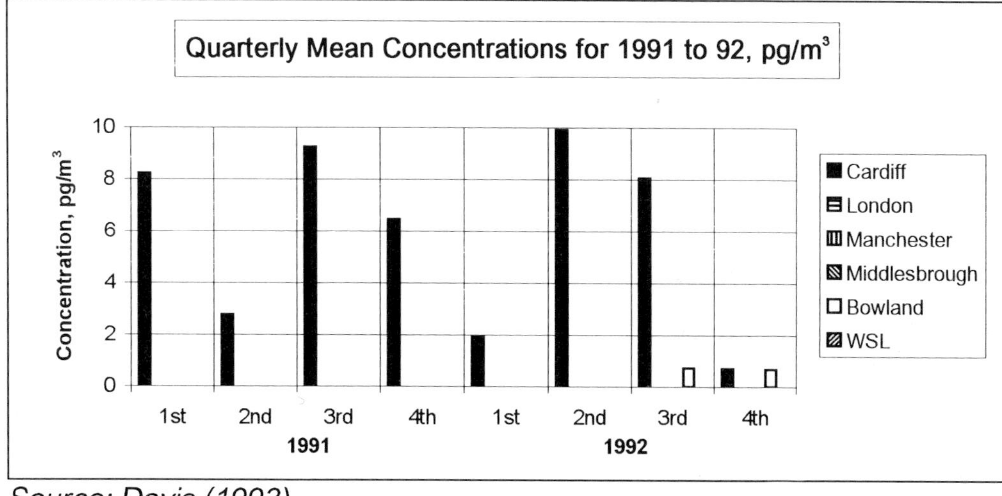

Source: Davis (1993)

2,2',3,4,4',5',6'-Heptachlorobiphenyl in deposition

Chemical formula : $C_{12}H_3Cl_7$

Alternative names : PCB-183

Type of pollutant : (PCB) polychlorinated biphenyl, air toxic

Structure :

Air quality data summary :

Location	Annual Mean ng/m²/day		
	1991	1992	1993
Bowland	*	*	2.03
Cardiff C	8.27	15.49	*
London	*	*	*
Manchester B	6.04	6.54	*
Middlesbrough	*	*	*
WSL	*	*	*

Source: Davis (1993)

Notes: * signifies no data available

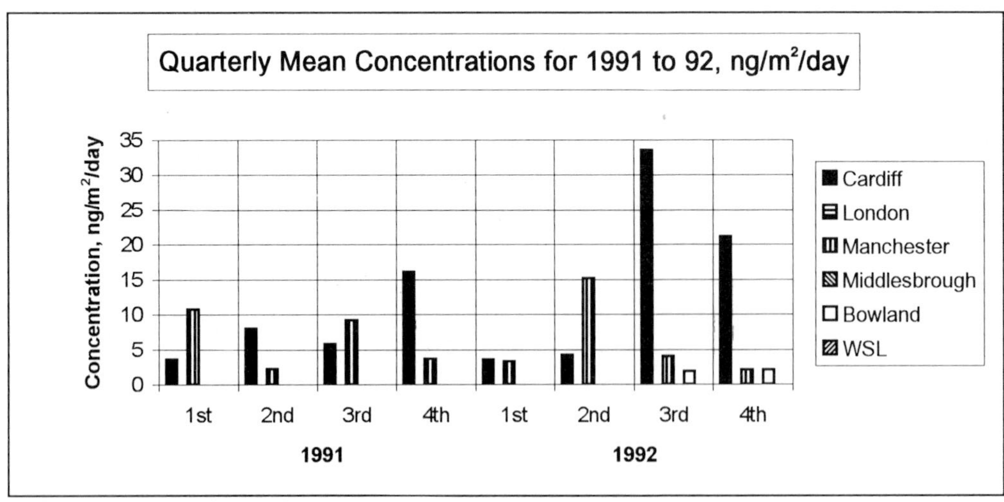

Source: Davis (1993)

2,2',3,4,5,5',6-Heptachlorobiphenyl in air

Chemical formula : $C_{12}H_3Cl_7$

Alternative names : PCB-185

Type of pollutant : (PCB) polychlorinated biphenyl, air toxic

Structure :

Air quality data summary :

Location	Annual Mean pg/m³		
	1991	1992	1993
Bowland	*	*	0.31
Cardiff C	6.56	2.85	*
London	*	*	*
Manchester B	8.50	4.29	0.72
Middlesbrough	*	*	*
WSL	*	*	*

Source: Davis (1993)

Notes: * signifies no data available

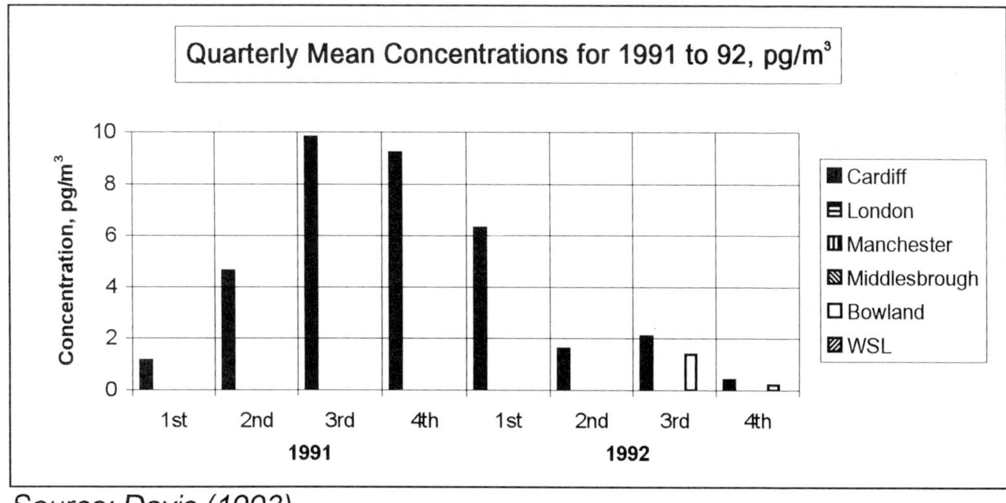

Source: Davis (1993)

2,2',3,4,5,5',6-Heptachlorobiphenyl in deposition

Chemical formula : $C_{12}H_3Cl_7$

Alternative names : PCB-185

Type of pollutant : (PCB) polychlorinated biphenyl, air toxic

Structure :

Air quality data summary :

Location	Annual Mean ng/m²/day		
	1991	1992	1993
Bowland	*	*	0.54
Cardiff C	5.68	5.69	*
London	*	*	*
Manchester B	5.77	2.48	*
Middlesbrough	*	*	*
WSL	*	*	*

Source: Davis (1993)

Notes: * signifies no data available

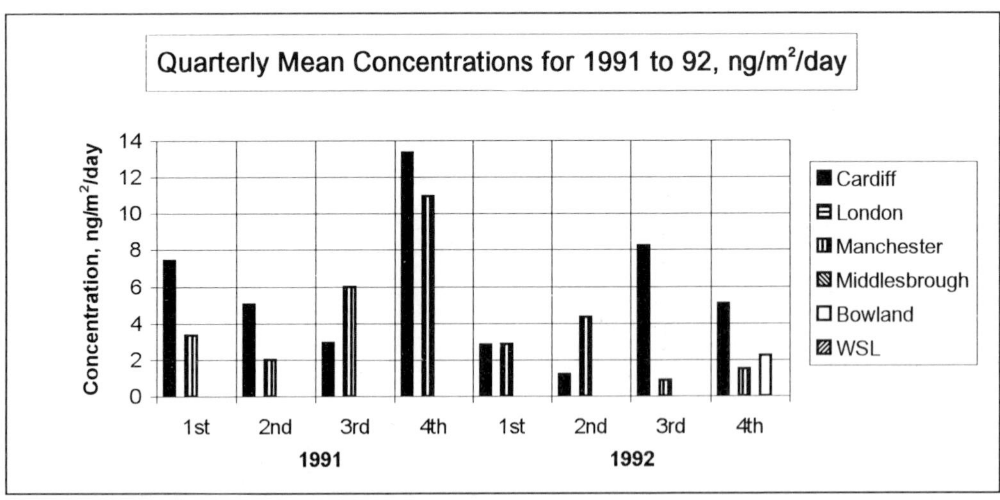

Source: Davis (1993)

2,2’,3,4’,5,5’,6-Heptachlorobiphenyl in air 98

Chemical formula : $C_{12}H_3Cl_7$

Alternative names : PCB-187

Type of pollutant : (PCB) polychlorinated biphenyl, air toxic

Structure :

Cl Cl Cl Cl Cl Cl Cl

Air quality data summary :

Location	Annual Mean pg/m^3		
	1991	1992	1993
Bowland	*	*	5.04
Cardiff C	9.81	11.91	*
London	*	*	*
Manchester B	15.14	19.13	16.46
Middlesbrough	*	*	*
WSL	*	*	*

Source: Davis (1993)

Notes: * signifies no data available

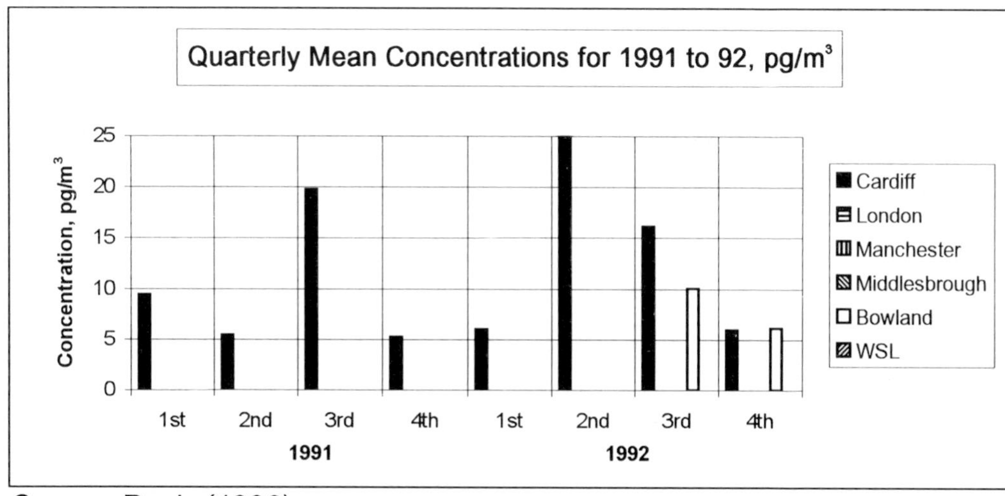

Source: Davis (1993)

2,2',3,4',5,5',6-Heptachlorobiphenyl in deposition 98

Chemical formula : $C_{12}H_3Cl_7$

Alternative names : PCB-187

Type of pollutant : (PCB) polychlorinated biphenyl, air toxic

Structure :

Air quality data summary :

Location	Annual Mean ng/m²/day		
	1991	1992	1993
Bowland	*	*	4.07
Cardiff C	14.79	31.31	*
London	*	*	*
Manchester B	16.14	11.26	*
Middlesbrough	*	*	*
WSL	*	*	*

Source: Davis (1993)

Notes: * signifies no data available

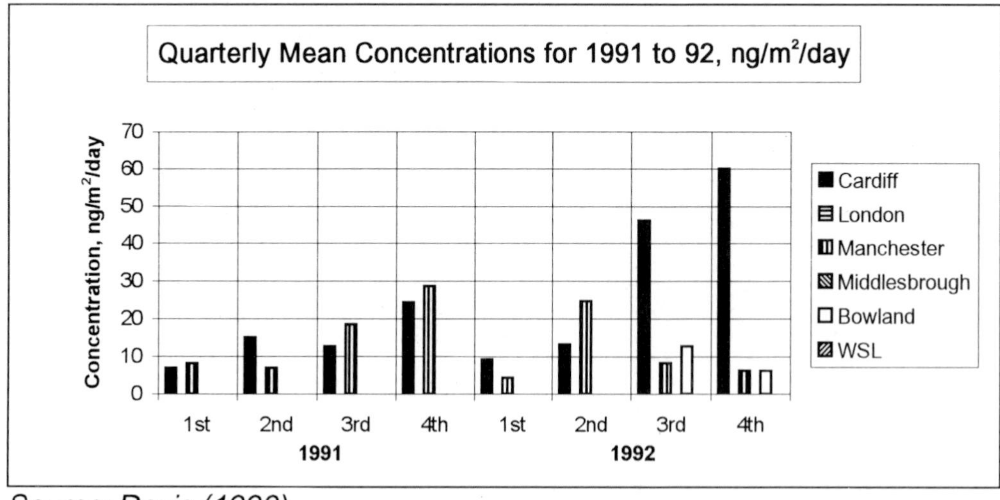

Source: Davis (1993)

Chemical formula : $C_{12}H_3Cl_7$

Alternative names : PCB-188

Type of pollutant : (PCB) polychlorinated biphenyl, air toxic

Structure :

Air quality data summary :

Location	Annual Mean pg/m³		
	1991	1992	1993
Bowland	*	*	1.65
Cardiff C	7.38	17.24	*
London	*	*	*
Manchester B	6.45	11.80	5.93
Middlesbrough	*	*	*
WSL	*	*	*

Source: Davis (1993)

Notes: * signifies no data available

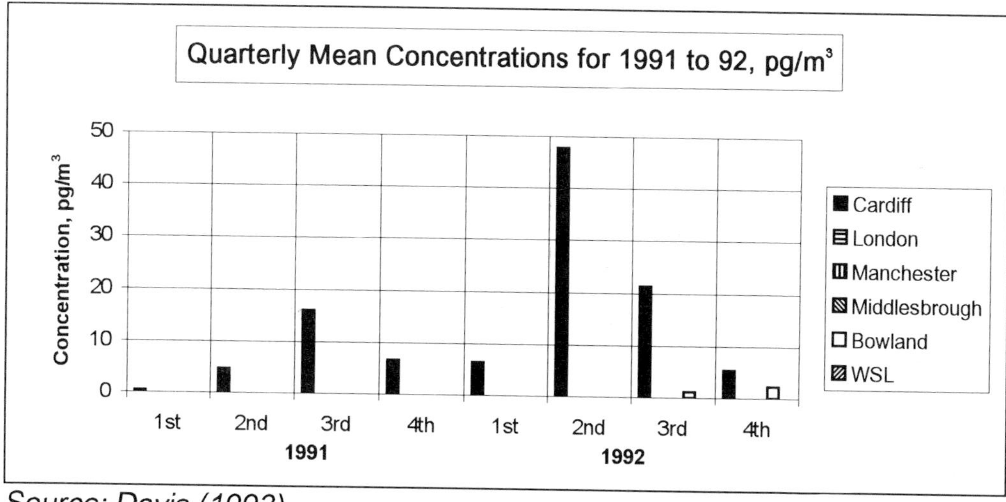

Source: Davis (1993)

2,2',3,4',5,6,6'-Heptachlorobiphenyl in deposition

Chemical formula : $C_{12}H_3Cl_7$

Alternative names : PCB-188

Type of pollutant : (PCB) polychlorinated biphenyl, air toxic

Structure :

Cl Cl Cl Cl Cl Cl Cl

Air quality data summary :

Location	Annual Mean ng/m²/day		
	1991	1992	1993
Bowland	*	*	2.21
Cardiff C	18.06	16.60	*
London	*	*	*
Manchester B	6.21	6.91	*
Middlesbrough	*	*	*
WSL	*	*	*

Source: Davis (1993)

Notes: * signifies no data available

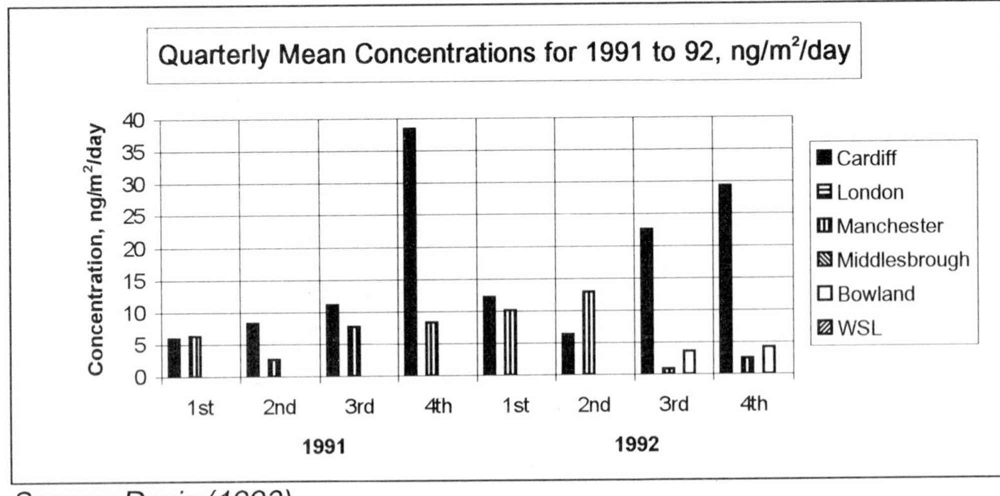

Source: Davis (1993)

1,2,3,4,6,7,8-Heptachlorodibenzofuran in air

Chemical formula : $C_{12}HCl_7O$

Alternative names : 1,2,3,4,6,7,8-HpCDF

Type of pollutant : Furan, air toxic

Structure :

Air quality data summary :

Urban concentrations

Location	Annual Mean pg/m^3		
	1991	1992	1993
Bowland	*	*	0.23
Cardiff C	0.47	0.25	*
London	0.48	0.26	0.16
Manchester B	0.63	0.81	1.05
Middlesbrough	*	*	0.20
WSL	0.29	*	*

Source: Davis (1993)

Note: * signifies no data available

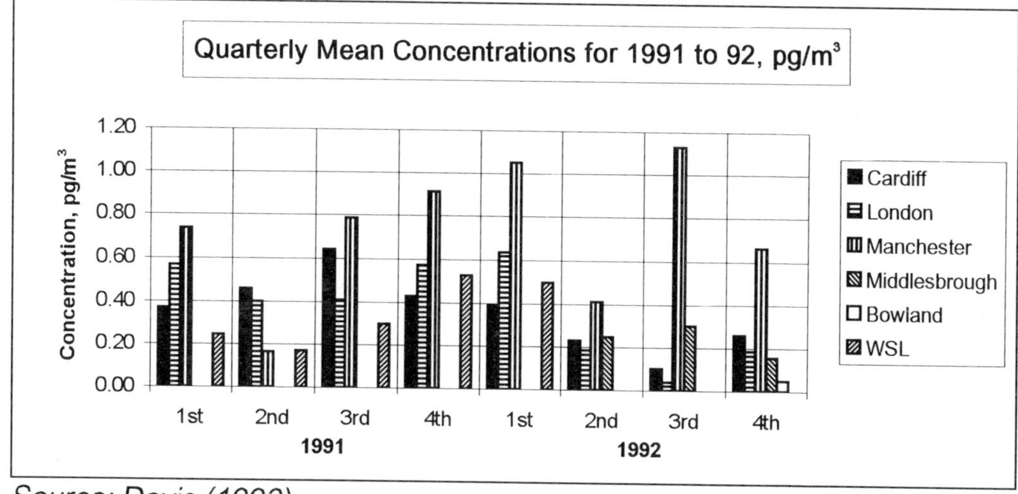

Source: Davis (1993)

1,2,3,4,6,7,8-Heptachlorodibenzofuran in deposition

Chemical formula : $C_{12}HCl_7O$

Alternative names : 1,2,3,4,6,7,8-HpCDF

Type of pollutant : Furan, air toxic

Structure :

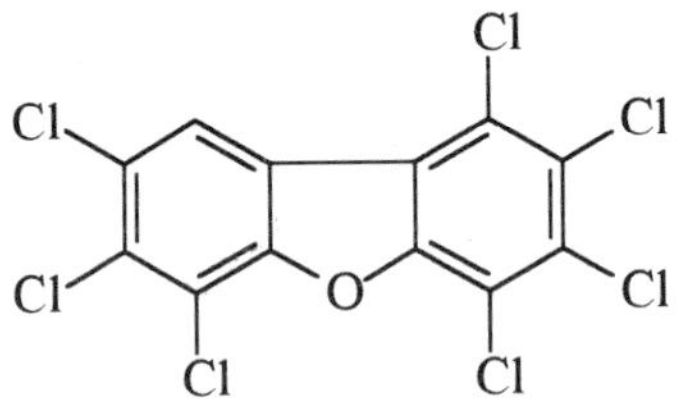

Air quality data summary :

Urban concentrations

Location	Annual Mean pg/m^2/day		
	1991	1992	1993
Bowland	*	*	*
Cardiff C	613.75	292.38	*
London	578.60	38.80	*
Manchester B	398.16	172.73	*
Middlesbrough	*	*	*
WSL	239.12	*	*

Source: Davis (1993)

Note: * signifies no data available

1,2,3,4,7,8,9-Heptachlorodibenzofuran in air 101

Chemical formula : $C_{12}HCl_7O$

Alternative names : 1,2,3,4,7,8,9-HpCDF

Type of pollutant : Furan, air toxic

Structure :

Air quality data summary :

Location	Annual Mean pg/m^3		
	1991	1992	1993
Bowland	*	*	0.00
Cardiff C	0.07	0.03	*
London	0.07	0.04	0.00
Manchester B	0.11	0.05	0.09
Middlesbrough	*	*	0.01
WSL	0.05	*	*

Source: Davis (1993)

Note: * signifies no data available

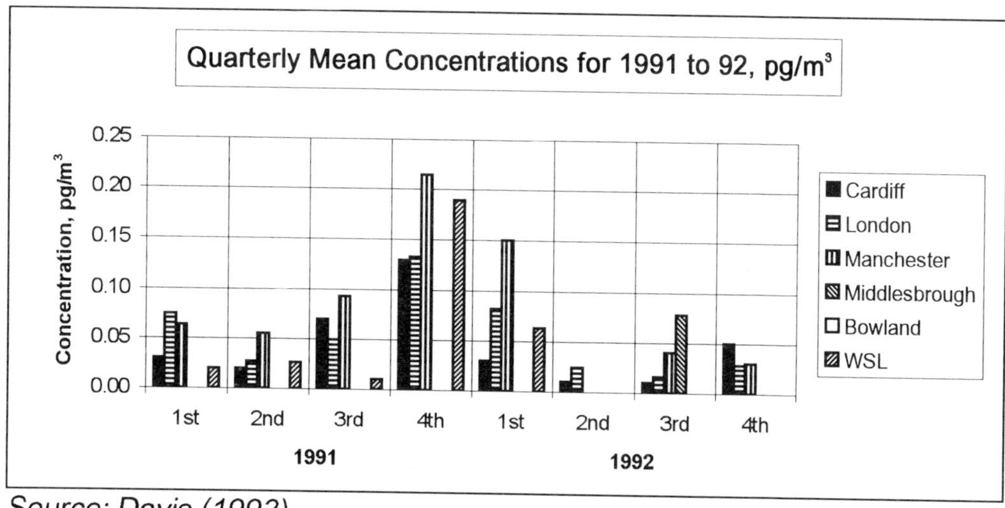

Source: Davis (1993)

1,2,3,4,7,8,9-Heptachlorodibenzofuran in deposition

Chemical formula : $C_{12}HCl_7O$

Alternative names : 1,2,3,4,7,8,9-HpCDF

Type of pollutant : Furan, air toxic

Structure :

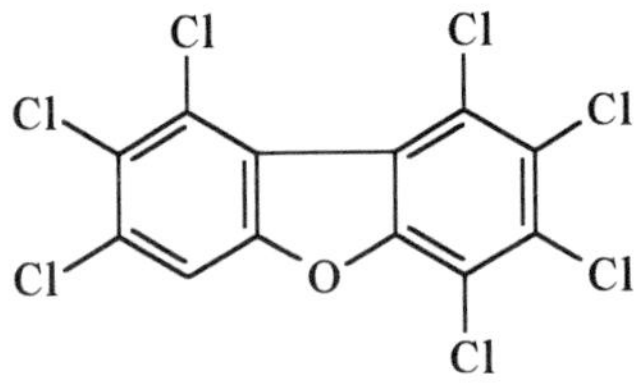

Air quality data summary :

Location	Annual Mean pg/m²/day		
	1991	1992	1993
Bowland	*	*	*
Cardiff C	126.05	80.70	*
London	68.50	2.10	*
Manchester B	83.58	12.73	*
Middlesbrough	*	*	*
WSL	26.40	*	*

Source: Davis (1993)

Note: * signifies no data available

Chemical formula : $C_{12}HCl_7O_2$

Alternative names : 1,2,3,4,6,7,8-HpCDD

Type of pollutant : Dioxin, air toxic

Structure :

Cl Cl Cl O Cl Cl O Cl Cl

Air quality data summary :

Location	Annual Mean pg/m³		
	1991	1992	1993
Bowland	*	*	1.09
Cardiff C	0.55	0.48	*
London	1.03	0.82	0.68
Manchester B	0.66	1.17	0.74
Middlesbrough	*	*	0.61
WSL	0.79	*	*

Source: Davis (1993)

Note: * signifies no data available

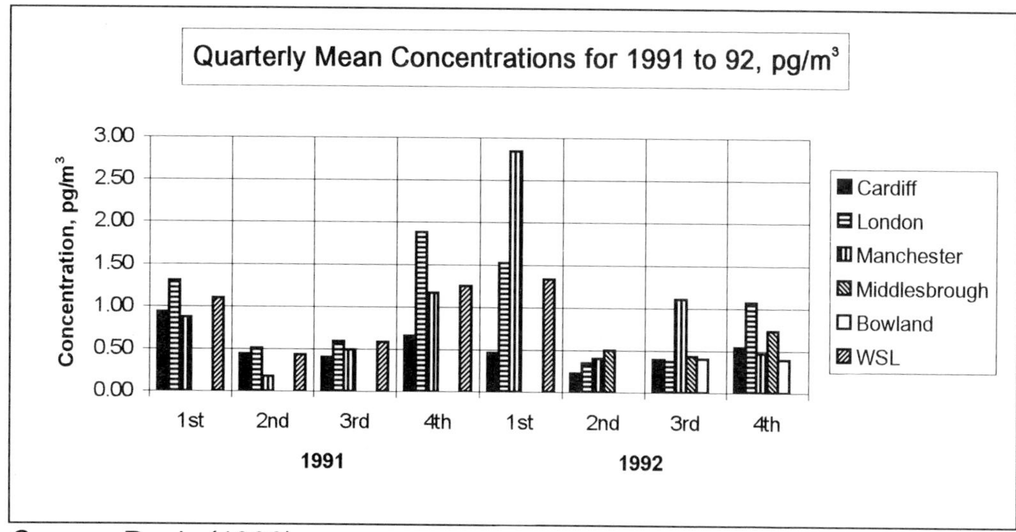

Source: Davis (1993)

1,2,3,4,6,7,8,-Heptachlorodibenzo-p-dioxin in deposition

Chemical formula : $C_{12}HCl_7O_2$

Alternative names : 1,2,3,4,6,7,8-HpCDD

Type of pollutant : Dioxin, air toxic

Structure :

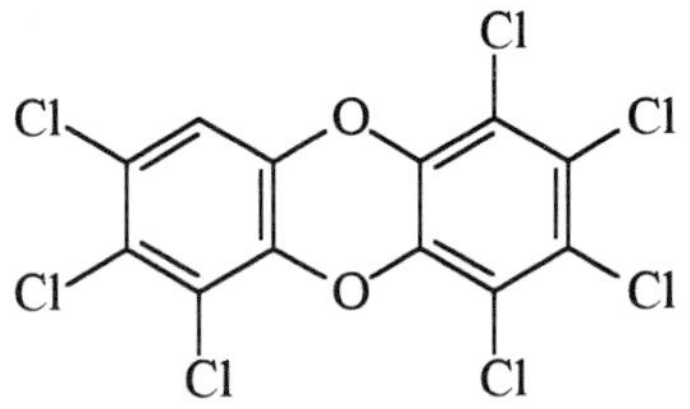

Air quality data summary :

Location	Annual Mean pg/m^2/day		
	1991	1992	1993
Bowland	*	*	*
Cardiff C	729.02	247.90	*
London	495.80	74.70	*
Manchester B	403.90	143.64	*
Middlesbrough	*	*	*
WSL	217.48	*	*

Source: Davis (1993)

Note: * signifies no data available

Chemical formula	:	C_7H_{16}
Alternative names	:	
Type of pollutant	:	(Volatile) organic compound (VOC), hydrocarbon
Structure	:	$CH_3CH_2CH_2CH_2CH_2CH_2CH_3$
Air quality data summary	:	

Remote rural concentrations

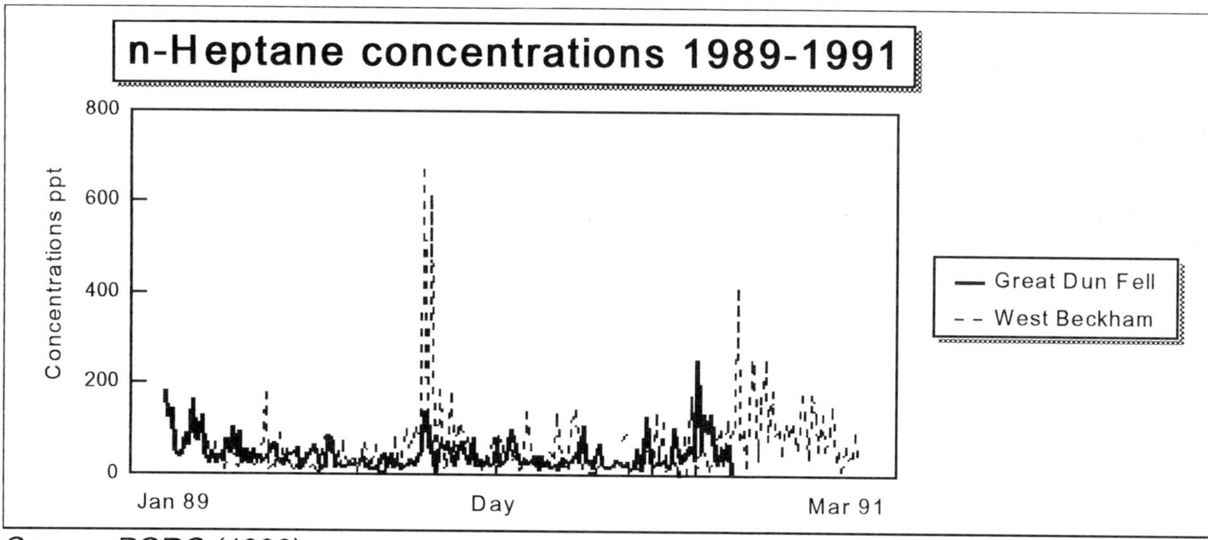

Source: PORG (1993)

Urban concentrations

Mean Air Concentration in Leeds, 19/8/94 to 8/9/94	
Location	**21 day mean, μg/m³**
Albion Street	0.152
Cliff Lane	0.108
EUN monitoring site	0.142
Kerbside site	0.191
Kirkstall Road	0.233
Park site	0.095
Queen Street	0.170
Vicar Lane	0.469

Source: Bartle et al. (1995)

1994-95 Monthly Means, ppb									
	Belfast C	Birmingham B	Bristol A	Cardiff B	Edinburgh A	Eltham	Harwell	Middlesbrough	UCL
Jan 94	0.22	0.28	-	0.39	0.35	0.14	-	0.10	0.36
Feb 94	0.31	0.37	-	0.37	0.22	0.19	-	0.41	0.54
Mar 94	0.09	0.18	-	0.16	0.13	0.24	-	0.88	0.14
Apr 94	0.08	0.19	0.17	0.15	0.15	0.43	-	0.80	0.48
May 94	0.10	0.26	0.17	0.24	0.36	0.68	-	0.13	0.54
Jun 94	0.08	0.19	0.13	0.14	0.09	0.06	-	0.26	0.32
Jul 94	0.10	0.25	0.10	0.16	0.15	0.11	-	0.35	0.40
Aug 94	0.13	0.54	0.12	0.19	0.15	0.17	-	0.29	0.25
Sep 94	0.20	0.20	0.18	0.18	0.19	0.11	-	1.48	0.27
Oct 94	0.26	0.35	0.63	0.51	0.22	0.15	-	0.53	0.36
Nov 94	0.21	0.31	0.31	0.36	0.18	0.25	-	0.29	0.27
Dec 94	0.22	0.33	0.19	0.30	0.18	0.17	-	0.07	0.20
Jan 95	0.17	0.14	0.15	0.21	0.11	0.22	0.06	0.04	0.08
Feb 95	0.15	0.12	0.15	0.18	0.08	0.11	0.06	0.05	0.11

Source: Dollard (1995)

Chemical formula : $C_{12}H_4Cl_6$

Alternative names : PCB-138

Type of pollutant : (PCB) polychlorinated biphenyl, air toxic

Structure :

Air quality data summary :

Location	Annual Mean pg/m³		
	1991	1992	1993
Bowland	*	*	2.63
Cardiff C	23.48	40.05	*
London	23.87	22.53	22.96
Manchester B	26.81	29.27	32.74
Middlesbrough	*	*	8.23
WSL	9.50	*	*

Source: Davis (1993)

Notes: * signifies no data available

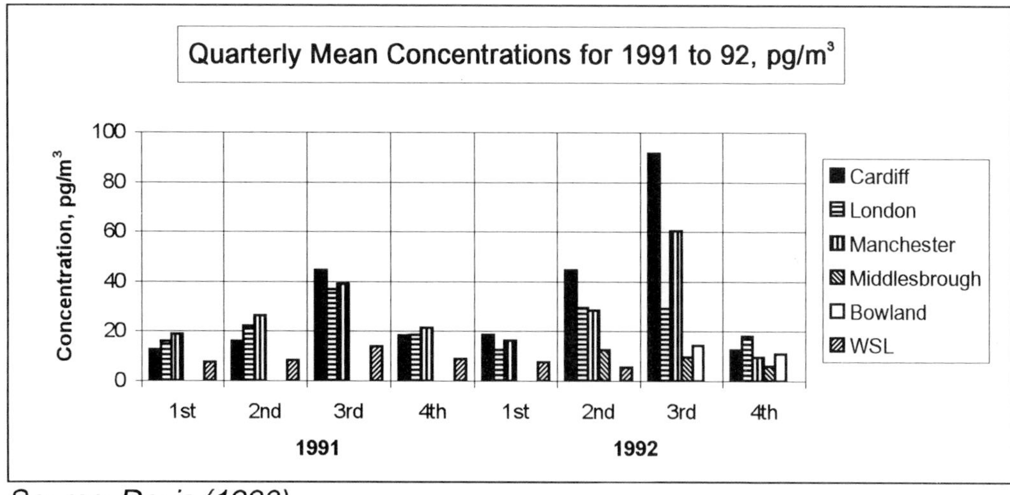

Source: Davis (1993)

Chemical formula : $C_{12}H_4Cl_6$

Alternative names : PCB-138

Type of pollutant : (PCB) polychlorinated biphenyl, air toxic

Structure :

Air quality data summary :

Location	Annual Mean ng/m^2/day		
	1991	1992	1993
Bowland	*	*	5.45
Cardiff C	120.64	46.02	*
London	22.50	9.87	*
Manchester B	18.96	25.04	*
Middlesbrough	*	*	*
WSL	7.12	*	*

Source: Davis (1993)

Notes: * signifies no data available

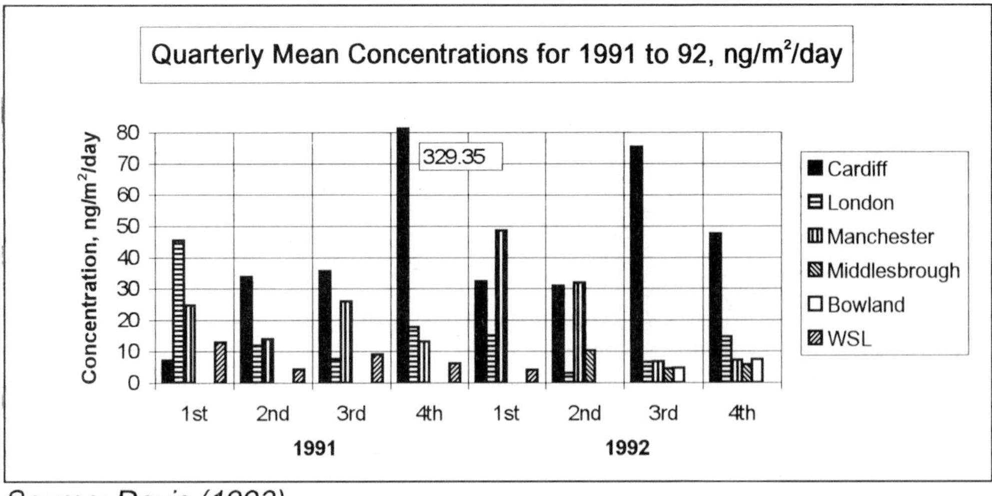

Source: Davis (1993)

Chemical formula : $C_{12}H_4Cl_6$

Alternative names : PCB-149

Type of pollutant : (PCB) polychlorinated biphenyl, air toxic

Structure :

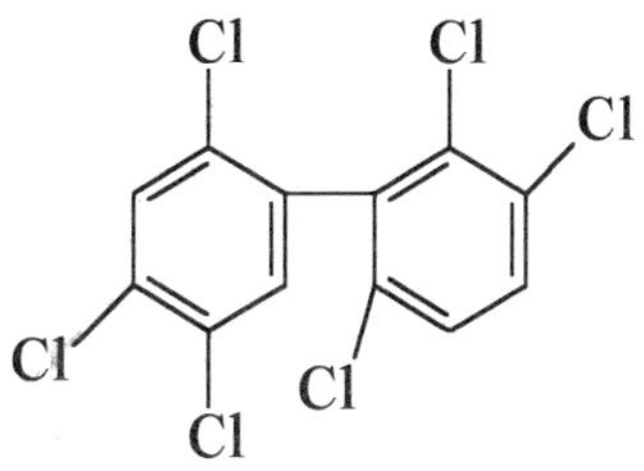

Air quality data summary :

Location	Annual Mean pg/m^3		
	1991	1992	1993
Bowland	*	*	11.17
Cardiff C	36.91	69.09	*
London	*	*	*
Manchester B	53.98	74.95	59.88
Middlesbrough	*	*	*
WSL	*	*	*

Source: Davis (1993)

Notes: * signifies no data available

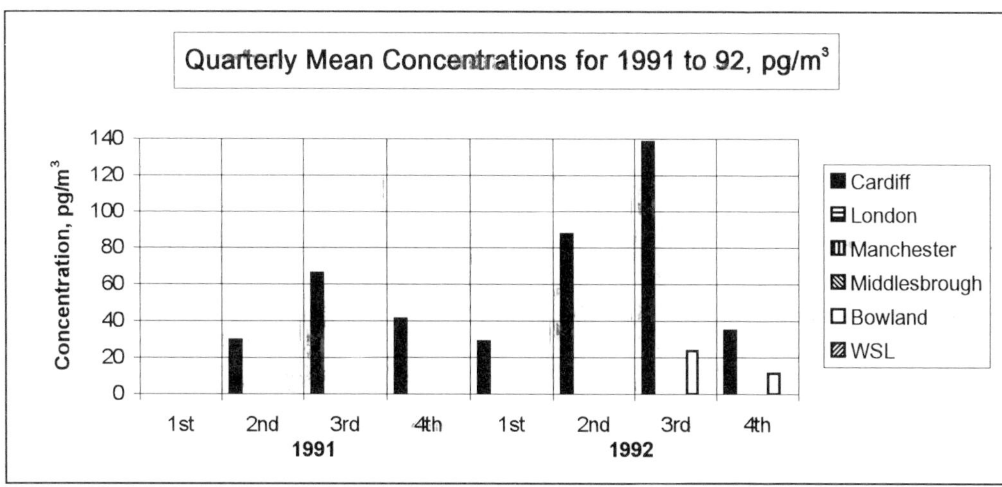

Source: Davis (1993)

Chemical formula : $C_{12}H_4Cl_6$

Alternative names : PCB-149

Type of pollutant : (PCB) polychlorinated biphenyl, air toxic

Structure :

Cl Cl Cl Cl Cl Cl

Air quality data summary :

Location	Annual Mean ng/m²/day		
	1991	1992	1993
Bowland	*	*	14.69
Cardiff C	43.97	56.31	*
London	*	*	*
Manchester B	32.15	34.73	*
Middlesbrough	*	*	*
WSL	*	*	*

Source: Davis (1993)

Notes: * signifies no data available

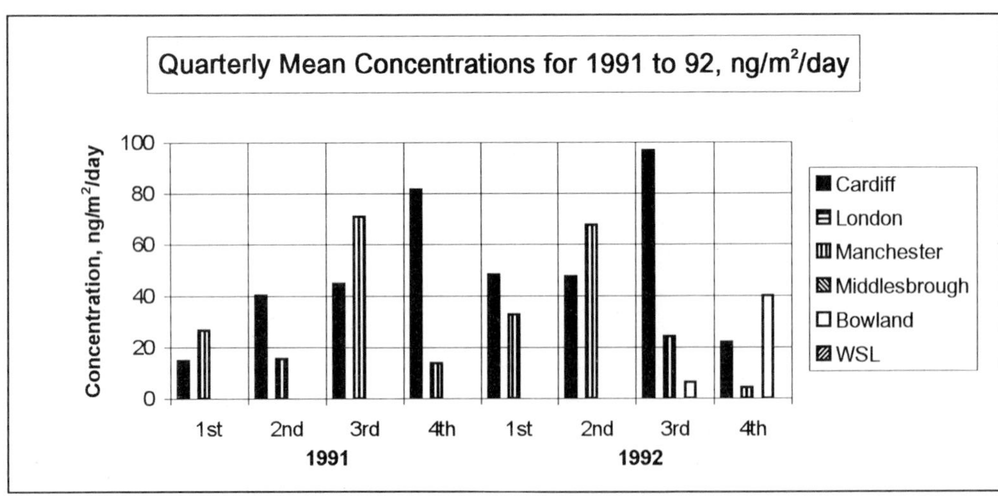

Source: Davis (1993)

2,2',4,4',5,5'-Hexachlorobiphenyl in air

Chemical formula : $C_{12}H_4Cl_6$

Alternative names : PCB-153

Type of pollutant : (PCB) polychlorinated biphenyl, air toxic

Structure :

Cl Cl
Cl Cl
Cl Cl

Air quality data summary :

Location	Annual Mean pg/m^3		
	1991	1992	1993
Bowland	*	*	4.39
Cardiff C	25.44	37.26	*
London	28.76	23.65	29.00
Manchester B	32.77	38.42	39.25
Middlesbrough	*	*	12.14
WSL	14.36	*	*

Source: Davis (1993)

Notes: * signifies no data available

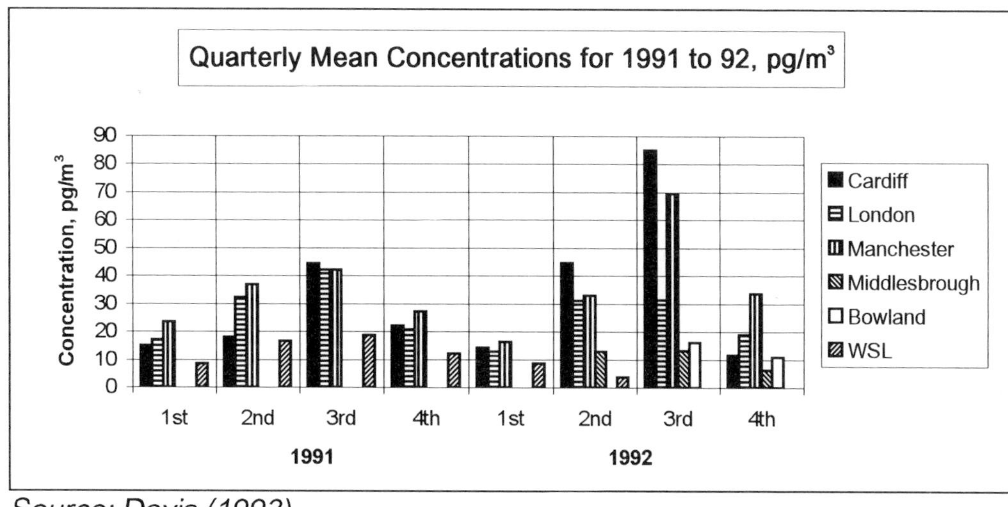

Source: Davis (1993)

Chemical formula : $C_{12}H_4Cl_6$

Alternative names : PCB-153

Type of pollutant : (PCB) polychlorinated biphenyl, air toxic

Structure :

Air quality data summary :

Location	Annual Mean ng/m²/day		
	1991	1992	1993
Bowland	*	*	12.92
Cardiff C	78.26	72.34	*
London	40.00	9.38	*
Manchester B	23.17	30.98	*
Middlesbrough	*	*	*
WSL	12.64	*	*

Source: Davis (1993)

Notes: * signifies no data available

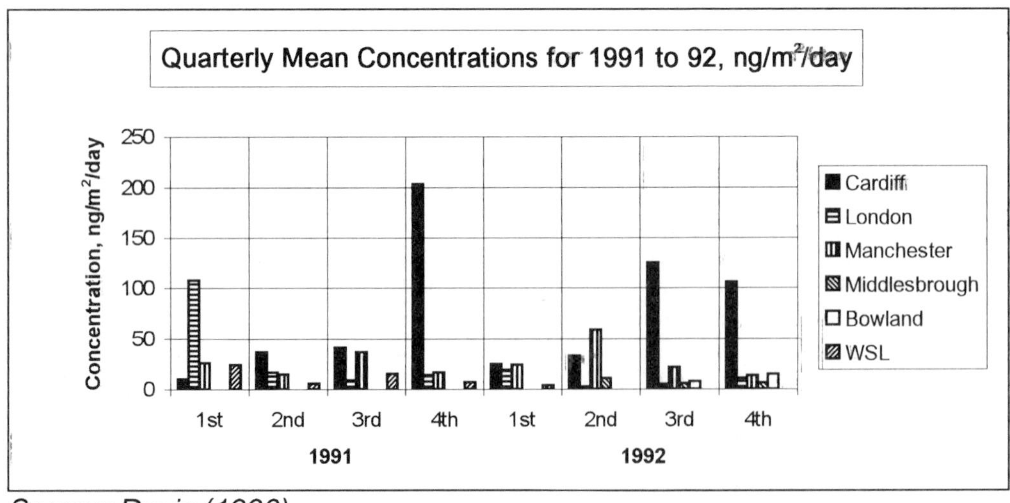

Source: Davis (1993)

3,3',4,4',5,5',-Hexachlorobiphenyl in air

Chemical formula : $C_{12}H_4Cl_6$

Alternative names : PCB-169

Type of pollutant : (PCB) polychlorinated biphenyl, air toxic

Structure :

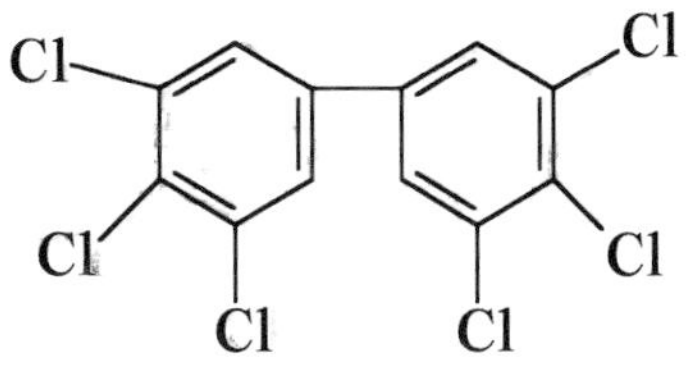

Air quality data summary :

Location	Annual Mean pg/m^3		
	1991	1992	1993
Bowland	*	*	*
Cardiff C	*	*	*
London	0.00	0.00	0.00
Manchester B	*	*	*
Middlesbrough	*	*	0.00
WSL	0.00	*	*

Source: Davis (1993)

Notes: * signifies no data available

3,3',4,4',5,5',-Hexachlorobiphenyl in deposition

Chemical formula : $C_{12}H_4Cl_6$

Alternative names : PCB-169

Type of pollutant : (PCB) polychlorinated biphenyl, air toxic

Structure :

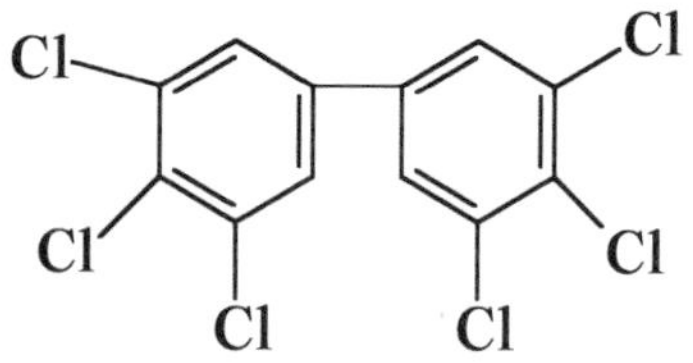

Air quality data summary :

Location	Annual Mean ng/m²/day		
	1991	1992	1993
Bowland	*	*	*
Cardiff C	*	*	*
London	0.00	0.00	*
Manchester B	*	*	*
Middlesbrough	*	*	*
WSL	0.00	*	*

Source: Davis (1993)

Notes: * signifies no data available

1,2,3,4,7,8-Hexachlorodibenzofuran in air 108

Chemical formula : $C_{12}H_2Cl_6O$

Alternative names : 1,2,3,4,7,8-HxCDF

Type of pollutant : Furan, air toxic

Structure :

Air quality data summary :

Location	Annual Mean pg/m^3		
	1991	1992	1993
Bowland	*	*	0.02
Cardiff C	0.18	0.19	*
London	0.13	0.11	0.02
Manchester B	0.51	0.53	0.44
Middlesbrough	*	*	0.08
WSL	0.10	*	*

Source: Davis (1993)

Note: * signifies no data available

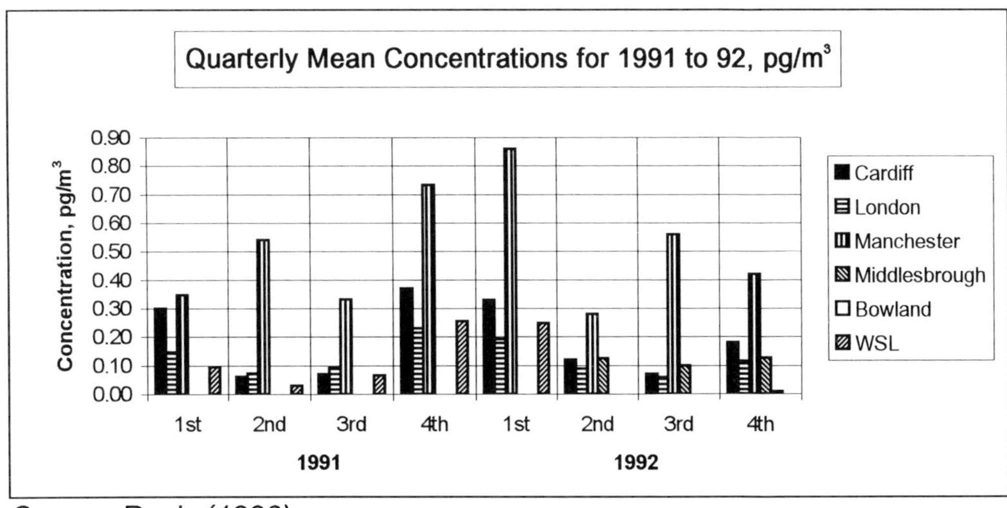

Source: Davis (1993)

1,2,3,4,7,8-Hexachlorodibenzofuran in deposition

Chemical formula : $C_{12}H_2Cl_6O$

Alternative names : 1,2,3,4,7,8-HxCDF

Type of pollutant : Furan, air toxic

Structure :

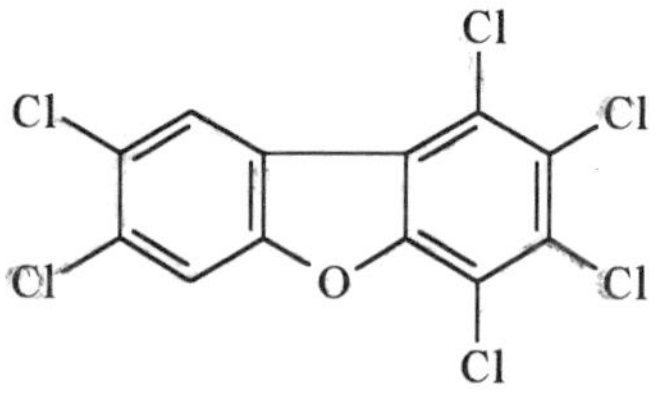

Air quality data summary :

Location	Annual Mean pg/m²/day		
	1991	1992	1993
Bowland	*	*	*
Cardiff C	161.77	59.55	*
London	128.06	9.80	*
Manchester B	92.08	70.91	*
Middlesbrough	*	*	*
WSL	44.94	*	*

Source: Davis (1993)

Note: * signifies no data available

Chemical formula : $C_{12}H_2Cl_6O$

Alternative names : 1,2,3,6,7,8-HxCDF

Type of pollutant : Furan, air toxic

Structure :

Air quality data summary :

Location	Annual Mean pg/m^3		
	1991	1992	1993
Bowland	*	*	0.04
Cardiff C	0.07	0.17	*
London	0.11	0.09	0.03
Manchester B	0.22	0.20	0.21
Middlesbrough	*	*	0.08
WSL	0.08	*	*

Source: Davis (1993)

Note: * signifies no data available

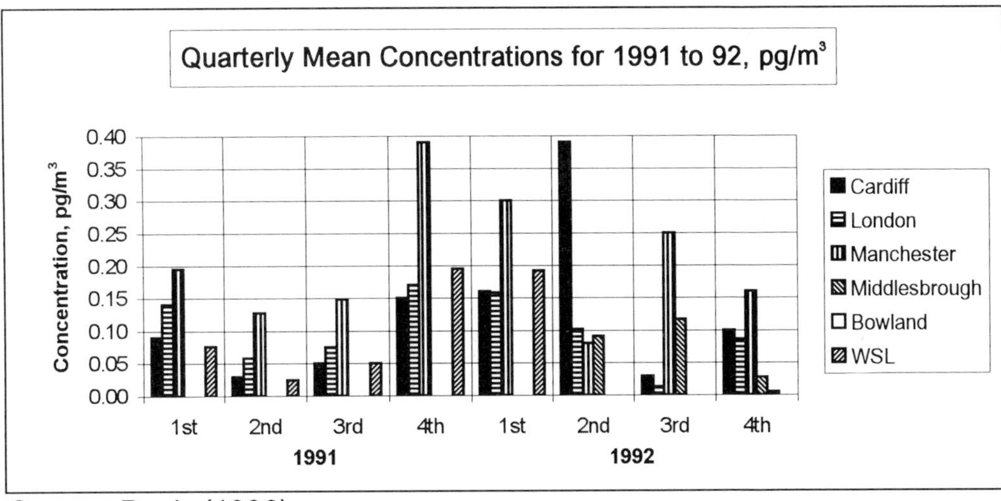

Source: Davis (1993)

Chemical formula : $C_{12}H_2Cl_6O$

Alternative names : 1,2,3,6,7,8-HxCDF

Type of pollutant : Furan, air toxic

Structure :

Air quality data summary :

Location	Annual Mean pg/m²/day		
	1991	1992	1993
Bowland	*	*	*
Cardiff C	109.26	27.94	*
London	125.86	9.60	*
Manchester B	42.40	30.91	*
Middlesbrough	*	*	*
WSL	46.40	*	*

Source: Davis (1993)

Note: * signifies no data available

1,2,3,7,8,9-Hexachlorodibenzofuran in air

Chemical formula : $C_{12}H_2Cl_6O$

Alternative names : 1,2,3,7,8,9-HxCDF

Type of pollutant : Furan, air toxic

Structure :

Air quality data summary :

Location	Annual Mean pg/m³		
	1991	1992	1993
Bowland	*	*	0.00
Cardiff C	0.02	0.01	*
London	0.01	0.02	0.00
Manchester B	0.05	0.02	0.01
Middlesbrough	*	*	0.01
WSL	0.00	*	*

Source: Davis (1993)

Note: * signifies no data available

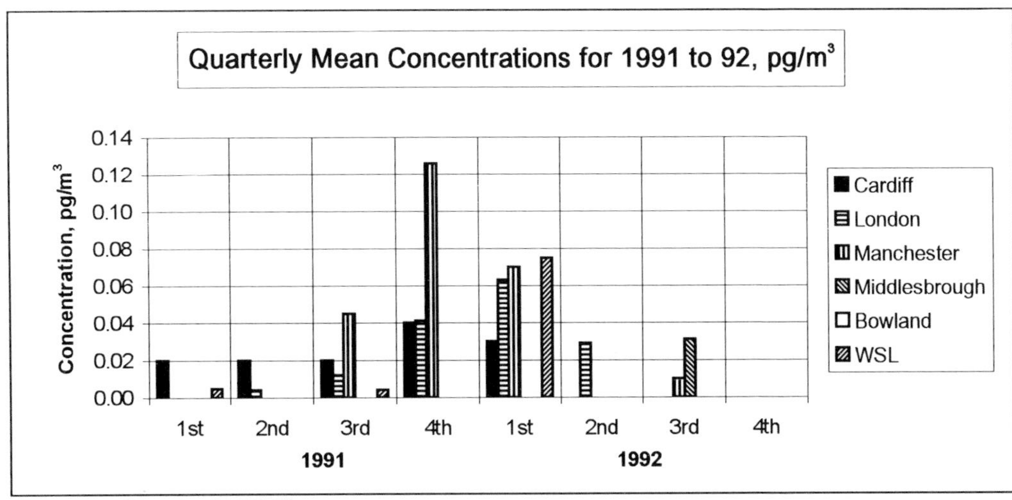

Source: Davis (1993)

1,2,3,7,8,9-Hexachlorodibenzofuran in deposition

Chemical formula : $C_{12}H_2Cl_6O$

Alternative names : 1,2,3,7,8,9-HxCDF

Type of pollutant : Furan, air toxic

Structure :

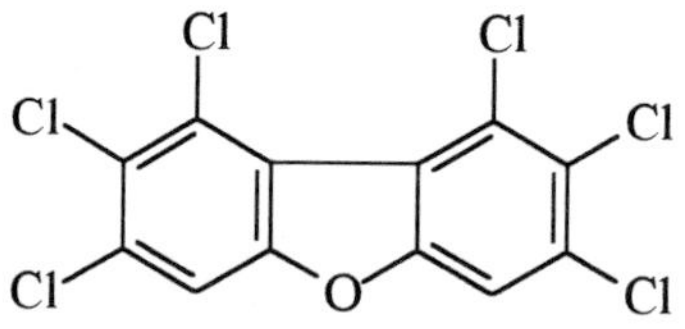

Air quality data summary :

Location	Annual Mean pg/m^2/day		
	1991	1992	1993
Bowland	*	*	*
Cardiff C	86.07	7.18	*
London	4.75	0.00	*
Manchester B	15.97	9.09	*
Middlesbrough	*	*	*
WSL	9.18	*	*

Source: Davis (1993)

Note: * signifies no data available

Chemical formula	:	$C_{12}H_2Cl_6O$
Alternative names	:	2,3,4,6,7,8-HxCDF
Type of pollutant	:	Furan, air toxic
Structure	:	

Air quality data summary :

Location	Annual Mean pg/m³		
	1991	1992	1993
Bowland	*	*	0.04
Cardiff C	0.08	0.08	*
London	0.12	0.13	0.04
Manchester B	0.24	0.23	0.28
Middlesbrough	*	*	0.15
WSL	0.09	*	*

Source: Davis (1993)

Note: * signifies no data available

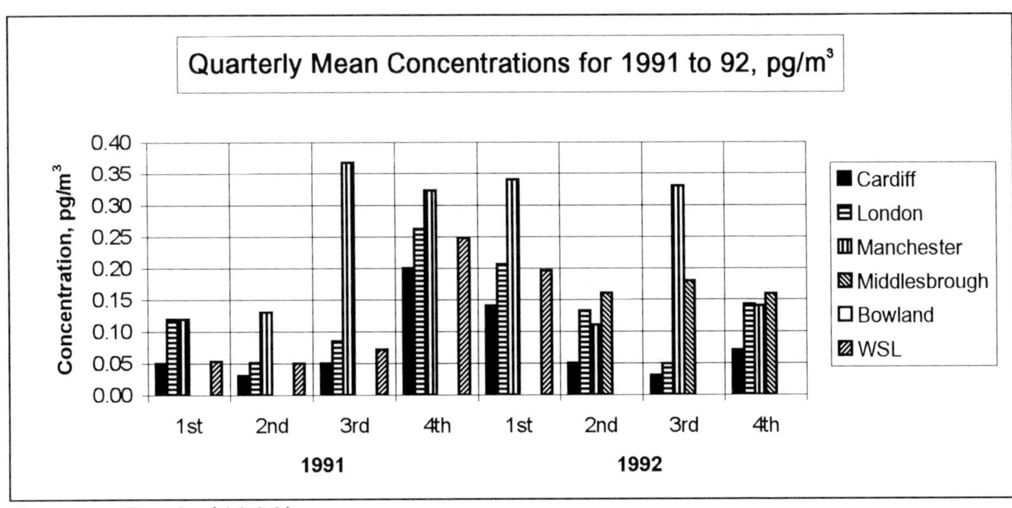

Source: Davis (1993)

Chemical formula : $C_{12}H_2Cl_6O$

Alternative names : 2,3,4,6,7,8-HxCDF

Type of pollutant : Furan, air toxic

Structure :

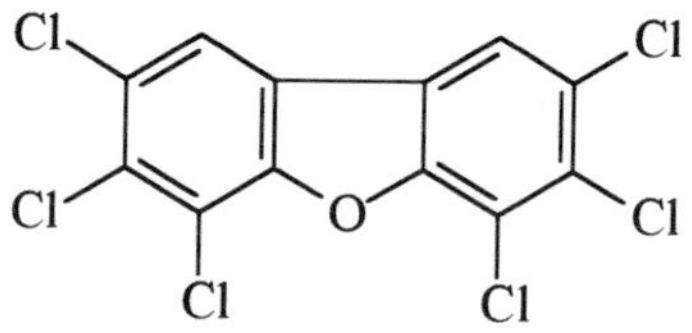

Air quality data summary :

Location	Annual Mean pg/m^2/day		
	1991	1992	1993
Bowland	*	*	*
Cardiff C	154.02	23.44	*
London	100.00	14.60	*
Manchester B	33.30	26.36	*
Middlesbrough	*	*	*
WSL	39.61	*	*

Source: Davis (1993)

Note: * signifies no data available

1,2,3,4,7,8-Hexachlorodibenzo-p-dioxin in air

Chemical formula : $C_{12}H_2Cl_6O_2$

Alternative names : 1,2,3,4,7,8-HxCDD

Type of pollutant : Dioxin, air toxic

Structure :

Air quality data summary :

Location	Annual Mean pg/m³		
	1991	1992	1993
Bowland	*	*	0.01
Cardiff C	0.03	0.02	*
London	0.03	0.03	0.04
Manchester B	0.05	0.05	0.03
Middlesbrough	*	*	0.02
WSL	0.03	*	*

Source: Davis (1993)

Note: * signifies no data available

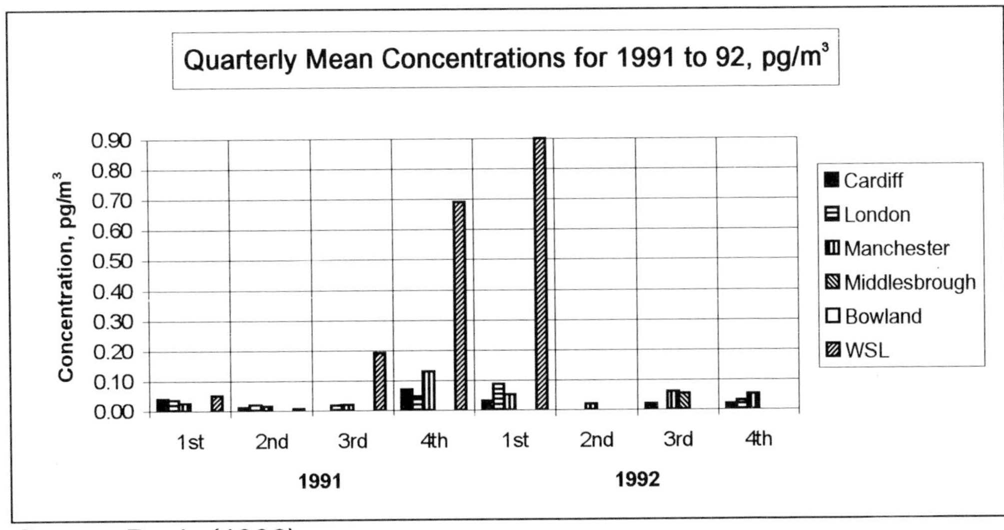

Source: Davis (1993)

Chemical formula : $C_{12}H_2Cl_6O_2$

Alternative names : 1,2,3,4,7,8-HxCDD

Type of pollutant : Dioxin, air toxic

Structure :

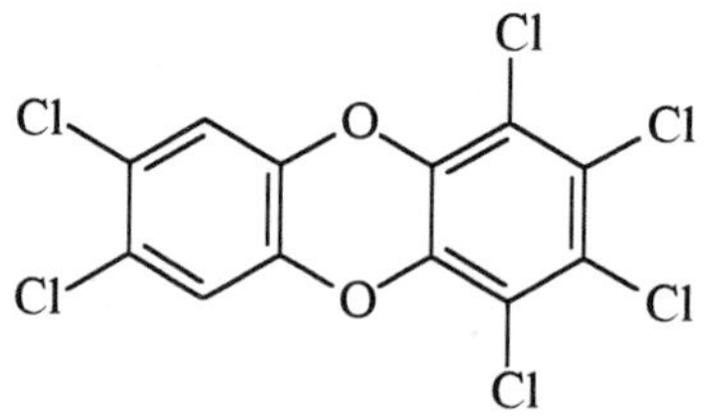

Air quality data summary :

Location	Annual Mean pg/m²/day		
	1991	1992	1993
Bowland	*	*	*
Cardiff C	79.05	59.85	*
London	59.45	0.00	*
Manchester B	23.71	15.45	*
Middlesbrough	*	*	*
WSL	23.05	*	*

Source: Davis (1993)

Note: * signifies no data available

Chemical formula : $C_{12}H_2Cl_6O_2$

Alternative names : 1,2,3,6,7,8-HxCDD

Type of pollutant : Dioxin, air toxic

Structure :

Air quality data summary :

Location	Annual Mean pg/m³		
	1991	1992	1993
Bowland	*	*	0.02
Cardiff C	0.03	0.03	*
London	0.06	0.04	0.02
Manchester B	0.06	0.06	0.03
Middlesbrough	*	*	0.03
WSL	0.06	*	*

Source: Davis (1993)

Note: * signifies no data available

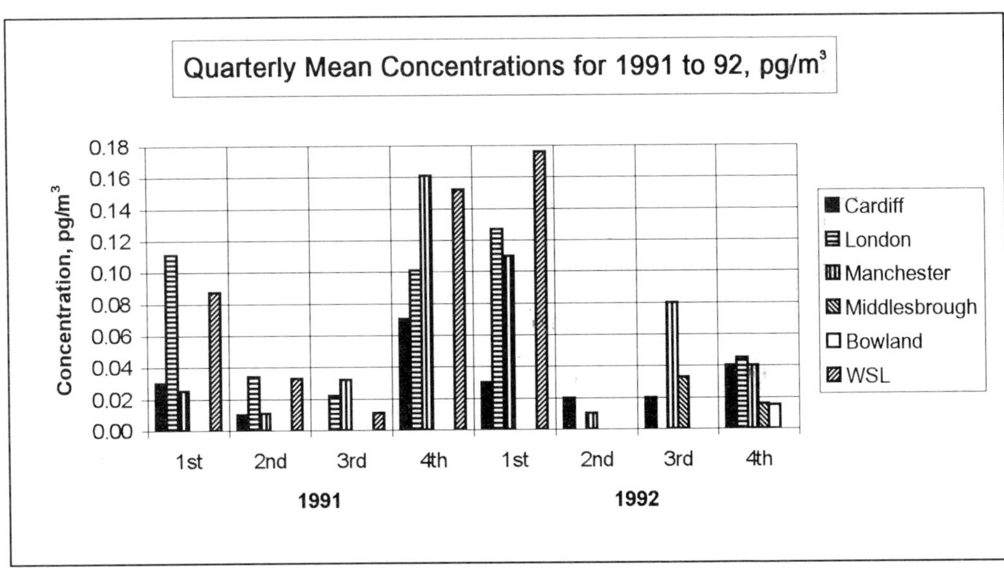

Source: Davis (1993)

Chemical formula : $C_{12}H_2Cl_6O_2$

Alternative names : 1,2,3,6,7,8-HxCDD

Type of pollutant : Dioxin, air toxic

Structure :

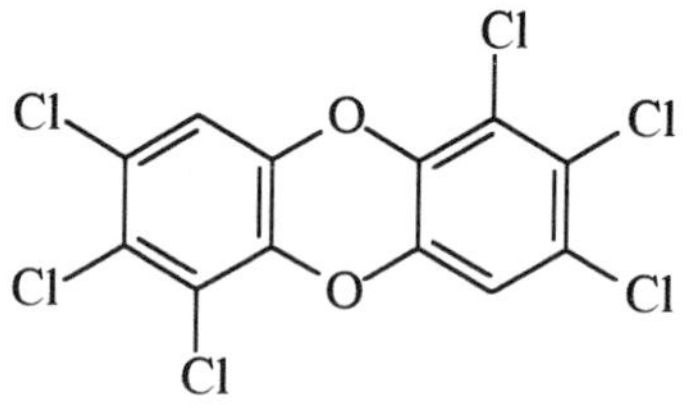

Air quality data summary :

Location	Annual Mean pg/m²/day		
	1991	1992	1993
Bowland	*	*	*
Cardiff C	79.05	13.49	*
London	99.19	0.00	*
Manchester B	22.74	15.45	*
Middlesbrough	*	*	*
WSL	26.35	*	*

Source: Davis (1993)

Note: * signifies no data available

1,2,3,7,8,9-Hexachlorodibenzo-p-dioxin in air

Chemical formula : $C_{12}H_2Cl_6O_2$

Alternative names : 1,2,3,7,8,9-HxCDD

Type of pollutant : Dioxin, air toxic

Structure :

Cl Cl Cl O Cl Cl O Cl

Air quality data summary :

Location	Annual Mean pg/m^3		
	1991	1992	1993
Bowland	*	*	0.00
Cardiff C	0.03	0.04	*
London	0.04	0.07	0.02
Manchester B	0.07	0.07	0.03
Middlesbrough	*	*	0.03
WSL	0.05	*	*

Source: Davis (1993)

Note: * signifies no data available

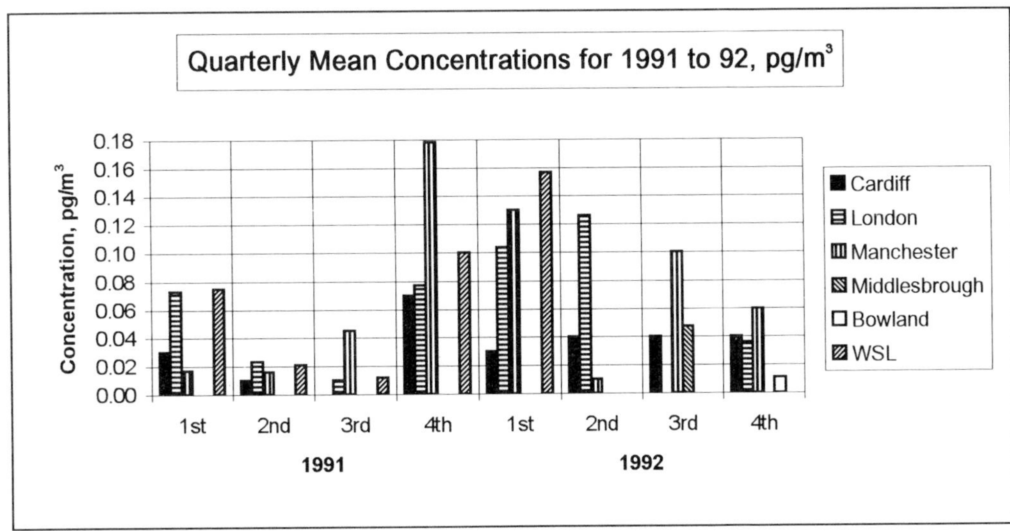

Source: Davis (1993)

Chemical formula : $C_{12}H_2Cl_6O_2$

Alternative names : 1,2,3,7,8,9-HxCDD

Type of pollutant : Dioxin, air toxic

Structure :

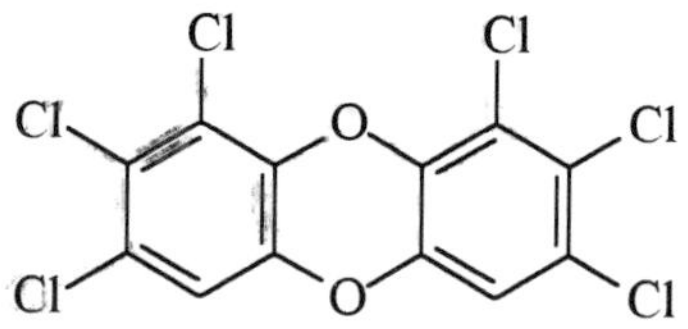

Air quality data summary :

Location	Annual Mean pg/m²/day		
	1991	1992	1993
Bowland	*	*	*
Cardiff C	79.05	13.49	*
London	62.02	0.00	*
Manchester B	21.81	15.45	*
Middlesbrough	*	*	*
WSL	16.76	*	*

Source: Davis (1993)

Note: * signifies no data available

Chemical formula : $C_6H_{12}O$

Alternative names : Caproaldehyde, n-caproic aldehyde

Type of pollutant : (Volatile) organic compound VOC, hydrocarbon, oxygenate

Structure :

$CH_3CH_2CH_2CH_2CH_2CHO$

Air quality data summary :

Rural Concentrations

Month 1993	Air Concentration at Harwell site, ppb
	Monthly Mean
August	0.074
September	0.022
October	0.014
November	0.014

Source: Solberg et al. (1994)

Chemical formula : C_6H_{14}

Alternative names :

Type of pollutant : (Volatile) organic compound VOC, hydrocarbon

Structure :

$CH_3CH_2CH_2CH_2CH_2CH_3$

Air quality data summary :

Remote rural concentrations

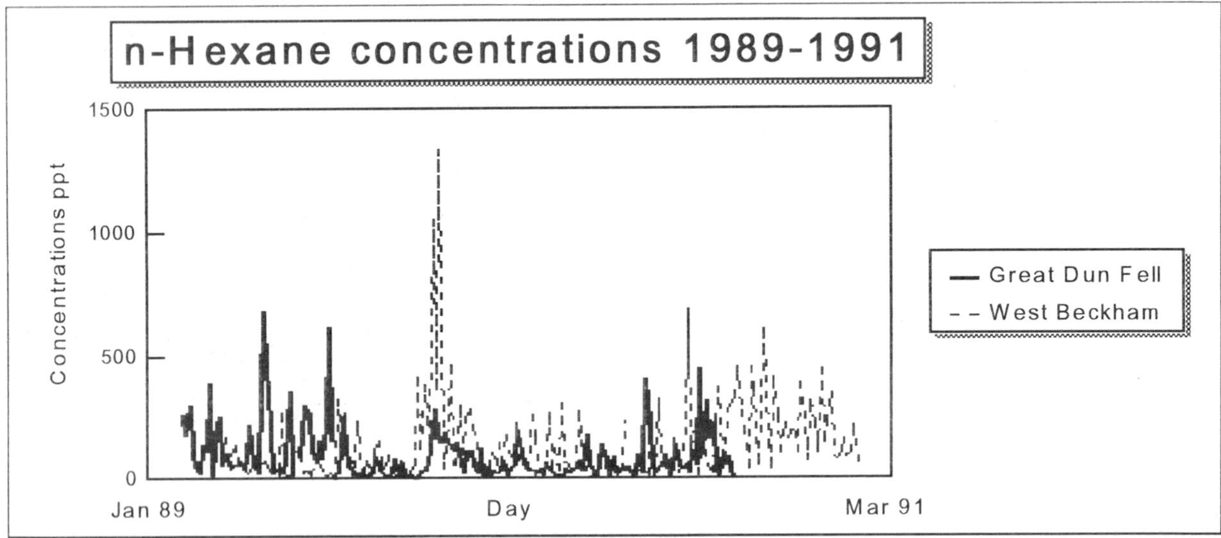

Source: PORG (1993)

Rural concentrations

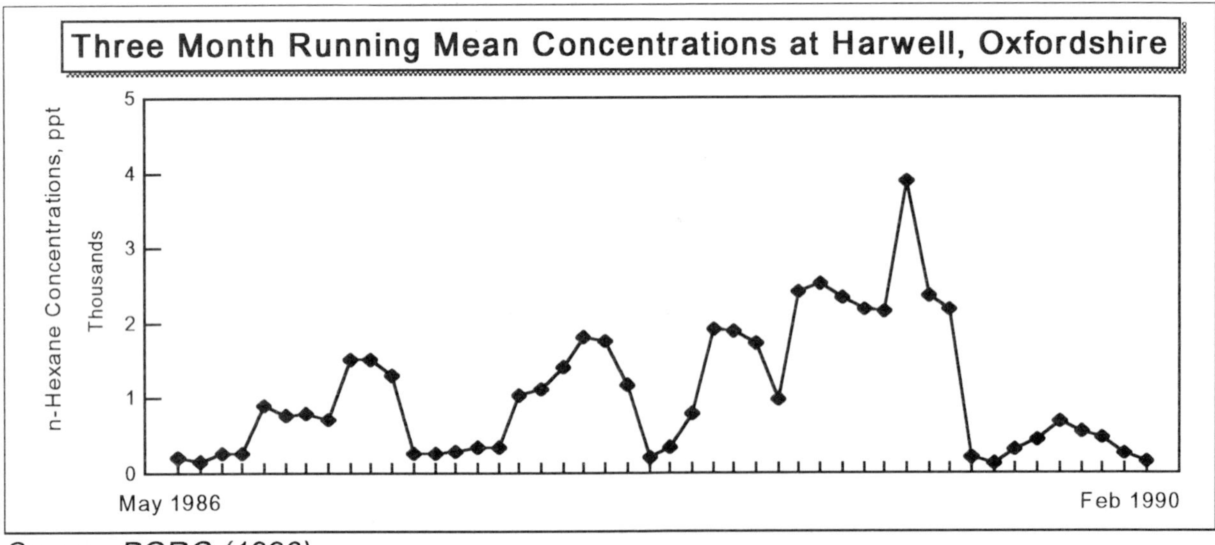

Source: PORG (1993)

Urban concentrations

	1994-95 Monthly Means, ppb								
	Belfast C	Birmingham B	Bristol A	Cardiff B	Edinburgh A	Eltham	Harwell	Middlesbrough	UCL
Jan 94	0.17	0.50	-	0.43	-	0.22	-	0.10	0.15
Feb 94	0.09	0.13	-	0.28	0.10	0.29	-	0.41	0.80
Mar 94	0.05	0.15	-	0.33	0.09	0.32	-	0.88	0.30
Apr 94	0.06	0.16	0.17	0.27	0.14	0.11	-	0.80	0.51
May 94	0.12	0.20	0.27	0.42	0.07	0.16	-	0.13	0.51
Jun 94	0.17	0.09	0.15	0.33	0.15	0.25	-	0.26	0.29
Jul 94	0.19	0.32	0.21	0.24	0.23	0.21	-	0.35	0.30
Aug 94	0.22	0.23	0.21	0.26	0.21	0.10	-	0.29	0.13
Sep 94	0.35	0.17	0.27	0.34	0.25	0.23	-	1.48	0.29
Oct 94	0.46	0.24	0.78	0.31	0.16	0.18	-	0.53	0.53
Nov 94	0.36	0.41	0.28	0.12	0.09	0.32	-	0.29	0.41
Dec 94	0.39	0.41	0.32	0.59	0.30	0.14	-	0.07	0.35
Jan 95	0.28	0.26	0.30	0.43	0.27	0.31	0.09	0.04	0.27
Feb 95	0.20	0.22	0.26	0.43	0.19	0.20	0.07	0.05	0.23

Source: Dollard (1995)

Mean Air Concentration in Leeds, 19/8/94 to 8/9/94	
Location	21 day mean, $\mu g/m^3$
Albion Street	0.277
Cliff Lane	0.180
EUN monitoring site	0.299
Kerbside site	0.438
Kirkstall Road	0.508
Park site	0.237
Queen Street	0.302
Vicar Lane	0.900

Source: Bartle et al. (1995)

Chemical formula	:	C_6H_{12}
Alternative names	:	hex-1-ene
Type of pollutant	:	(Volatile) organic compound VOC, hydrocarbon
Structure	:	$CH_2{=}CHCH_2CH_2CH_2CH_3$
Air quality data summary	:	

Remote rural concentrations

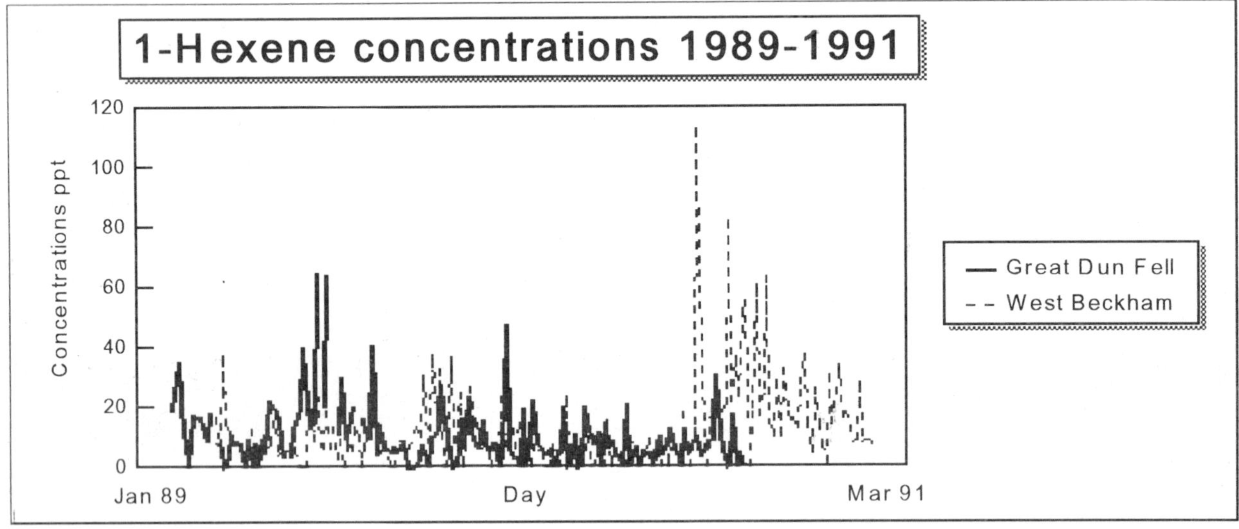

Source: PORG (1993)

Chemical formula	:	C_6H_{12}
Alternative names	:	
Type of pollutant	:	(Volatile) organic compounds VOC, hydrocarbons
Air quality data summary	:	

Mean Air Concentration in Leeds, 19/8/94 to 8/9/94, $\mu g/m^3$	
Location	21 day mean
Albion Street	0.033
Cliff Lane	0.024
EUN monitoring site	0.035
Kerbside site	0.053
Kirkstall Road	0.073
Park site	0.016
Queen Street	0.037
Vicar Lane	0.113

Source: Bartle et al. (1995)

Mean Air Concentration in Leeds, 19/8/94 to 8/9/94, $\mu g/m^3$	
Location	21 day mean
Albion Street	0.098
Cliff Lane	0.074
EUN monitoring site	0.095
Kerbside site	0.100
Kirkstall Road	0.126
Park site	0.084
Queen Street	0.093
Vicar Lane	0.188

Source: Bartle et al. (1995)

Note: These data represent different isomers of hexene, each table representing a different isomer.

Chemical formula	:	HCl
Alternative names	:	Hydrochloric acid gas or vapour
Type of pollutant	:	Trace gas
Structure	:	HCl
Air quality data summary	:	

Rural Concentrations

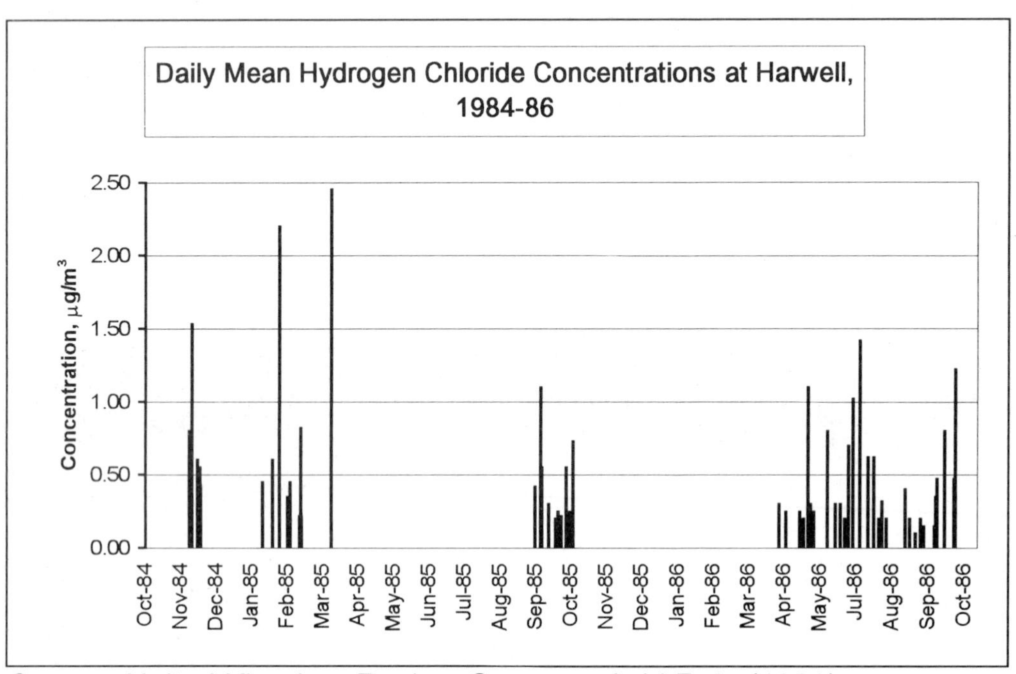

Source: United Kingdom Review Group on Acid Rain (1990)

Chemical formula : H

Alternative names : Precipitation acidity, rainfall pH, acid rain

Type of pollutant : Trace contaminant of rain

Air quality data summary :

Rural Concentrations

Location	Annual Average Rainfall Concentration, µg per litre *	
	1972-1981	1982-1991
Harwell, Oxon.	4.0	4.6
Styrrup, Nottinghamshire.	4.0	4.3
Wraymires, Cumbria.	4.0	4.3

Source: Cawse et al. (1994)

*based on soluble fraction only

Site	Precipitation-weighted Annual Mean Acidity, 1986-93, (μ eql^{-1})								
	OS Grid Ref	1986	1987	1988	1989	1990	1991	1992	1993
Achanarras	ND 152552	10	19	25	25	19	20	24	22
Balquhidder	NN 521506	21	32	24	20	16	22	20	24
Bannisdale	NY 515043	30	27	28	24	18	22	25	31
Barcombe Mills	TQ 437149	19	22	13	15	12	20	17	24
Beddgelert	SH 556518	17	19	17	15	12	16	14	18
Bottesford	SK 797376	61	76	81	48	42	62	68	62
Compton	SU 512804	25	28	16	25	14	18	35	34
Cow Green Reservoir	NY 817298	27	31	34	23	21	24	28	33
Driby	TF 386744	42	43	42	47	41	41	45	35
Eskdalemuir	NT 234028	21	25	27	20	24	22	22	26
Flatford Mill	TM 077333	33	43	35	35	27	43	36	25
Glen Dye	NO 642864	-	45	46	36	39	44	41	35
Goonhilly	SW 723214	20	23	15	19	14	26	15	17
High Muffles	SE 776939	58	63	72	55	55	58	59	47
Hillsborough Forest	J 243577	-	-	-	13	7	12	12	17
Jenny Hurn	SK 816986	89	100	85	63	53	80	81	67
Llyn Brianne	SN 822507	16	21	18	19	17	24	20	19
Loch Dee	NX 468779	29	23	19	15	15	19	17	22
Lough Navar	H 065545	11	9	10	10	8	6	8	11
Plynlimon	SN 823854	-	-	-	14	12	16	18	19

Site	Precipitation-weighted Annual Mean Acidity, 1986-93, (μ eql^{-1})								
	OS Grid Ref	1986	1987	1988	1989	1990	1991	1992	1993
Redesdale	NY 833954	41	44	52	32	30	33	42	31
River Mharcaidh	NH 876052	22	22	21	20	18	17	17	17
Stoke Ferry	TL 700988	35	36	30	40	18	22	30	27
Strathvaich Dam	NH 347750	-	16	16	13	11	15	20	13
Thorganby	SE 676428	75	73	88	84	64	55	82	80
Tycanol Wood	SN 093364	16	17	15	18	14	21	21	17
Wardlow Hay Cop	SK 177739	29	45	33	37	24	33	34	36
Whiteadder	NT 664633	40	36	47	35	31	36	45	34
Woburn	SP 964361	45	50	37	37	28	35	37	27
Yarner Wood	SX 867890	17	20	14	20	13	17	18	17

Source: Campbell et al. (1994a)

Location	1992 Monthly Weighted Mean pH of Precipitation											
	Jan	Feb	Mar	Apr	May	Jun	Jul	Aug	Sep	Oct	Nov	Dec
Eskdalemuir	4.89	4.77	4.70	4.84	4.78	3.66	4.32	4.78	4.66	4.87	4.79	4.80
High Muffles	4.34	4.24	4.33	4.30	4.34	4.13	4.16	4.29	4.23	4.21	4.06	4.19
Lough Navar	5.03	5.13	5.02	5.24	4.65	4.45	4.76	5.05	5.02	5.13	5.15	5.20
Strath Vaich	4.88	5.24	4.84	4.93	4.13	4.11	4.70	4.73	4.55	4.96	5.12	5.14
Yarner Wood	4.87	5.02	4.91	4.84	4.44	4.36	4.51	4.79	4.49	4.45	4.77	4.89

Source: Schaug et al. (1994)

Chemical formula	:	H_2O_2
Alternative names	:	
Type of pollutant	:	Photochemical oxidant
Structure	:	H_2O_2
Air quality data summary	:	

Rural Concentrations

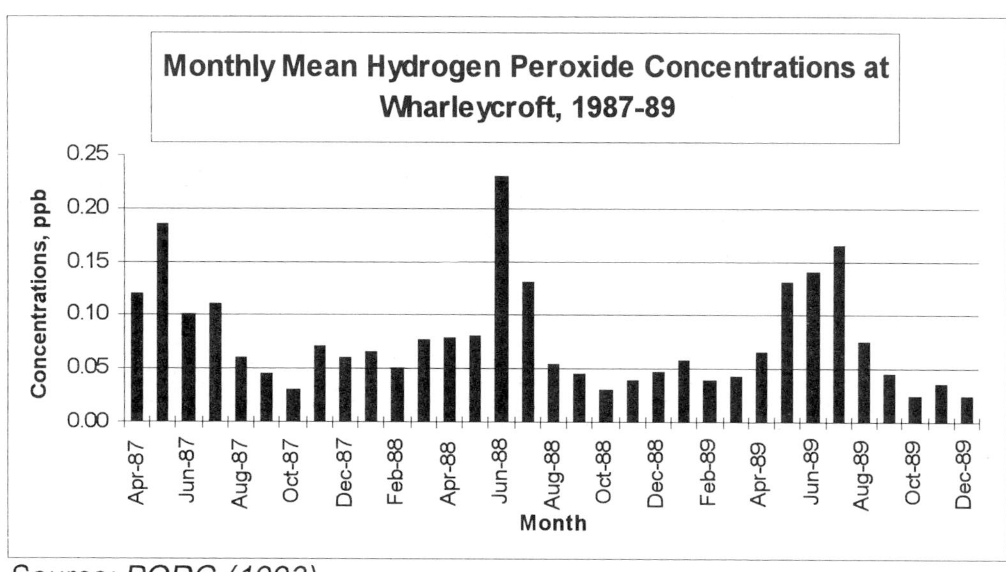

Source: PORG (1993)

Chemical formula : C_9H_{10}

Alternative names :

Type of pollutant : (Volatile) organic compound (VOC), hydrocarbon

Structure :

$$\text{benzene ring fused to } CH_2-CH_2-CH_2 \text{ (five-membered ring)}$$

Air quality data summary :

Mean Air Concentration in Leeds, 19/8/94 to 8/9/94	
Location	21 day mean, $\mu g/m^3$
Albion Street	0.128
Cliff Lane	0.049
EUN monitoring site	0.069
Kerbside site	0.113
Kirkstall Road	0.140
Park site	0.081
Queen Street	0.089
Vicar Lane	0.253

Source: Bartle et al. (1995)

Chemical formula : $C_{22}H_{12}$

Alternative names : PAH EPA no.83

Type of pollutant : Polynuclear Aromatic Hydrocarbon (PAH)

Structure :

Air quality data summary :

Location	Annual Mean ng/m³		
	1991	1992	1993
Bowland	*	*	*
Cardiff C	*	*	*
London	2.19	1.78	0.69
Manchester B	*	*	*
Middlesbrough	*	*	1.15
WSL	1.88	*	*

Source: Davis (1993)

Notes: * signifies no data available

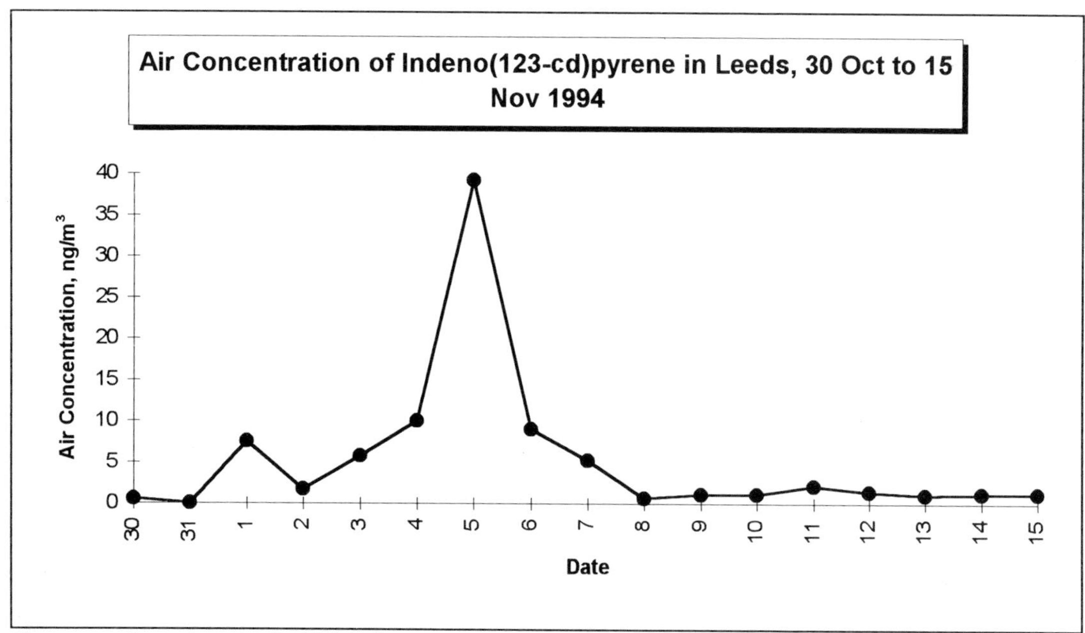

Source: Lewis et al. (1995)

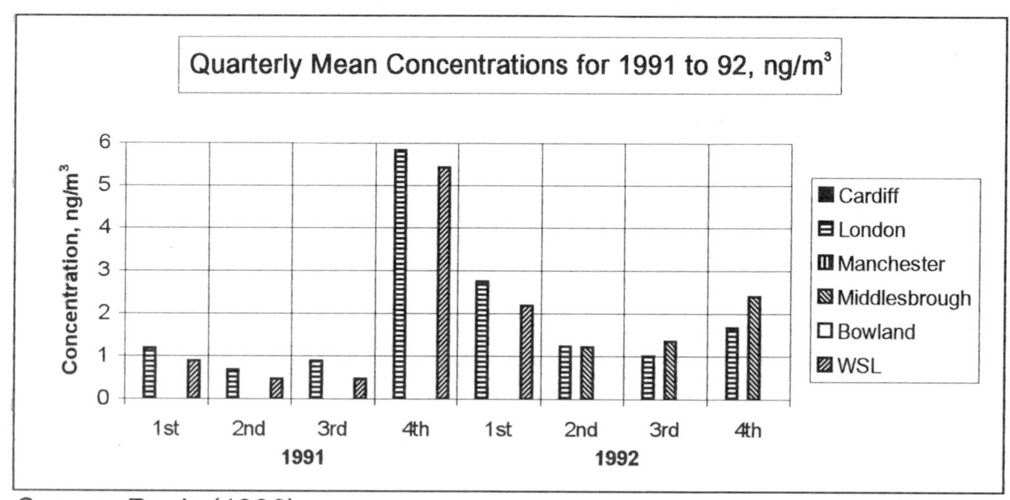

Source: Davis (1993)

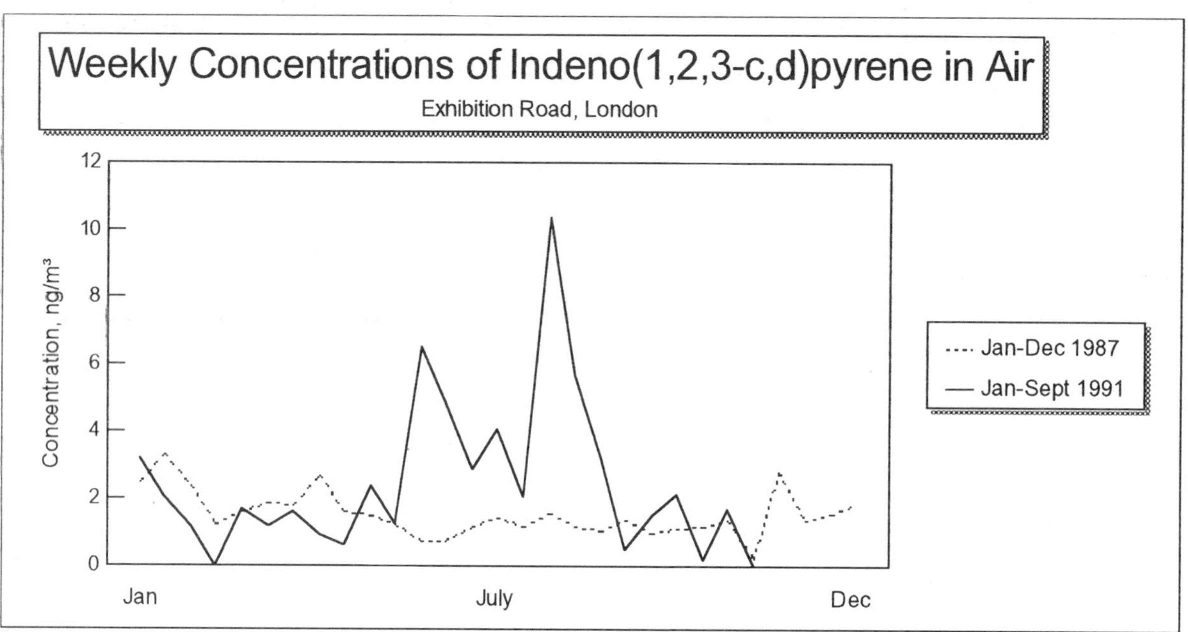

Source: Brown et al. (1995)

Location	Season 1992	Total Concentration in Air ng/m³
Edgbaston	Winter (February)	1.96
Edgbaston	Summer (August)	0.42
Wasthills	Summer (August)	0.11

Source: Smith and Harrison (1994)

Chemical formula	:	$C_{22}H_{12}$
Alternative names	:	PAH EPA no.83
Type of pollutant	:	Polynuclear Aromatic Hydrocarbon (PAH)
Structure	:	

Air quality data summary :

Location	Annual Mean ng/m²/day		
	1991	1992	1993
Bowland	*	*	*
Cardiff C	*	*	*
London	119.50	497.30	*
Manchester B	*	*	*
Middlesbrough	*	*	*
WSL	44.19	*	*

Source: Davis (1993)

Notes: * signifies no data available

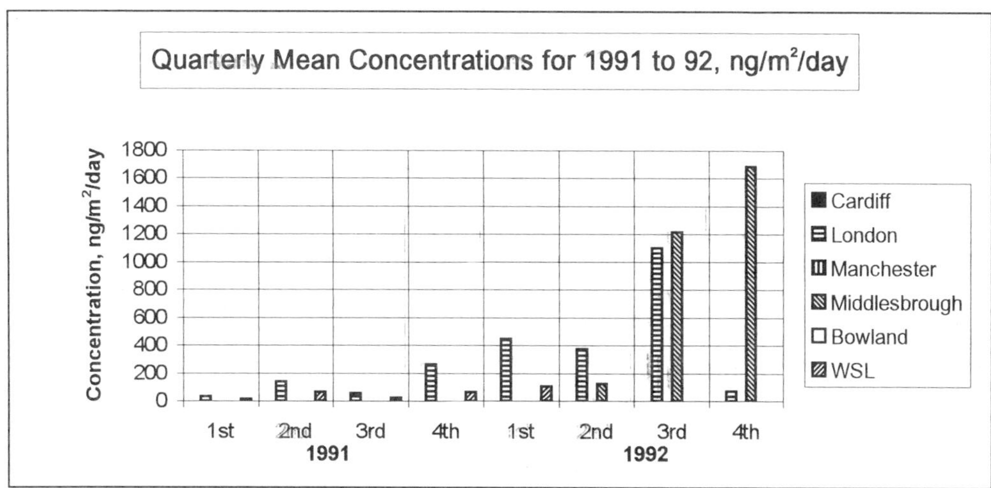

Source: Davis (1993)

Chemical formula : In

Alternative names : Particulate indium

Type of pollutant : Suspended particulate matter, trace element

Air quality data summary :

Rural Concentrations

Location	Concentrations, ng/m^3				
	Mean	Trend	Mean		Trend
	1975-1981	%/yr	1982-1991		%/yr
Harwell, Oxfordshire.	0.073	nst	0.031	*	-6.8
Styrrup, Nottinghamshire.	0.120	nst	0.081	**	-18.3
Trebanos, Glamorgan.	0.061	-	-		-
Wraymires, Cumbria.	0.088	nst	0.037	***	nst

Source: Cawse et al. (1994)

Note: * only 38% of measurements were positive.

** only 85% of measurements were positive.

*** 85% of measurements were below limits of detection during the period 1982-1991.

nst=no significant trend

Chemical formula : In

Alternative names : Precipitation indium

Type of pollutant : Trace contaminant of rain, trace element

Air quality data summary :

Rural Concentrations

Location	Average Annual Rainfall Concentration, μg per litre	
	1972-1981	1982-1991 *
Harwell, Oxfordshire.	<0.2	<0.3
Styrrup, Nottinghamshire.	<0.2	<0.4
Wraymires, Cumbria.	0.14	<0.4

Source: Cawse et al. (1994)

Note: total deposition expressed as apparent rainfall concentration.
* based on soluble fraction only.

Iodide aerosol

Chemical formula : I

Alternative names : Particulate iodide

Type of pollutant : Suspended particulate matter, trace element

Air quality data summary :

Rural Concentrations

Location	Concentrations, ng/m^3			
	Mean	Trend	Mean	Trend
	1972-1981	%/yr	1982-1991	%/yr
Harwell, Oxfordshire.	<3.6	-	1.96	-
Styrrup, Nottinghamshire.	<4.9	-	<2.4	-
Wraymires, Cumbria.	<1.2	-	<1.2	-

Source: Cawse et al. (1994)

Iodide in rain

Chemical formula : I

Alternative names : Precipitation iodide

Type of pollutant : Trace contaminant of rain, trace element

Air quality data summary :

Rural Concentrations

Location	Average Annual Rainfall Concentration, µg per litre	
	1972 - 1981	1982-1991*
Harwell, Oxfordshire	<5	<3
Styrrup, Nottinghamshire	<7	<3
Wraymires, Cumbria	<4	<3

Source: Cawse et al. (1994)

Note: total deposition expressed as apparent rainfall concentration
* based on soluble fraction only

Chemical formula : Fe

Alternative names : Particulate iron

Type of pollutant : Suspended particulate matter, trace element

Air quality data summary :

Rural Concentrations

Location	Concentrations, ng/m^3			
	Mean	Trend	Mean	Trend
	1972-1981	%/yr	1982-1991	%/yr
Harwell, Oxfordshire.	285	-6.0	172	3.3
Styrrup, Nottinghamshire.	682	-11.2	460	-5.2
Trebanos, Glamorgan.	372	-9.1	318	-
Wraymires, Cumbria.	242	nst	98	-4.2

Source: Cawse et al. (1994)
nst=no significant trend

Urban Concentrations

Location	Mean Annual Concentrations, ng/m^3						
	1972-1981	1985	1986	1987	1988	1989	1990
Swansea	31.0						
Central London		803.7	941.7	1015.1	1130.3	1140.3	1686.9
Brent		529.0	526.7	607.0	506.3	350.2	573.2
Motherwell		2061.7	1648.8	1547.6	2216.3	1789.0	1780.4
Glasgow C		534.0	424.6	510.0	481.4	425.8	538.6
Leeds		642.2	636.0	691.9	520.2	475.7	656.5

Source: Pattenden (1974), DoE (1992)

Location	Nature of site	Measurement period	Mean concentration ng/m^3
Altrincham	Residential	1978-1989	737
Brent	Residential	1975-1989	938
Chilton	Rural	1971-1989	242
Flixton	Residential	1975-1989	737
Lambeth	Residential	1976-1982	1031
Manchester City North	Industrial/ Residential	1975-1988	1013
Manchester City South	Residential	1975-1989	667
Walsall	Industrial	1976-1989	1687
Wraymires	Rural	1970-1989	156

Source: Lee et al. (1994)

Iron in rain

Chemical formula : Fe

Alternative names : Precipitation iron

Type of pollutant : Trace contaminant of rain, trace element

Air quality data summary :

Rural Concentrations

Location	Average Annual Rainfall Concentration, µg per litre	
	1972-1981	1982-1991 *
Harwell, Oxfordshire.	328	27
Styrrup, Nottinghamshire.	983	65
Wraymires, Cumbria.	78	18

Source: Cawse et al. (1994)

Note: total deposition expressed as apparent rainfall concentration.
* based on soluble fraction only.

Chemical formula : C_5H_8

Alternative name : 2-methylbuta-1,3-diene

Type of pollutant : (Volatile) organic compound VOC, natural biogenic hydrocarbon, hemiterpene

Structure :

$$CH_2{=}\underset{\displaystyle CH_3}{\underset{|}{C}}{-}CH{=}CH_2$$

Air quality data summary :

Remote rural concentrations

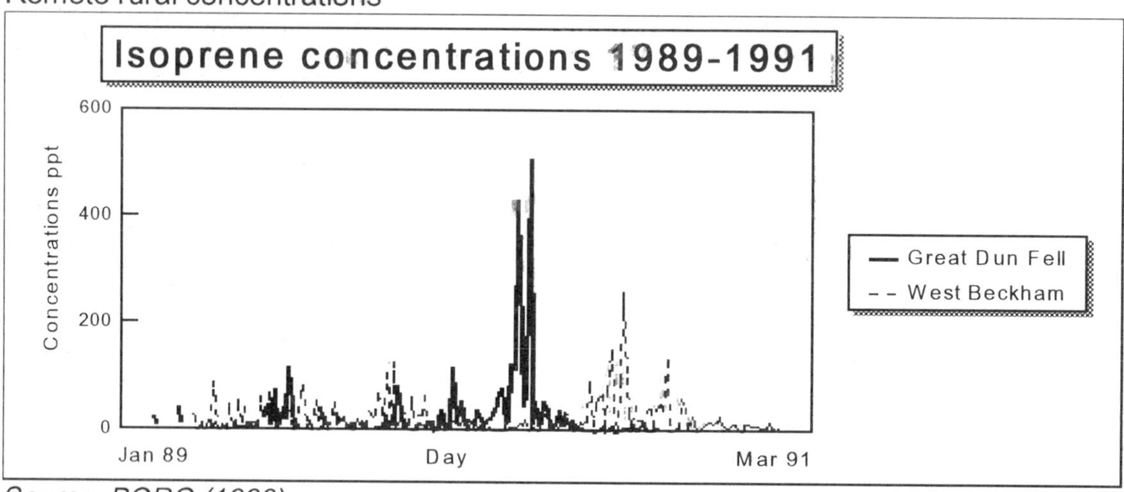

Source: PORG (1993)

Urban Concentrations

1994-95 Monthly Means, ppb									
	Belfast C	Birmingham B	Bristol A	Cardiff B	Edinburgh A	Eltham	Harwell	Middlesbrough	UCL
Jan 94	-	0.69	-	0.42	-	-	-	-	-
Feb 94	-	0.19	-	0.38	-	-	-	-	-
Mar 94	-	0.07	-	0.57	-	-	-	-	-
Apr 94	-	0.06	-	0.09	-	-	-	-	-
May 94	-	0.10	-	0.29	-	-	-	-	-
Jun 94	-	0.18	-	0.10	-	0.10	-	0.05	-
Jul 94	-	0.32	0.14	0.12	-	0.21	-	0.14	0.51
Aug 94	0.09	0.49	0.16	0.32	-	0.18	-	0.21	0.28
Sep 94	0.13	0.18	0.20	0.27	-	0.11	-	2.67	0.26
Oct 94	0.16	0.62	0.98	0.77	-	0.37	-	0.68	0.46
Nov 94	0.14	0.35	0.28	0.71	-	0.45	-	0.31	0.41
Dec 94	0.14	0.27	0.57	0.10	-	0.12	-	0.09	0.48
Jan 95	0.09	0.11	-	0.13	0.03	0.21	-	0.10	0.10
Feb 95	0.09	0.27	0.19	0.08	0.03	0.09	-	0.07	0.10

Source: Dollard (1995)

Chemical formula : La

Alternative names : Particulate lanthanum

Type of pollutant : Suspended particulate matter, trace element

Air quality data summary :

Rural concentrations

Location	Concentrations, ng/m^3			
	Mean	Trend	Mean	Trend
	1972-1981	%/yr	1982-1991	%/yr
Harwell, Oxfordshire.	0.59	-	0.25	-10.4
Styrrup, Nottinghamshire.	0.86	-	0.39	-12.2
Trebanos, Glamorgan.	0.84	-	0.35	-26.4
Wraymires, Cumbria.	0.51	-	0.13	-16.1

Source: Cawse et al. (1994)

Chemical formula : La

Alternative names : Precipitation lanthanum

Type of pollutant : Trace contaminant of rain, trace element

Air quality data summary :

Rural Concentrations

Location	Average Annual Rainfall Concentration, µg per litre	
	1972-1981	1982-1989 *
Harwell, Oxfordshire.	<0.8	<0.1
Styrrup, Nottinghamshire.	<1.7	<0.2
Wraymires, Cumbria.	<0.4	<0.1

Source: Cawse et al. (1994)

Note: total deposition expressed as apparent rainfall concentration.
* based on soluble fraction only.

Lanthanum not analysed in rainwater in 1990 and 1991.

Chemical formula	:	Pb
Alternative name	:	Particulate lead
Type of pollutant	:	Suspended particulate matter, trace element
Air quality data summary	:	

Rural Concentrations:

Location	Concentrations, ng/m^3			
	Mean	Trend	Mean	Trend
	1972-1981	%/yr	1982-1991	%/yr
Harwell, Oxfordshire.	124	-9.6	58	-7.4
Styrrup, Nottinghamshire.	242	-12.4	102	-10.6
Trebanos, Glamorgan.	143	-12.9	66	-6.2
Wraymires, Cumbria.	68	nst	28	-12.5

Source: Cawse et al. (1994)

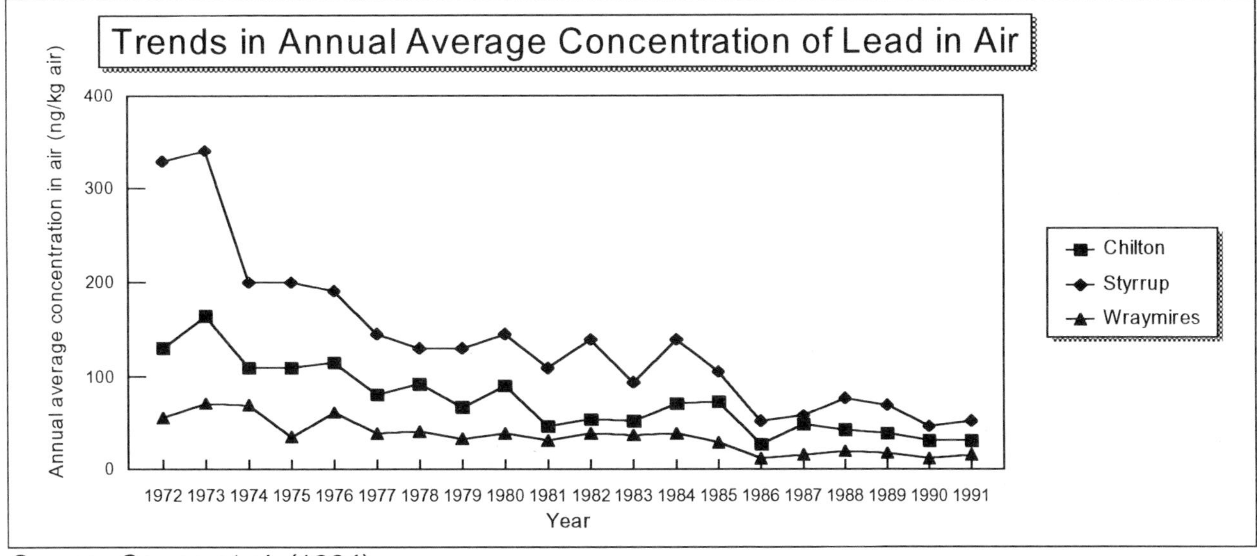

Source: Cawse et al. (1994)

Location		Mean Annual Concentration, ng/m^3			
		1984	1985	1986	1987
Plynlimon, Powys	Rural	46	23	14	11
Trebanos, West Glamorgan	Rural	98	81	39	48
Queensferry, Clwyd	Urban	547	645	248	219
Wrexham, Clwyd	Urban	211	224	92	110
Bedwas, Mid Glamorgan	Urban	222	224	88	103
Port Talbot, West Glamorgan	Urban	144	146	69	71

Source: Baker et al. (1988)

Location	Nature of site	Measurement period	Mean concentration ng/m^3
Altrincham	Residential	1978-1989	267
Brent	Residential	1975-1989	670
Chilton	Rural	1971-1989	100
Flixton	Residential	1975-1989	427
Lambeth	Residential	1976-1982	529
Manchester City North	Industrial/residential	1975-1988	380
Manchester City South	Residential	1975-1989	341
Walsall	Industrial	1976-1989	1316
Wraymires	Rural	1970-1989	53

Source: Lee et al. (1995)

Location	Annual Mean Concentration at Lead in Petrol sites, ng/m^3									
		1984	1985	1986	1987	1988	1989	1990	1991	1992
Cottered	Rural	130	130	77	98	76	75	41	45	44
N. Petherton	Rural	-	-	70	65	69	81	53	62	-
Cardiff D	Kerbside	-	1280	630	670	620	570	460	440	384
Manchester C	Kerbside	-	2040	810	810	760	640	510	460	339
Newcastle B	Urban	-	180	130	150	110	110	70	70	67
N. Tyneside	Urban	-	290	150	190	140	120	81	100	83
Eskdalemuir	Rural	-	29	8	13	14	13	10	13	10

Source: DoE (1992)

Urban Concentrations:

Location	Mean Annual Concentrations, ng/m^3					
	1972-1981	1980	1985	1990	1991	1992
Swansea	620.0	-	-	-	-	-
Central London	-	640	480	-	120	99
Brent	-	770	640	220	200	174
Motherwell	-	260	260	200	160	50
Glasgow C	-	460	270	95	92	93
Leeds	-	650	310	120	-	-

Source: Pattenden (1974), DoE (1992)

Chemical formula : Pb

Alternative name : Precipitation lead

Type of pollutant : Trace contaminant of rain, trace element

Air quality data summary :

Rural Concentrations

Location	Average Annual Rainfall Concentration, µg per litre	
	1972 - 1981	1982-1991*
Harwell, Oxfordshire	37	15
Styrrup, Nottinghamshire	60	21
Wraymires, Cumbria	16	5.2

Source: Cawse et al. (1994)

Note: total deposition expressed as apparent rainfall concentration
* based on soluble fraction only

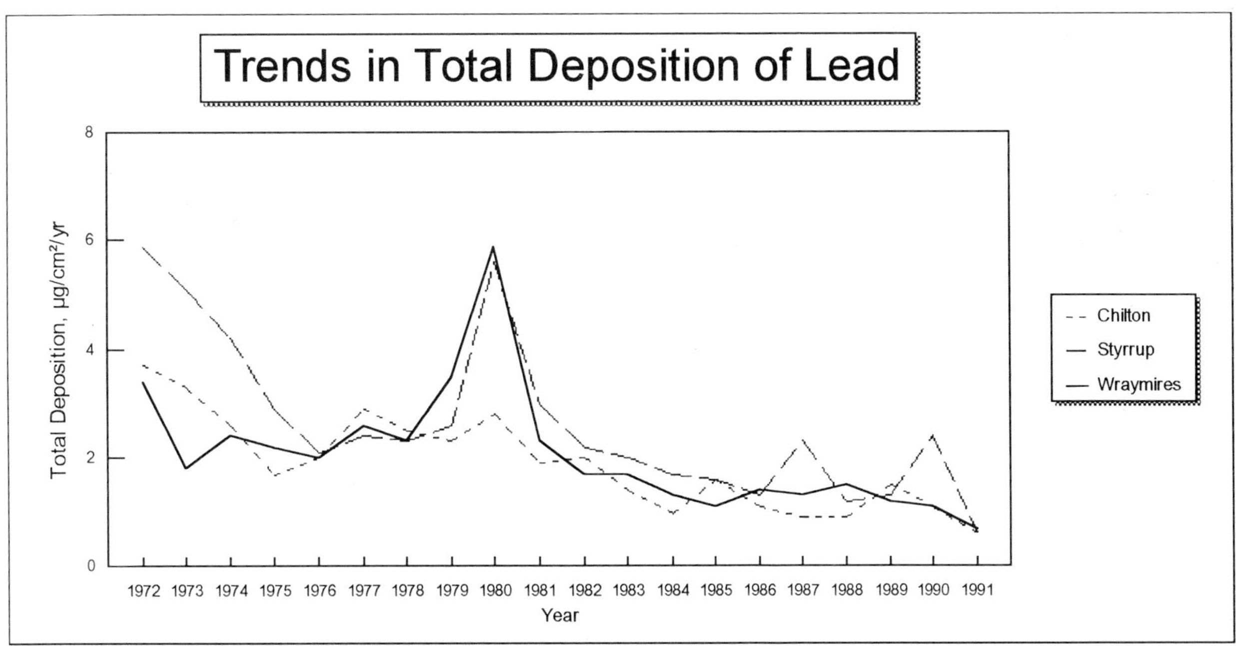

Source: Cawse et al. (1994)

Chemical formula : Mg

Alternative name : Particulate magnesium

Type of pollutant : Suspended particulate matter, trace element

Air quality data summary :

Rural Concentrations

Location	Average Annual Concentrations, ng/m^3			
	Mean	Trend	Mean	Trend
	1975-1981	%/yr	1982-1991	%/yr
Harwell, Oxfordshire.	335	nst	<83	nst
Styrrup, Nottinghamshire.	1004	nst	<190	-12.3
Trebanos, Glamorgan.	347	-	-	-
Wraymires, Cumbria.	335	-14.4	<140	nst

Source: Cawse et al. (1994)

>75% of measurements at each location were below limits of detection during the period 1982-1991.

nst=no significant trend

Magnesium in rain

Chemical formula : Mg

Alternative name : Precipitation magnesium

Type of pollutant : Trace contaminant of rain, trace element

Air quality data summary :

Rural Concentrations

Location	Average Annual Rainfall Concentrations, µg per litre	
	1972 - 1981	1982-1991*
Harwell, Oxfordshire	806	590
Styrrup, Nottinghamshire	1000	620
Wraymires, Cumbria	583	410

Source: Cawse et al. (1994)

Note: total deposition expressed as apparent rainfall concentration
*based on soluble fraction only

Site	Precipitation-weighted Annual Mean Magnesium Concentration, 1986-93, (μ eql^{-1})								
	OS Grid ref	1986	1987	1988	1989	1990	1991	1992	1993
Achanarras	ND 151550	55	37	46	64	49	54	46	56
Balquhidder	NN 521206	29	11	14	26	24	21	16	37
Bannisdale	NY 515043	29	15	33	27	38	43	23	27
Barcombe Mills	TQ 437149	44	62	35	49	85	34	33	28
Beddgelert	SH 556518	29	18	26	31	44	37	24	29
Bottesford	SK 797376	26	11	18	16	18	16	11	10
Compton	SU 512804	13	19	21	21	31	18	11	15
Cow Green Reservoir	NY 817298	17	10	17	18	22	20	19	19
Driby	TF 386744	24	14	18	27	27	26	18	22
Eskdalemuir	NT 235028	20	9	15	20	21	25	14	17
Flatford Mill	TM 077333	32	17	16	23	22	19	15	15
Glen Dye	NO 642864	-	12	18	21	21	19	16	22
Goonhilly	SW 723214	61	48	49	63	19	77	57	54
High Muffles	SE 776939	15	17	19	23	29	27	19	30
Hillsborough Forest	J 243577	-	-	-	21	31	24	20	25
Jenny Hurn	SK 816986	36	16	30	25	35	21	14	16
Llyn Brianne	SN 822507	21	16	20	27	36	27	19	26
Loch Dee	NX 468779	29	12	31	31	35	29	22	22
Lough Navar	H 065545	57	24	80	32	60	47	34	48
Plynlimon	SN 823854	-	-	-	24	32	23	19	20

Site	Precipitation-weighted Annual Mean Magnesium Concentration, 1986-93, (μ eql^{-1})								
	OS Grid ref	1986	1987	1988	1989	1990	1991	1992	1993
Polloch	NM 792689	-	-	-	-	-	48	30	52
Preston Montford	SJ 432143	21	11	22	11	24	43	11	18
Redesdale	NY 833954	26	12	19	23	18	19	15	20
River Mharcaidh	NH 876052	21	8	12	20	15	11	14	35
Stoke Ferry	TL 700988	20	12	13	16	23	18	16	15
Strathvaich Dam	NH 347750	-	20	25	28	39	32	31	51
Thorganby	SE 676428	22	16	17	23	27	31	16	15
Tycanol Wood	SN 093364	27	21	24	53	54	39	29	31
Wardlow Hay Cop	SK 177739	18	15	25	17	35	32	15	25
Whiteadder	NT 664633	26	13	22	23	20	15	19	26
Woburn	SP 964361	9	11	13	18	24	14	9	12
Yarner Wood	SX 867890	23	30	35	38	58	32	26	28

Source: Campbell et al. (1994a)

Location	1992 Monthly Weighted Mean Concentration in Precipitation, mg/l											
	Jan	Feb	Mar	Apr	May	Jun	Jul	Aug	Sep	Oct	Nov	Dec
Eskdalemuir	0.34	0.20	0.20	0.18	0.21	0.21	0.14	0.12	0.13	0.13	0.26	0.12
High Muffles	0.19	0.22	0.26	0.31	0.12	0.28	0.12	0.06	0.03	0.23	0.08	0.07
Lough Navar	0.15	0.50	0.91	0.41	0.54	0.04	0.13	0.22	0.37	0.53	0.59	0.30
Strath Vaich	0.49	0.57	0.33	0.38	0.19	0.08	0.22	0.03	0.15	0.51	0.46	0.16
Yarner Wood	0.20	0.19	0.39	0.26	0.26	0.04	0.07	0.24	0.18	0.91	0.30	0.27

Source: Schaug et al. (1994)

Chemical formula	:	Mn
Alternative name	:	Particulate manganese
Type of pollutant	:	Trace element

Air quality data summary :

Rural Concentrations

Location	Average Annual Concentrations, ng/m^3			
	Mean	Trend	Mean	Trend
	1972-1981	%/yr	1982-1991	%/yr
Harwell, Oxfordshire.	14.9	-11.0	6.4	nst
Styrrup, Nottinghamshire.	43.4	-10.5	25.1	-5.1
Trebanos, Glamorgan.	14.9	-9.0	-	
Wraymires, Cumbria.	10.9	-8.9	3.9	-7.9

Source: Cawse et al. (1994)

Urban Concentrations

Location	Mean Annual Concentrations, ng/m^3						
	1972-1981	1985	1986	1987	1988	1989	1990
Swansea	31.0						
Central London		16.9	16.7	17.8	18.4	19.7	25.0
Brent		12.1	14.4	17.1	13.5	6.7	10.7
Motherwell		65.9	47.4	51.8	51.3	60.7	57.9
Glasgow C		14.8	15.1	19.1	14.0	13.5	13.4
Leeds		35.6	32.7	33.3	25.9	21.9	24.2

Source: Pattenden (1974), DoE (1992)

Chemical formula : Mn

Alternative name : Precipitation manganese

Type of pollutant : Trace contaminant of rain, trace element

Air quality data summary :

Rural Concentrations

Location	Average Annual Rainfall Concentration, µg per litre	
	1972-1981	1982-1991 *
Harwell, Oxfordshire.	14	8.2
Styrrup, Nottinghamshire.	34	15.0
Wraymires, Cumbria.	6	2.2

Source: Cawse et al. (1994)

Note: total deposition expressed as apparent rainfall concentration.
* based on soluble fraction only.

Chemical formula : Hg

Alternative name : Particulate mercury

Type of pollutant : Suspended particulate matter, trace element

Air quality data summary :

Rural Concentrations

Location	Average Annual Concentrations, ng/m^3	
	Mean	Mean
	1972-1981	1982-1991
Harwell, Oxfordshire.	<0.009	0.10
Styrrup, Nottinghamshire.	<0.5	0.26
Trebanos, Glamorgan.	<0.2	-
Wraymires, Cumbria.	<0.1	0.086

Source: Cawse et al. (1994)

Location	Nature of site	Measurement period	Mean concentration ng/m^3
Altrincham	Residential	1978-1989	0.22
Brent	Residential	1975-1989	0.28
Chilton	Rural	1971-1989	0.08
Flixton	Residential	1975-1989	0.34
Lambeth	Residential	1976-1982	0.22
Manchester City North	Industrial/ Residential	1975-1988	0.30
Manchester City South	Residential	1975-1989	0.22
Walsall	Industrial	1976-1989	0.54
Wraymires	Rural	1970-1989	0.09

Source: Lee et al. (1994)

Chemical formula : Hg

Alternative name : Precipitation mercury

Type of pollutant : Trace contaminant of rain, trace element

Air quality data summary :

Rural Concentrations

Location	Average Annual Rainfall Concentration, µg per litre	
	1972-1981	1982-1991 *
Harwell, Oxfordshire.	<0.2	0.67
Styrrup, Nottinghamshire.	<0.2	0.74
Wraymires, Cumbria.	0.09	0.60

Source: Cawse et al. (1994)

Note: total deposition expressed as apparent rainfall concentration.
* based on soluble fraction only.

Chemical formula : CH_4

Alternative name :

Type of pollutant : (Volatile) organic compound (VOC), hydrocarbon, radiatively active trace gas, greenhouse gas

Structure :

CH_4

Air quality data summary :

Remote Rural Concentrations

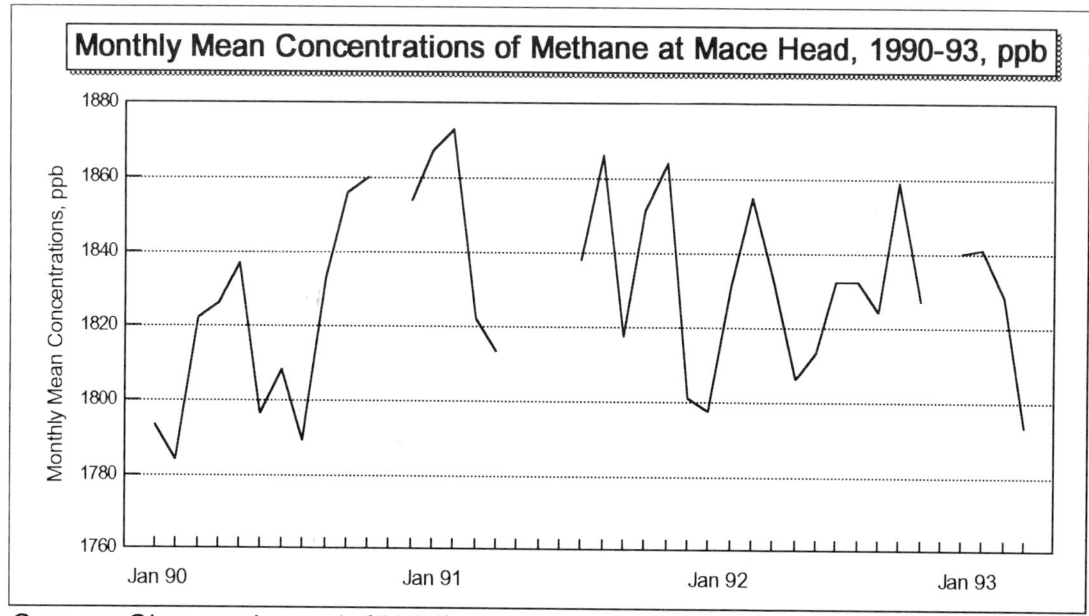

Source: Simmonds et al. (1994)

Chemical formula : $C_{19}H_{14}$

Alternative names :

Type of pollutant : Polynuclear Aromatic Hydrocarbon (PAH)

Structure :

Air quality data summary :

Urban Concentrations:

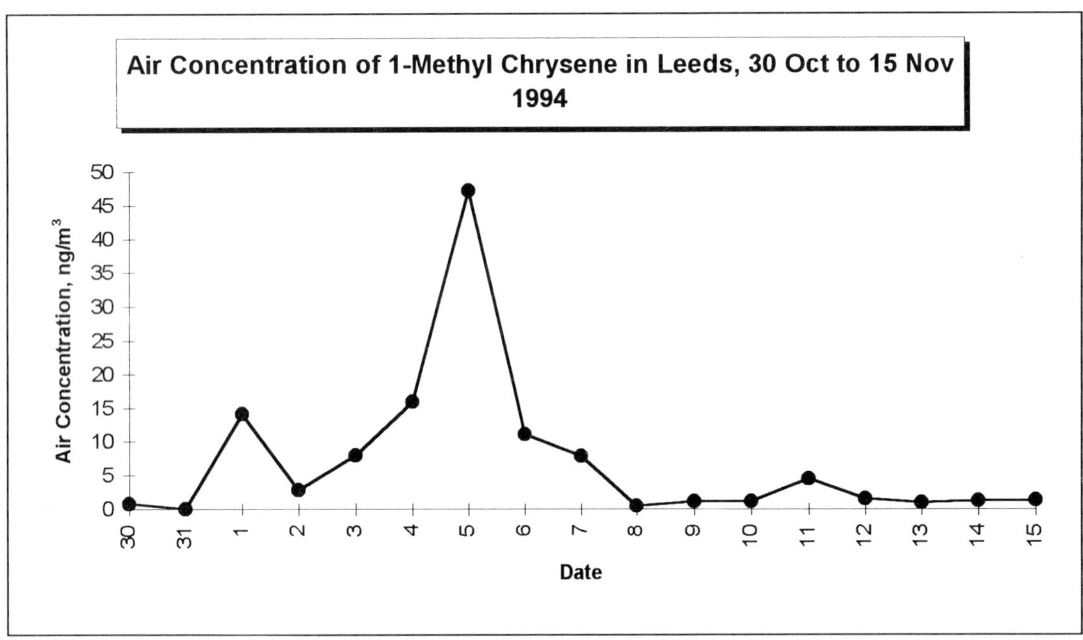

Source: Lewis et al. (1995)

5-Methyl Chrysene

Chemical formula : $C_{19}H_{14}$

Alternative names :

Type of pollutant : Polynuclear Aromatic Hydrocarbon (PAH)

Structure :

CH_3

Air quality data summary :

Urban Concentrations:

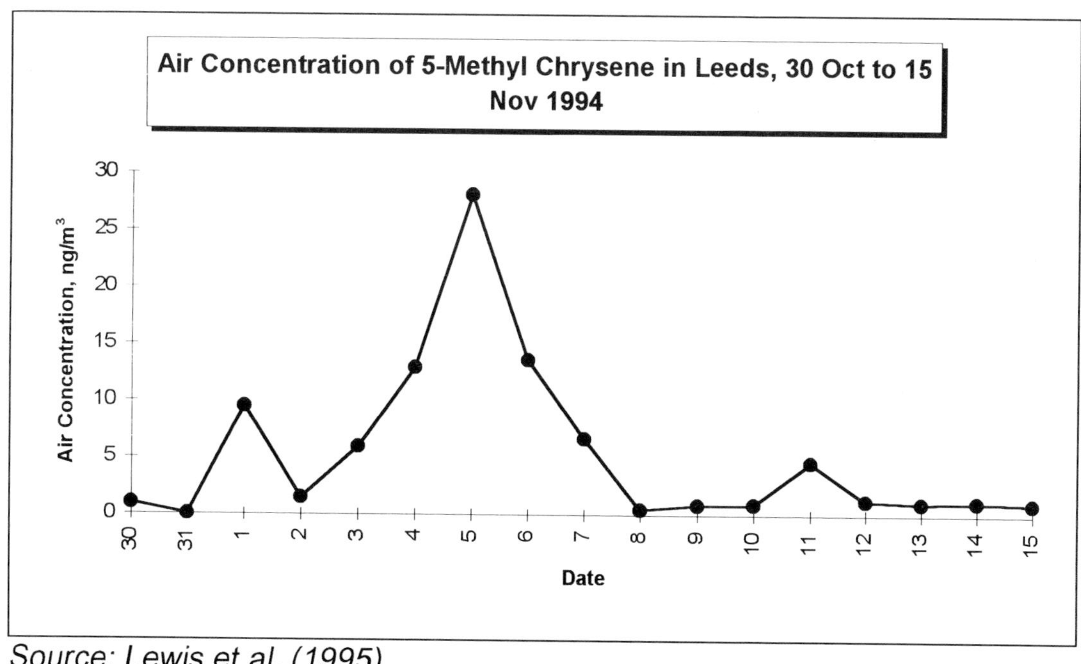

Source: Lewis et al. (1995)

Methylcyclohexane

Chemical formula : C_7H_{14}

Alternative name : Hexahydrotoluene

Type of pollutant : (Volatile) organic compound (VOC), hydrocarbon

Structure :

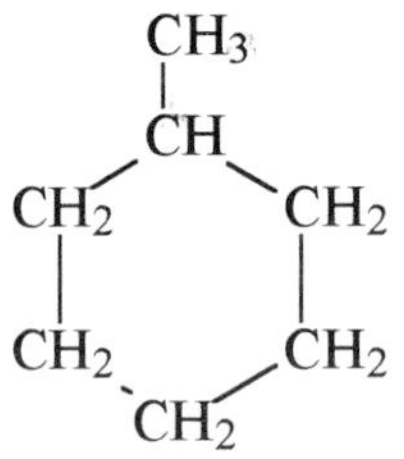

$$
\begin{array}{ccccc}
 & & CH_3 & & \\
 & & | & & \\
 & & CH & & \\
 & / & & \backslash & \\
CH_2 & & & & CH_2 \\
| & & & & | \\
CH_2 & & & & CH_2 \\
 & \backslash & & / & \\
 & & CH_2 & &
\end{array}
$$

Air quality data summary :

Mean Air Concentration in Leeds, 19/8/94 to 8/9/94	
Location	21 day mean, μg/m^3
Albion Street	0.110
Cliff Lane	0.065
EUN monitoring site	0.089
Kerbside site	0.113
Kirkstall Road	0.149
Park site	0.050
Queen Street	0.112
Vicar Lane	0.269

Source: Bartle et al. (1995)

Chemical formula	:	C_6H_{12}
Alternative name	:	Methylpentamethylene
Type of pollutant	:	(Volatile) organic compound (VOC), hydrocarbon
Structure	:	

$$
\begin{array}{c}
CH_3 \\
| \\
CH \\
H_2C \diagup \quad \diagdown CH_2 \\
\diagdown \qquad \diagup \\
H_2C\text{-}CH_2
\end{array}
$$

Air quality data summary :

Mean Air Concentration in Leeds, 19/8/94 to 8/9/94	
Location	21 day mean, $\mu g/m^3$
Albion Street	0.129
Cliff Lane	0.091
EUN monitoring site	0.121
Kerbside site	0.164
Kirkstall Road	0.224
Park site	0.105
Queen Street	0.159
Vicar Lane	0.431

Source: Bartle et al. (1995)

3-Methylcyclopentene

Chemical formula : C_6H_{10}

Alternative name :

Type of pollutant : (Volatile) organic compound (VOC), hydrocarbon

Structure :

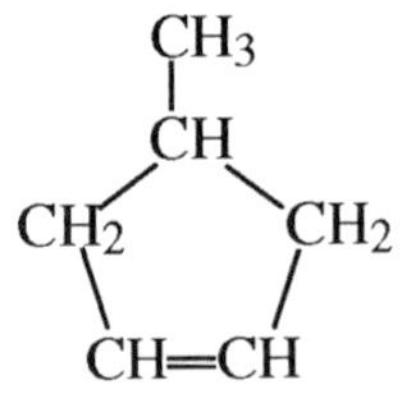

```
      CH3
      |
      CH
    /    \
 CH2      CH2
   \      /
   CH═CH
```

Air quality data summary :

Mean Air Concentration in Leeds, 19/8/94 to 8/9/94	
Location	21 day mean, $\mu g/m^3$
Albion Street	0.037
Cliff Lane	0.036
EUN monitoring site	0.080
Kerbside site	0.060
Kirkstall Road	0.078
Park site	0.080
Queen Street	0.043
Vicar Lane	0.153

Source: Bartle et al. (1995)

Methylglyoxal

Chemical formula : $C_3H_4O_2$

Alternative names : Propan-1-al-2-one

Type of pollutant : (Volatile) organic compound (VOC), hydrocarbon, oxygenate

Structure :

$$CHO-\underset{\underset{O}{\|}}{C}-CH_3$$

Air quality data summary :

Month 1993	Air Concentration at Harwell site, ppb
	Monthly Mean
August	0.017
September	0.013
October	0.013
November	0.037
December	0.017

Source: Solberg et al. (1994)

2-Methylheptane

Chemical formula : C_8H_{18}

Alternative name :

Type of pollutant : (Volatile) organic compound (VOC), hydrocarbon

Structure :

$$CH_3-\underset{\displaystyle CH_3}{\underset{|}{C}H}-CH_2-CH_2-CH_2-CH_2-CH_3$$

Air quality data summary :

Mean Air Concentration in Leeds, 19/8/94 to 8/9/94	
Location	21 day mean, µg/m^3
Albion Street	0.092
Cliff Lane	0.053
EUN monitoring site	0.085
Kerbside site	0.126
Kirkstall Road	0.135
Park site	0.045
Queen Street	0.118
Vicar Lane	0.349

Source: Bartle et al. (1995)

Chemical formula : C_8H_{18}

Alternative name :

Type of pollutant : (Volatile) organic compound (VOC), hydrocarbon

Structure :

$$CH_3-CH_2-\underset{\displaystyle CH_3}{\underset{|}{CH}}-CH_2-CH_2-CH_2-CH_3$$

Air quality data summary :

Mean Air Concentration in Leeds, 19/8/94 to 8/9/94	
Location	21 day mean, $\mu g/m^3$
Albion Street	0.067
Cliff Lane	0.051
EUN monitoring site	0.068
Kerbside site	0.119
Kirkstall Road	0.115
Park site	0.034
Queen Street	0.108
Vicar Lane	0.311

Source: Bartle et al. (1995)

Chemical formula : C_8H_{18}

Alternative name :

Type of pollutant : (Volatile) organic compound (VOC), hydrocarbon

Structure :

$$CH_3-CH_2-CH_2-\underset{\displaystyle CH_3}{\underset{|}{CH}}-CH_2-CH_2-CH_3$$

Air quality data summary :

Mean Air Concentration in Leeds, 19/8/94 to 8/9/94	
Location	21 day mean, μg/m^3
Albion Street	0.032
Cliff Lane	0.035
EUN monitoring site	0.036
Kerbside site	0.049
Kirkstall Road	0.049
Park site	0.035
Queen Street	0.044
Vicar Lane	0.145

Source: Bartle et al. (1995)

Chemical formula : C_7H_{16}

Alternative name : i-heptane

Type of pollutant : (Volatile) organic compound (VOC), hydrocarbon

Structure :

$$CH_3-\underset{\displaystyle CH_3}{\underset{|}{CH}}-CH_2-CH_2-CH_2-CH_3$$

Air quality data summary :

Mean Air Concentration in Leeds, 19/8/94 to 8/9/94	
Location	21 day mean, $\mu g/m^3$
Albion Street	0.165
Cliff Lane	0.119
EUN monitoring site	0.166
Kerbside site	0.264
Kirkstall Road	0.289
Park site	0.083
Queen Street	0.231
Vicar Lane	0.660

Source: Bartle et al. (1995)

Chemical formula : C_7H_{16}

Alternative name :

Type of pollutant : (Volatile) organic compound (VOC), hydrocarbon

Structure :

$$CH_3{-}CH_2{-}\underset{\displaystyle CH_3}{\underset{|}{CH}}{-}CH_2{-}CH_2{-}CH_3$$

Air quality data summary :

Mean Air Concentration in Leeds, 19/8/94 to 8/9/94	
Location	21 day mean, $\mu g/m^3$
Albion Street	0.178
Cliff Lane	0.127
EUN monitoring site	0.179
Kerbside site	0.260
Kirkstall Road	0.296
Park site	0.096
Queen Street	0.243
Vicar Lane	0.678

Source: Bartle et al. (1995)

Chemical formula	:	CH_3I
Alternative name	:	Iodomethane
Type of pollutant	:	Natural biogenic halocarbon
Structure	:	CH_3I
Air quality data summary	:	

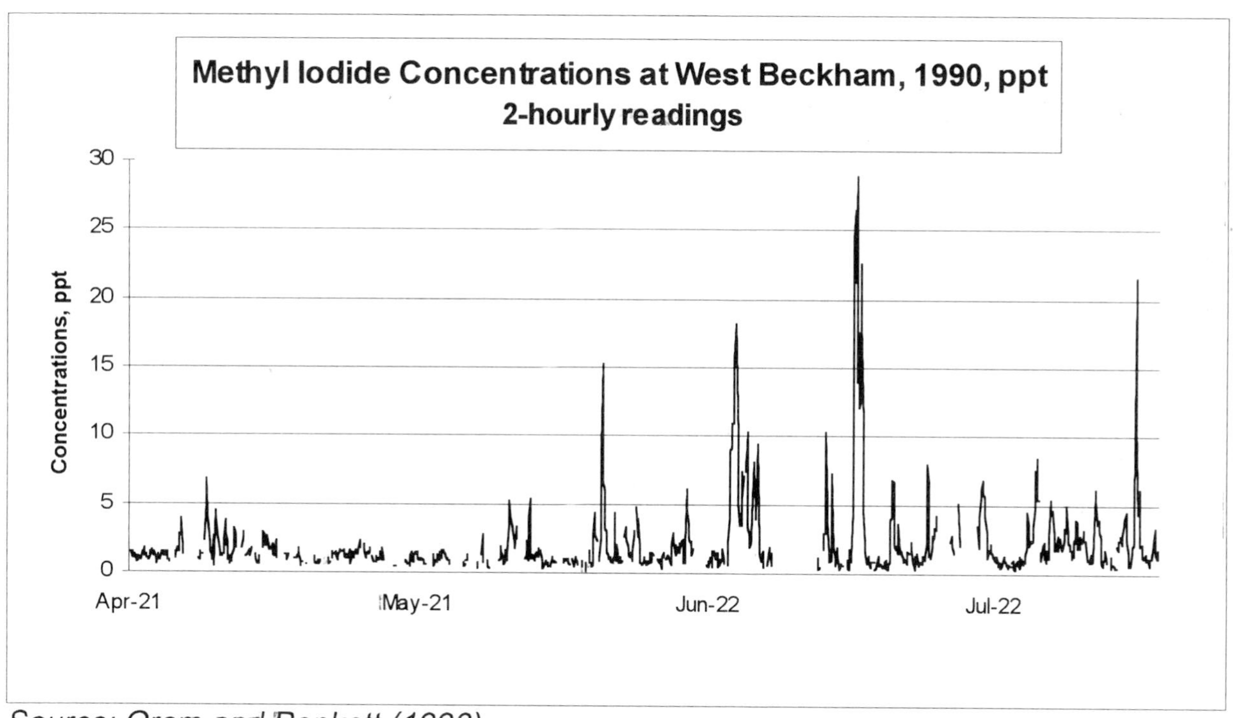

Source: Oram and Penkett (1993)

Chemical formula : $C_{10}H_{22}$

Alternative name :

Type of pollutant : (Volatile) organic compound (VOC), hydrocarbon

Structure :

$$CH_3-\underset{\underset{CH_3}{|}}{CH}-CH_2-CH_2-CH_2-CH_2-CH_2-CH_2-CH_3$$

Air quality data summary :

Mean Air Concentration in Leeds, 19/8/94 to 8/9/94	
Location	21 day mean, $\mu g/m^3$
Albion Street	0.104
Cliff Lane	0.068
EUN monitoring site	0.095
Kerbside site	0.160
Kirkstall Road	0.218
Park site	0.136
Queen Street	0.118
Vicar Lane	0.294

Source: Bartle et al. (1995)

Chemical formula : $C_{10}H_{22}$

Alternative name :

Type of pollutant : (Volatile) organic compound (VOC), hydrocarbon

Structure :

$$CH_3-CH_2-CH_2-\underset{\displaystyle CH_3}{\underset{|}{CH}}-CH_2-CH_2-CH_2-CH_2-CH_3$$

Air quality data summary :

Mean Air Concentration in Leeds, 19/8/94 to 8/9/94	
Location	21 day mean, $\mu g/m^3$
Albion Street	0.234
Cliff Lane	0.161
EUN monitoring site	0.245
Kerbside site	0.428
Kirkstall Road	0.609
Park site	0.230
Queen Street	0.338
Vicar Lane	0.950

Source: Bartle et al. (1995)

Note: Data represents concentrations of 4-methyl nonane and 1,3,5-trimethylbenzene mixture.

2-Methyloctane

Chemical formula : C_9H_{20}

Alternative name :

Type of pollutant : (Volatile) organic compound (VOC), hydrocarbon

Structure :

$$CH_3-\underset{\displaystyle CH_3}{\underset{|}{C}H}-CH_2-CH_2-CH_2-CH_2-CH_2-CH_3$$

Air quality data summary :

Mean Air Concentration in Leeds, 19/8/94 to 8/9/94	
Location	21 day mean, $\mu g/m^3$
Albion Street	0.096
Cliff Lane	0.071
EUN monitoring site	0.103
Kerbside site	0.153
Kirkstall Road	0.173
Park site	0.103
Queen Street	0.141
Vicar Lane	0.351

Source: Bartle et al. (1995)

Note: Data represents concentrations of 2-methyloctane and 4-methyloctane mixture.

3-Methyloctane

Chemical formula : C_9H_{20}

Alternative name :

Type of pollutant : (Volatile) organic compound (VOC), hydrocarbon

Structure :

$$CH_3-CH_2-\underset{\displaystyle CH_3}{\underset{|}{C}H}-CH_2-CH_2-CH_2-CH_2-CH_3$$

Air quality data summary :

Mean Air Concentration in Leeds, 19/8/94 to 8/9/94	
Location	21 day mean, $\mu g/m^3$
Albion Street	0.050
Cliff Lane	0.047
EUN monitoring site	0.044
Kerbside site	0.068
Kirkstall Road	0.082
Park site	0.051
Queen Street	0.060
Vicar Lane	0.148

Source: Bartle et al. (1995)

4-Methyloctane

Chemical formula : C_9H_{20}

Alternative name :

Type of pollutant : (Volatile) organic compound (VOC), hydrocarbon

Structure :

$$CH_3-CH_2-CH_2-\underset{\displaystyle CH_3}{\underset{|}{CH}}-CH_2-CH_2-CH_2-CH_3$$

Air quality data summary :

Mean Air Concentration in Leeds, 19/8/94 to 8/9/94	
Location	21 day mean, µg/m³
Albion Street	0.096
Cliff Lane	0.071
EUN monitoring site	0.103
Kerbside site	0.153
Kirkstall Road	0.173
Park site	0.103
Queen Street	0.141
Vicar Lane	0.351

Source: Bartle et al. (1995)

Note: Data represents concentrations of 2-methyloctane and 4-methyloctane mixture.

2-Methylpentane

Chemical formula : C_6H_{14}

Alternative names : i-hexane

Type of pollutant : (Volatile) organic compound (VOC), hydrocarbon

Structure :

$$CH_3\underset{\displaystyle CH_3}{\underset{|}{C}}HCH_2CH_2CH_3$$

Air quality data summary :

Rural concentrations

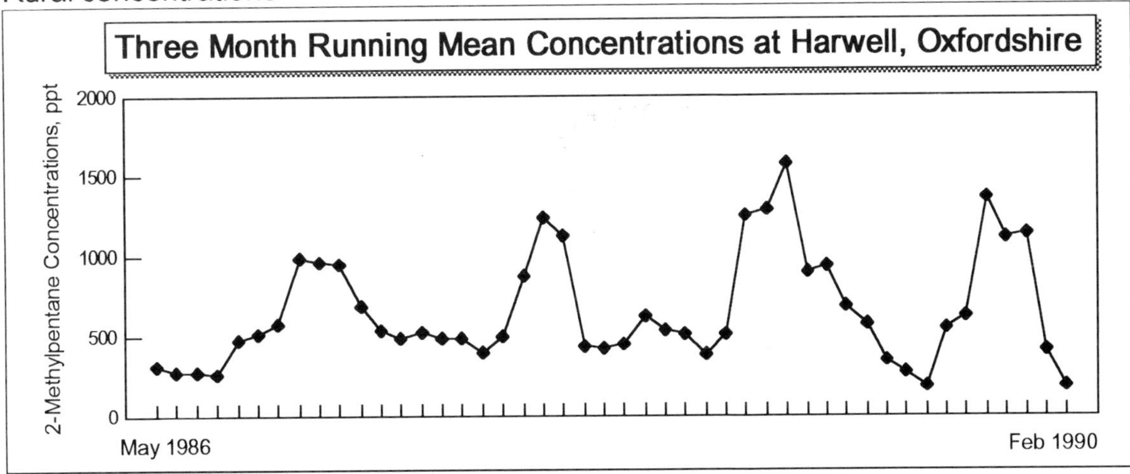

Source: PORG (1993)

Urban Concentrations

1994-95 Monthly Means, ppb									
	Belfast C	Birmingham B	Bristol A	Cardiff B	Edinburgh A	Eltham	Harwell	Middlesbrough	UCL
Jan 94	0.37	0.65	-	0.77	-	0.39	-	0.56	0.75
Feb 94	0.55	0.92	-	0.78	0.24	0.43	-	0.82	1.34
Mar 94	0.22	0.39	-	0.47	0.19	0.38	-	0.94	0.60
Apr 94	0.24	0.38	0.19	0.51	0.26	0.63	-	2.04	0.87
May 94	0.39	0.45	0.42	0.95	0.48	0.92	-	0.25	1.42
Jun 94	0.37	0.43	0.35	0.53	0.30	0.40	-	0.14	0.75
Jul 94	0.29	0.50	0.18	0.66	0.39	0.61	-	1.14	0.73
Aug 94	0.32	0.77	0.49	0.64	0.45	0.33	-	0.56	0.36
Sep 94	0.65	0.84	0.56	0.48	0.47	0.62	-	2.35	0.80
Oct 94	0.78	0.91	1.12	0.80	0.59	0.63	-	1.16	1.26
Nov 94	0.66	1.08	0.79	0.82	0.32	0.74	-	1.24	1.38
Dec 94	0.65	1.79	0.69	1.02	0.51	0.78	-	0.36	1.15
Jan 95	0.40	0.53	0.61	0.69	0.33	0.78	0.15	0.39	0.48
Feb 95	0.29	0.49	0.50	0.64	0.23	0.61	0.10	0.34	0.46

Source: Dollard (1995)

Chemical formula : C_6H_{14}

Alternative names :

Type of pollutant : (Volatile) organic compound (VOC), hydrocarbon

Structure :

$$CH_3CH_2\underset{\displaystyle CH_3}{\underset{|}{C}}HCH_2CH_3$$

Air quality data summary :

Rural concentrations

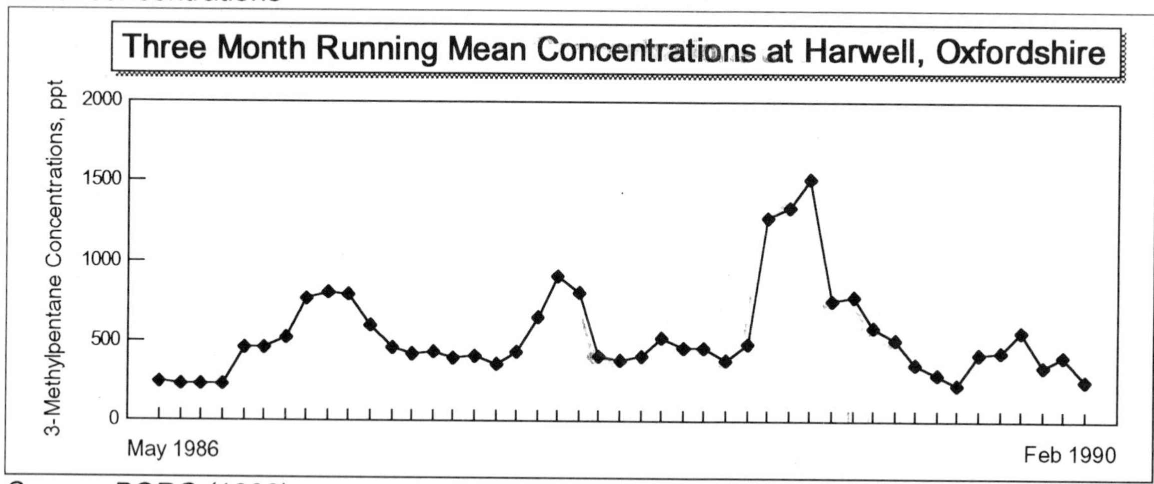

Source: PORG (1993)

Urban Concentrations

1994-95 Monthly Means, ppb									
	Belfast C	Birmingham B	Bristol A	Cardiff B	Edinburgh A	Eltham	Harwell	Middlesbrough	UCL
Jan 94	0.14	0.28	-	0.32	-	0.30	-	0.38	0.25
Feb 94	0.16	0.13	-	0.23	0.27	0.40	-	0.73	1.04
Mar 94	0.06	0.40	-	0.15	0.12	0.34	-	0.70	0.24
Apr 94	0.06	0.39	0.09	0.30	0.15	0.66	-	1.36	0.10
May 94	0.15	0.44	0.44	0.52	0.09	0.22	-	0.22	0.21
Jun 94	0.26	0.30	0.36	0.37	0.22	0.46	-	0.16	0.69
Jul 94	0.30	0.52	0.49	0.48	0.43	0.34	-	0.60	0.72
Aug 94	0.35	0.45	0.48	0.25	0.37	0.05	-	0.29	0.36
Sep 94	0.49	0.28	0.53	0.20	0.42	0.34	-	1.72	0.66
Oct 94	0.78	0.19	1.33	0.09	0.06	0.23	-	1.17	1.11
Nov 94	0.59	0.85	0.81	0.12	0.11	0.75	-	1.03	1.30
Dec 94	0.46	0.63	0.88	0.74	0.44	0.25	-	0.36	0.76
Jan 95	0.38	0.31	0.63	0.54	0.29	0.58	0.07	0.41	0.50
Feb 95	0.29	0.29	0.34	0.48	0.21	0.36	0.05	0.30	0.45

Source: Dollard (1995)

2-Methyl-2-pentene

Chemical formula : C_6H_{12}

Alternative name : 2-methylpent-2-ene

Type of pollutant : (Volatile) organic compound (VOC), hydrocarbon

Structure :

$$CH_3-\underset{\displaystyle CH_3}{\underset{|}{C}}=CH-CH_2-CH_3$$

Air quality data summary :

Mean Air Concentration in Leeds, 19/8/94 to 8/9/94	
Location	21 day mean, $\mu g/m^3$
Albion Street	0.052
Cliff Lane	0.034
EUN monitoring site	0.046
Kerbside site	0.066
Kirkstall Road	0.094
Park site	0.053
Queen Street	0.043
Vicar Lane	0.161

Source: Bartle et al. (1995)

3-Methyl-cis-2-pentene

Chemical formula : C_6H_{12}

Alternative name : 3-methyl cis pent-2-ene

Type of pollutant : (Volatile) organic compound (VOC), hydrocarbon

Structure :

$$CH_3—CH_2—\underset{\displaystyle CH_3}{\underset{|}{C}}{=}\underset{\displaystyle CH_3}{\underset{|}{CH}}$$

Air quality data summary :

Mean Air Concentration in Leeds, 19/8/94 to 8/9/94	
Location	21 day mean, $\mu g/m^3$
Albion Street	0.061
Cliff Lane	0.043
EUN monitoring site	0.053
Kerbside site	0.070
Kirkstall Road	0.117
Park site	0.048
Queen Street	0.053
Vicar Lane	0.206

Source: Bartle et al.(1995)

Chemical formula : C_6H_{12}

Alternative name : 3-methyl-trans-pent-2-ene

Type of pollutant : (Volatile) organic compound (VOC), hydrocarbon

Structure :

$$CH_3-CH_2-\underset{\displaystyle CH_3}{\underset{|}{C}}=\overset{\displaystyle CH_3}{\overset{|}{CH}}$$

Air quality data summary :

Mean Air Concentration in Leeds, 19/8/94 to 8/9/94	
Location	21 day mean, $\mu g/m^3$
Albion Street	0.044
Cliff Lane	0.040
EUN monitoring site	0.041
Kerbside site	0.064
Kirkstall Road	0.096
Park site	0.045
Queen Street	0.053
Vicar Lane	0.181

Source: Bartle et al. (1995)

Chemical formula : C_4H_6O

Alternative names : Methacrolein

Type of pollutant : (Volatile) organic compound (VOC), hydrocarbon, oxygenate

Structure :

$$CH_2{=}C(CH_3){-}CHO$$

Air quality data summary :

Month 1993	Air Concentration at Harwell site, ppb
	Monthly Mean
August	0.014
September	0.007

Source: Solberg et al. (1994)

1-Methyl-3-n-propylbenzene

Chemical formula : $C_{10}H_{14}$

Alternative name : m-methylpropylbenzene

Type of pollutant : (Volatile) organic compound (VOC), hydrocarbon

Structure :

CH_3

$CH_2CH_2CH_3$

Air quality data summary :

Mean Air Concentration in Leeds, 19/8/94 to 8/9/94	
Location	21 day mean, $\mu g/m^3$
Albion Street	0.058
Cliff Lane	0.033
EUN monitoring site	0.054
Kerbside site	0.085
Kirkstall Road	0.116
Park site	0.060
Queen Street	0.071
Vicar Lane	0.224

Source: Bartle et al. (1995)

Methyl(1)pyrene

Chemical formula : $C_{17}H_{12}$

Alternative names :

Type of pollutant : Polynuclear Aromatic Hydrocarbon (PAH)

Structure :

CH3

Air quality data summary :

Urban Concentrations:

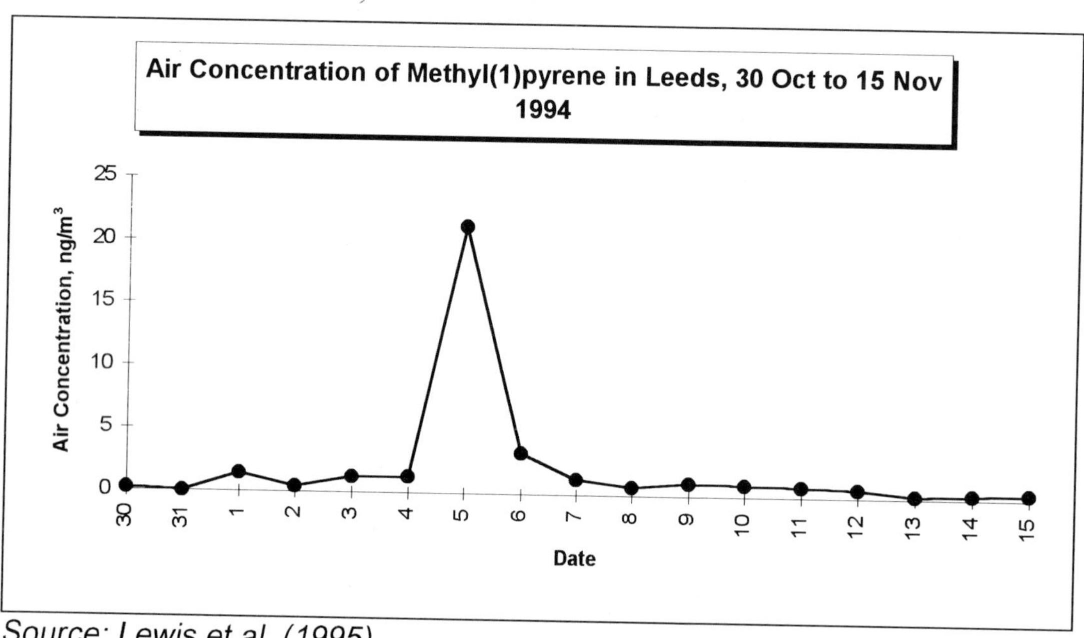

Source: Lewis et al. (1995)

Methyl(2)pyrene

Chemical formula : $C_{17}H_{12}$

Alternative names :

Type of pollutant : Polynuclear Aromatic Hydrocarbon (PAH)

Structure :

Air quality data summary :

Urban Concentrations:

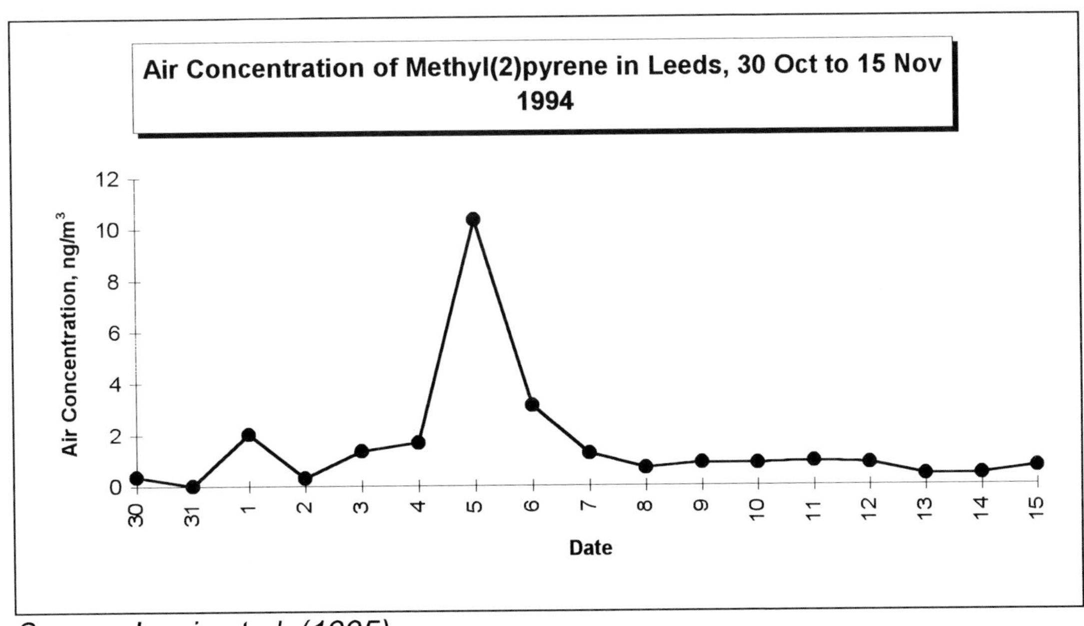

Source: Lewis et al. (1995)

Chemical formula : Mo

Alternative names : Particulate molybdenum

Type of pollutant : Suspended particulate matter, trace element

Air quality data summary :

Rural Concentrations

Location	Average Annual Concentrations, ng/m^3	
	Mean	Mean
	1972-1981	1982-1991
Harwell, Oxfordshire.	<0.7	<1
Styrrup, Nottinghamshire.	<1	<4
Trebanos, Glamorgan.	<0.8	-
Wraymires, Cumbria.	<0.5	<1

Source: Cawse et al. (1994)

Molybdenum in rain

Chemical formula : Mo

Alternative names : Precipitation molybdenum

Type of pollutant : Trace contaminant of rain, trace element

Air quality data summary :

Rural Concentrations

Location	Average Annual Rainfall Concentration, µg per litre	
	1972-1981	1982-1991 *
Harwell, Oxfordshire.	<1	<1
Styrrup, Nottinghamshire.	<2	<1
Wraymires, Cumbria.	<0.6	<0.7

Source: Cawse et al. (1994)

Note: total deposition expressed as apparent rainfall concentration.
* based on soluble fraction only.

Chemical formula : $C_{10}H_8$

Alternative names : PAH EPA no.55

Type of pollutant : Polynuclear Aromatic Hydrocarbon (PAH)

Structure :

Air quality data summary :

Location	Season 1992	Total Concentration in Air ng/m^3
Edgbaston	Winter (February)	13.24
Edgbaston	Summer (August)	1.87
Wasthills	Summer (August)	0.34

Source: Smith and Harrison (1994)

Mean Air Concentration in Leeds, 19/8/94 to 8/9/94	
Location	21 day mean, µg/m^3
Albion Street	0.236
Cliff Lane	0.051
EUN monitoring site	0.096
Kerbside site	0.168
Kirkstall Road	0.136
Park site	0.077
Queen Street	0.086
Vicar Lane	0.272

Source: Bartle et al. (1995)

Chemical formula : Ni

Alternative names : Particulate nickel

Type of pollutant : Suspended particulate matter, trace element

Air quality data summary :

Rural Concentrations

Location	Average Annual Concentrations, ng/m^3				
	Mean	Trend	Mean		Trend
	1972-1981	%/yr	1982-1991		%/yr
Harwell, Oxfordshire.	6.6	nst	3.3	*	-6.4
Styrrup, Nottinghamshire.	9.4	-6.8	5.6		-4.3
Trebanos, Glamorgan.	91.7	-	45.4		-7.3
Wraymires, Cumbria.	4.6	nst	2.6	**	-5.2

Source: Cawse et al. (1994)

Note: * only 80% of measurements were positive.
** only 58% of measurements were positive.
nst=no significant trend

Urban Concentrations

Location	Mean Annual Concentrations, ng/m^3						
	1972-1981	1985	1986	1987	1988	1989	1990
Brent	-	8.6	7.1	8.8	20.8	6.0	12.8
Central London	-	7.6	8.5	8.8	10.1	8.8	8.6
Glasgow C	-	8.5	4.1	8.1	11.1	9.4	8.3
Leeds	-	14.8	10.1	13.1	10.0	12.0	10.0
Motherwell	-	18.5	16.0	19.1	21.1	23.0	18.8
Swansea	81.8	-	-	-	-	-	-

Source: DoE (1992), Pattenden (1974).

Location	Nature of site	Measurement period	Mean concentration ng/m^3
Altrincham	Residential	1978-1989	17.2
Brent	Residential	1975-1989	11.9
Flixton	Residential	1975-1989	9.8
Lambeth	Residential	1976-1982	14.5
Manchester City North	Industrial/ Residential	1975-1988	13.2
Manchester City South	Residential	1975-1989	13.2
Walsall	Industrial	1976-1989	31.2
Wraymires	Rural	1970-1989	3.1

Source: Lee et al. (1994)

Nickel in rain

Chemical formula : Ni

Alternative names : Precipitation nickel

Type of pollutant : Trace contaminant of rain, trace element

Air quality data summary :

Rural Concentrations

Location	Average Annual Rainfall Concentration µg per litre	
	1972-1981	1982-1991 *
Harwell, Oxfordshire.	11	3.0
Styrrup, Nottinghamshire.	10	5.6
Wraymires, Cumbria.	6.1	3.5

Source: Cawse et al. (1994)

Note: total deposition expressed as apparent rainfall concentration.
* based on soluble fraction only.

Nitrate aerosol

Chemical formula : NO_3

Alternative names : Particulate nitrate

Type of pollutant : Suspended particulate matter

Air quality data summary :

Location	1992 Monthly Mean Concentration in Air, µg/m³											
	Jan	Feb	Mar	Apr	May	Jun	Jul	Aug	Sep	Oct	Nov	Dec
Eskdalemuir	0.89	0.54	0.29	0.45	0.01	0.36	0.23	0.15	0.64	0.24	0.17	0.57
High Muffles	1.19	1.24	0.87	1.04	0.52	0.88	0.49	0.60	1.18	0.60	0.53	1.13

Source: Schaug et al. (1994)

Note: These data represent results for a mixture of nitric acid and nitrate in aerosol.

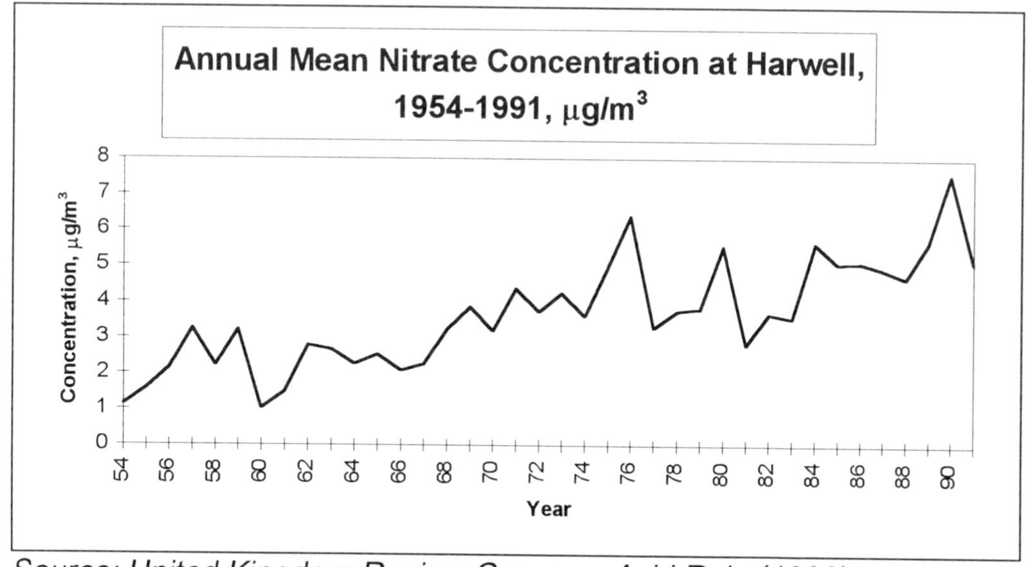

Source: United Kingdom Review Group on Acid Rain (1990)

Chemical formula : NO_3

Alternative names : Precipitation nitrate

Type of pollutant : Trace contaminant of rain

Air quality data summary :

Rural Concentrations

Location	Average Annual Rainfall Concentration, µg per litre	
	1972 - 1981	1982-1991*
Harwell, Oxfordshire	1314	5680
Styrrup, Nottinghamshire	1402	5870
Wraymires, Cumbria	552	2220

Source: Cawse et al. (1994)

Note: total deposition expressed as apparent rainfall concentration
*based on soluble fraction only

Site	Precipitation-weighted Annual Mean Nitrate Concentration, 1986-93, (μ eql^{-1})								
	OS Grid ref	1986	1987	1988	1989	1990	1991	1992	1993
Achanarras	ND 151550	14	22	24	25	18	22	16	18
Balquhidder	NN 521206	13	21	16	13	10	17	13	18
Bannisdale	NY 515043	20	18	21	19	17	21	19	23
Barcombe Mills	TQ 437149	27	31	25	30	24	36	25	19
Beddgelert	SH 556518	17	16	13	11	10	12	10	14
Bottesford	SK 797376	41	41	44	50	34	43	36	34
Compton	SU 512804	38	46	38	36	28	36	39	28
Cow Green Reservoir	NY 817298	19	21	25	20	20	21	23	25
Driby	TF 386744	39	44	47	48	46	50	46	38
Eskdalemuir	NT 235028	15	18	19	18	15	19	16	19
Flatford Mill	TM 077333	39	45	43	56	38	44	40	30
Glen Dye	NO 642864	-	31	32	31	29	33	28	33
Goonhilly	SW 723214	19	27	16	22	20	31	17	23
High Muffles	SE 776939	37	43	47	45	38	47	37	36
Hillsborough Forest	J 243577	-	-	-	26	16	23	16	21
Jenny Hurn	SK 816986	44	48	44	51	43	45	42	33
Llyn Brianne	SN 822507	12	14	13	14	16	18	16	14
Loch Dee	NX 468779	14	19	18	14	14	16	15	19
Lough Navar	H 065545	8	8	7	9	7	9	9	10

Site	Precipitation-weighted Annual Mean Nitrate Concentration, 1986-93, (μ eql^{-1})								
	OS Grid ref	1986	1987	1988	1989	1990	1991	1992	1993
Plynlimon	SN 823854	-	-	-	10	9	14	13	13
Polloch	NM 792689	-	-	-	-	-	9	9	9
Preston Montford	SJ 432143	22	32	26	31	20	35	38	27
Redesdale	NY 833954	34	26	33	31	26	31	36	26
River Mharcaidh	NH 876052	10	12	10	10	9	10	8	7
Stoke Ferry	TL 700988	48	44	39	55	46	48	43	36
Strathvaich Dam	NH 347750	-	10	8	7	6	9	9	8
Thorganby	SE 676428	41	43	42	49	40	50	42	46
Tycanol Wood	SN 093364	12	15	12	15	11	18	14	12
Wardlow Hay Cop	SK 177739	25	36	31	36	26	38	29	33
Whiteadder	NT 664633	34	29	42	34	23	32	35	29
Woburn	SP 964361	39	40	39	47	35	40	36	31
Yarner Wood	SX 867890	16	24	14	18	13	19	16	20

Source: Campbell et al. (1994a)

Location	1992 Monthly Weighted Mean Concentration in Precipitation, mg/l											
	Jan	Feb	Mar	Apr	May	Jun	Jul	Aug	Sep	Oct	Nov	Dec
Eskdalemuir	0.29	0.21	0.26	0.19	0.26	2.48	0.38	0.13	0.19	0.17	0.16	0.19
High Muffles	0.28	0.43	0.57	0.33	0.67	0.39	0.38	0.40	0.47	0.35	0.36	0.31
Lough Navar	0.12	0.07	0.08	0.06	0.18	0.66	0.14	0.05	0.06	0.06	0.06	0.08
Strath Vaich	0.24	0.07	0.10	0.09	0.46	0.63	0.17	0.12	0.17	0.09	0.04	0.05
Yarner Wood	0.18	0.13	0.16	0.15	1.05	0.44	0.28	0.13	0.35	0.37	0.10	0.13

Source: Schaug et al. (1994)

Chemical formula : HNO_3

Alternative names : Nitric acid gas or vapour

Type of pollutant : Trace gas of NO_y family

Structure : HNO_3

Air quality data summary :

Rural Concentrations

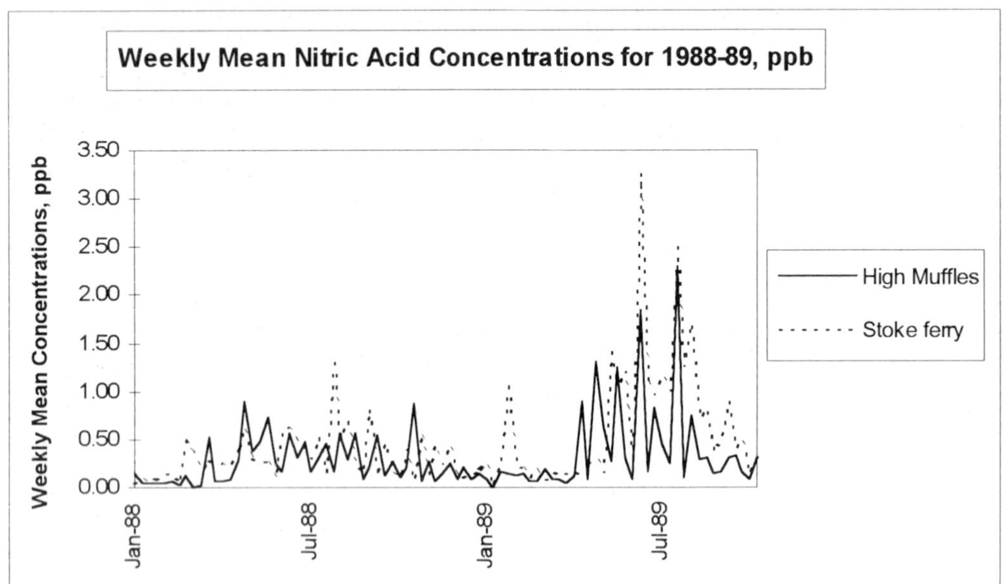

Source: United Kingdom Review Group on Acid Rain (1990)

Chemical formula : NO

Alternative name :

Type of pollutant : Trace gas of NO_x family

Structure :

NO

Air quality data summary :

Urban Concentrations

Nitric Oxide Calendar Year Statistics							
Site	Year	Annual mean (ppb)	Max. run. 8 hour (ppb)	Site	Year	Annual mean (ppb)	Max.run. 8 hour (ppb)
Belfast B	92	23	563	Bridge Place	93	39	625
	93	24	501	(cont.)	94	37	718
	94	21	753				
				Bristol B	93	42	416
Bexley	94	28	420		94	39	588
Billingham	87	28	445	Canvey	78	17	419
	88	21	312		79	12	159
	89	21	274		80	13	323
	90	21	427				
	91	27	539	Cardiff A	92	30	361
	92	27	412		93	22	379
	93	20	351		94	23	407
	94	19	219				
				Central London	72	49	481
Birmingham A	92	31	918		73	49	568
	93	24	240		74	48	205
	94	22	717		75	49	541
					76	65	306
Birmingham B	94	18	975		77	60	638
					78	51	391
Bloomsbury	92	41	404		79	42	423
	93	39	541		80	31	323
	94	39	759		81	46	580
					82	50	844
Bridge Place	90	52	769		83	41	755
	91	59	1002		84	34	334
	92	49	504		85	37	402

Nitric Oxide Calendar Year Statistics							
Site	Year	Annual mean (ppb)	Max. run 8 hour (ppb)	Site	Year	Annual mean (ppb)	Max. run. 8 hour (ppb)
Central London	86	38	294	Harrow	79	30	312
(cont.)	87	51	697		80	26	341
	88	47	589				
	89	48	951	Hull	94	30	520
	90	31	383				
				Islington	77	31	388
Cromwell Road	73	87	834		78	26	439
	74	109	766				
	75	146	846	Ladybower	91	3	56
	76	230	1031		92	2	63
	77	154	645		93	5	94
	78	155	830		94	2	60
	79	127	606				
	82	188	1008	Leeds	93	42	668
	83	208	1453		94	42	942
	84	157	751				
	85	152	594	Leicester	94	21	540
	86	158	750				
	89	221	1603	Liverpool	93	38	449
	90	210	1163		94	33	328
	91	230	1172				
	92	200	837	Lullington Heath	91	2	42
	93	177	899		92	2	176
	94	161	902		93	2	57
					94	1	33
Edinburgh B	93	36	518				
	94	30	348	Manchester A	87	40	869
					88	42	910
Glasgow A	87	53	661		89	43	795
	88	50	460		90	35	677
	89	55	938		91	35	436
	90	54	721		92	44	1039
	91	62	1041		93	35	372
	92	56	672		94	38	711
	93	58	505				
	94	43	574	Newcastle A	92	37	370
					93	44	622
Glasgow B	79	155	952		94	32	358
	81	221	1173				
	82	169	1058	Sheffield	91	65	549
					92	73	897
					93	53	490

Nitric Oxide Calendar Year Statistics							
Site	Year	Annual mean (ppb)	Max. run. 8 hour (ppb)	Site	Year	Annual mean (ppb)	Max. run. 8 hour (ppb)
Sheffield (cont.)	94	53	683	Strath Vaich	91	0.3	3
					92	0.2	1
Sibton	78	2	27		93	0.2	1
	79	4	22		94	0.2	3
Southampton	94	35	621	Walsall	87	55	762
					88	56	1017
Stevenage	77	31	371		89	51	1123
	78	33	410		90	41	946
	79	33	590		91	52	707
	80	27	307		92	53	1130
	81	42	349		93	40	669
	82	38	727		94	36	1104
	83	39	826				
	84	39	542	West London	87	66	890
	85	29	380		88	63	741
	86	38	396		89	80	1160
	87	46	559		90	47	820
	88	45	587		91	59	1107
	89	53	787		92	51	540
	90	45	492		93	42	649
	91	51	720		94	39	655
	92	49	565				
	93	37	379				
	94	33	294				

Source: Bower et al. (1995)

Data displayed for data captures $\geq$ 25 %

Chemical formula : NO_2

Alternative name :

Type of pollutant : Trace gas of NO_x family

Structure :

NO_2

Air quality data summary :

Rural Concentrations

Month	Monthly Mean Concentrations, ppb					
	Ladybower		Lullington Heath		Strath Vaich	
	1992	1993	1992	1993	1992	1993
January	14.0	8.2	27.1	7.4	1.3	0.6
February	10.8	13.2	11.8	18.4	0.6	0.9
March	8.2	11.7	6.0	12.2	0.6	1.3
April	6.9	10.0	6.6	8.9	0.6	1.3
May	8.1	8.0	6.4	8.5	0.9	0.8
June	8.6	10.9	5.0	7.0	0.5	0.6
July	7.8	-	5.4	4.9	0.3	-
August	6.3	5.7	4.7	6.1	0.3	-
September	9.7	8.7	4.4	9.9	1.1	-
October	8.8	9.7	8.9	8.1	0.4	-
November	7.7	17.4	6.8	13.6	0.5	-
December	11.3	6.5	16.0	6.7	1.0	-

Source: Bower et al. (1995)

Nitrogen Dioxide Calendar Year Urban Statistics							
Site	Year	Annual mean (ppb)	Max. run 8 hour (ppb)	Site	Year	Annual mean (ppb)	Max. run 8 hour (ppb)
Belfast B	92	23	78	Central London	72	47	155
	93	22	89		73	38	189
	94	21	80		74	28	142
					75	54	263
Bexley	94	22	76		76	48	140
					77	45	131
Billingham	87	23	80		78	39	121
	88	21	100		79	34	98
	89	22	89		80	34	101
	90	21	93		81	35	90
	91	19	77		82	43	205
	92	18	63		83	39	172
	93	16	50		84	44	103
	94	17	56		85	32	98
					86	35	139
Birmingham A	92	24	82		87	39	184
	93	25	97		88	35	148
	94	24	110		89	37	137
					90	35	93
Birmingham B	94	20	156				
				Cromwell Road	73	52	353
Bloomsbury	92	35	87		74	89	511
	93	34	100		75	112	463
	94	35	171		77	43	158
					78	44	132
Bridge Place	90	37	140		79	36	121
	91	43	335		82	46	803
	92	39	129		83	68	335
	93	34	110		84	50	167
	94	34	245		85	48	223
					86	40	146
Bristol B	93	26	65		89	45	250
	94	23	71		90	42	142
					91	43	340
Canvey	78	19	120		92	41	120
	79	16	53		93	40	153
	80	13	51		94	44	224
Cardiff A	92	25	57	Edinburgh B	93	27	73
	93	23	63		94	27	61
	94	22	114				

Nitrogen Dioxide Calendar Year Urban Statistics							
Site	Year	Annual mean (ppb)	Max run. 8 hour (ppb)	Site	Year	Annual mean (ppb)	Max run. 8 hour (ppb)
Glasgow A	87	31	155	Manchester	91	27	96
	88	30	88		92	31	209
	89	27	195		93	26	104
	90	26	76		94	26	282
	91	26	143				
	92	25	68	Newcastle A	92	27	72
	93	27	77		93	28	75
	94	26	91		94	24	114
Glasgow B	81	50	381	Sheffield	91	28	104
	82	41	261		92	31	103
					93	28	91
Harrow	79	24	73		94	28	86
	80	20	110				
				Sibton	78	8	38
Hull	94	24	71		79	5	39
Islington	77	26	69	Southampton	94	23	67
	78	23	108				
				Stevenage	77	23	64
Ladybower	91	11	41		78	23	83
	92	9	49		79	25	139
	93	10	50		80	18	94
	94	9	48		81	18	89
					82	22	106
Leeds	93	26	61		83	20	56
	94	29	120		84	23	88
					85	25	68
Leicester	94	23	74		86	21	77
					87	27	106
Liverpool	93	27	80		88	24	120
	94	26	85		89	25	131
					90	25	85
Lullington Heath	91	8	48		91	24	90
	92	7	67		92	22	58
	93	9	41		93	21	58
	94	8	59		94	24	61
Manchester A	87	29	185	Strath Vaich	91	2.0	21
	88	28	215		92	0.7	11
	89	25	185		93	1.0	12
	90	28	150		94	1.0	15

Nitrogen Dioxide Calendar Year Urban Statistics							
Site	Year	Annual mean (ppb)	Max. run. 8 hour (ppb)	Site	Year	Annual mean (ppb)	Max. run. 8 hour (ppb)
Walsall	87	30	86	West London	87	35	196
	88	27	88		88	37	163
	89	29	159		89	43	263
	90	25	121		90	35	134
	91	26	97		91	35	339
	92	27	205		92	32	94
	93	24	79		93	31	114
	94	25	158		94	31	187

Source: Bower et al. (1995)

Data displayed for data captures ≥ 25 %

Urban and suburban NO_2 concentrations

Key to site types:
21 >50 metres from nearest road
22 <50 metres
23 kerbside
99 indeterminate

Six month mean concentrations over the period July-December in ppb

East	North	Site Name	Type	1986	1991
3929	8057	ABERDEEN 2	22	12.9	10.3
3758	4285	ACCRINGTON 5	21	16.0	24.8
4440	4167	ACKWORTH 1	22	22.2	24.0
5208	1824	ACTON 13	23		49.0
5052	1646	ADDLESTONE 1	22	18.2	35.0
4417	3555	ALFRETON 4	21	19.0	
4417	4279	ALLERTON BYWATER 1	22	17.3	21.3
4404	4293	ALLERTON BYWATER 2	22	19.3	
2885	6930	ALLOA 6	22		20.5
4187	6132	ALNWICK 2	21	6.8	11.0
4726	1401	ALTON 2	22	12.3	16.0
2880	6970	ALVA 3	22		16.3
2163	2079	AMROTH (Dyfed) 1	21	4.2	5.8
3687	5208	APPELBY 1	21		11.8
4284	5871	ASHINGTON 4	21		12.5
3576	3991	ASHTON-IN-MAKERFIELD 1	21	24.0	29.4
4561	4131	ASKERN 8	23	20.2	
3870	4228	BACUP 4	22	16.8	
5460	1831	BARKING 15	22		37.2
3894	3385	BARLASTON 1	21	15.3	19.3
4342	4067	BARNSLEY 12	21	15.0	23.8
4348	4094	BARNSLEY 8	22	19.4	28.1
4370	4055	BARNSLEY 9	21		26.0
3197	4697	BARROW-IN-FURNESS 3	21	11.2	19.6
3754	1656	BATH 6	22	18.4	31.8
4243	4242	BATLEY 2	22	17.5	23.9
5056	2486	BEDFORD 10	22	20.0	24.6
4266	5821	BEDLINGTON 7	21	12.5	15.8
		BELFAST 11	21	17.9	23.7
		BELFAST 12	21	18.0	20.1
		BELFAST 13	22		23.9
		BELFAST 14	21	13.7	16.4
		BELFAST 15	22	18.2	25.6
		BELFAST 17	21	12.2	
		BELFAST 18	21	10.5	
		BELFAST 33	21	11.9	24.0
		BELFAST 39	23	16.4	22.2

East	North	Site Name	Type	1986	1991
		BELFAST 40	21	10.0	14.9
3965	2943	BILSTON 19	21	19.2	24.4
3315	3882	BIRKENHEAD 2	22	15.0	24.4
4115	2889	BIRMINGHAM 26	21	23.5	25.3
3678	4281	BLACKBURN 16	22	19.2	
3702	4270	BLACKBURN 21	21	15.6	
3317	4367	BLACKPOOL 6	22	15.3	
4857	2337	BLETCHLEY 2	21	15.4	
4314	5817	BLYTH 15	21	13.5	
4307	5818	BLYTH 16	21		15.0
2989	6808	BONESS 2	22	10.2	19.9
2842	6811	BONNYBRIDGE 1	21	11.1	30.0
3345	3948	BOOTLE 6	22	19.7	
4154	4273	BRADFORD 17	22	16.0	
4133	4334	BRADFORD 19	22		22.7
4151	4351	BRADFORD 20	21	13.7	19.3
4155	4333	BRADFORD 21	21		
4158	4320	BRADFORD 22	22	17.3	26.1
4186	4331	BRADFORD 23	23		24.2
4163	4329	BRADFORD 6	22	19.8	31.8
5757	2235	BRAINTREE 8	21	17.2	23.0
3296	1369	BRIDGWATER 2	21	13.0	
3918	2874	BRIERLEY HILL 15	22	18.0	24.2
4405	3736	BRIMINGTON 1	21	18.2	23.5
3634	1763	BRISTOL 26	21	14.8	20.2
3590	1732	BRISTOL 28	99		
3080	6723	BROXBURN 2	22		25.5
6340	2895	BUNGAY 1	21	13.1	
5730	1619	BURHAM 1	21	17.0	20.0
4047	3087	BURNTWOOD 1	21	14.4	24.6
4240	3235	BURTON-UPON-TRENT 12	22	19.8	24.6
3811	4125	BURY 8	21		
3819	4116	BURY 9	21		24.3
4993	3900	CAENBY (LINCS) 1	21	16.0	18.1
5343	1735	CAMBERWELL 4	22	27.0	
1628	407	CAMBORNE 1	21		7.2
5458	2573	CAMBRIDGE 14	99		

East	North	Site Name	Type	1986	1991
2278	6543	CAMPHILL 1	21		6.4
3989	3117	CANNOCK 18	22		22.7
3193	1773	CARDIFF 12	21	21.5	
5079	2468	CARDINGTON 2	21	13.3	16.7
3401	5572	CARLISLE 10	21	14.2	16.0
3407	5555	CARLISLE 12	23	16.7	18.9
3398	5550	CARLISLE 13	22	12.0	17.1
		CARRICKFERGUS 2	21	5.6	8.4
4434	4255	CASTLEFORD 9	22	21.0	
4437	4257	CASTLEFORD 10	99		24.4
5291	1790	CENTRAL LONDON	22		44.3
3909	4053	CHADDERTON 4	99	26.2	
4356	3962	CHAPELTOWN 3	22		
3859	3886	CHEADLE & GATLEY 6	21		22.8
5271	1781	CHELSEA 6	21	29.4	40.0
4273	5507	CHESTER-LE-STREET 4	21	14.0	18.9
4372	3709	CHESTERFIELD 18	22	16.2	24.2
3585	4178	CHORLEY 6	22	19.1	25.7
4192	4254	CLECKHEATON 5	21	20.5	25.3
4428	3142	COALVILLE 5	22	20.9	24.0
2738	6652	COATBRIDGE 11	22	18.2	
2712	6638	COATBRIDGE 5	21	16.4	22.4
2717	6669	COATBRIDGE 9	21	41.2	
4513	3987	CONISBROUGH 7	22		
4501	3996	CONISBROUGH 8	21	16.0	
4337	2788	COVENTRY 13	21	20.5	26.1
4297	5814	COWPEN 1	21	10.1	
5269	1362	CRAWLEY 3	21	14.2	19.3
2064	2062	CRESSELLY (Dyfed) 1	21	4.3	9.1
3703	3550	CREWE 9	21		20.1
3321	3990	CROSBY 3	21	12.5	20.1
4388	4092	CUDWORTH 1	22	23.8	26.9
2293	6492	DALRY 1	22		15.9
2288	6492	DALRY 2	22		
3986	2991	DARLASTON 3	21		
3978	2968	DARLASTON 6	21		
4289	5149	DARLINGTON 10	22		21.9
5543	1744	DARTFORD 9	21		34.5
4309	4099	DARTON 1	22	20.0	26.8
5376	1775	DEPTFORD 3	21	25.6	
4353	3342	DERBY 17	22		31.8
4345	3333	DERBY 18	22		
4224	4203	DEWSBURY 10	21	18.8	24.8

East	North	Site Name	Type	1986	1991
4411	1068	DIBDEN PURLIEU 1	21	10.3	14.2
4528	3861	DINNINGTON 4	21		
4591	4043	DONCASTER 19	23	24.5	28.0
4577	4030	DONCASTER 27	22	24.0	
4552	4028	DONCASTER 28	22	25.0	
4623	4051	DONCASTER 29	22	19.7	
4613	3983	DONCASTER 32	23		20.5
4532	4075	DONCASTER 33	21	18.2	21.5
5175	1807	EALING 3	22		39.0
4420	5435	EASINGTON 1	21	13.8	20.0
5608	992	EASTBOURNE 4	23	14.5	22.7
3363	3815	EASTHAM (WIRRAL) 1	21	13.1	20.3
3230	6765	EDINBURGH 12	22	11.6	
3254	6734	EDINBURGH 14	23	18.6	25.9
3009	5107	EGREMONT 1	21	8.1	
4086	4214	ELLAND 14	21	13.4	
4109	4209	ELLAND 2	22	19.2	23.2
3398	3759	ELLESMERE PORT 12	22	17.0	28.2
3384	3775	ELLESMERE PORT 2	99		
3441	3759	ELLESMERE PORT 9	21		23.3
5338	1958	ENFIELD 14	21		27.0
3235	6026	ESKDALEMUIR 1	21	2.7	
4535	5206	ESTON 9	21		
2883	6802	FALKIRK 5	21	13.6	20.1
2888	6821	FALKIRK 6	22	12.9	21.5
4429	4195	FEATHERSTONE 1	21	19.8	22.8
4294	5324	FERRYHILL 1	21		16.0
3606	3926	FIDDLERS FERRY 3	21	22.8	27.1
4402	4324	GARFORTH 1	21	18.5	27.0
4254	5615	GATESHEAD 8	22	15.5	
4256	3619	GATESHEAD 10	22		24.3
2595	6653	GLASGOW 20	22	23.7	
2572	6681	GLASGOW 42	21		27.9
2638	6638	GLASGOW 47	21	14.3	20.8
2533	6641	GLASGOW 51	22	14.8	23.4
2594	6643	GLASGOW 52	22	19.7	27.0
2520	6712	GLASGOW 66	22	16.1	22.0
2613	6673	GLASGOW 68	21	18.8	
2568	6663	GLASGOW 69	22	20.5	26.1
2612	6627	GLASGOW 73	21	13.3	18.7
2651	6621	GLASGOW 80	21		18.0
2593	6679	GLASGOW 86	21	16.7	24.0
2617	6654	GLASGOW 87	21	19.6	26.9

East	North	Site Name	Type	1986	1991
2600	6643	GLASGOW 91	21	13.8	22.8
2620	6639	GLASGOW 92	22	15.2	25.2
2585	6617	GLASGOW 93	23	18.8	28.2
2679	6642	GLASGOW 95	21	14.2	17.0
2574	6659	GLASGOW 96	22	19.6	28.3
2611	6678	GLASGOW 98	22		24.0
3832	2179	GLOUCESTER 4	22	15.5	22.5
3854	2189	GLOUCESTER 6	21	16.4	19.4
4462	4043	GOLDTHORPE 1	22	20.3	27.6
2929	6815	GRANGEMOUTH 2	21	14.5	21.8
2923	6805	GRANGEMOUTH 4	22	14.4	
2947	6830	GRANGEMOUTH 8	22	19.2	
5382	1773	GREENWICH 9	21		34.2
4414	4091	GRIMETHORPE 2	22	16.8	
4406	4080	GRIMETHORPE 3	21	19.5	21.9
5359	1862	HACKNEY 11	21	28.0	
5356	1853	HACKNEY 4	21	30.3	
5351	1854	HACKNEY 9	23	31.6	
4093	4254	HALIFAX 16	22	22.8	35.7
4091	4240	HALIFAX 9	21	11.8	
2720	6550	HAMILTON 5	22	10.3	
5227	1785	HAMMERSMITH 6	22	31.0	40.1
4484	4023	HARLINGTON, YORKS 1	21	16.3	
5160	1904	HARROW 7	21		
4489	3807	HARTHILL(S.YORKS) 1	21	18.8	22.5
4505	5326	HARTLEPOOL 12	21	17.6	21.8
4488	5294	HARTLEPOOL 14	21	17.2	
4397	3697	HASLAND 1	21	15.5	20.2
3785	4234	HASLINGDEN 4	22	17.7	22.1
4058	8373	HATTON 1	22		8.8
4434	3464	HEANOR 7	21		21.7
4428	4134	HEMSWORTH 3	22		
4355	5469	HETTON-LE-HOLE 3	22	15.0	17.3
4428	2938	HINCKLEY 1	21	18.5	21.8
4472	3093	HINCKLEY 5	21	13.9	18.8
4144	4085	HOLMFIRTH 5	21	14.1	18.2
4292	4184	HORBURY 4	22		
4340	5501	HOUGHTON-LE-SPRINGS 2	22		20.8
4373	4005	HOYLAND NETHER 5	22	18.5	20.3
4143	4164	HUDDERSFIELD 19	21	18.7	29.5
4158	4165	HUDDERSFIELD 6	22	23.2	29.0
4964	2361	HUSBORNE CRAWLEY 1	99		
5440	1864	ILFORD 6	21	29.0	38.7

East	North	Site Name	Type	1986	1991
4466	3418	ILKESTON 7	21	13.7	25.6
4468	3425	ILKESTON 8	21	19.1	25.2
5175	4150	IMMINGHAM 5	21	14.6	18.7
3594	4048	INCE-IN-MAKERFIELD 1	22	16.5	23.2
2296	6714	INVERKIP 11	21		
2243	6723	INVERKIP 5	21	5.9	
2200	6609	INVERKIP 6	22	4.6	
2210	6739	INVERKIP 7	21	5.0	
2202	6674	INVERKIP 9	21	5.9	
6160	2447	IPSWICH 14	21	20.2	26.8
5316	1842	ISLINGTON 9	22	31.4	34.1
4054	4408	KEIGHLEY 10	22	13.7	26.4
4061	4412	KEIGHLEY 11	23	16.0	22.9
5254	1797	KENSINGTON 11	22	31.2	42.1
5243	1813	KENSINGTON 12	23	39.2	53.7
5267	1791	KENSINGTON 8	21		35.0
4869	2782	KETTERING 5	23	18.7	22.4
3836	3541	KIDSGROVE 1	21		19.8
2317	6545	KILBIRNIE 2	99		
2427	6380	KILMARNOCK 2	23	19.2	19.6
1894	2008	KILPAISON BURROWS 1	21	3.8	7.2
2722	6780	KILSYTH 1	21	9.7	17.4
5078	4281	KINGSTON-UPON-HULL 12	21	16.4	
5181	1685	KINGSTON-UPON-THAMES 14	21	16.0	
4416	4303	KIPPAX 1	22	22.3	22.4
5056	3271	KIRKBY UNDERWOOD 1	21	12.4	
4181	4181	KIRKHEATON 1	21	20.2	24.4
4177	4185	KIRKHEATON 2	22		20.8
2659	6739	KIRKINTILLOCH 5	21	9.7	18.4
4493	4233	KNOTTINGLEY 1	21	20.7	28.0
5304	1758	LAMBETH 7	21	30.8	41.6
4586	3873	LANGOLD (BASSETLAW) 1	22	17.1	30.3
4282	4342	LEEDS 24	22	23.7	32.2
4321	4348	LEEDS 26	22	21.8	26.7
4269	4369	LEEDS 28	21	14.8	
4271	4335	LEEDS 34	22	19.4	
4299	4274	LEEDS 36	22	19.0	
4267	4367	LEEDS 37	21		17.8
4304	4335	LEEDS 4	23	28.3	27.9
2653	6769	LENNOXTOWN 7	21	9.4	15.2
4456	11394	LERWICK 3	21	2.2	
5381	1749	LEWISHAM 14	99	26.2	32.8
5382	1864	LEYTON 14	21	26.8	33.1

East	North	Site Name	Type	1986	1991
4991	2390	LIDLINGTON 2	22	19.0	21.1
4974	3714	LINCOLN 5	21	17.7	19.9
5971	2312	LITTLE HORKESLEY 1	21	13.8	17.5
3938	4164	LITTLEBOROUGH 5	21	21.7	24.1
3345	3908	LIVERPOOL 16	22	20.7	29.1
3425	3866	LIVERPOOL 18	23	17.8	24.8
3409	3944	LIVERPOOL 19	21	14.3	20.9
3371	3875	LIVERPOOL 21	23	16.7	25.1
3384	3922	LIVERPOOL 22	22	26.2	33.5
5324	1814	LONDON CITY 16	99	31.0	44.2
5325	1818	LONDON CITY 17	99	34.5	38.4
		LONDONDERRY 11	22		17.8
4489	3339	LONG EATON 1	22	21.7	33.5
4038	8473	LONGSIDE 1	99		5.6
4295	5912	LYNEMOUTH 2	21	10.2	11.1
3919	3726	MACCLESFIELD 4	21		21.0
3916	3745	MACCLESFIELD 5	99		
5754	1555	MAIDSTONE 7	22	23.2	33.9
4530	3922	MALTBY 2	22	20.8	23.1
3838	3981	MANCHESTER 11	23	33.3	38.8
3836	3925	MANCHESTER 13	21	22.2	26.6
3875	3985	MANCHESTER 15	22	27.8	30.1
3865	4009	MANCHESTER 19	21	22.8	26.4
3847	4023	MANCHESTER 21	21	23.5	23.4
3835	3965	MANCHESTER 22	21	22.2	29.1
3852	3962	MANCHESTER 24	22	23.8	29.3
4538	3642	MANSFIELD WOODHOUSE 2	21		22.5
4567	3681	MANSFIELD 7	23	18.8	23.7
4566	3604	MANSFIELD 8	22	16.0	23.3
3255	1830	MARSHFIELD 1	21	16.4	
3042	5361	MARYPORT 1	99		
4472	4005	MEXBOROUGH 19	21	15.2	19.7
4495	5208	MIDDLESBROUGH 29	21	22.8	23.3
3871	4063	MIDDLETON 3	22	23.5	31.5
3932	4122	MILNROW 2	21	21.0	27.3
2052	2136	MINWEAR 1	21	3.1	5.0
2700	6708	MOODIESBURN 1	21	15.5	18.6
2662	6686	MOODIESBURN 4	22	18.0	23.1
4695	4155	MOORENDS 1	23	18.8	20.5
4263	4278	MORLEY 4	21	19.8	27.1
2757	6564	MOTHERWELL 14	22	15.6	33.2
2760	6596	MOTHERWELL 16	99		17.9
2760	6596	MOTHERWELL 17	22		17.2

East	North	Site Name	Type	1986	1991
4668	3686	NEW OLLERTON 1	21	20.2	
4664	3682	NEW OLLERTON 2	21		21.4
4309	5879	NEWBIGGIN 1	22		13.7
4199	5671	NEWBURN 2	22	13.4	19.6
4248	5652	NEWCASTLE UPON TYNE 17	22	24.0	29.1
4251	5645	NEWCASTLE UPON TYNE 27	23	22.8	28.6
4214	5636	NEWCASTLE UPON TYNE 31	21	14.3	19.5
4286	5645	NEWCASTLE UPON TYNE 32	22		
3835	3489	NEWCASTLE-U-LYME 10	22	22.5	23.0
3822	3466	NEWCASTLE-U-LYME 11	21		
3848	3462	NEWCASTLE-U-LYME 13	22	24.5	26.7
3851	3489	NEWCASTLE-U-LYME 19	22	15.7	22.9
3310	1880	NEWPORT (Gwent) 22	22	19.4	
		NEWRY 3	22	14.7	14.1
		NEWRY 4	22	20.4	24.3
1964	2052	NEYLAND 1	23	5.0	8.4
4385	4224	NORMANTON 3	21	21.3	23.8
6233	3099	NORWICH 7	21		29.7
4557	3401	NOTTINGHAM 18	23	22.4	23.7
4538	3452	NOTTINGHAM 19	99	21.2	
4575	3403	NOTTINGHAM 20	99		31.2
4540	3449	NOTTINGHAM 2	22		
4576	3403	NOTTINGHAM 3	22	28.0	
4558	3419	NOTTINGHAM 4	21	20.7	25.6
4530	3398	NOTTINGHAM 6	21	19.5	22.4
4591	3416	NOTTINGHAM 9	22	20.6	23.0
3920	4057	OLDHAM 13	21		24.8
3944	4058	OLDHAM 17	22	23.2	23.9
3929	4054	OLDHAM 3	21	20.2	26.8
3538	4049	ORRELL 1	22	21.3	18.8
4203	4457	OTLEY 3	22	14.9	21.6
4510	2060	OXFORD 18	22	15.0	24.1
4251	5532	PELTON 1	22	12.1	15.8
4246	4030	PENISTONE 2	99	15.8	
4136	8461	PETERHEAD 1	23		20.3
4113	8465	PETERHEAD 2	21		10.6
4125	8448	PETERHEAD 3	21		8.6
4425	3622	PILSLEY 7	21	16.0	
2475	547	PLYMOUTH 11	22		25.4
4455	4220	PONTEFRACT 9	22	19.0	26.2
3297	2005	PONTYPOOL 13	21	13.2	13.1
3282	2009	PONTYPOOL 7	22	16.2	19.9
2780	1883	PORT TALBOT 14	22	11.9	22.0

East	North	Site Name	Type	1986	1991
		PORTADOWN 4	22	8.9	19.4
4652	1019	PORTSMOUTH 10	21		27.6
4408	3278	RATCLIFFE 13	21	13.3	
4438	3955	RAWMARSH 8	22	19.0	
3812	4229	RAWTENSTALL 7	22	20.8	25.8
4446	3779	RENISHAW 1	22	16.0	
4707	3811	RETFORD 3	23	22.8	
2456	2261	RHYDARGEAU 1	21	3.6	4.5
4399	3500	RIPLEY 6	22		22.9
3899	4124	ROCHDALE 7	21	18.2	30.8
4429	3931	ROTHERHAM 14	21	22.6	
3511	3833	RUNCORN 10	22	24.2	
3519	3821	RUNCORN 9	21	17.5	
4240	5473	SACRISTON 2	22		22.2
3783	3913	SALE (TRAFFORD) 7	23	19.3	
3823	3990	SALFORD 21	21		
5036	4885	SCARBOROUGH 1	22		20.2
4891	4113	SCUNTHORPE 15	22	18.6	25.4
4308	5753	SEATON DELAVAL 1	21	12.8	14.4
3919	2934	SEDGLEY 5	22	17.4	27.5
4612	4321	SELBY 3	21	19.2	
4616	4324	SELBY 4	21		21.0
4364	3888	SHEFFIELD 40	21		28.5
4355	3871	SHEFFIELD 82	22		28.7
4352	3854	SHEFFIELD 83	23		42.2
4237	5263	SHILDON 1	21	11.3	13.4
5333	1826	SHOREDITCH 2	21	32.6	
4232	4106	SKELMANTHORPE 1	21	18.2	24.3
4962	1819	SLOUGH 16	21	25.8	31.2
4017	2871	SMETHWICK 9	22	23.5	26.6
5149	4161	SOUTH KILLINGHOME 1	21	12.4	19.3
4456	4112	SOUTH KIRKBY 1	22	15.5	24.4
4365	5658	SOUTH SHIELDS 4	22		
4418	1122	SOUTHAMPTON 37	21	22.0	
5873	1862	SOUTHEND-ON-SEA 2	21	20.2	25.1
5318	1800	SOUTHWARK 11	99	40.2	
5322	1786	SOUTHWARK 3	22	33.3	
4247	5329	SPENNYMOOR 2	22	11.6	14.6
4246	4117	STAINFORTH 1	21		22.2
5153	2073	ST ALBANS 3	22	24.3	27.8
1999	518	ST AUSTELL 1	22	8.2	
3519	3977	ST HELENS 29	21		23.5
3534	3936	ST HELENS 36	22		26.8

East	North	Site Name	Type	1986	1991
3513	3955	ST HELENS 38	22		35.9
3510	3943	ST HELENS 41	21	18.8	
3510	3950	ST HELENS 42	21	20.5	
4434	3749	STAVELEY 11	21	16.0	21.9
5361	1824	STEPNEY 5	22	34.0	38.4
2795	6934	STIRLING (BURGH) 4	23	15.3	
2797	6946	STIRLING (BURGH) 5	21	9.3	17.0
4441	5186	STOCKTON-ON-TEES 10	21	17.6	
4446	5193	STOCKTON-ON-TEES 11	21		26.4
4436	5207	STOCKTON-ON-TEES 8	21	17.9	19.6
5330	1865	STOKE NEWINGTON 5	23	34.2	
3866	3447	STOKE-ON-TRENT 11	21		
3888	3475	STOKE-ON-TRENT 20	22	24.4	
3875	3450	STOKE-ON-TRENT 21	22	19.4	
3858	3515	STOKE-ON-TRENT 22	22	24.0	
3861	3505	STOKE-ON-TRENT 3	99	20.6	
4410	3595	STONEBROOM 1	21	17.2	
1464	9332	STORNOWAY 4	21	3.1	
5388	1841	STRATFORD 2	22	32.2	
3801	3966	STRETFORD (TRAFFORD) 12	22	25.0	
4398	5570	SUNDERLAND 12	22	22.5	27.4
4350	5590	SUNDERLAND 15	22	17.5	21.1
4404	5584	SUNDERLAND 16	99		19.9
4366	5563	SUNDERLAND 6	21	16.5	
4407	5558	SUNDERLAND 7	22		
4391	5585	SUNDERLAND 8	22	23.6	22.7
4108	2942	SUTTON COLDFIELD 5	21	23.4	23.3
4297	3196	SWADLINCOTE 6	22	18.3	23.1
4384	4304	SWILLINGTON 1	21	17.8	21.6
4147	1858	SWINDON 2	22	17.3	23.1
4460	3992	SWINTON (YORKS) 7	22	21.2	22.2
4486	4434	TADCASTER 1	21	15.5	17.2
5159	1710	TEDDINGTON 3	22	22.0	38.6
4689	4130	THORNE 2	22		19.2
5623	1785	THURROCK 7	22	22.5	
5337	1894	TOTTENHAM 6	21	27.3	
3810	3958	TRAFFORD 1	22	23.6	29.1
4432	3878	TREETON 3	99		
3746	3944	URMSTON (TRAFFORD) 10	23		25.8
3733	3924	URMSTON (TRAFFORD) 15	99	17.7	
3778	3975	URMSTON (TRAFFORD) 16	21	21.3	
3766	3949	URMSTON (TRAFFORD) 9	22	20.0	24.5
4352	4132	WAKEFIELD 24	21	12.7	15.3

East	North	Site Name	Type	1986	1991
4331	4208	WAKEFIELD 26	22	21.4	27.0
3316	3909	WALLASEY 9	21	17.6	
4304	5664	WALLSEND 7	22	20.5	24.3
3995	3005	WALSALL 13	21		28.5
4009	2973	WALSALL 15	22		33.7
4014	2987	WALSALL 18	21	20.8	29.2
4002	2982	WALSALL 19	21	24.4	29.1
5374	1887	WALTHAMSTOW 8	22	32.8	33.1
4433	4009	WATH-UPON-DEARNE 6	21	18.0	21.3
3946	3002	WEDNESFIELD 2	21	18.6	26.6
3228	3073	WELSHPOOL 1	21		12.6
5188	1853	WEMBLEY 7	22	28.8	39.5
4587	3377	WEST BRIDGFORD 4	22	19.4	18.3
4007	2933	WEST BROMWICH 16	21	18.0	
3022	6634	WEST CALDER 1	21	9.1	12.2
4504	1875	WEST HAGBOURNE 1	21	14.6	16.6
4903	5106	WHITBY 4	22		12.4
2984	5156	WHITEHAVEN 4	21	8.2	
3513	3854	WIDNES 8	22	27.2	31.1
3528	3866	WIDNES 9	21	16.7	23.9
3584	4075	WIGAN 6	22	17.5	
3965	2983	WILLENHALL 15	22		
5257	1705	WIMBLEDON 5	21	27.0	
3898	3958	WOLVERHAMPTON 7	21	14.0	18.0
4401	4030	WOMBWELL 2	22	20.0	25.7
5441	1769	WOOLWICH 9	99		27.6
3003	5287	WORKINGTON 4	22	8.7	
4353	4037	WORSBROUGH BRIDGE 1	22	17.2	
3337	3505	WREXHAM 7	22	15.0	22.7
3292	3464	WREXHAM 9	21	7.6	10.6
4606	4514	YORK 6	22	19.3	21.0
4573	4507	YORK 7	21	14.3	19.6
4607	4536	YORK 8	21	16.4	19.3
4601	4521	YORK 9	99	19.8	

Source: Bower et al. (1989)
Campbell et al. (1994b)

Chemical formula : N_2O

Alternative name : Laughing gas

Type of pollutant : Radiatively active trace gas, greenhouse gas

Structure :

N_2O

Air quality data summary :

Remote Rural Concentrations

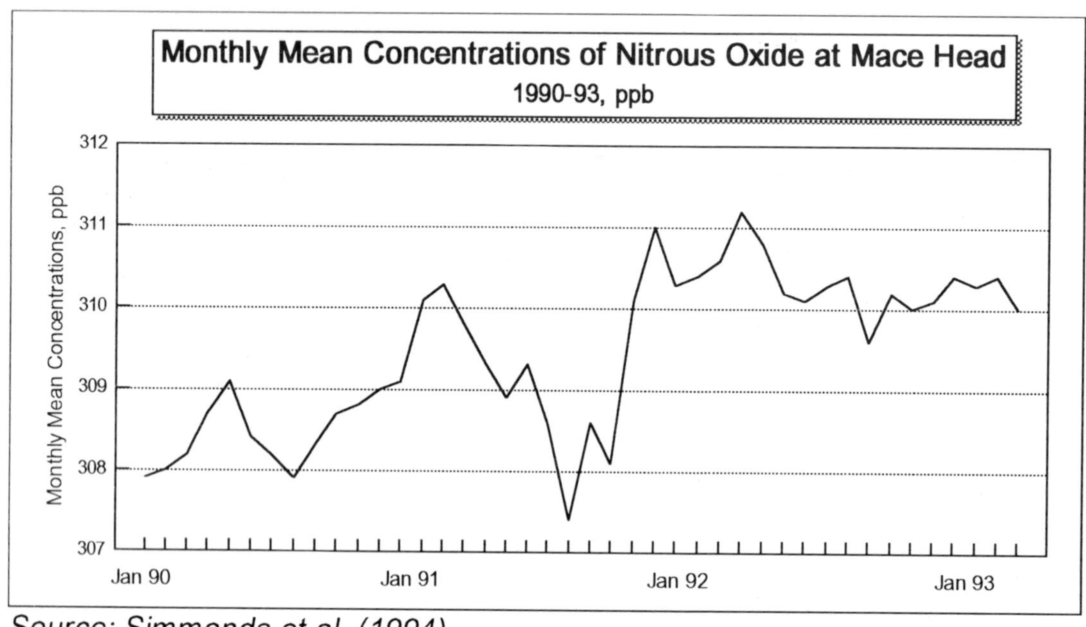

Source: Simmonds et al. (1994)

2,2',3,3',4,4',5,5',6-Nonachlorobiphenyl in air

Chemical formula : $C_{12}HCl_9$

Alternative names : PCB-206

Type of pollutant : (PCB) polychlorinated biphenyl, air toxic

Structure :

Cl Cl Cl Cl Cl Cl Cl Cl Cl

Air quality data summary :

Location	Annual Mean pg/m³		
	1991	1992	1993
Bowland	*	*	0.56
Cardiff C	0.55	1.36	*
London	*	*	*
Manchester B	1.58	1.17	0.00
Middlesbrough	*	*	*
WSL	*	*	*

Source: Davis (1993)

Notes: * signifies no data available

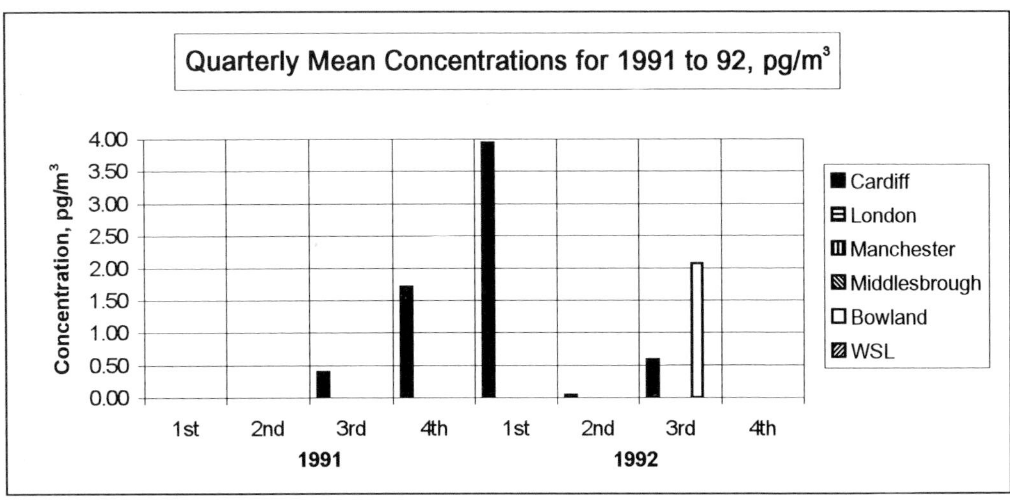

Source: Davis (1993)

Chemical formula	:	$C_{12}HCl_9$
Alternative names	:	PCB-206
Type of pollutant	:	(PCB) polychlorinated biphenyl, air toxic
Structure	:	

Air quality data summary :

Location	Annual Mean ng/m²/day		
	1991	1992	1993
Bowland	*	*	0.15
Cardiff C	0.81	8.68	*
London	*	*	*
Manchester B	0.90	2.25	*
Middlesbrough	*	*	*
WSL	*	*	*

Source: Davis (1993)

Notes: * signifies no data available

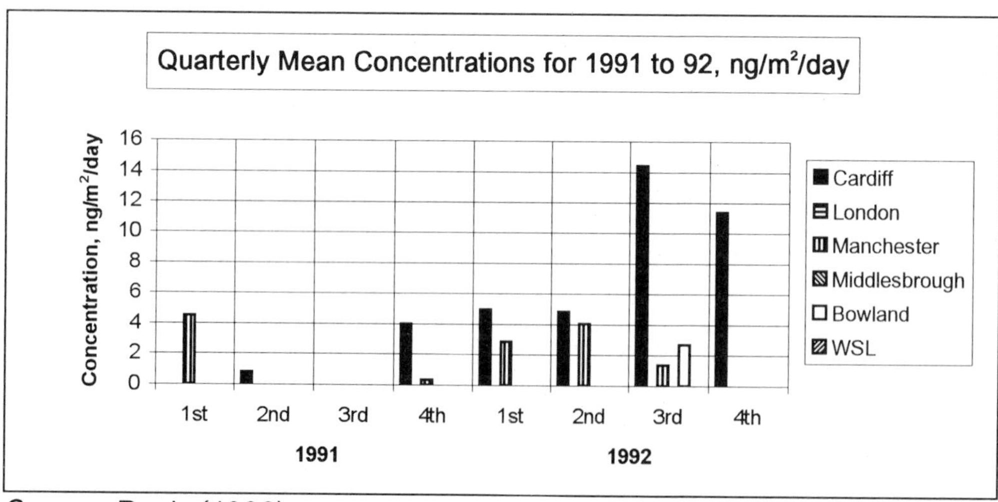

Source: Davis (1993)

2,2',3,3',4,5,5',6,6'-Nonachlorobiphenyl in air

Chemical formula : $C_{12}HCl_9$

Alternative names : PCB-208

Type of pollutant : (PCB) polychlorinated biphenyl, air toxic

Structure :

Air quality data summary :

Location	Annual Mean pg/m^3		
	1991	1992	1993
Bowland	*	*	*
Cardiff C	0.43	1.19	*
London	*	*	*
Manchester B	1.33	1.66	4.00
Middlesbrough	*	*	*
WSL	*	*	*

Source: Davis (1993)

Notes: * signifies no data available

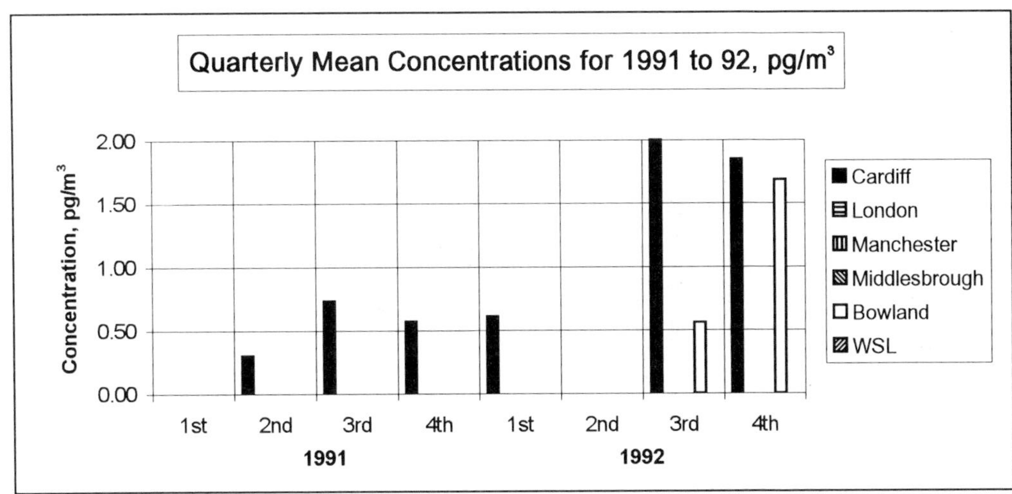

Source: Davis (1993)

Chemical formula : $C_{12}HCl_9$

Alternative names : PCB-208

Type of pollutant : (PCB) polychlorinated biphenyl, air toxic

Structure :

Air quality data summary :

Location	Annual Mean ng/m²/day		
	1991	1992	1993
Bowland	*	*	0.39
Cardiff C	1.17	10.45	*
London	*	*	*
Manchester B	2.02	2.56	*
Middlesbrough	*	*	*
WSL	*	*	*

Source: Davis (1993)

Notes: * signifies no data available

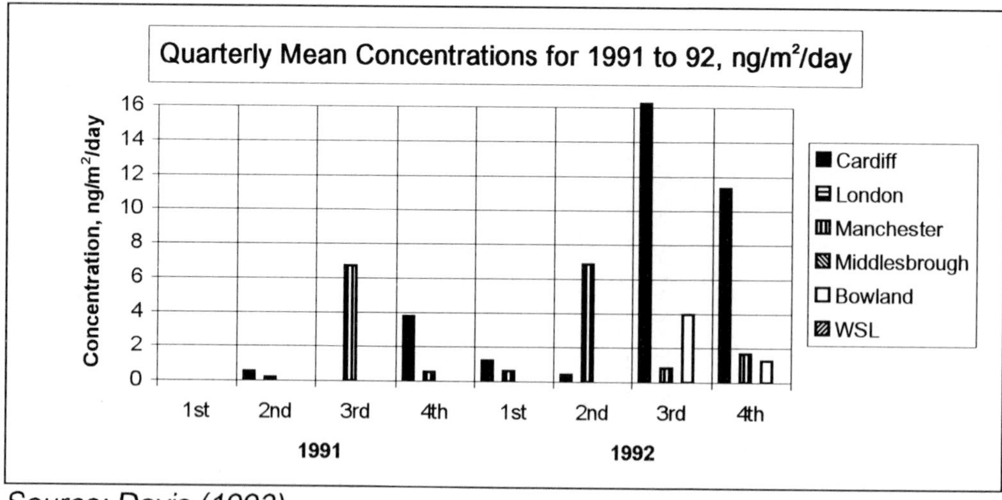

Source: Davis (1993)

n-Nonane

Chemical formula : C_9H_{20}

Alternative name :

Type of pollutant : (Volatile) organic compound (VOC), hydrocarbon

Structure :

$CH_3CH_2\,CH_2\,CH_2\,CH_2\,CH_2\,CH_2\,CH_2CH_3$

Air quality data summary :

Urban concentrations

Mean Air Concentration in Leeds, 19/8/94 to 8/9/94	
Location	21 day mean, $\mu g/m^3$
Albion Street	0.159
Cliff Lane	0.129
EUN monitoring site	0.143
Kerbside site	0.213
Kirkstall Road	0.295
Park site	0.259
Queen Street	0.171
Vicar Lane	0.232

Source: Bartle et al. (1995)

Chemical formula	:	$C_{12}H_2Cl_8$
Alternative names	:	PCB-198
Type of pollutant	:	(PCB) polychlorinated biphenyl, air toxic
Structure	:	

Air quality data summary :

Location	Annual Mean pg/m^3		
	1991	1992	1993
Bowland	*	*	0.96
Cardiff C	0.73	2.40	*
London	*	*	*
Manchester B	1.51	1.16	2.26
Middlesbrough	*	*	*
WSL	*	*	*

Source: Davis (1993)

Notes: * signifies no data available

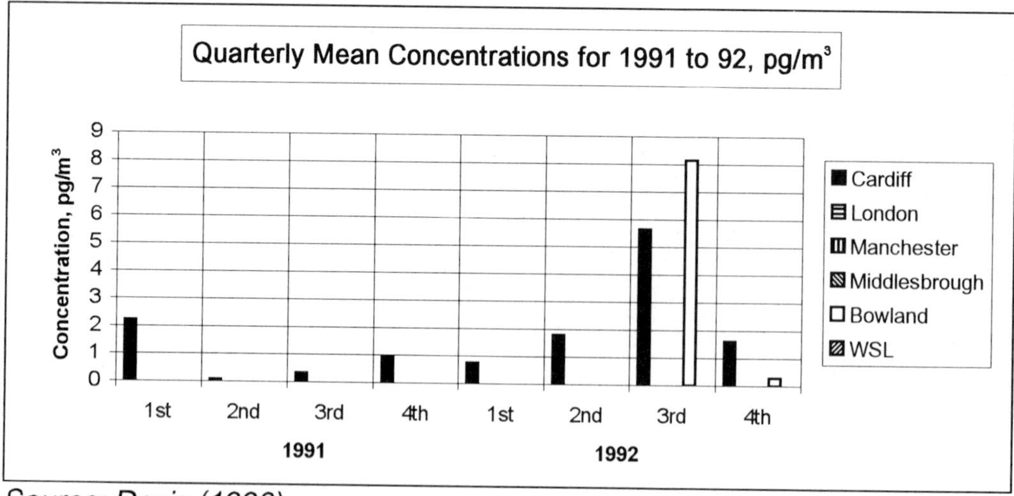

Source: Davis (1993)

Chemical formula : $C_{12}H_2Cl_8$

Alternative names : PCB-198

Type of pollutant : (PCB) polychlorinated biphenyl, air toxic

Structure :

Air quality data summary :

Location	Annual Mean ng/m²/day		
	1991	1992	1993
Bowland	*	*	1.41
Cardiff C	0.42	6.12	*
London	*	*	*
Manchester B	1.11	3.85	*
Middlesbrough	*	*	*
WSL	*	*	*

Source: Davis (1993)

Notes: * signifies no data available

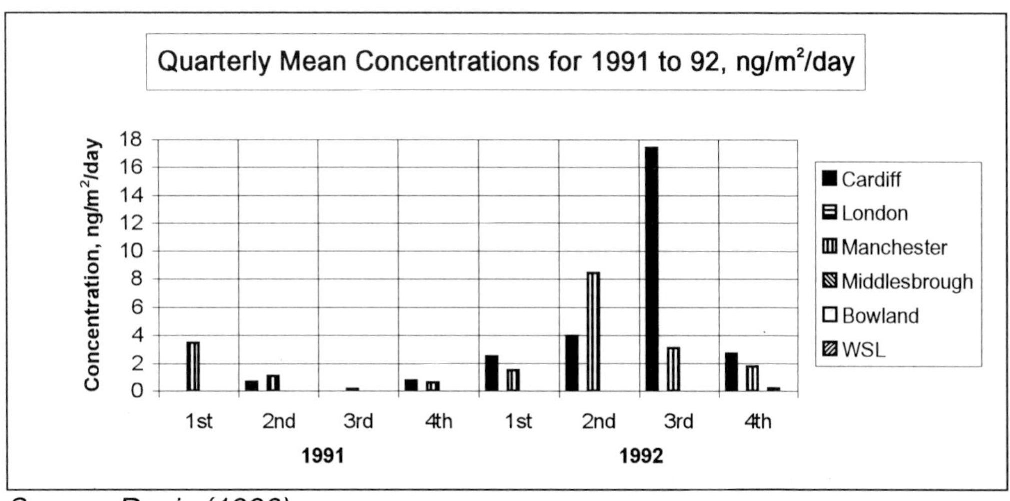

Source: Davis (1993)

Chemical formula : $C_{12}H_2Cl_8$

Alternative names : PCB-201

Type of pollutant : (PCB) polychlorinated biphenyl, air toxic

Structure :

Air quality data summary :

Location	Annual Mean pg/m³		
	1991	1992	1993
Bowland	*	*	0.73
Cardiff C	1.35	0.90	*
London	*	*	*
Manchester B	5.35	1.95	2.74
Middlesbrough	*	*	*
WSL	*	*	*

Source: Davis (1993)

Notes: * signifies no data available

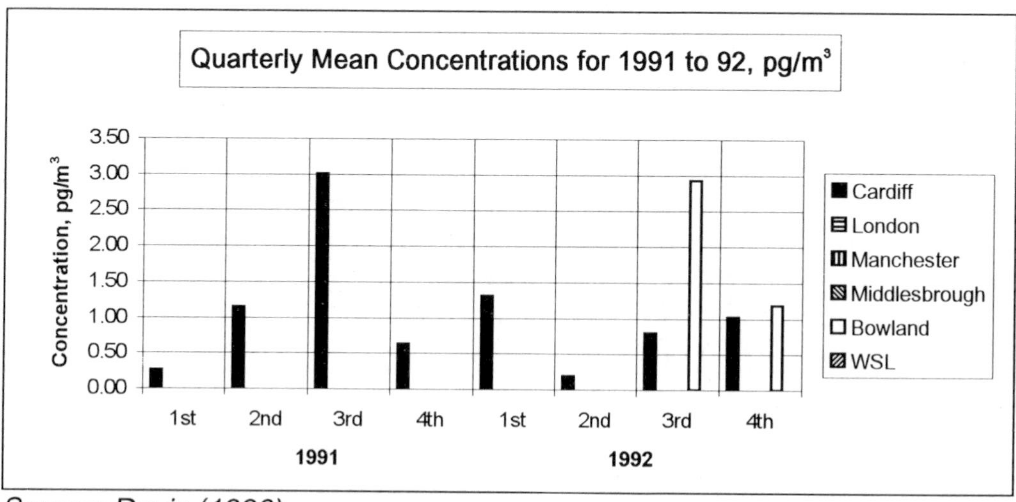

Source: Davis (1993)

Chemical formula : $C_{12}H_2Cl_8$

Alternative names : PCB-201

Type of pollutant : (PCB) polychlorinated biphenyl, air toxic

Structure :

Cl Cl Cl Cl Cl Cl Cl Cl

Air quality data summary :

Location	Annual Mean ng/m²/day		
	1991	1992	1993
Bowland	*	*	0.48
Cardiff C	7.19	17.34	*
London	*	*	*
Manchester B	5.98	3.88	*
Middlesbrough	*	*	*
WSL	*	*	*

Source: Davis (1993)

Notes: * signifies no data available

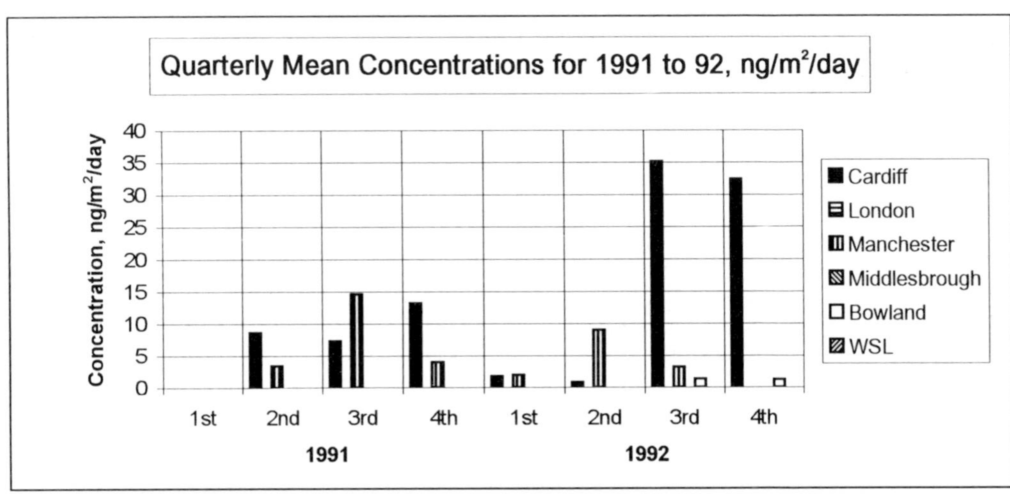

Source: Davis (1993)

2,2',3,4,4',5,6,6'-Octachlorobiphenyl in air

Chemical formula : $C_{12}H_2Cl_8$

Alternative names : PCB-204

Type of pollutant : (PCB) polychlorinated biphenyl, air toxic

Structure :

Air quality data summary :

Location	Annual Mean pg/m³		
	1991	1992	1993
Bowland	*	*	0.33
Cardiff C	1.39	1.61	*
London	*	*	*
Manchester B	2.36	2.47	0.70
Middlesbrough	*	*	*
WSL	*	*	*

Source: Davis (1993)

Notes: * signifies no data available

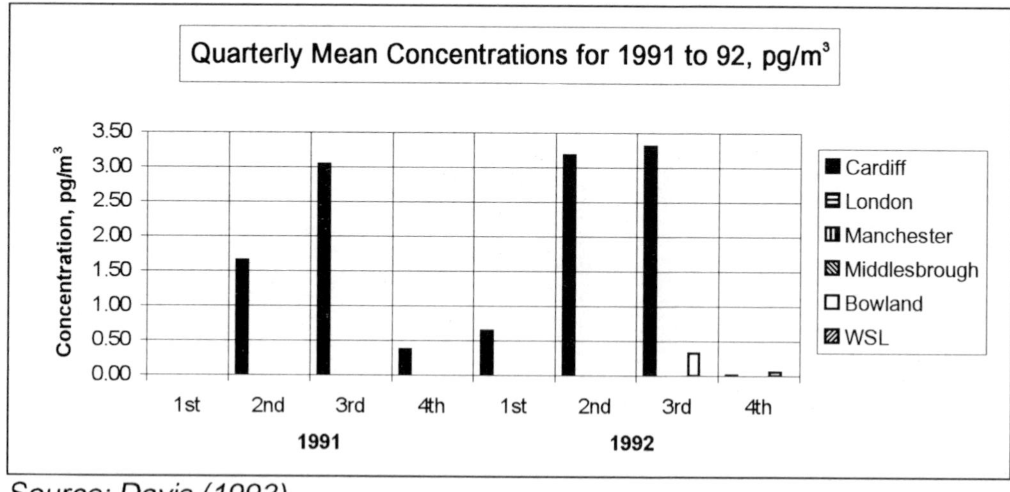

Source: Davis (1993)

2,2',3,4,4',5,6,6'-Octachlorobiphenyl in deposition

Chemical formula : $C_{12}H_2Cl_8$

Alternative names : PCB-204

Type of pollutant : (PCB) polychlorinated biphenyl, air toxic

Structure :

Air quality data summary :

Location	Annual Mean ng/m²/day		
	1991	1992	1993
Bowland	*	*	0.51
Cardiff C	2.26	5.51	*
London	*	*	*
Manchester B	0.87	1.28	*
Middlesbrough	*	*	*
WSL	*	*	*

Source: Davis (1993)

Notes: * signifies no data available

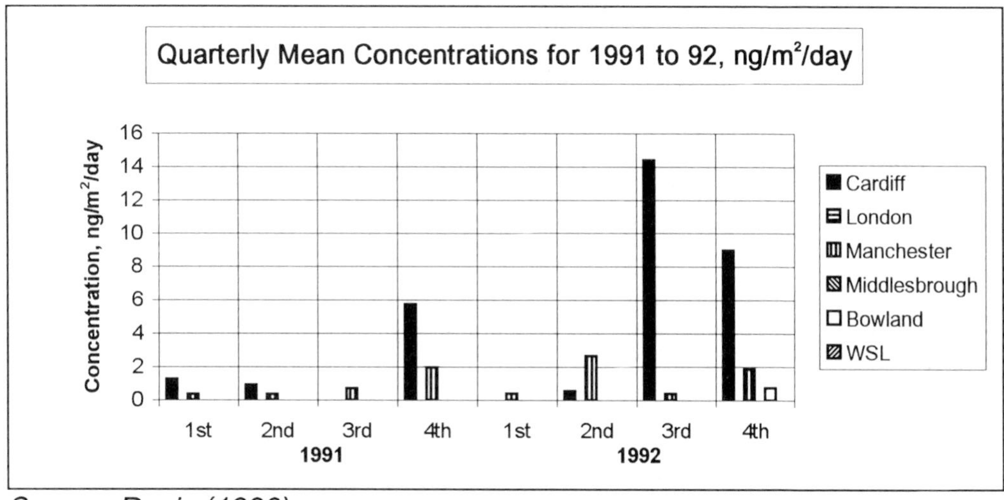

Source: Davis (1993)

Chemical formula : $C_{12}Cl_8O$

Alternative names : OCDF

Type of pollutant : Furan, air toxic

Structure :

Air quality data summary :

Location	Annual Mean pg/m^3		
	1991	1992	1993
Bowland	*	*	0.00
Cardiff C	0.43	0.31	*
London	0.09	0.17	0.11
Manchester B	0.75	0.66	0.19
Middlesbrough	*	*	0.27
WSL	0.08	*	*

Source: Davis (1993)

Note: * signifies no data available

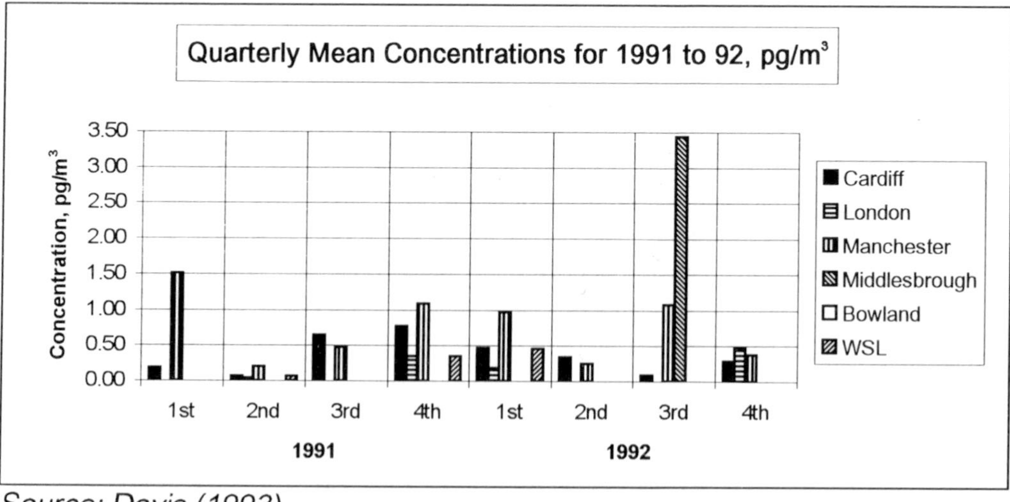

Source: Davis (1993)

Octachlorodibenzofuran in deposition

Chemical formula : $C_{12}Cl_8O$

Alternative names : OCDF

Type of pollutant : Furan, air toxic

Structure :

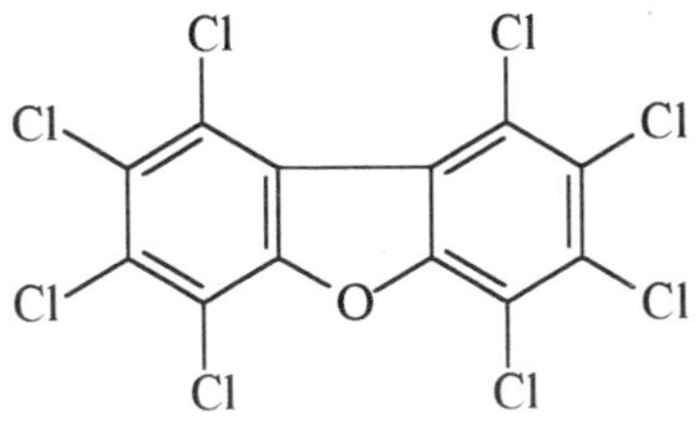

Air quality data summary :

Location	Annual Mean $pg/m^2/day$		
	1991	1992	1993
Bowland	*	*	*
Cardiff C	1635.27	318.77	*
London	43.11	208.60	*
Manchester B	627.72	143.64	*
Middlesbrough	*	*	*
WSL	0.00	*	*

Source: Davis (1993)

Note: * signifies no data available

Chemical formula : $C_{12}Cl_8O_2$

Alternative names : OCDD

Type of pollutant : Dioxin, air toxic

Structure :

Air quality data summary :

Location	Annual Mean pg/m^3		
	1991	1992	1993
Bowland	*	*	5.32
Cardiff C	2.91	8.27	*
London	2.40	2.54	2.78
Manchester B	3.11	3.85	8.13
Middlesbrough	*	*	3.01
WSL	1.84	*	*

Source: Davis (1993)

Note: * signifies no data available

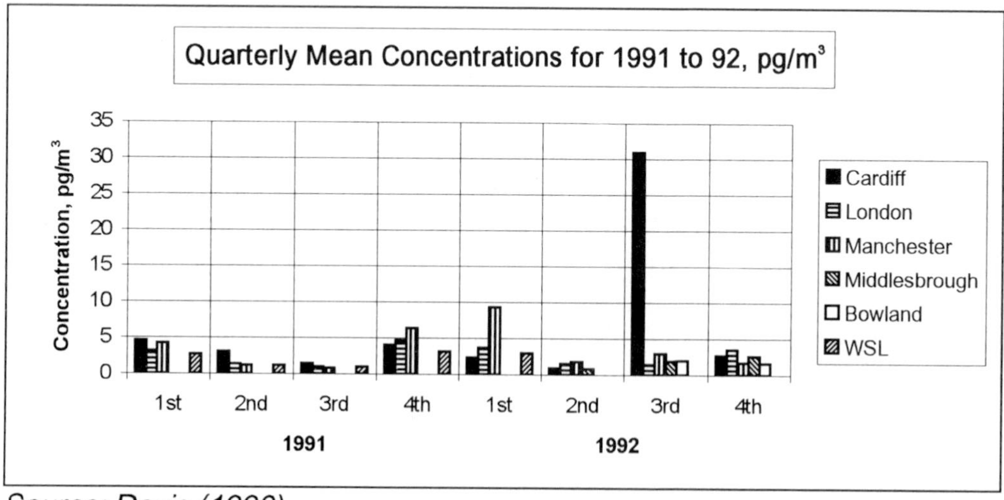

Source: Davis (1993)

Octachlorodibenzo-p-dioxin in deposition

Chemical formula : $C_{12}Cl_8O_2$

Alternative names : OCDD

Type of pollutant : Dioxin, air toxic

Structure :

Cl Cl Cl Cl O O Cl Cl Cl Cl

Air quality data summary :

Location	Annual Mean pg/m²/day		
	1991	1992	1993
Bowland	*	*	*
Cardiff C	3485.50	1250.00	*
London	1493.00	966.50	*
Manchester B	2231.92	933.64	*
Middlesbrough	*	*	*
WSL	621.23	*	*

Source: Davis (1993)

Note: * signifies no data available

Chemical formula : C_8H_{18}

Alternative names :

Type of pollutant : (Volatile) organic compound (VOC), hydrocarbon

Structure : $CH_3CH_2\ CH_2\ CH_2\ CH_2\ CH_2\ CH_2CH_3$

Air quality data summary :

Remote rural concentrations

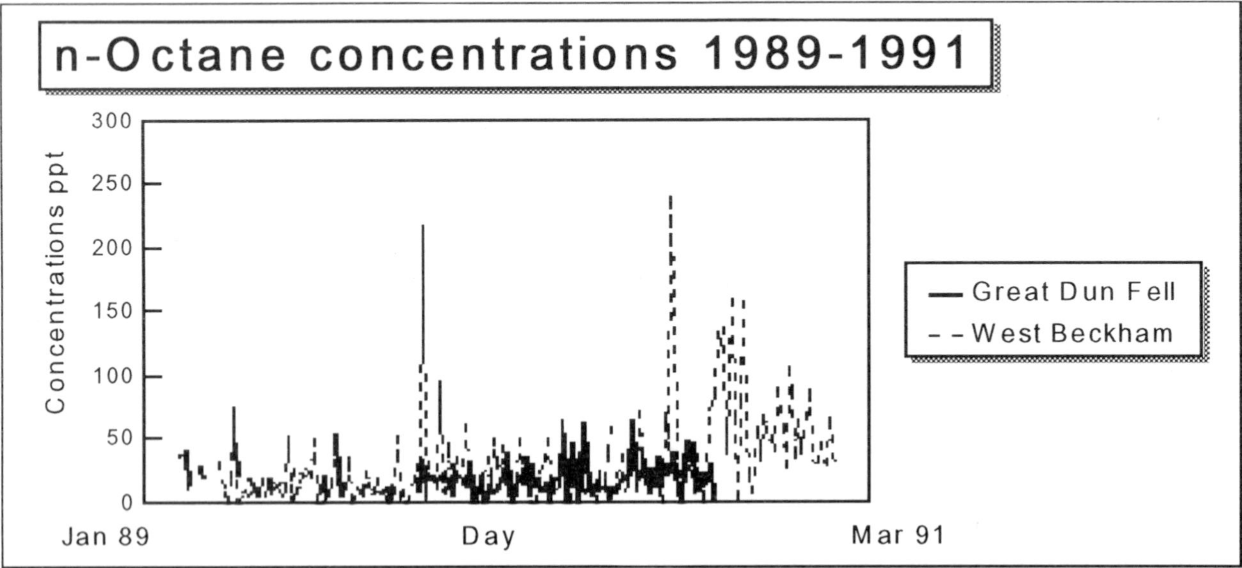

Source: PORG (1993)

Mean Air Concentration in Leeds, 19/8/94 to 8/9/94	
Location	21 day mean, µg/m³
Albion Street	0.091
Cliff Lane	0.102
EUN monitoring site	0.108
Kerbside site	0.140
Kirkstall Road	0.151
Park site	0.096
Queen Street	0.140
Vicar Lane	0.238

Source: Bartle et al. (1995)

Chemical formula : O_3

Alternative names :

Type of pollutant : Photochemical oxidant, radiatively active trace gas, greenhouse gas

Structure : O_3

Air quality data summary :

Remote rural concentrations:

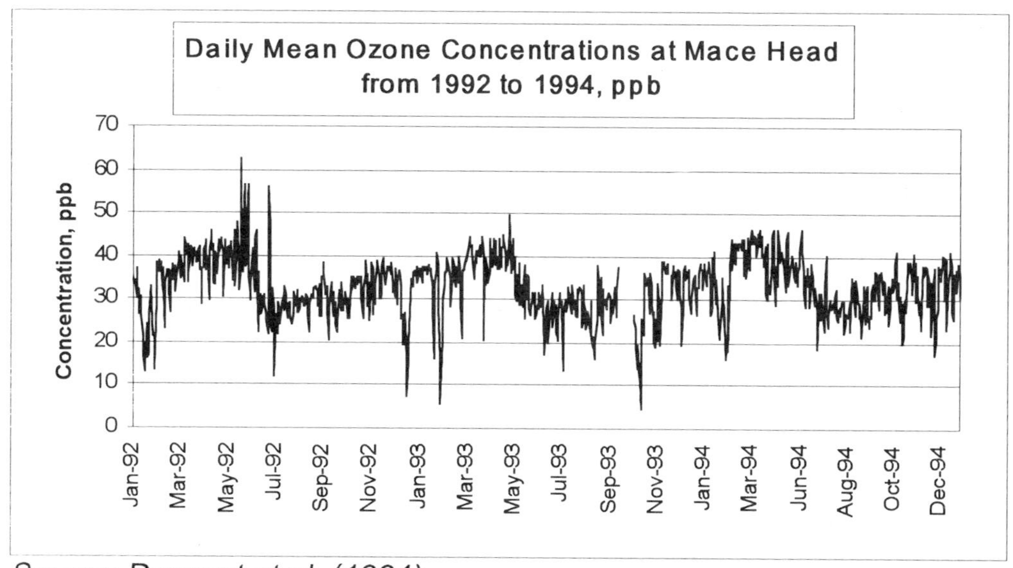

Source: Derwent et al. (1994)

Rural concentrations:

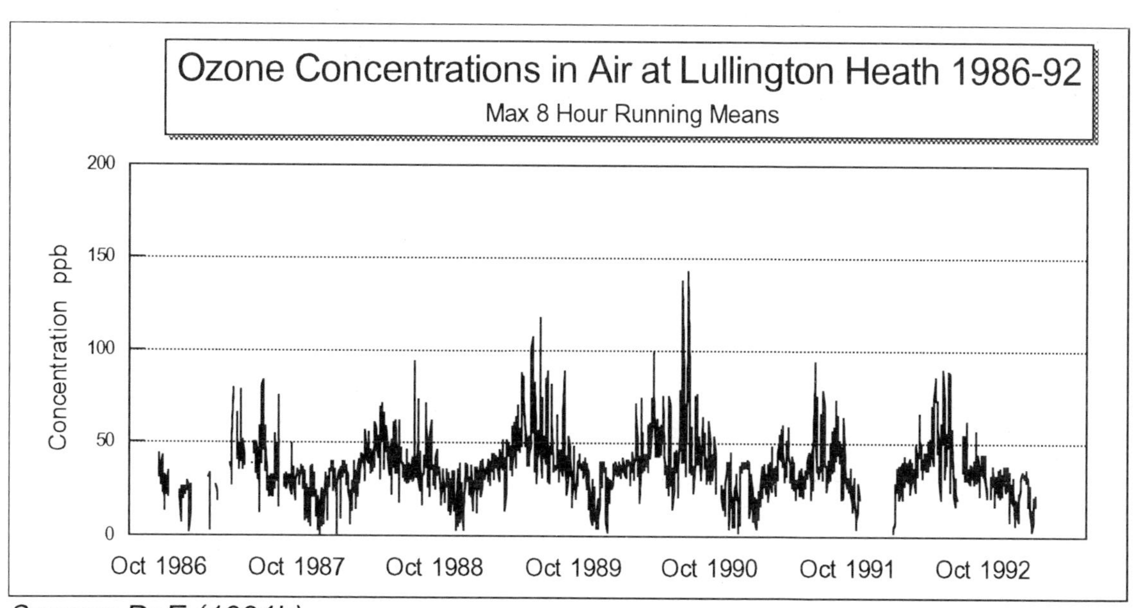

Source: DoE (1994b)

Ozone Calendar Year Statistics

Site	Year	Annual mean (ppb)	Max. run. 8 hour (ppb)
Aston Hill	86	25	99
	87	24	68
	88	30	95
	89	31	102
	90	33	115
	91	30	63
	92	28	86
	93	28	80
	94	31	84
Belfast B	92	18	54
	93	16	44
	94	18	53
Bexley	94	16	90
Birmingham A	92	15	69
	93	14	68
	94	17	57
Birmingham B	94	17	83
Bloomsbury	92	10	65
	93	9	81
	94	11	73
Bottesford	81	19	71
	82	22	94
	83	22	89
	84	21	105
	85	20	105
	86	23	86
	87	18	90
	88	17	60
	89	17	71
	90	18	118
	91	12	44
	92	15	75
	93	15	78
	94	20	78

Site	Year	Annual mean (ppb)	Max. run. 8 hour (ppb)
Bridge Place	90	10	94
	91	10	49
	92	11	57
	93	11	79
	94	13	86
Bristol B	93	16	74
	94	19	61
Bush	86	26	61
	87	23	88
	88	27	70
	89	27	90
	90	28	93
	91	23	67
	92	26	67
	93	24	46
	94	27	65
Canvey	77	33	128
	78	23	128
	79	18	81
	80	14	64
Cardiff D	74	11	62
Cardiff A	92	14	93
	93	15	77
	94	17	95
Central London	72	12	98
	73	13	116
	74	16	122
	75	10	76
	76	16	114
	77	13	86
	78	14	99
	79	12	73
	80	9	66
	81	7	97
	82	9	56

Ozone Calendar Year Statistics

Site	Year	Annual mean (ppb)	Max. run. 8 hour (ppb)	Site	Year	Annual mean (ppb)	Max. run. 8 hour (ppb)
Central London	83	10	52	Great Dun Fell	91	30	87
(cont.)	84	11	56	(cont.)	92	29	110
	85	16	113		93	30	97
	86	11	80		94	31	75
	87	5	58				
	88	7	54	Harrow	79	8	64
	89	10	81		80	13	57
	90	12	75				
				Harwell	83	34	112
Chilworth	75	38	142		84	26	94
					85	27	91
Cromwell Road	73	7	72		86	23	113
	74	5	29		87	21	84
					88	24	68
East Kilbride	75	28	97		89	21	105
					90	25	111
Edinburgh B	93	13	38		91	25	78
	94	15	48		92	25	98
					93	23	83
Eskdalemuir	86	21	96		94	24	93
	87	21	80				
	88	26	69	High Muffles	87	18	47
	89	28	84		88	24	70
	90	28	90		89	26	91
	91	26	64		90	26	101
	92	25	68		91	26	73
	93	23	93		92	28	85
	94	26	65		93	27	96
					94	27	82
Glazebury	88	20	68				
	89	17	75	Hull	94	16	87
	90	19	82				
	91	14	62	Islington	76	10	90
	92	17	94		77	10	101
	93	15	72		78	9	68
	94	17	60				
				Ladybower	88	24	87
Great Dun Fell	86	22	90		89	26	101
	87	29	87		90	26	105
	88	30	73		91	23	70
	89	31	94		92	22	91
	90	32	101		93	23	75

Ozone Calendar Year Statistics

Site	Year	Annual mean (ppb)	Max. 8 hour (ppb)	Site	Year	Annual mean (ppb)	Max. run. 8 hour (ppb)
Ladybower (cont.)	94	26	79	Sibton (cont.)	85	18	77
					87	22	82
Leeds	93	13	50		88	24	86
	94	14	62		89	25	107
					90	25	127
Leicester	94	17	80		91	26	69
					92	24	102
Liverpool	93	14	42		93	25	100
	94	17	53		94	25	103
Lough Navar	87	22	78	Southampton	94	18	77
	88	25	72				
	89	25	98	Stevenage	77	23	111
	90	26	85		78	16	84
	91	22	75		79	14	85
	92	24	75		80	10	67
	93	23	51		81	7	60
	94	24	62		82	17	119
					83	20	120
Lullington	87	23	83		84	20	153
	88	27	94		85	15	102
	89	31	118		86	13	96
	90	32	143		87	10	70
	91	26	94		88	12	58
	92	29	90		89	13	84
	93	26	92		90	15	114
	94	29	91		91	13	75
					92	14	82
Newcastle A	92	15	50		93	15	103
	93	15	43		94	17	40
	94	15	52				
				Strath Vaich	87	31	81
Sibton	75	38	148		88	34	67
	76	24	96		89	32	72
	77	29	102		90	33	73
	78	31	96		91	31	66
	79	22	80		92	32	68
	80	16	55		93	32	58
	81	24	178		94	33	66
	82	25	105				
	83	28	110	Wharley Croft	86	15	69
	84	23	104		87	19	80

Ozone Calendar Year Statistics							
Site	Year	Annual mean (ppb)	Max 8 hour (ppb)	Site	Year	Annual mean (ppb)	Max. run 8 hour (ppb)
Warley Croft	88	25	63	Yarner Wood	87	21	80
(cont.)	89	26	96		88	29	93
	90	27	90		89	32	121
	91	29	70		90	33	121
	92	27	93		91	31	106
	93	26	98		92	28	95
	94	28	71		93	26	83
					94	28	96
Wray	85	28	79				
	86	27	62				
	87	25	88				

Source: Bower et al. (1995)

Data displayed for data captures $\geq$ 25 %

Chemical formula : $C_2H_3O_5N$

Alternative names : Peroxyacetylnitrate

Type of pollutant : Photochemical oxidant, member of NO_Y family

Structure :

$$CH_3-\overset{\overset{O}{\|}}{C}-O-O-\underset{\underset{O}{\|}}{\overset{\overset{O}{\|}}{N}}$$

Air quality data summary :

Rural Concentrations

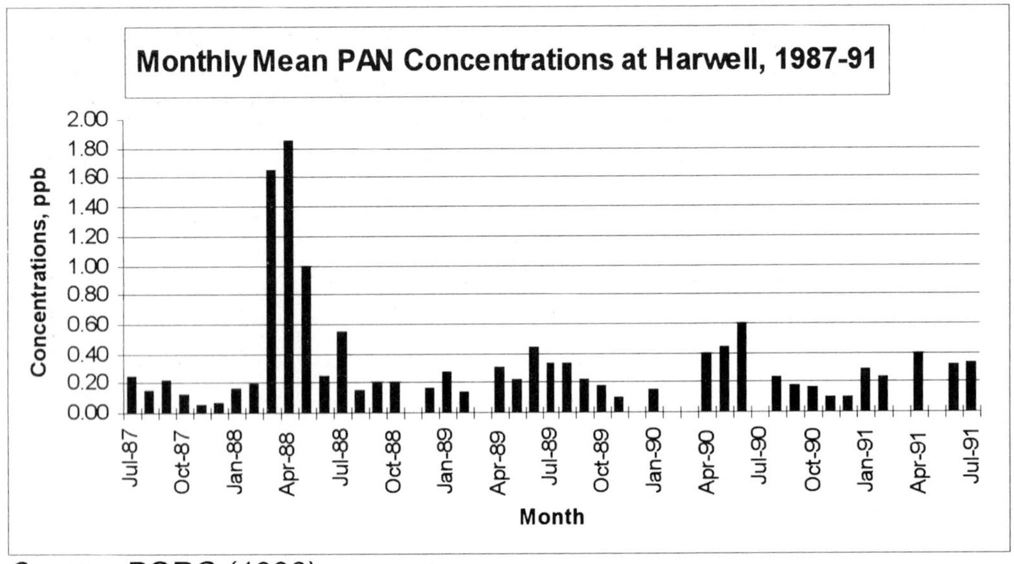

Source: PORG (1993)

Chemical formula : $C_{12}H_5Cl_5$

Alternative names : PCB-101

Type of pollutant : (PCB) polychlorinated biphenyl, air toxic

Structure :

Cl Cl Cl Cl Cl

Air quality data summary :

Location	Annual Mean pg/m³		
	1991	1992	1993
Bowland	*	*	9.80
Cardiff C	74.52	100.80	*
London	127.48	104.27	112.61
Manchester B	87.53	81.62	55.75
Middlesbrough	*	*	21.59
WSL	31.22	*	*

Source: Davis (1993)

Notes: * signifies no data available

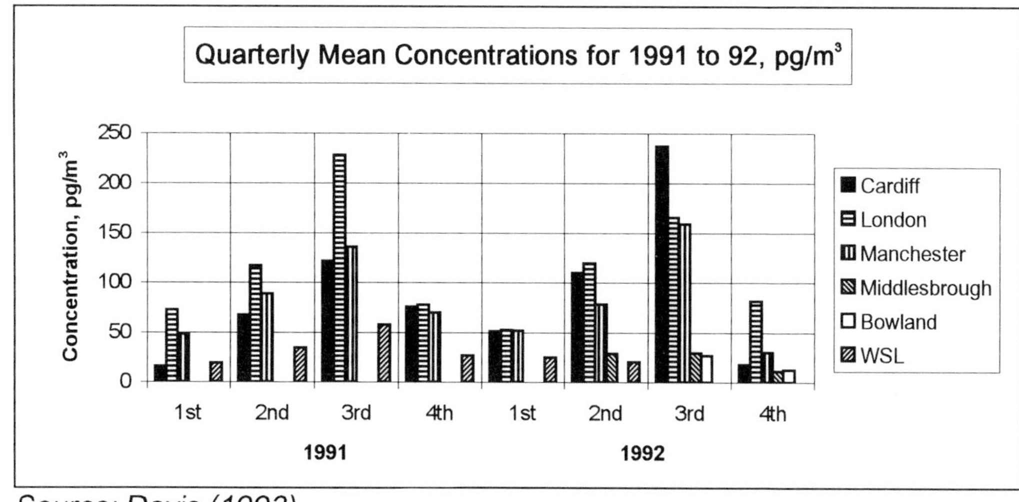

Source: Davis (1993)

Chemical formula	:	$C_{12}H_5Cl_5$
Alternative names	:	PCB-101
Type of pollutant	:	(PCB) polychlorinated biphenyl, air toxic
Structure	:	

Cl Cl Cl Cl Cl

Air quality data summary :

Location	Annual Mean ng/m²/day		
	1991	1992	1993
Bowland	*	*	17.35
Cardiff C	161.08	115.61	*
London	68.00	10.53	*
Manchester B	17.67	38.07	*
Middlesbrough	*	*	*
WSL	22.44	*	*

Source: Davis (1993)

Notes: * signifies no data available

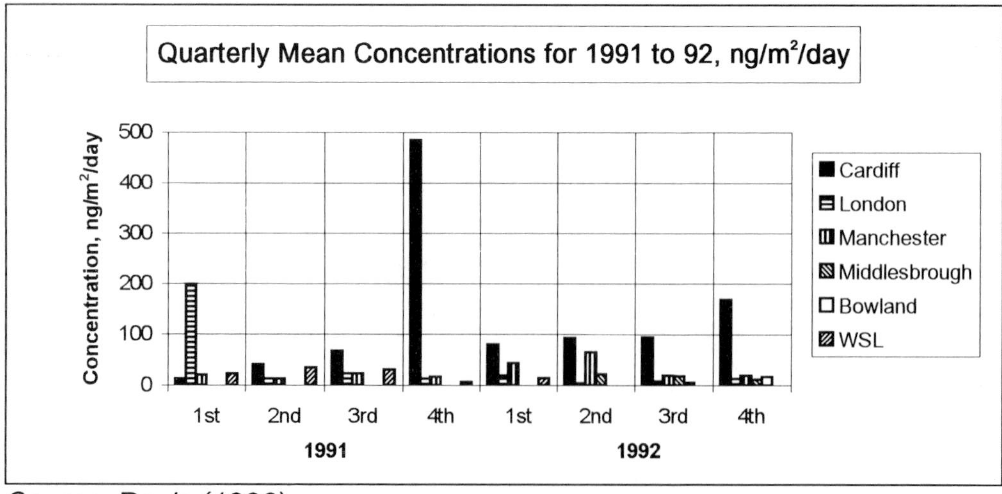

Source: Davis (1993)

2,2',4,6,6'-Pentachlorobiphenyl in air

Chemical formula : $C_{12}H_5Cl_5$

Alternative names : PCB-104

Type of pollutant : (PCB) polychlorinated biphenyl, air toxic

Structure :

Cl Cl Cl Cl Cl

Air quality data summary :

Location	Annual Mean pg/m³		
	1991	1992	1993
Bowland	*	*	1.66
Cardiff C	17.82	2.96	*
London	*	*	*
Manchester B	11.77	5.43	3.71
Middlesbrough	*	*	*
WSL	*	*	*

Source: Davis (1993)

Notes: * signifies no data available

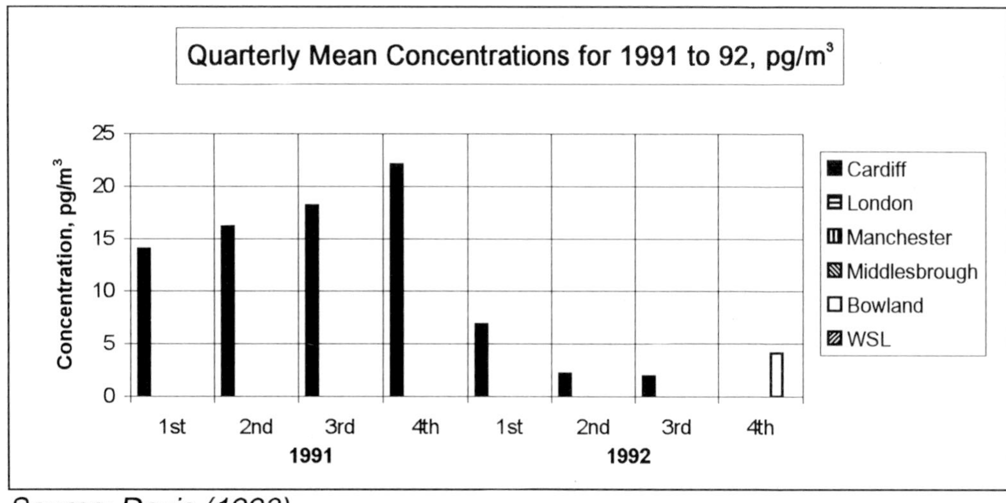

Source: Davis (1993)

2,2',4,6,6'-Pentachlorobiphenyl in deposition

Chemical formula : $C_{12}H_5Cl_5$

Alternative names : PCB-104

Type of pollutant : (PCB) polychlorinated biphenyl, air toxic

Structure :

Air quality data summary :

Location	Annual Mean ng/m²/day		
	1991	1992	1993
Bowland	*	*	0.31
Cardiff C	449.73	59.94	*
London	*	*	*
Manchester B	12.14	17.89	*
Middlesbrough	*	*	*
WSL	*	*	*

Source: Davis (1993)

Notes: * signifies no data available

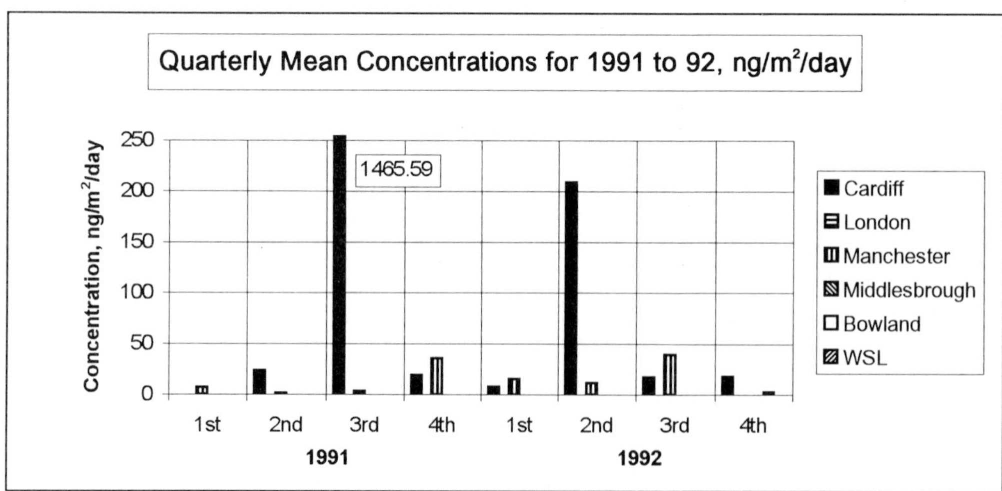

Source: Davis (1993)

Chemical formula	:	$C_{12}H_5Cl_5$
Alternative names	:	PCB-105
Type of pollutant	:	(PCB) polychlorinated biphenyl, air toxic
Structure	:	

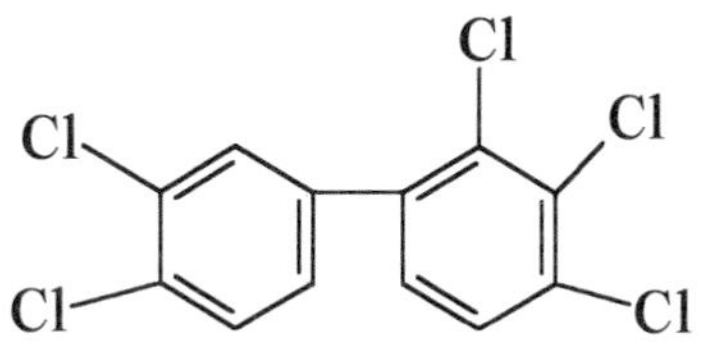

Air quality data summary :

Location	Annual Mean pg/m^3		
	1991	1992	1993
Bowland	*	*	6.72
Cardiff C	16.97	36.84	*
London	*	*	*
Manchester B	17.57	34.91	27.67
Middlesbrough	*	*	*
WSL	*	*	*

Source: Davis (1993)

Notes: * signifies no data available

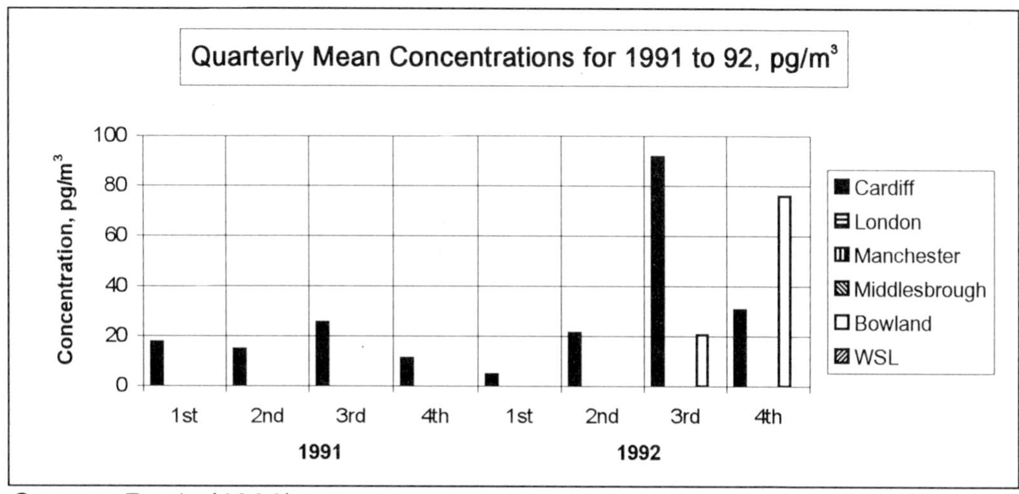

Source: Davis (1993)

Chemical formula : $C_{12}H_5Cl_5$

Alternative names : PCB-105

Type of pollutant : (PCB) polychlorinated biphenyl, air toxic

Structure :

Cl Cl Cl Cl Cl

Air quality data summary :

Location	Annual Mean ng/m²/day		
	1991	1992	1993
Bowland	*	*	5.22
Cardiff C	90.08	28.14	*
London	*	*	*
Manchester B	10.04	15.47	*
Middlesbrough	*	*	*
WSL	*	*	*

Source: Davis (1993)

Notes: * signifies no data available

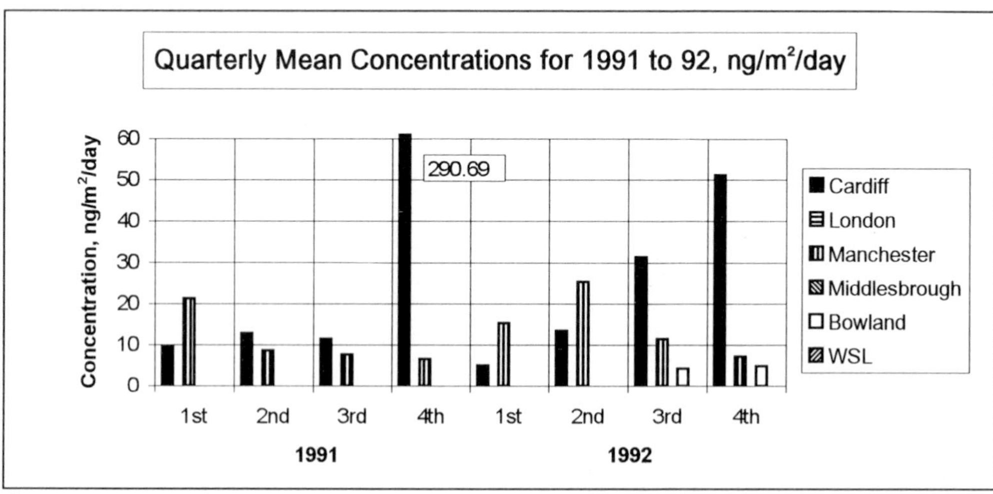

Source: Davis (1993)

Chemical formula : $C_{12}H_5Cl_5$

Alternative names : PCB-110

Type of pollutant : (PCB) polychlorinated biphenyl, air toxic

Structure :

Cl Cl Cl Cl Cl

Air quality data summary :

Location	Annual Mean pg/m³		
	1991	1992	1993
Bowland	*	*	7.86
Cardiff C	70.71	118.28	*
London	18.36	13.89	14.30
Manchester B	84.39	71.23	58.52
Middlesbrough	*	*	5.82
WSL	3.10	*	*

Source: Davis (1993)

Notes: * signifies no data available. These data represent results for a mixture of PCB-77 and PCB-110 since the separate peaks are not normally resolvable.

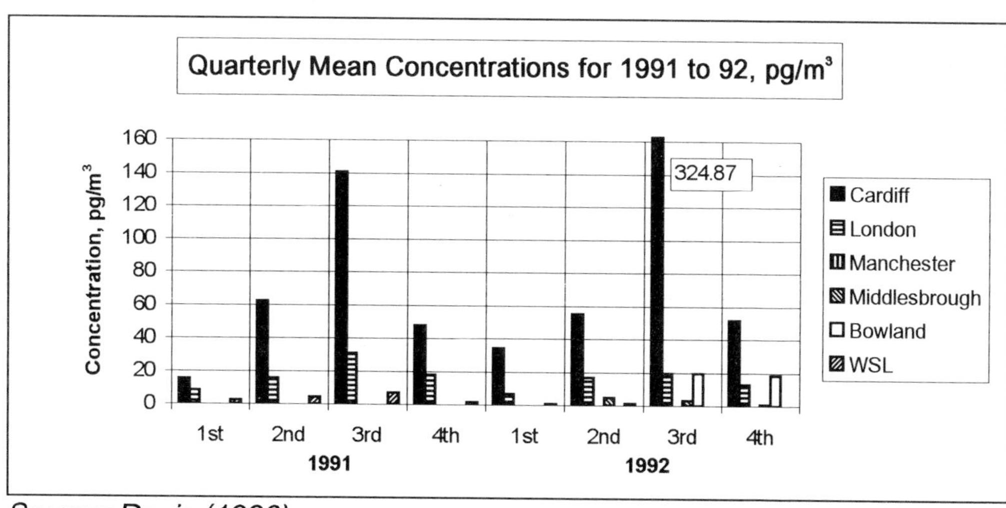

Source: Davis (1993)

2,3,3',4',6-Pentachlorobiphenyl in deposition 182

Chemical formula : $C_{12}H_5Cl_5$

Alternative names : PCB-110

Type of pollutant : (PCB) polychlorinated biphenyl, air toxic

Structure :

Cl Cl Cl Cl Cl

Air quality data summary :

Location	Annual Mean ng/m^2/day		
	1991	1992	1993
Bowland	*	*	15.02
Cardiff C	191.97	101.20	*
London	16.34	2.88	*
Manchester B	24.72	32.47	*
Middlesbrough	*	*	*
WSL	5.33	*	*

Source: Davis (1993)

Notes: * signifies no data available. These data represent results for a mixture of PCB-77 and PCB-110 since the separate peaks are not normally resolvable.

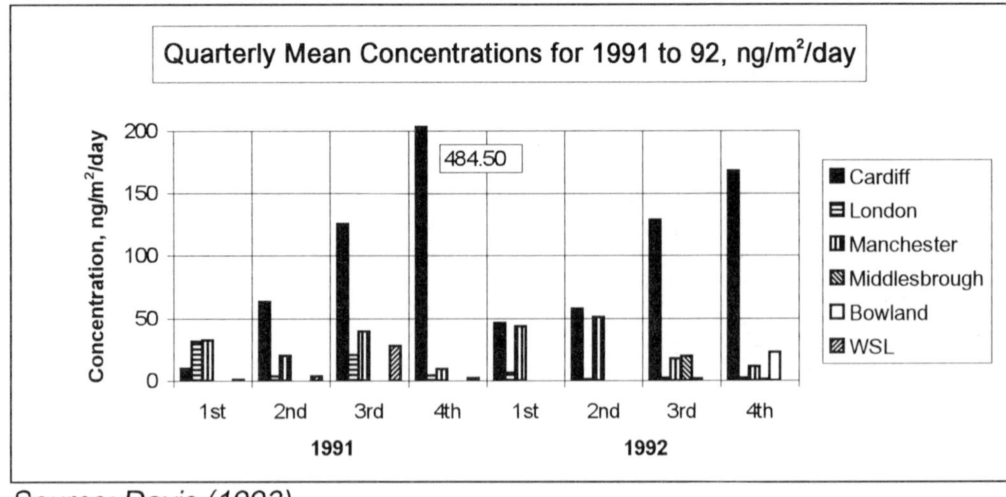

Source: Davis (1993)

Chemical formula : $C_{12}H_5Cl_5$

Alternative names : PCB-118

Type of pollutant : (PCB) polychlorinated biphenyl, air toxic

Structure :

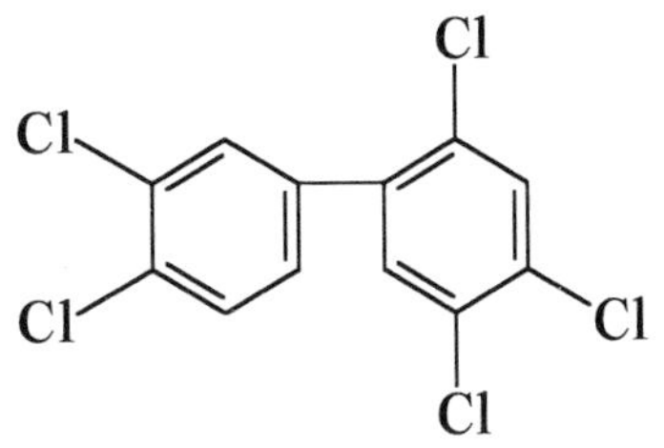

Air quality data summary :

Location	Annual Mean pg/m³		
	1991	1992	1993
Bowland	*	*	7.27
Cardiff C	21.35	54.02	*
London	54.25	44.00	47.99
Manchester B	22.33	35.16	27.21
Middlesbrough	*	*	7.61
WSL	11.94	*	*

Source: Davis (1993)

Notes: * signifies no data available

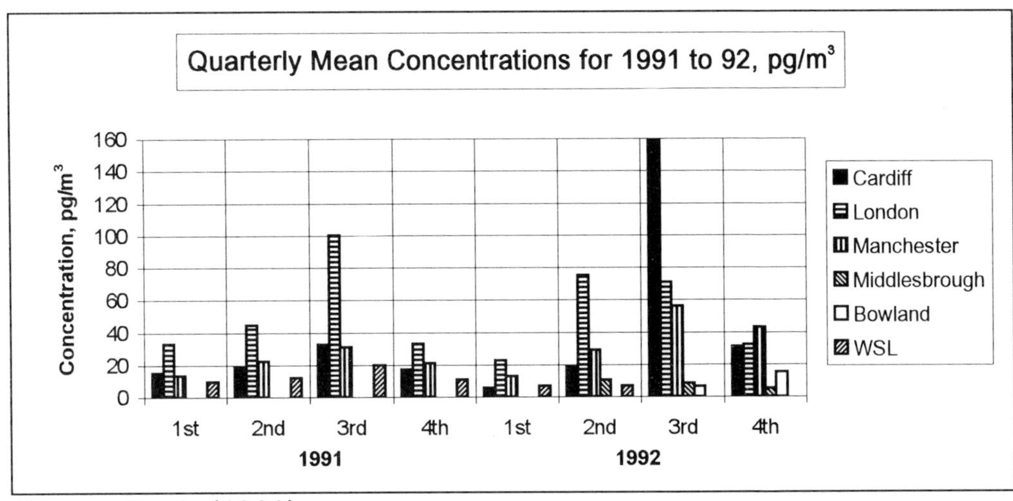

Source: Davis (1993)

2,3',4,4',5-Pentachlorobiphenyl in deposition

Chemical formula : $C_{12}H_5Cl_5$

Alternative names : PCB-118

Type of pollutant : (PCB) polychlorinated biphenyl, air toxic

Structure :

Air quality data summary :

Location	Annual Mean ng/m²/day		
	1991	1992	1993
Bowland	*	*	20.61
Cardiff C	80.28	50.80	*
London	28.59	15.11	*
Manchester B	16.43	13.67	*
Middlesbrough	*	*	*
WSL	11.82	*	*

Source: Davis (1993)

Notes: * signifies no data available

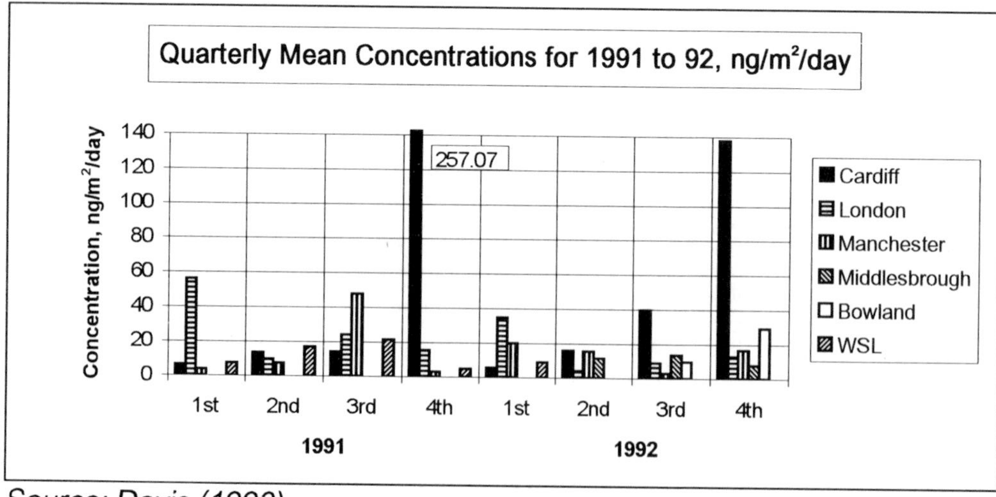

Source: Davis (1993)

3,3',4,4',5-Pentachlorobiphenyl in air

Chemical formula : $C_{12}H_5Cl_5$

Alternative names : PCB-126

Type of pollutant : (PCB) polychlorinated biphenyl, air toxic

Structure :

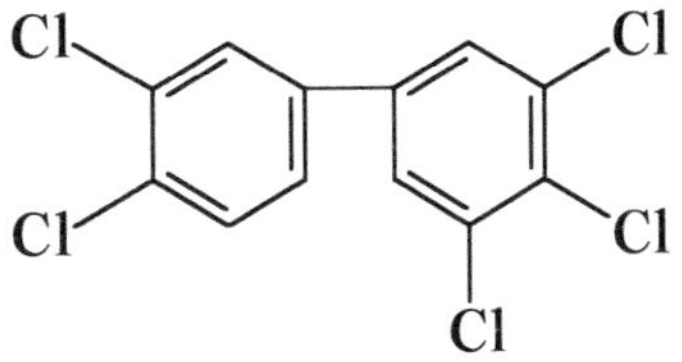

Air quality data summary :

Location	Annual Mean pg/m^3		
	1991	1992	1993
Bowland	*	*	*
Cardiff C	*	*	*
London	0.16	0.004	0.00
Manchester B	*	*	*
Middlesbrough	*	*	0.00
WSL	0.00	*	*

Source: Davis (1993)

Notes: * signifies no data available

3,3',4,4',5-Pentachlorobiphenyl in deposition

Chemical formula : $C_{12}H_5Cl_5$

Alternative names : PCB-126

Type of pollutant : (PCB) polychlorinated biphenyl, air toxic

Structure :

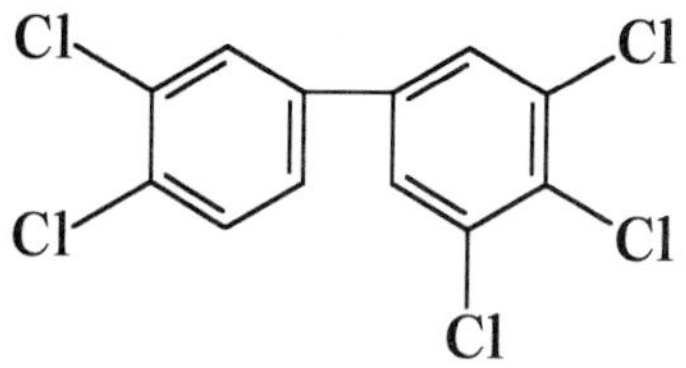

Air quality data summary :

Location	Annual Mean ng/m²/day		
	1991	1992	1993
Bowland	*	*	*
Cardiff C	*	*	*
London	1.14	0.02	*
Manchester B	*	*	*
Middlesbrough	*	*	*
WSL	0.00	*	*

Source: Davis (1993)

Notes: * signifies no data available

Chemical formula : $C_{12}H_3Cl_5O$

Alternative names : 1,2,3,7,8-PeCDF

Type of pollutant : Furan, air toxic

Structure :

Cl Cl Cl Cl Cl O

Air quality data summary :

Location	Annual Mean pg/m^3		
	1991	1992	1993
Bowland	*	*	0.00
Cardiff C	0.05	0.02	*
London	0.10	0.07	0.03
Manchester B	0.08	0.06	0.08
Middlesbrough	*	*	0.06
WSL	0.06	*	*

Source: Davis (1993)

Note: * signifies no data available

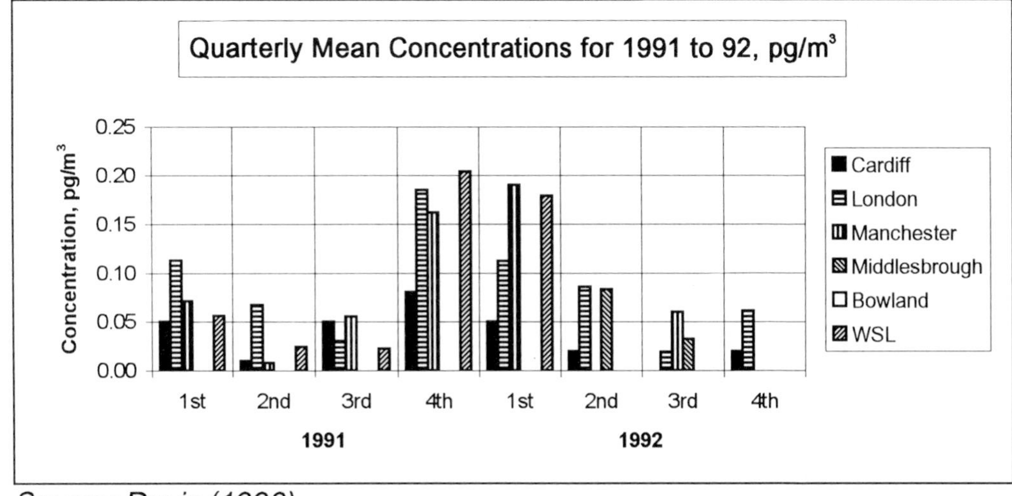

Source: Davis (1993)

Chemical formula : $C_{12}H_3Cl_5O$

Alternative names : 1,2,3,7,8-PeCDF

Type of pollutant : Furan, air toxic

Structure :

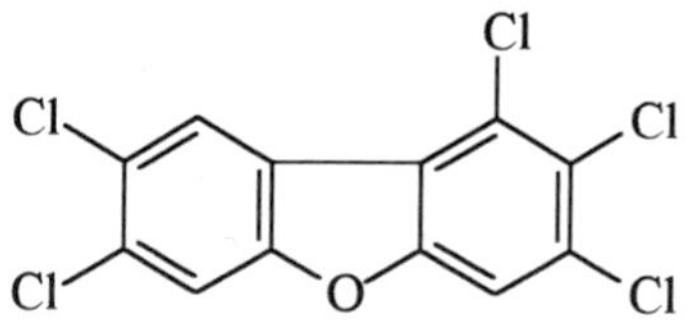

Air quality data summary :

Location	Annual Mean pg/m²/day		
	1991	1992	1993
Bowland	*	*	*
Cardiff C	50.94	8.12	*
London	67.97	4.50	*
Manchester B	18.83	27.27	*
Middlesbrough	*	*	*
WSL	27.54	*	*

Source: Davis (1993)

Note: * signifies no data available

2,3,4,7,8-Pentachlorodibenzofuran in air 186

Chemical formula	:	$C_{12}H_3Cl_5O$
Alternative names	:	2,3,4,7,8-PeCDF
Type of pollutant	:	Furan, air toxic
Structure	:	

Air quality data summary :

Location	Annual Mean pg/m^3		
	1991	1992	1993
Bowland	*	*	0.00
Cardiff C	0.06	0.04	*
London	0.10	0.07	0.02
Manchester B	0.09	0.08	0.09
Middlesbrough	*	*	0.10
WSL	0.07	*	*

Source: Davis (1993)

Note: * signifies no data available

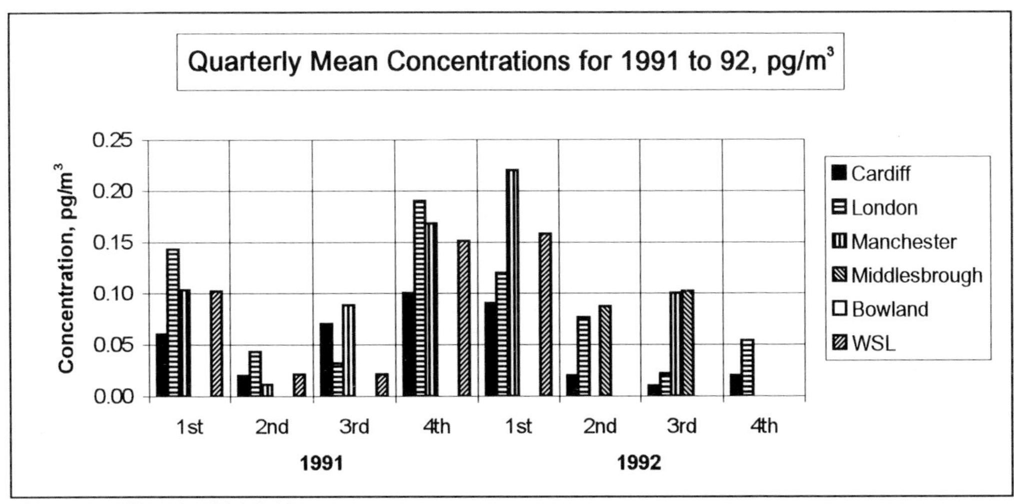

Source: Davis (1993)

2,3,4,7,8-Pentachlorodibenzofuran in deposition

Chemical formula : $C_{12}H_3Cl_5O$

Alternative names : 2,3,4,7,8-PeCDF

Type of pollutant : Furan, air toxic

Structure :

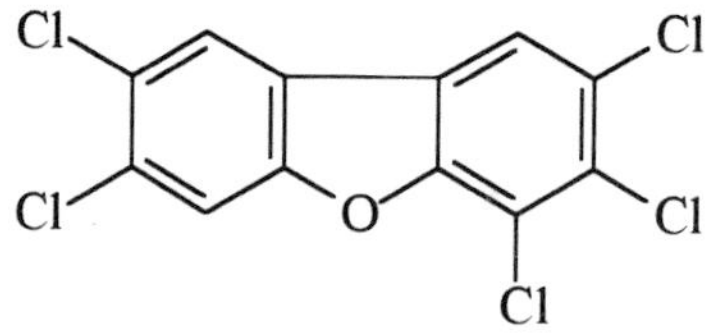

Air quality data summary :

Location	Annual Mean pg/m^2/day		
	1991	1992	1993
Bowland	*	*	*
Cardiff C	48.30	9.91	*
London	67.42	5.60	*
Manchester B	27.12	45.45	*
Middlesbrough	*	*	*
WSL	23.52	*	*

Source: Davis (1993)

Note: * signifies no data available

Chemical formula : $C_{12}H_3Cl_5O_2$

Alternative names : 1,2,3,7,8-PeCDD

Type of pollutant : Dioxin, air toxic

Structure :

Cl Cl Cl Cl Cl O O

Air quality data summary :

Location	Annual Mean pg/m³		
	1991	1992	1993
Bowland	*	*	0.02
Cardiff C	0.03	0.01	*
London	0.02	0.02	0.01
Manchester B	0.04	0.03	0.02
Middlesbrough	*	*	0.02
WSL	0.02	*	*

Source: Davis (1993)

Note: * signifies no data available

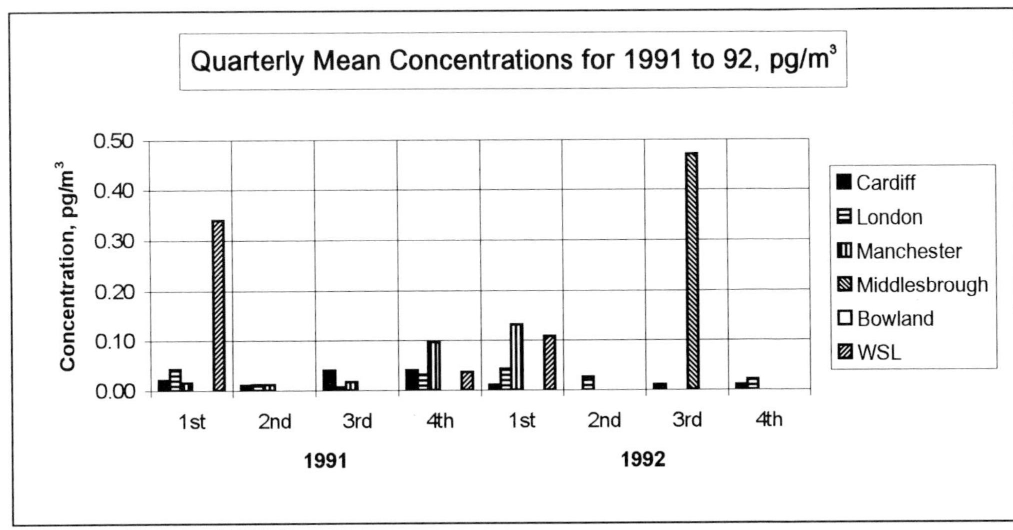

Source: Davis (1993)

Chemical formula : $C_{12}H_3Cl_5O_2$

Alternative names : 1,2,3,7,8-PeCDD

Type of pollutant : Dioxin, air toxic

Structure :

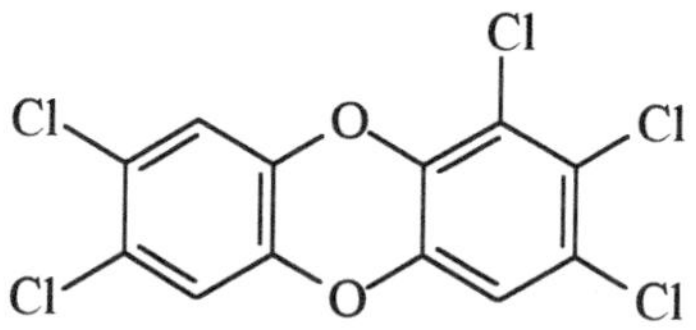

Air quality data summary :

Location	Annual Mean pg/m²/day		
	1991	1992	1993
Bowland	*	*	*
Cardiff C	100.13	9.00	*
London	70.38	0.00	*
Manchester B	48.22	15.45	*
Middlesbrough	*	*	*
WSL	17.82	*	*

Source: Davis (1993)

Note: * signifies no data available

Chemical formula : $C_5H_{10}O$

Alternative names : Valeral, valeraldehyde

Type of pollutant : (Volatile) organic compound (VOC), hydrocarbon, oxygenate

Structure :

$CH_3CH_2CH_2CH_2CHO$

Air quality data summary :

Rural Concentrations

Month 1993	Air Concentration at Harwell site, ppb
	Monthly Mean
August	0.028
September	0.019
October	0.019
November	0.017

Source: Schaug et al. (1994)

Chemical formula	:	i-C_5H_{12}
Alternative names	:	2-methylbutane
Type of pollutant	:	(Volatile) organic compound (VOC), hydrocarbon
Structure	:	

$$CH_3\underset{\displaystyle CH_3}{\underset{|}{C}}HCH_2CH_3$$

Air quality data summary :

Remote rural concentrations

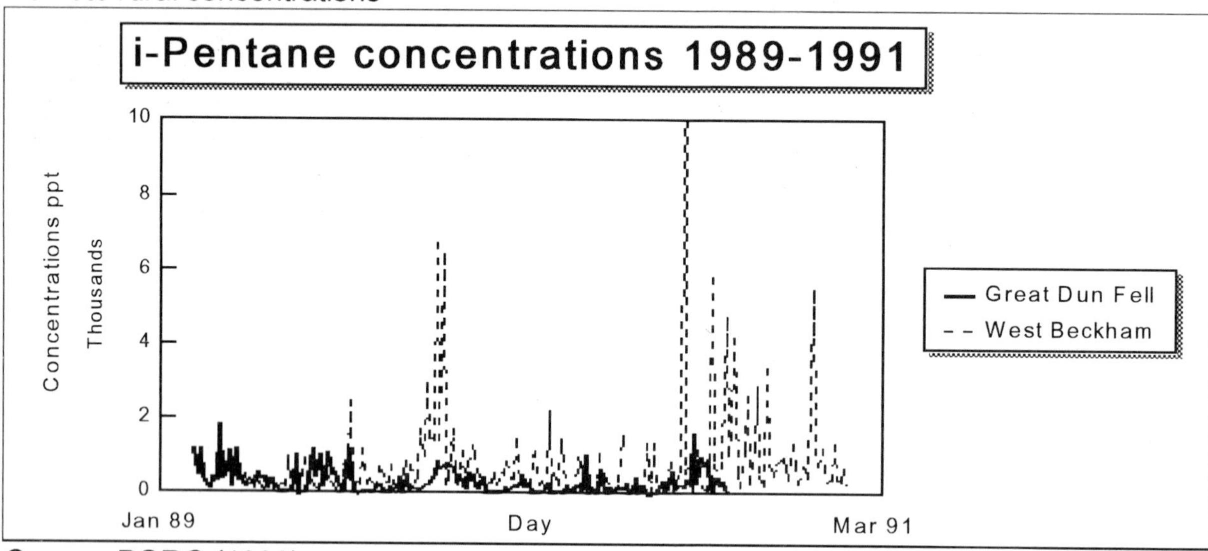

Source: PORG (1993)

Rural concentrations

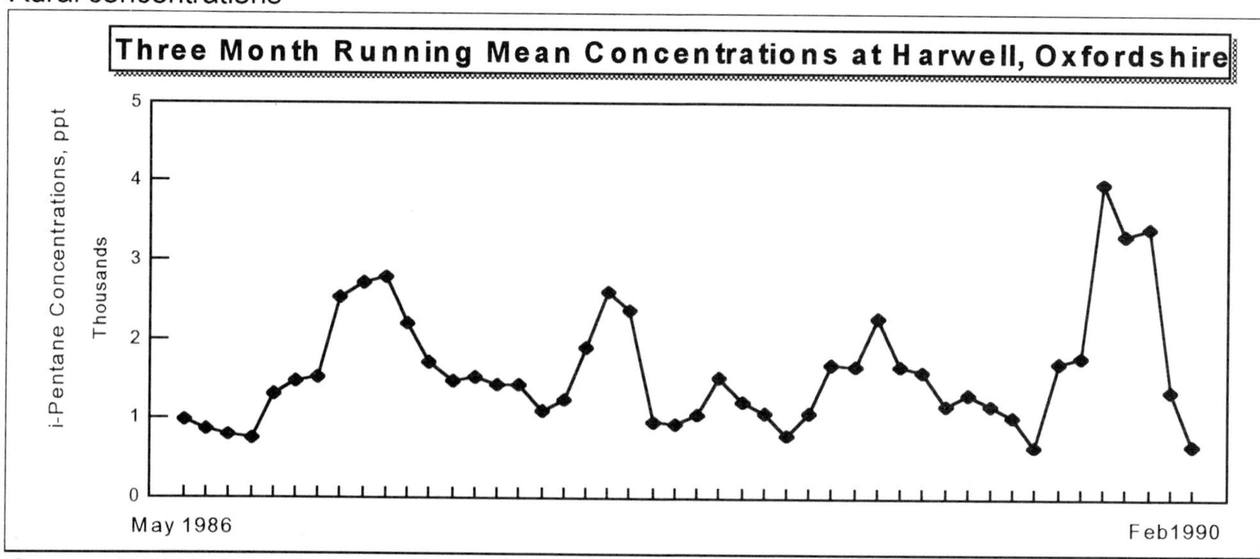

Source: PORG (1993)

Urban concentrations

	1994-95 Monthly Means, ppb								
	Belfast C	Birmingham B	Bristol A	Cardiff B	Edinburgh A	Eltham	Harwell	Middlesbrough	UCL
Jan 94	1.70	3.78	-	1.68	-	1.36	-	2.16	0.14
Feb 94	0.57	2.50	-	0.87	0.19	1.55	-	3.05	5.17
Mar 94	0.26	1.91	-	0.82	0.11	0.86	-	0.46	2.10
Apr 94	0.19	2.07	0.11	1.72	0.14	0.75	-	8.07	2.71
May 94	0.68	2.54	2.34	3.34	0.23	1.13	-	0.76	3.13
Jun 94	1.51	2.19	0.83	2.39	1.08	1.08	-	0.92	4.06
Jul 94	1.49	3.46	0.68	3.13	2.10	2.63	-	4.93	5.17
Aug 94	1.61	2.00	2.12	2.73	1.88	0.76	-	3.27	1.29
Sep 94	2.28	2.44	1.98	2.83	2.03	2.14	-	6.87	4.01
Oct 94	3.10	4.50	4.35	4.16	2.35	3.40	-	7.22	5.30
Nov 94	2.92	3.62	2.61	2.18	1.32	4.02	-	5.19	4.65
Dec 94	1.80	1.27	2.71	4.07	1.78	0.73	-	1.42	3.50
Jan 95	1.69	1.80	2.28	2.68	1.33	2.53	0.40	2.90	2.82
Feb 95	1.30	1.44	2.10	2.38	0.90	2.11	0.34	1.29	2.76

Source: Dollard (1995)

Chemical formula : $n\text{-}C_5H_{12}$

Alternative names :

Type of pollutant : (Volatile) organic compound (VOC), hydrocarbon

Structure :

$CH_3CH_2CH_2CH_2CH_3$

Air quality data summary :

Remote rural concentrations

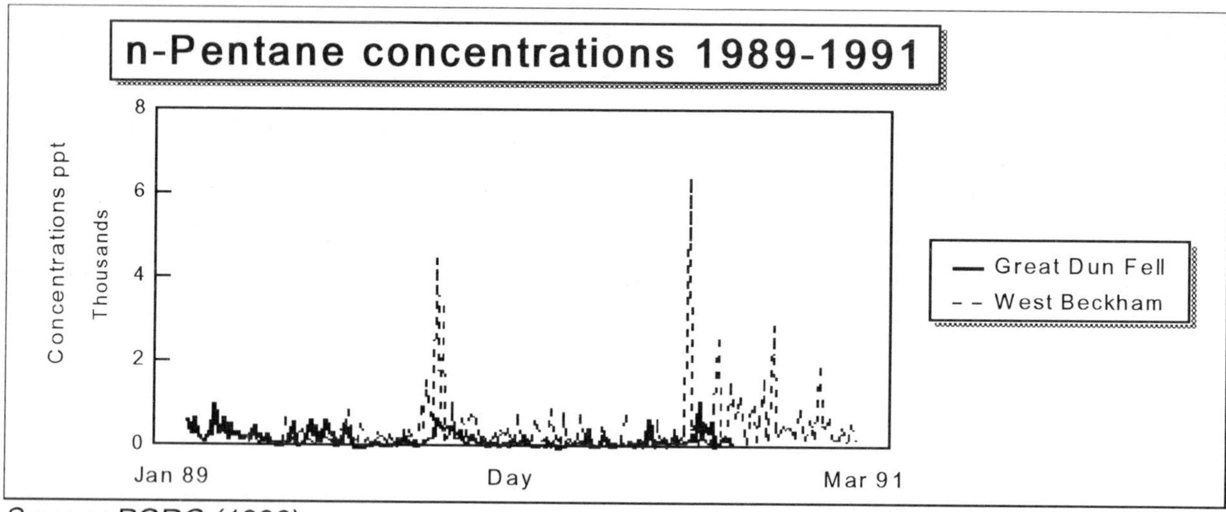

Source: PORG (1993)

Rural concentrations

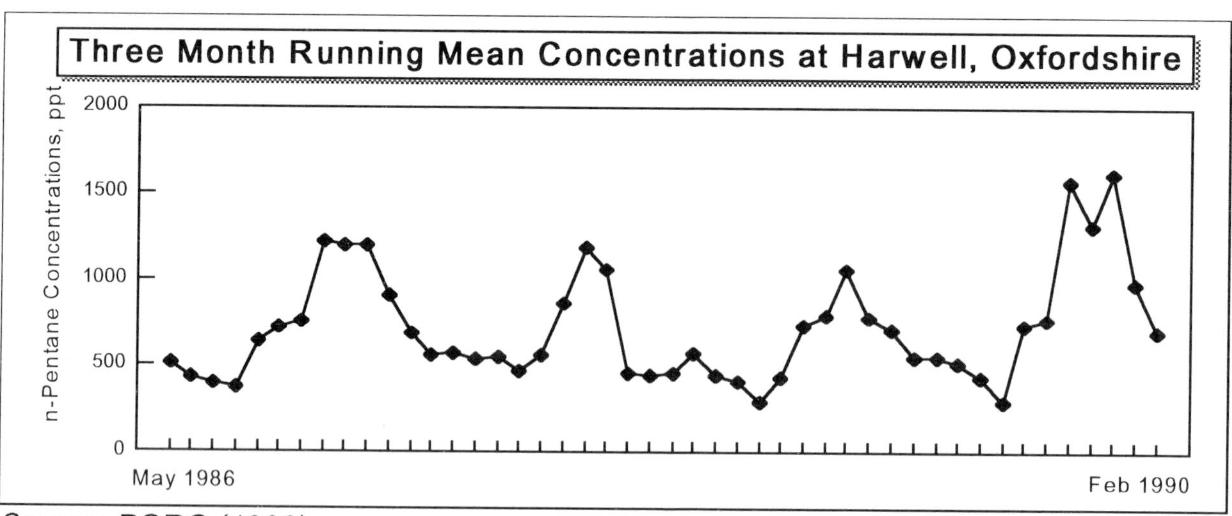

Source: PORG (1993)

Urban concentrations

	1994-95 Monthly Means, ppb								
	Belfast C	Birmingham B	Bristol A	Cardiff B	Edinburgh A	Eltham	Harwell	Middlesbrough	UCL
Jan 94	0.89	1.16	-	1.26	-	0.34	-	0.12	0.41
Feb 94	1.15	1.20	-	1.24	0.86	0.48	-	0.68	1.27
Mar 94	0.53	0.53	-	0.82	0.49	0.35	-	0.85	0.70
Apr 94	0.56	0.54	1.46	0.55	0.54	0.30	-	4.45	0.91
May 94	0.69	0.68	1.21	1.06	0.39	0.48	-	0.44	1.51
Jun 94	0.55	0.51	0.43	0.57	0.53	0.43	-	0.40	0.90
Jul 94	0.59	0.52	1.20	0.80	0.94	0.62	-	2.24	1.21
Aug 94	0.64	0.58	0.54	0.82	0.91	0.52	-	1.32	0.26
Sep 94	0.97	0.59	0.45	0.84	1.16	0.61	-	4.69	1.05
Oct 94	1.24	1.17	0.91	1.21	1.26	0.96	-	2.80	1.59
Nov 94	0.99	1.17	0.99	1.32	0.78	0.86	-	2.14	1.53
Dec 94	0.99	1.31	0.98	1.11	0.76	1.04	-	0.63	0.94
Jan 95	0.64	0.55	0.84	0.75	0.64	0.65	0.18	1.50	0.86
Feb 95	0.49	0.31	0.62	0.67	0.44	0.47	0.14	0.63	0.76

Source: Dollard (1995)

Chemical formula : C_5H_{10}

Alternative names : pent-1-ene

Type of pollutant : (Volatile) organic compound (VOC), hydrocarbon

Structure :

$CH_2=CHCH_2CH_2CH_3$

Air quality data summary :

Remote rural concentrations

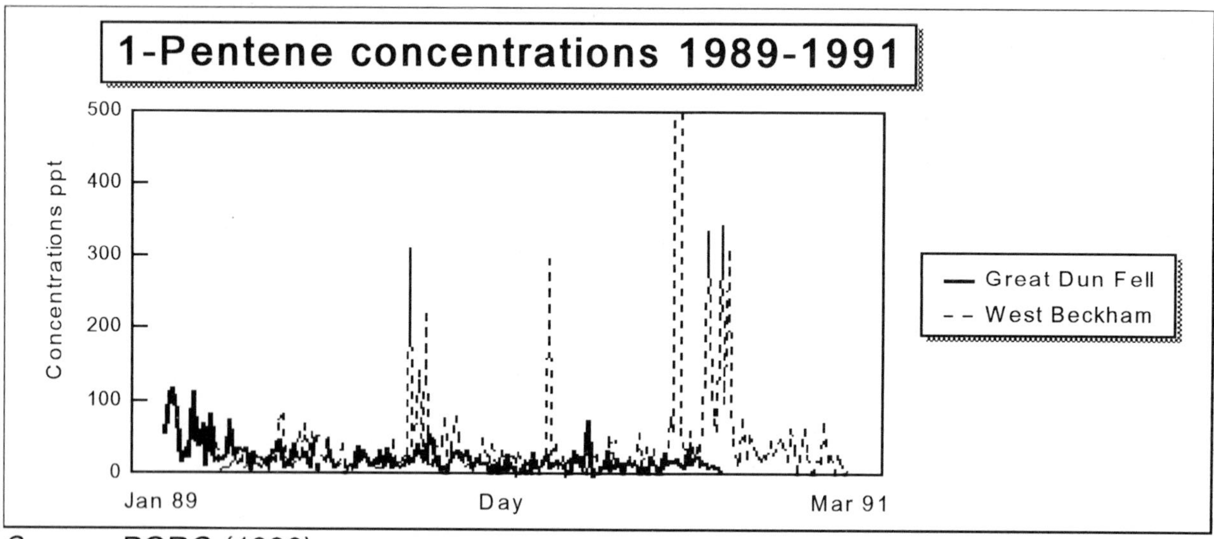

Source: PORG (1993)

Chemical formula	:	$C_{20}H_{12}$
Alternative names	:	*peri*-Dinaphthalene
Type of pollutant	:	Polynucleated aromatic hydrocarbon (PAH)
Structure	:	

Air quality data summary :

Urban concentrations :

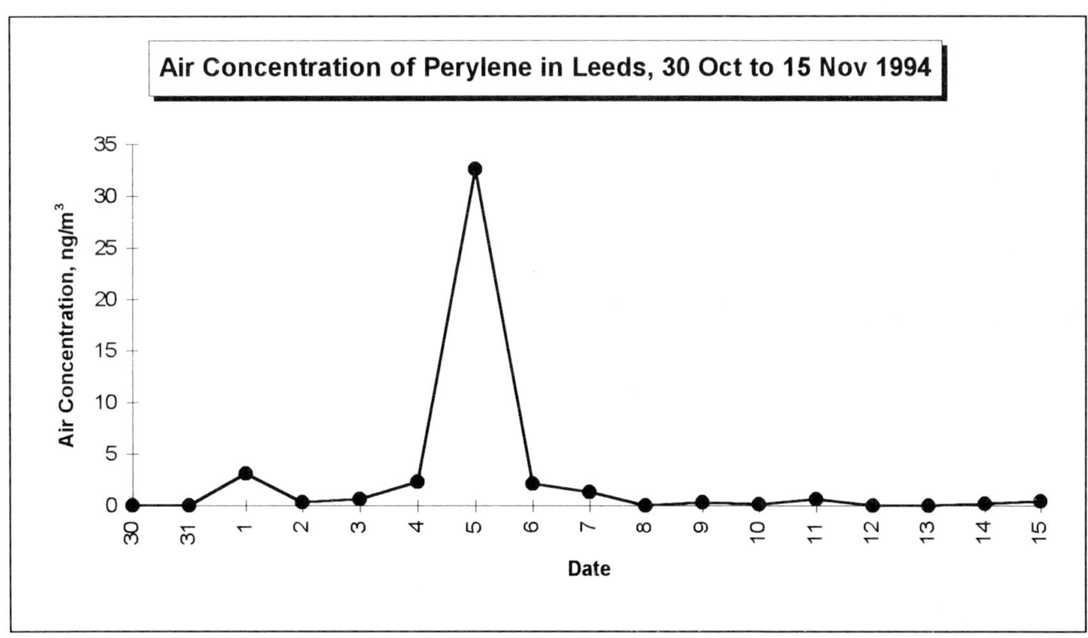

Source: Lewis et al. (1995)

Chemical formula : $C_{14}H_{10}$

Alternative names : PAH EPA no.81

Type of pollutant : Polynuclear Aromatic Hydrocarbon (PAH)

Structure :

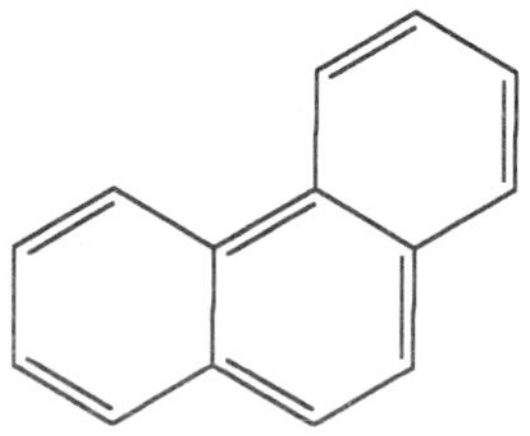

Air quality data summary :

Location	Annual Mean ng/m^3		
	1991	1992	1993
Bowland	*	*	156.28
Cardiff C	52.08	28.60	*
London	83.70	80.38	98.33
Manchester B	63.76	37.40	35.15
Middlesbrough	*	*	91.05
WSL	45.51	*	*

Source: Davis (1993)

Notes: * signifies no data available

Location	Season 1992	Total Concentration in Air ng/m^3
Edgbaston	Winter (February)	24.11
Edgbaston	Summer (August)	3.84
Wasthills	Summer (August)	0.60

Source: Smith and Harrison (1994)

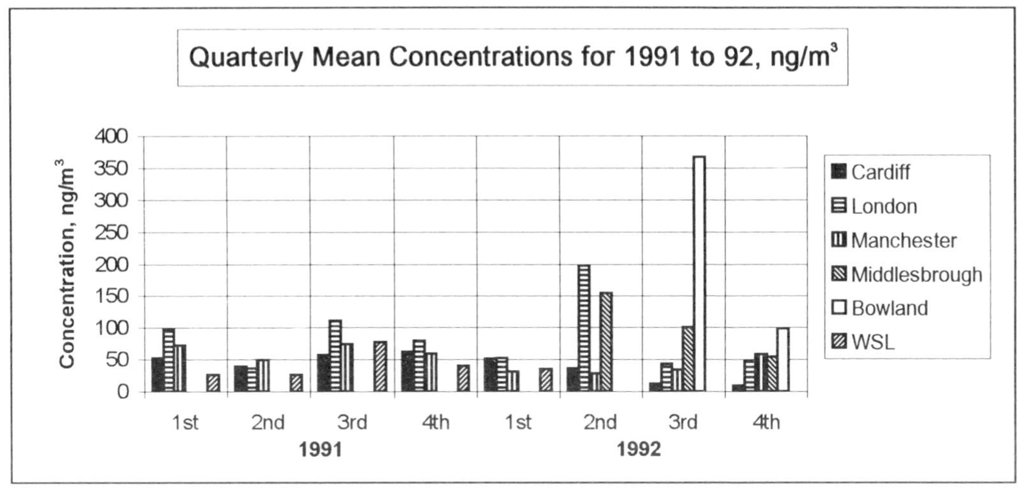

Source: Davis (1993)

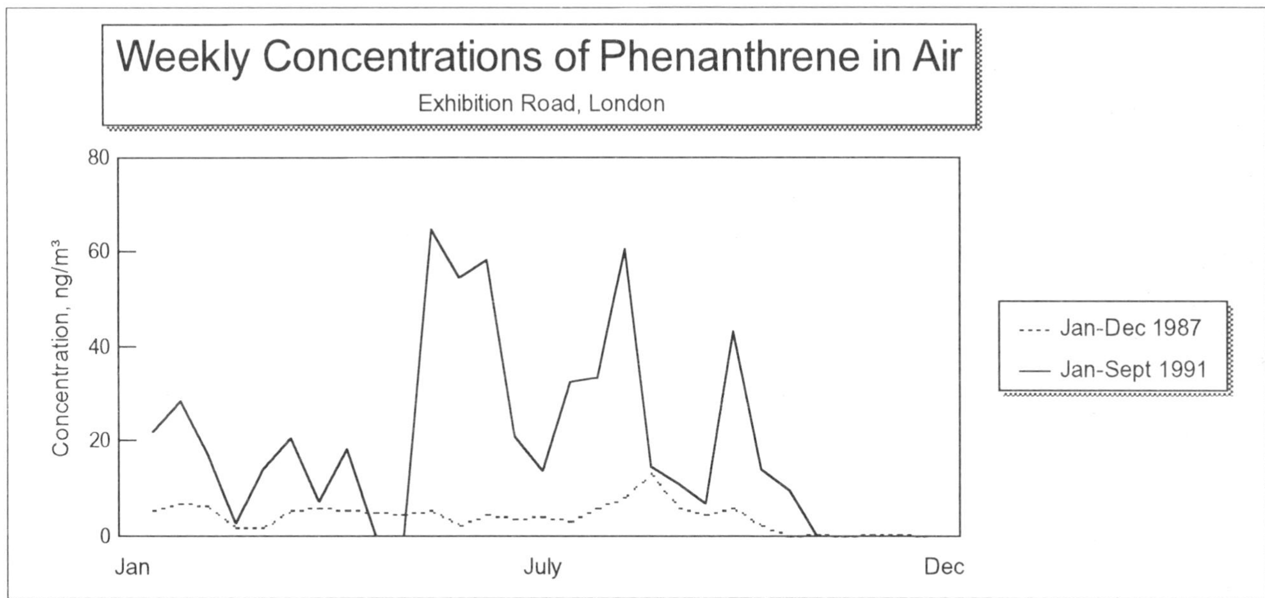

Source: Brown et al. (1995)

Phenanthrene in deposition

Chemical formula : $C_{14}H_{10}$

Alternative names : PAH EPA no.81

Type of pollutant : Polynuclear Aromatic Hydrocarbon (PAH)

Structure :

Air quality data summary :

Location	Annual Mean ng/m²/day		
	1991	1992	1993
Bowland	*	*	677.86
Cardiff C	1194.73	642.05	*
London	1997.50	36160.30	*
Manchester B	1603.93	495.77	*
Middlesbrough	*	*	*
WSL	2399.13	*	*

Source: Davis (1993)

Notes: * signifies no data available

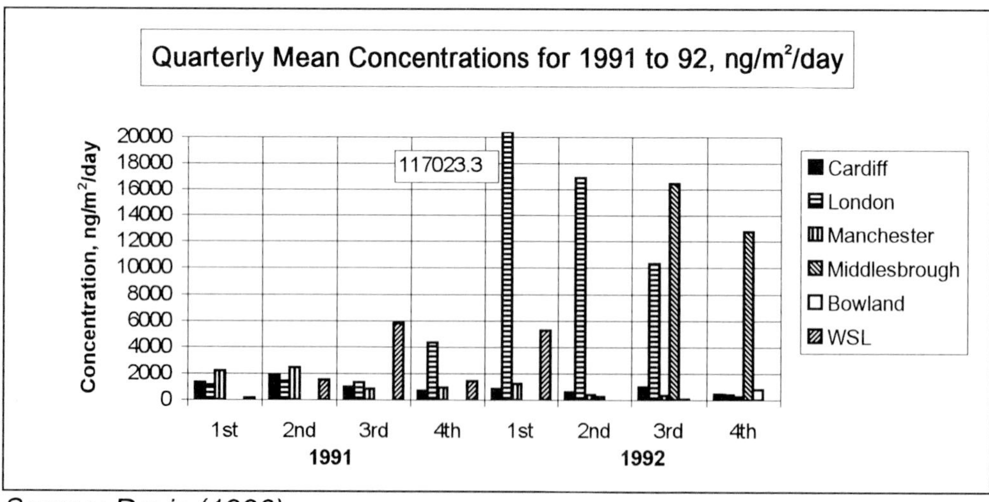

Source: Davis (1993)

Chemical formula : $C_{10}H_{16}$

Alternative names :

Type of pollutant : Terpene, natural biogenic hydrocarbon

Structure :

H_3C H H H H CH_3 CH_3 H H H

Air quality data summary :

Mean Air Concentration in Leeds, 19/8/94 to 8/9/94	
Location	21 day mean, $\mu g/m^3$
Albion Street	0.071
Cliff Lane	0.038
EUN monitoring site	0.029
Kerbside site	0.044
Kirkstall Road	0.054
Park site	0.058
Queen Street	0.045
Vicar Lane	0.074

Source: Bartle et al. (1995)

Chemical formula :

Alternative name : Particulate matter less than 10 micron size

Type of pollutant : Suspended particulate matter

Air quality data summary :

Urban Concentrations

PM_{10} Calendar Year Statistics, µg/m^3							
Location	Year	Annual Mean	Max. Daily Mean	Location	Year	Annual Mean	Max. Daily Mean
Belfast B	92	27	248	Edinburgh B	93	23	66
	93	32	120		94	20	65
	94	26	191				
				Hull	94	26	84
Bexley	94	25	70				
				Leeds	93	27	96
Birmingham A	92	26	131		94	26	114
	93	26	102				
	94	23	113	Leicester	94	21	65
Birmingham B	94	21	106	Liverpool	93	29	163
					94	25	84
Bloomsbury	92	30	94				
	93	29	100	Newcastle	92	28	72
	94	27	93		93	29	79
					94	26	77
Bristol B	93	27	81				
	94	24	83	Southampton	94	23	63
Cardiff A	92	26	85				
	93	31	89				
	94	34	96				

Source: Bower et al. (1995)

Location	Year	Maximum Daily Mean PM_{10} Concentration 1992-94, µg/m^3											
		Jan	Feb	Mar	Apr	May	Jun	Jul	Aug	Sep	Oct	Nov	Dec
Belfast B	92	-	-	-	30	56	45	28	28	95	136	95	248
	93	120	61	66	73	78	107	25	42	65	118	98	40
	94	-	162	38	40	57	49	42	30	66	83	54	191

Location	Year	Maximum Daily Mean PM_{10} Concentration 1992-94, $\mu g/m^3$											
		Jan	Feb	Mar	Apr	May	Jun	Jul	Aug	Sep	Oct	Nov	Dec
Bexley	94	-	-	-	-	-	44	57	33	41	70	58	49
Birmingham A	92	-	-	-	68	77	64	71	60	57	59	34	131
	93	-	-	56	102	57	-	27	40	66	44	71	27
	94	-	63	30	30	43	43	46	39	36	71	56	113
Birmingham B	93	-	-	-	-	-	-	-	-	-	-	-	31
	94	51	57	26	26	37	41	45	32	33	62	79	106
Bloomsbury	92	-	68	51	-	-	75	68	-	66	44	43	79
	93	66	76	68	75	81	100	54	50	44	48	81	29
	94	42	75	31	41	57	54	58	41	46	93	58	91
Bristol	93	37	-	53	-	57	61	58	44	61	49	81	49
	94	53	71	34	33	47	42	41	40	40	83	49	52
Cardiff A	92	-	-	-	-	-	-	36	45	52	-	69	85
	93	-	-	59	89	65	75	-	-	-	-	-	45
	94	60	68	59	64	58	81	82	96	80	76	72	41
Edinburgh	92	-	-	-	-	-	-	-	-	-	-	-	72
	93	36	-	-	43	41	46	-	37	32	45	66	35
	94	33	43	25	25	42	38	41	28	34	65	38	48
Hull	94	-	73	34	37	58	37	52	46	48	84	62	55
Leeds	93	-	62	-	-	-	-	-	52	60	51	96	43
	94												
Leicester	94	59	50	25	30	36	39	42	40	33	51	52	65
Liverpool	93	-	-	-	-	74	-	-	44	85	48	163	49
	94	-	76	32	29	52	39	47	39	58	84	59	76
Newcastle	92	-	-	37	71	-	-	-	51	67	40	40	-
	93	42	62	54	65	45	79	-	-	-	-	73	43
	94	50	63	33	43	52	-	51	37	53	77	58	59
Southampton	94	50	-	-	55	39	45	48	35	40	63	52	43

Source: Bower (1995)

Data displayed for $\geq 75\%$ valid days of > 15 hours.

Chemical formula : K

Alternative names : Particulate potassium

Type of pollutant : Suspended particulate matter, trace element

Air quality data summary :

Rural Concentrations

Location	Average Annual Concentrations, ng/m^3			
	Mean	Trend	Mean	Trend
	1972-1981	%/yr	1982-1991	%/yr
Harwell, Oxfordshire.	731	nst	<478	-14.2
Styrrup, Nottinghamshire.	1041	-12.6	<662	-9.9
Trebanos, Glamorgan.	992	-	-	-
Wraymires, Cumbria.	717	nst	<564	-10.1

Source: Cawse et al. (1994)

Note: >70% of measurements at each location were below limits of detection during the period 1982-1991.
nst=no significant trend

Chemical formula : K

Alternative names : Precipitation potassium

Type of pollutant : Trace contaminant of rain, trace element

Air quality data summary :

Rural Concentrations

Location	Average Annual Rainfall Concentration, µg per litre	
	1972 - 1981	1982-1991*
Harwell, Oxfordshire	2388	<1400
Styrrup, Nottinghamshire	1586	<1250
Wraymires, Cumbria	1111	<1200

Source: Cawse et al. (1994)

Note: total deposition expressed as apparent rainfall concentration
*based on soluble fraction only

Location	1992 Monthly Weighted Mean Concentration in Precipitation, mg/l											
	Jan	Feb	Mar	Apr	May	Jun	Jul	Aug	Sep	Oct	Nov	Dec
Eskdalemuir	0.1	0.1	0.0	0.0	0.1	1.2	0.2	0.1	0.0	0.5	0.0	0.0
High Muffles	0.1	0.1	0.1	0.1	0.1	0.1	0.1	0.1	0.0	0.1	0.0	0.0
Lough Navar	0.1	0.2	0.2	0.1	0.1	0.0	0.0	0.1	0.1	0.1	0.1	0.1
Strath Vaich	0.2	0.3	0.1	0.1	0.0	0.1	0.2	0.0	0.1	0.1	0.1	0.0
Yarner Wood	0.1	0.1	0.1	0.1	0.1	0.0	0.1	0.1	0.1	0.3	0.1	0.1

Source: Schaug et al. (1994)

Chemical formula : C_3H_6O

Alternative names : Propionaldehyde, propional

Type of pollutant : (Volatile) organic compound (VOC), hydrocarbon, oxygenate

Structure : CH_3CH_2CHO

Air quality data summary :

Rural Concentrations

Month 1993	Air Concentration at Harwell site, ppb
	Monthly Mean
August	0.108
September	0.083
October	0.066
November	0.120
December	0.029

Source: Solberg et al. (1994)

Chemical formula : C_3H_8

Alternative names :

Type of pollutant : (Volatile) organic compound (VOC), hydrocarbon

Structure : $CH_3CH_2CH_3$

Air quality data summary :

Remote rural concentrations

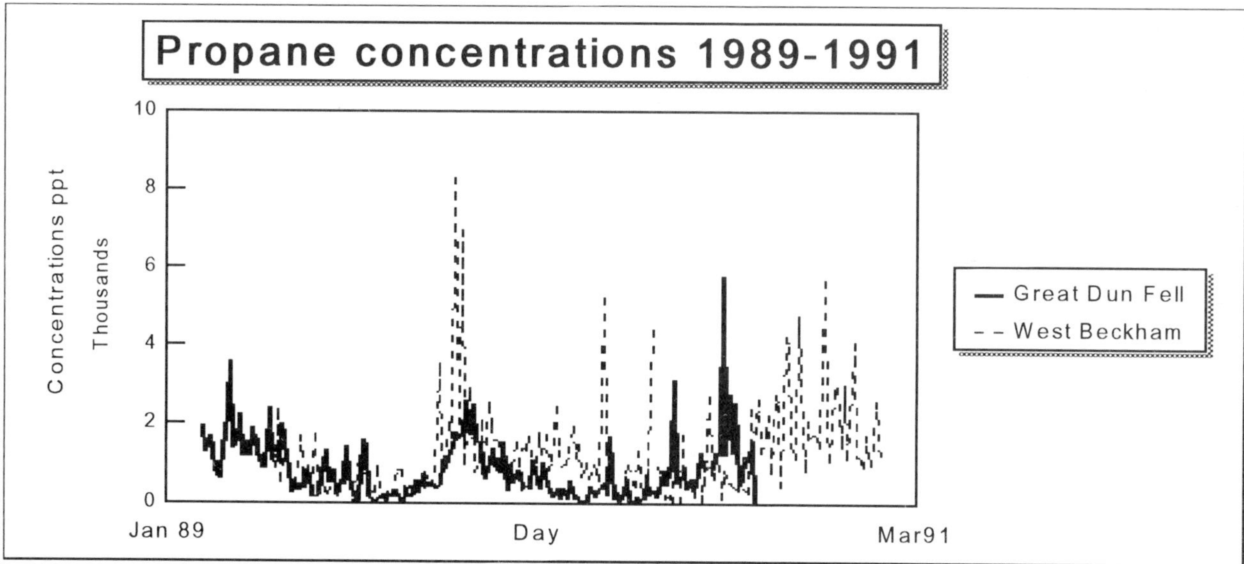

Source: PORG (1993)

Rural concentrations

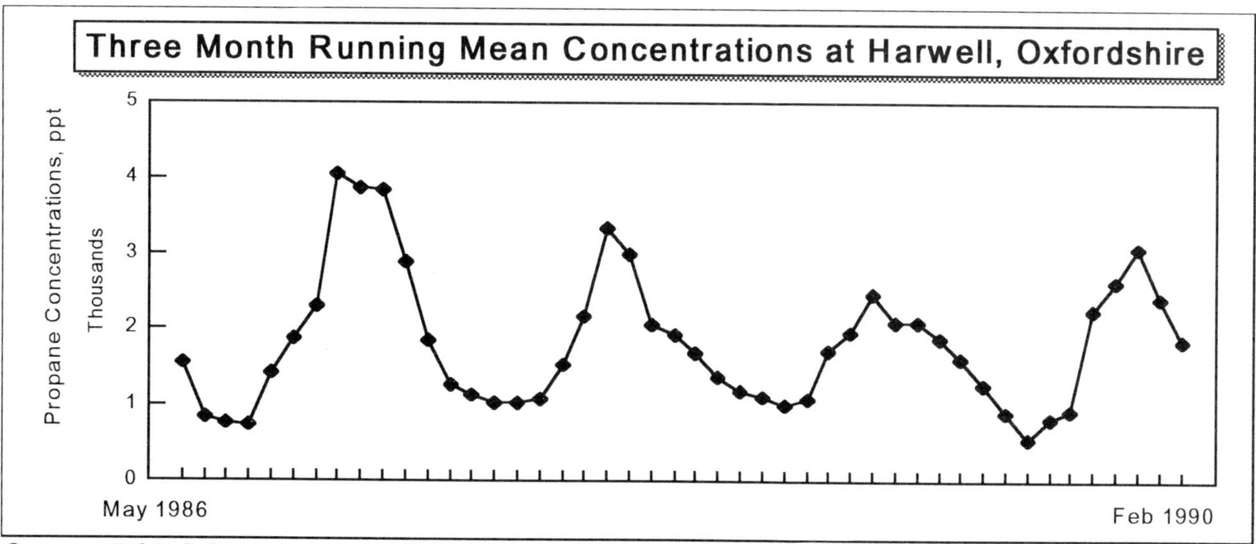

Source: PORG (1993)

Urban Concentrations

	1994-95 Monthly Means, ppb								
	Belfast C	Birmingham B	Bristol A	Cardiff B	Edinburgh A	Eltham	Harwell	Middlesbrough	UCL
Jan 94	5.06	4.63	-	3.02	-	1.21	-	4.66	3.18
Feb 94	6.91	5.22	-	3.44	3.79	1.69	-	5.22	4.19
Mar 94	2.92	2.84	-	2.52	1.71	0.78	-	1.11	2.30
Apr 94	3.33	2.71	0.01	1.59	1.81	1.89	-	6.96	2.64
May 94	4.85	3.26	1.86	7.84	-	1.65	-	4.82	2.58
Jun 94	2.66	2.76	0.76	2.21	1.02	0.93	-	1.84	1.78
Jul 94	3.05	3.28	1.28	1.99	2.35	1.09	-	7.93	2.10
Aug 94	2.77	3.53	1.41	1.89	2.52	1.03	-	3.74	0.42
Sep 94	4.51	2.69	1.51	1.66	4.01	1.20	-	6.29	2.35
Oct 94	6.50	5.13	3.10	3.15	4.23	1.94	-	5.18	3.45
Nov 94	25.67	4.34	2.56	3.40	2.33	1.81	-	5.82	3.48
Dec 94	26.36	4.80	2.13	2.97	2.85	2.40	-	3.35	3.14
Jan 95	15.73	2.85	2.38	2.74	3.51	2.08	1.28	4.27	2.65
Feb 95	14.49	2.61	2.15	2.67	2.02	1.58	1.09	4.09	2.34

Source: Dollard (1995)

Chemical formula : C_3H_6O

Alternative names : Acetone

Type of pollutant : (Volatile) organic compound (VOC), hydrocarbon, oxygenate

Structure :

$$CH_3\underset{\underset{O}{||}}{C}CH_3$$

Air quality data summary :

Rural Concentrations

Month 1993	Air Concentration at Harwell site, ppb
	Monthly Mean
September	0.608
October	0.596
November	0.902
December	0.319

Source: Solberg et al. (1994)

Propenal

Chemical formula : C_3H_4O

Alternative names : Acrolein, acrylaldehyde

Type of pollutant : (Volatile) organic compound (VOC), hydrocarbon, oxygenate

Structure :

$CH_2{=}CH{-}CHO$

Air quality data summary :

Rural Concentrations

Month 1993	Air Concentration at Harwell site, ppb
	Monthly Mean
August	0.021
September	0.030
October	0.030
November	0.056

Source: Solberg et al. (1994)

Chemical formula : C_9H_{12}

Alternative names :

Type of pollutant : (Volatile) organic compound (VOC), hydrocarbon

Structure :

$CH_2CH_2CH_3$ (attached to benzene ring)

Air quality data summary :

Mean Air Concentration in Leeds, 19/8/94 to 8/9/94	
Location	**21 day mean, µg/m^3**
Albion Street	0.122
Cliff Lane	0.081
EUN monitoring site	0.102
Kerbside site	0.162
Kirkstall Road	0.228
Park site	0.088
Queen Street	0.135
Vicar Lane	0.364

Source: Bartle et al. (1995)

i-Propylbenzene

Chemical formula : C_9H_{12}

Alternative names :

Type of pollutant : (Volatile) organic compound (VOC), hydrocarbon

Structure :

$CH(CH_3)_2$

Air quality data summary :

Mean Air Concentration in Leeds, 19/8/94 to 8/9/94	
Location	21 day mean, $\mu g/m^3$
Albion Street	0.039
Cliff Lane	0.038
EUN monitoring site	0.038
Kerbside site	0.044
Kirkstall Road	0.054
Park site	0.034
Queen Street	0.033
Vicar Lane	0.093

Source: Bartle et al. (1995)

Propylcyclohexane

Chemical formula : C_9H_{18}

Alternative names :

Type of pollutant : (Volatile) organic compound (VOC), hydrocarbon

Structure :

C_3H_7 | CH, CH_2, CH_2, CH_2, CH_2, CH_2 (cyclohexane ring)

Air quality data summary :

Mean Air Concentration in Leeds, 19/8/94 to 8/9/94	
Location	21 day mean, $\mu g/m^3$
Albion Street	0.053
Cliff Lane	0.037
EUN monitoring site	0.039
Kerbside site	0.066
Kirkstall Road	0.098
Park site	0.083
Queen Street	0.045
Vicar Lane	0.074

Source: Bartle et al. (1995)

Chemical formula : C_3H_6

Alternative names : Propene

Type of pollutant : (Volatile) organic compound (VOC), hydrocarbon

Structure :

$CH_2{=}CHCH_3$

Air quality data summary :

Remote rural concentrations

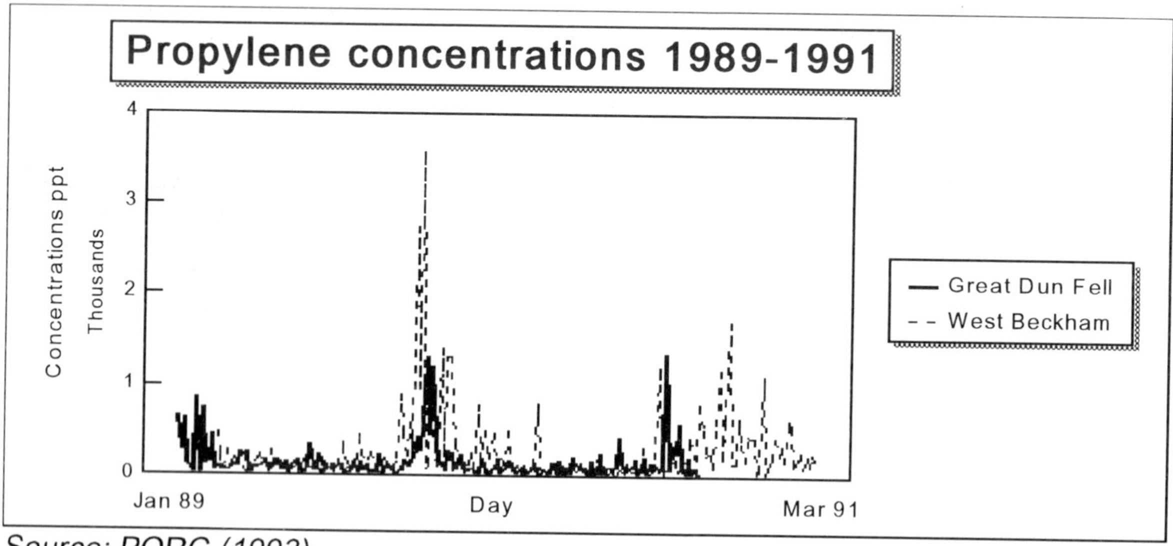

Source: PORG (1993)

Rural concentrations

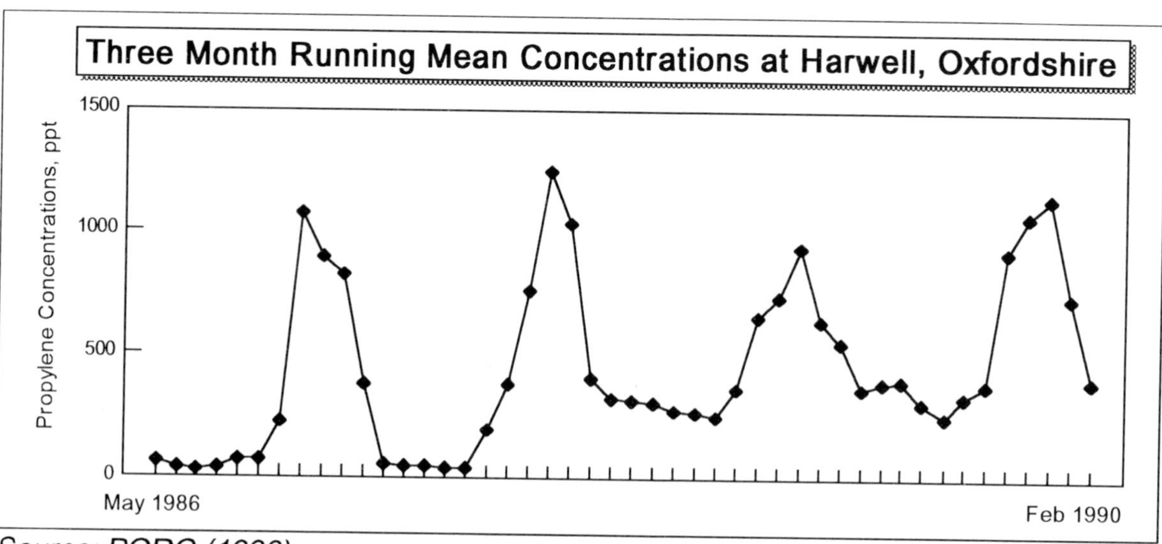

Source: PORG (1993)

Urban Concentrations

	1994-95 Monthly Means, ppb								
	Belfast C	Birmingham B	Bristol A	Cardiff B	Edinburgh A	Eltham	Harwell	Middlesbrough	UCL
Jan 94	1.26	2.25	-	2.39	-	0.99	-	1.97	2.13
Feb 94	1.62	2.25	-	2.16	1.13	0.86	-	2.08	3.34
Mar 94	0.88	1.61	-	1.31	0.71	0.52	-	9.79	1.46
Apr 94	0.99	1.86	1.02	1.07	0.75	1.57	-	5.77	1.86
May 94	1.25	1.79	1.78	1.28	-	0.97	-	2.78	2.78
Jun 94	1.07	1.43	1.32	1.23	0.89	1.07	-	1.20	1.79
Jul 94	1.03	1.61	1.53	1.51	1.13	1.08	-	4.68	2.07
Aug 94	0.62	1.69	1.42	1.44	1.05	0.96	-	2.03	0.92
Sep 94	1.37	1.95	1.28	1.13	1.08	1.11	-	2.34	2.44
Oct 94	1.78	3.28	2.37	1.80	1.28	1.52	-	2.22	3.33
Nov 94	1.77	2.98	1.66	1.93	1.19	1.79	-	2.19	3.23
Dec 94	1.87	3.05	1.64	1.66	1.10	2.11	-	1.32	2.72
Jan 95	1.23	1.34	1.42	1.25	0.75	1.56	0.44	1.68	1.82
Feb 95	0.95	1.35	1.29	1.16	0.60	1.20	0.46	1.61	1.58

Source: Dollard (1995)

Chemical formula : $C_{16}H_{10}$

Alternative names : PAH EPA no.84

Type of pollutant : Polynuclear Aromatic Hydrocarbon (PAH)

Structure :

Air quality data summary :

Location	Annual Mean ng/m³		
	1991	1992	1993
Bowland	*	*	5.24
Cardiff C	11.11	4.89	*
London	12.69	6.82	5.38
Manchester B	11.95	5.94	5.82
Middlesbrough	*	*	5.49
WSL	6.03	*	*

Source: Davis (1993)

Notes: * signifies no data available

Location	Season 1992	Total Concentration in Air ng/m³
Edgbaston	Winter (February)	38.04
Edgbaston	Summer (August)	3.33
Wasthills	Summer (August)	1.00

Source: Smith and Harrison (1994)

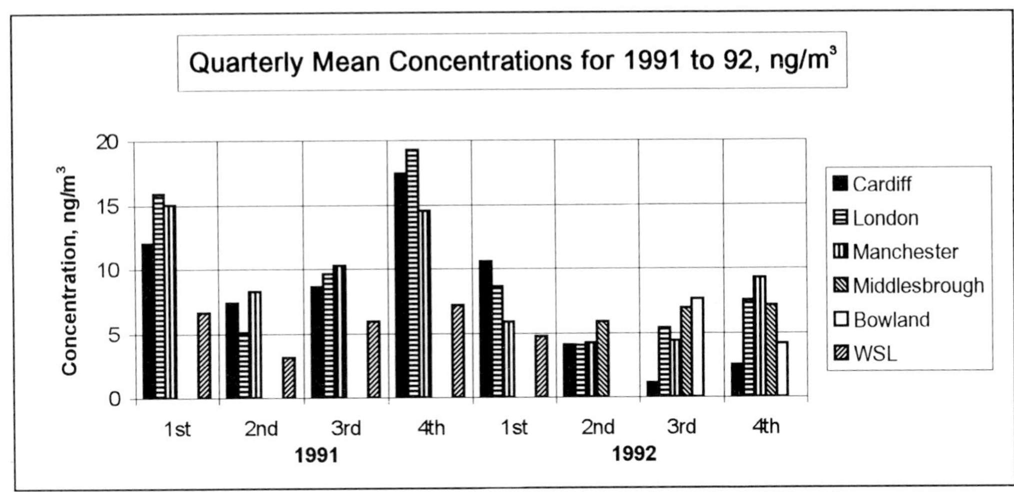

Source: Davis (1993)

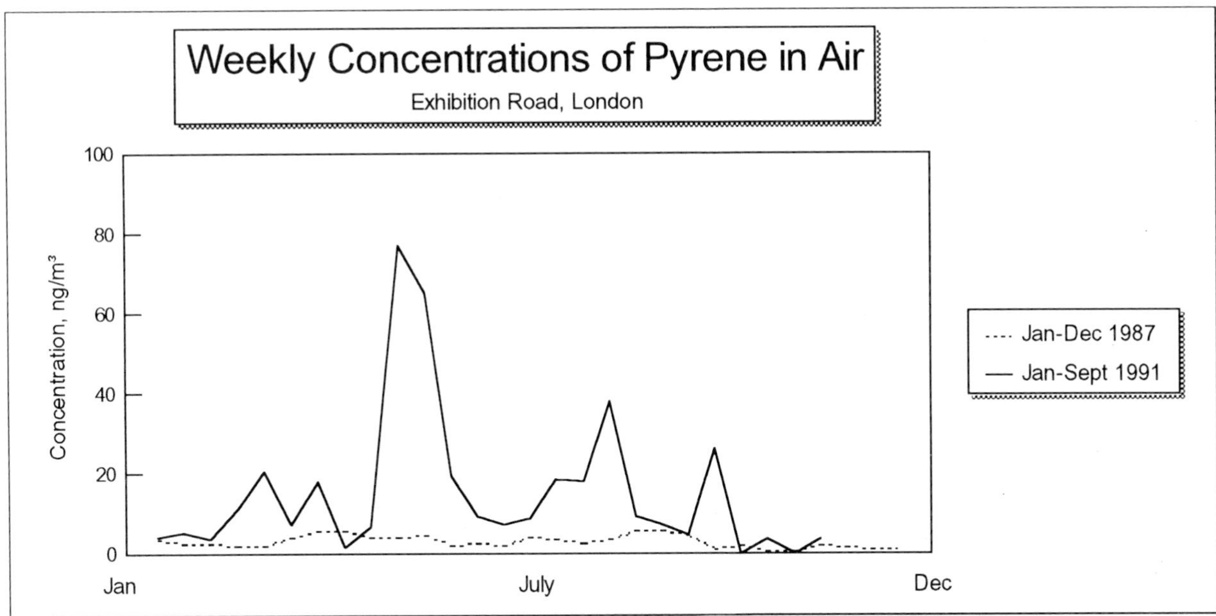

Source: Brown et al. (1995)

Chemical formula : $C_{16}H_{10}$

Alternative names : PAH EPA no.84

Type of pollutant : Polynuclear Aromatic Hydrocarbon (PAH)

Structure :

Air quality data summary :

Location	Annual Mean ng/m²/day		
	1991	1992	1993
Bowland	*	*	157.73
Cardiff C	807.09	223.66	*
London	678.10	2174.20	*
Manchester B	1553.63	289.42	*
Middlesbrough	*	*	*
WSL	398.04	*	*

Source: Davis (1993)

Notes: * signifies no data available

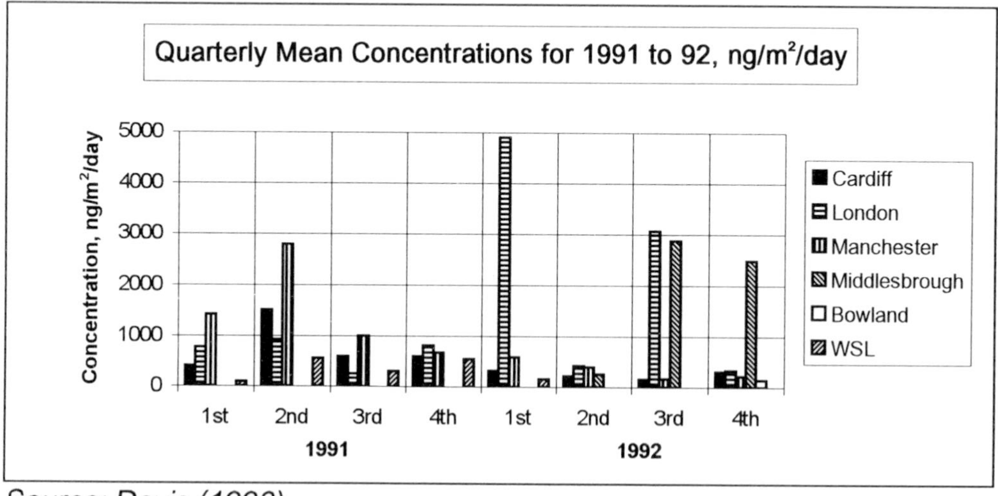

Source: Davis (1993)

Chemical formula : Rb

Alternative names : Particulate rubidium

Type of pollutant : Suspended particulate matter, trace element

Air quality data summary :

Rural concentrations

Location	Average Annual Concentrations, ng/m^3	
	Mean	Mean
	1972-1981	1982-1991
Harwell, Oxfordshire.	<2	<0.9
Styrrup, Nottinghamshire.	<5	<2
Trebanos, Glamorgan.	<5	-
Wraymires, Cumbria.	<1	<0.9

Source: Cawse et al. (1994)

Chemical formula : Rb

Alternative names : Precipitation rubidium

Type of pollutant : Trace contaminant of rain, trace element

Air quality data summary :

Rural Concentrations

Location	Average Annual Rainfall Concentration µg per litre	
	1972-1981	1982-1989 *
Harwell, Oxfordshire.	<2	<0.7
Styrrup, Nottinghamshire.	<7	<1
Wraymires, Cumbria.	<1	<0.7

Source: Cawse et al. (1994)

Note: total deposition expressed as apparent rainfall concentration.
* based on soluble fraction only.

Rubidium not analysed in rainwater in 1990 and 1991.

Chemical formula : Sm

Alternative names : Particulate samarium

Type of pollutant : Suspended particulate matter, trace element

Air quality data summary :

Rural concentrations

Location	Average Annual Concentrations, ng/m^3			
	Mean	Trend	Mean	Trend
	1975-1981	%/yr	1982-1991	%/yr
Harwell, Oxfordshire.	0.026	-	0.022	-6.1
Styrrup, Nottinghamshire.	0.059	-	0.042	-6.8
Trebanos, Glamorgan.	0.037	-	0.039	-20.5
Wraymires, Cumbria.	0.026	-	0.015	-10.5

Source: Cawse et al. (1994)

Location	Nature of site	Measurement period	Mean concentration ng/m^3
Altrincham	Residential	1978-1989	0.062
Brent	Residential	1975-1989	0.065
Chilton	Rural	1971-1989	0.028
Flixton	Residential	1975-1989	0.092
Lambeth	Residential	1976-1982	0.085
Manchester City North	Industrial/ Residential	1975-1988	0.081
Manchester City South	Residential	1975-1989	0.073
Walsall	Industrial	1976-1989	0.086
Wraymires	Rural	1970-1989	0.018

Source: Lee et al. (1994)

Chemical formula : Sm

Alternative names : Precipitation samarium

Type of pollutant : Trace contaminant of rain, trace element

Air quality data summary :

Rural Concentrations

Location	Average Annual Rainfall Concentration µg per litre	
	1972-1981	1982-1989 *
Harwell, Oxfordshire.	0.06	<0.01
Styrrup, Nottinghamshire.	0.09	<0.01
Wraymires, Cumbria.	<0.02	<0.01

Source: Cawse et al. (1994)

Note: total deposition expressed as apparent rainfall concentration.
* based on soluble fraction only.

Samarium not analysed in rainwater in 1990 and 1991.

Chemical formula	:	Sc
Alternative names	:	Particulate scandium
Type of pollutant	:	Suspended particulate matter, trace element

Air quality data summary :

Rural concentrations

Location	Average Annual Concentrations, ng/m^3			
	Mean	Trend	Mean	Trend
	1972-1981	%/yr	1982-1991	%/yr
Harwell, Oxfordshire.	0.07	-3.2	0.039	-
Styrrup, Nottinghamshire.	0.14	-7.6	0.091	-7.2
Trebanos, Glamorgan.	0.08	-7.3	0.064	-
Wraymires, Cumbria.	0.05	nst	0.026	-5.6

Source: Cawse et al. (1994)

nst=no significant trend

Location	Nature of site	Measurement period	Mean concentration ng/m^3
Altrincham	Residential	1978-1989	0.166
Brent	Residential	1975-1989	0.133
Chilton	Rural	1971-1989	0.058
Flixton	Residential	1975-1989	0.189
Lambeth	Residential	1976-1982	0.183
Manchester City North	Industrial/ Residential	1975-1988	0.185
Manchester City South	Residential	1975-1989	0.148
Swansea	Urban	1972-1981	0.200
Walsall	Industrial	1976-1989	0.263
Wraymires	Rural	1970-1989	0.047

Source: Lee et al. (1994), Pattenden (1974).

Chemical formula : Sc

Alternative names : Precipitation scandium

Type of pollutant : Trace contaminant of rain, trace element

Air quality data summary :

Rural Concentrations

Location	Average Annual Rainfall Concentration µg per litre	
	1972-1981	1982-1989 *
Harwell, Oxfordshire.	0.06	0.047
Styrrup, Nottinghamshire.	0.21	<0.006
Wraymires, Cumbria.	0.02	<0.002

Source: Cawse et al. (1994)

Note: total deposition expressed as apparent rainfall concentration.
* based on soluble fraction only.

Scandium not analysed in rainwater in 1990 and 1991.

Chemical formula : Se

Alternative names : Particulate selenium

Type of pollutant : Suspended particulate matter, trace element

Air quality data summary :

Rural Concentrations

Location	Average Annual Concentrations, ng/m^3			
	Mean	Trend	Mean	Trend
	1972-1981	%/yr	1982-1991	%/yr
Harwell, Oxfordshire.	2	nst	1.1	nst
Styrrup, Nottinghamshire.	4	nst	3.9	nst
Trebanos, Glamorgan.	2	-6.2	1.2	-
Wraymires, Cumbria.	1	nst	0.86	-4.5

Source: Cawse et al. (1994)

nst=no significant trend

Location	Nature of site	Measurement period	Mean concentration ng/m^3
Altrincham	Residential	1978-1989	2.6
Brent	Residential	1975-1989	2.3
Chilton	Rural	1971-1989	1.3
Flixton	Residential	1975-1989	2.8
Lambeth	Residential	1976-1982	2.5
Manchester City North	Industrial/ Residential	1975-1988	2.9
Manchester City South	Residential	1975-1989	2.7
Swansea	Urban	1972-1981	3.0
Walsall	Industrial	1976-1989	16.7
Wraymires	Rural	1970-1989	0.9

Source: Lee et al. (1994), Pattenden (1974).

Chemical formula : Se

Alternative names : Precipitation selenium

Type of pollutant : Trace contaminant of rain, trace element

Air quality data summary :

Rural Concentrations

Location	Average Annual Rainfall Concentration μg per litre	
	1972-1981	1982-1989 *
Harwell, Oxfordshire.	0.4	0.6
Styrrup, Nottinghamshire.	0.9	0.6
Wraymires, Cumbria.	0.2	0.1

Source: Cawse et al. (1994)

Note: total deposition expressed as apparent rainfall concentration.
* based on soluble fraction only.

Selenium not analysed in rainwater in 1990 and 1991.

Chemical formula : Ag

Alternative names : Particulate silver

Type of pollutant : Suspended particulate matter, trace element

Air quality data summary :

Rural Concentrations

Location	Concentrations, ng/m^3				
	Mean	Trend	Mean		Trend
	1975-1981	%/yr	1982-1991		%/yr
Harwell, Oxfordshire.	0.30	-	0.13	*	-
Styrrup, Nottinghamshire.	0.50	-	0.37	**	-24.7
Trebanos, Glamorgan.	0.29	-			-
Wraymires, Cumbria.	0.16	-	0.071	***	-16.1

Source: Cawse et al. (1994)

* only 63% of results were positive.
** only 55% of results were positive.
*** only 33% of results were positive.

Location	Nature of site	Measurement period	Mean concentration ng/m^3
Altrincham	Residential	1978-1989	0.3
Brent	Residential	1975-1989	1.1
Chilton	Rural	1971-1989	0.2
Flixton	Residential	1975-1989	0.5
Lambeth	Residential	1976-1982	0.9
Manchester City North	Industrial/ Residential	1975-1988	0.5
Manchester City South	Residential	1975-1989	0.3
Walsall	Industrial	1976-1989	5.3
Wraymires	Rural	1970-1989	<0.1

Source: Lee et al. (1994)

Chemical formula : Ag

Alternative names : Precipitation silver

Type of pollutant : Trace contaminant of rain, trace element

Air quality data summary :

Rural Concentrations

Location	Average Annual Rainfall Concentration μg/m^3	
	1972-1981	1982-1991 *
Harwell, Oxfordshire.	<0.1	<0.06
Styrrup, Nottinghamshire.	<0.2	<0.1
Wraymires, Cumbria.	<0.06	<0.1

Source: Cawse et al. (1994)

Note: total deposition expressed as apparent rainfall concentration.
* based on soluble fraction only.

Chemical formula :

Alternative names : Black smoke, smoke stain reflectance

Type of pollutant : Suspended particulate matter

Air quality data summary :

Black Smoke Annual Mean Concentrations (µg/m³) 1986 to 1994										
SITE NAME & NUMBER	GRID EAST	GRID NORTH	1986/7	1987/8	1988/9	1989/90	1990/1	1991/2	1992/3	1993/4
				Annual Mean	(µg/m³)					
ABERDEEN 2	3929	8057	10	13	7	9	11	6		
ABERDEEN 3	3931	8062						13	6	11
ACCRINGTON 5	3758	4285	14	11	9	11	12	12	9	11
ACKWORTH 1	4440	4167	32	44	37	35	34	30	14	11
ACTON 13	5208	1824	12							
ACTON 14	5206	1822	20	14						
ACTON 15	5209	1825			17	15	19	18	14	14
ADDLESTONE 1	5052	1646	7	6	22	11	10	11	9	8
ALFRETON 4	4417	3555	38	34	50	33	19	30	21	21
ALLERTON BYWATER 1	4417	4279	28	25	30	21	21			
ALLERTON BYWATER 2	4404	4293	21	17	17					
ALLOA 6	2885	6930	19	10						
ALNWICK 1	4187	6136	6							
ALNWICK 2	4187	6132	23	14						
ALSAGER 1	3797	3555	19							
ALTON 2	4726	1401	5	4						
ALVA 3	2880	6970	20	15	6					
AMROTH (Dyfed) 1	2163	2079	3							
APPLEBY 1	3687	5208	5	6						
ARMADALE 2	2945	6681					19	9	7	9
ARMADALE 3	2938	6685					22	11	8	9
ARMAGH 1	92877	93450						26	10	11
ASHINGTON 4	4284	5871	58	44	14	12	13	12	9	9
ASHTON-IN-MAKERFIELD 1	3576	3991	24	28				17	13	11
ASHTON-UNDER-LYNE 8	3939	3992	18	22	22	14	19	17	12	11
ASKERN 6	4557	4136		59	27	15	15	14		
ASKERN 8	4561	4131	43							
ATHERTON 5	3678	4034	18	17						
AWSWORTH 1	4482	3438	22							
BACUP 4	3870	4228	13	12	11	9	11	10	9	8
BALLINGRY 2	3178	6978		18	7	15	10	15	9	6
BALMEDIE 1	3956	8186			3	3	3	3	2	1
BANFF 1	3690	8639	4	5	5	3	4	4	3	2
BANGOR (CO DOWN) 4			5	5						
BARKING 15	5460	1831	15							
BARLASTON 1	3894	3385	12							
BARNSLEY 8	4348	4094	29	28	24	22	25	23	18	16

SITE NAME & NUMBER	GRID EAST	GRID NORTH	1986/7	1987/8	1988/9	1989/90	1990/1	1991/2	1992/3	1993/4
				Annual Mean		(µg/m³)				
BARNSLEY 9	4370	4055	43	42	31	27	25	24	20	17
BARNSLEY 12	4342	4067	12	12	10	18	18	20	12	11
BARROW-IN-FURNESS 3	3197	4697	22	21	19	18				
BARROW-IN-FURNESS 4	3214	4692						16	13	11
BATH 6	3754	1656	19	16	17	23	17	17	16	14
BATLEY 2	4243	4242	16	18						
BEDFORD 10	5056	2486	11	10	14	9	11	11	9	7
BEDLINGTON 7	4266	5821	42	34	27	15	23			
BEESTON & STAPLEFORD 1	4526	3370	15	18	21	12	13	19	13	14
BEESTON & STAPLEFORD 2	4490	3368	17	21						
BELFAST 11	93337	93742	29	33	15	30	26	17	17	18
BELFAST 12	93324	93737	40	31	30	22	40	23	13	20
BELFAST 13	93357	93740	40	37	29	37	29	23	23	17
BELFAST 14			12	13	11					
BELFAST 15	93317	93708	35	44	27	31	30	25	21	26
BELFAST 17			26	24						
BELFAST 18			17	22	21					
BELFAST 33	93346	93755	25	29	26	25	33	25	22	19
BELFAST 39			50	53	43	35				
BELFAST 40			11	16	15					
BELFAST 41	93336	93765		52	25	29	24	17	14	11
BELFAST 42	93322	93748				43	39	25	23	22
BIDDULPH 2	3884	3577	41	39	40	31	32	34	16	11
BILSTON 19	3965	2943	15	14						
BIRCOTES 1	4627	3920		34	24	25	26	19	12	11
BIRKENHEAD 2	3315	3882	14	14						
BIRMINGHAM 26	4115	2889	14	13	14	15	14	14	11	11
BISHOPBRIGGS 1	2612	6713	15	16	11					
BLACKBURN 16	3678	4281	15							
BLACKBURN 21	3702	4270	9	8						
BLACKPOOL 6	3317	4367	14	17	19	15	16	14	13	13
BLACKROD 1	3613	4109	13	12						
BLETCHLEY 2	4857	2337	10	8	9	8	10	12	8	7
BLOOMSBURY,EUN. 1	5302	1820								14
BLYTH 15	4314	5817	21	19	12					
BLYTH 16	4307	5818	51	26	15					
BOLSOVER 5	4475	3706	44	43	33	27	29	26	17	11
BOLTON 24	3715	4092	17	17	15	14	14	15	13	14
BOLTON 27	3690	4078	14	14						
BOLTON 28	3713	4117	19							
BOLTON 29	3741	4096	18	16						
BO'NESS 2	2989	6808	25	14	7	10	8	8	6	7
BONNYRIGG 1	3309	6651			33	36	30	26	17	14
BOOTLE 6	3345	3948	17	16	14					
BRADFORD 6	4163	4329	17	22	19	8	16	16	18	16
BRADFORD 17	4154	4273	11	14						
BRADFORD 19	4133	4334	9	7	7					
BRADFORD 20	4151	4351	10	12						
BRADFORD 22	4158	4320	19	22						
BRADFORD 23	4186	4331	14	14	13					
BRAINTREE 8	5757	2235	9	10	12	9	7	6		
BRAMPTON 1	4414	4019				52	38	24	18	23
BRIDGWATER 2	3296	1369	14	10	10	8	7	5		
BRIDGWATER 3	3298	1373						12	8	9
BRIERLEY HILL 15	3918	2874	13							
BRIMINGTON 1	4405	3736	12							

SITE NAME & NUMBER	GRID EAST	GRID NORTH	1986/7	1987/8	1988/9	1989/90	1990/1	1991/2	1992/3	1993/4
				Annual Mean ($\mu g/m^3$)						
BRISTOL 26	3634	1763	12	10	9	9	8	8	6	7
BRISTOL 28	3590	1732	10							
BROCKHILL 1	4002	2702		10	6	6	4			
BROXBURN 2	3080	6723	13	9						
BUNGAY 1	6340	2895	9	8						
BURHAM 1	5730	1619	7	8	8	5	6			
BURNLEY 12	3841	4324							16	10
BURNTWOOD 1	4047	3087	13	15						
BURTON-UPON-TRENT 12	4240	3235	19	17	18	15	17	15	11	8
BURTON-UPON-TRENT 13	4242	3233								9
BURY 8	3811	4125	6	6						
BURY 9	3819	4116	8	8	5	5	3	8	8	12
CAENBY, LINCS 1	4993	3900	8	10	9	8	7			
CAMBERWELL 4	5343	1735	13	11	12		11	17		
CAMBORNE 1	1628	407	3	2	3	2	3			
CAMPHILL 1	2278	6543			3	3	3			
CANNOCK 18	3989	3117	55	49	46	37	30	16	17	13
CARDIFF 12	3193	1773	15	14	12	10	14	12	11	10
CARDINGTON 2	5079	2468	10	7	7	7	7			
CARLISLE 12	3407	5555	9							
CARLISLE 13	3398	5550	26	17	13	14	15	13	12	10
CARRICKFERGUS 2			12		8	7	10			
CASTLEFORD 9	4434	4255	36	36	32	21	12			
CASTLEFORD 10	4437	4257					15	13	11	7
CHADDERTON 4	3909	4053	23	22						
CHAPELTOWN 3	4356	3962	16							
CHEADLE 3	4010	3437	32	29	38	24	27	22	15	11
CHEADLE & GATLEY 6	3859	3886	7	7	5	9	3	8	9	6
CHELSEA 6	5271	1781	17	19						
CHESTERFIELD 18	4372	3709	15	8	6	5	4	3	5	7
CHESTER-LE-STREET 4	4273	5507	38	36	28	24	23	23	17	14
CHORLEY 6	3585	4178	27	15	13	10	11	7	16	13
CLIPSTONE 1	4588	3632	38	28	34					
COALVILLE 5	4428	3142	15	17	11	19	15	17	13	14
COATBRIDGE 5	2712	6638	26	24	14	19	22	10	9	7
COATBRIDGE 9	2717	6669	14	17	11					
COATBRIDGE 11	2738	6652	15	11	9	12	11	12	8	5
CONGLETON 2	3860	3629	27							
CONISBROUGH 7	4513	3987	20	24						
CONISBROUGH 8	4501	3996	25	24	31					
CORPACH 1	2055	7780		2			3			
COTTAM 20	4708	3822	18	18						
COVENTRY 13	4337	2788	11	11	11	11	12	12	8	
COWDENBEATH 1	3165	6912		23	8	15	17	20	14	11
COWPEN 1	4297	5814	31							
CRAWLEY 3	5269	1362	8	9	6	9	8	9	8	8
CRESSELLY (Dyfed) 1	2064	2062	3	3	3	3	4			
CREWE 9	3703	3550	18	12	15	17	22	10	14	13
CREWE 17	3710	3567	40	25	25	19	24	12	12	10
CREWE 18	3696	3568	21	14						
CROOK 1	4167	5356	25							
CROSBY 3	3321	3990	15	13	12	13	15	14	11	11
CROWDEN 1	4069	3995	5	5						
CROYDON 15	5325	1653	13	12	8	6	14	14	12	11
CUDWORTH 1	4388	4092	41	40	39	31	32	20		
CUDWORTH 2	4387	4091						31	20	16

SITE NAME & NUMBER	GRID EAST	GRID NORTH	1986/7	1987/8	1988/9	1989/90	1990/1	1991/2	1992/3	1993/4
				Annual	Mean	(µg/m³)				
CWMGWRACH 1	2868	2053					8	7	4	4
DALKEITH 1	3341	6670			29	32	26	21	16	16
DALRY 1	2293	6492	11	11	9					
DALRY 2	2288	6492	11	7	6					
DARLASTON 3	3986	2991	24							
DARLINGTON 10	4289	5149	11	12						
DARLINGTON 11	4290	5149			15	13	15	9		
DARLINGTON 12	4292	5145						22	12	9
DARTFORD 9	5543	1744	13	15	16	16	14	13	11	12
DARTON 1	4309	4099	24	27						
DEPTFORD 1	5353	1773	19							
DEPTFORD 3	5376	1775	17	15						
DERBY 17	4353	3342	11							
DERBY 18	4345	3333	16	10						
DERBY 23	4355	3363			12	23	22	27	22	23
DEWSBURY 10	4224	4203	17	21						
DEWSBURY 12	4235	4212			12	26	14	13	9	10
DIBDEN PURLIEU 1	4411	1068	7	5						
DIDCOT 1	4493	1808	7	6	5	6	6	8	6	6
DIDCOT 4	4462	1927	6	5	5	6	7	6	5	5
DIDCOT 6	4423	1995	6	5	5	7	6	6	6	5
DIDCOT 9	4562	2010	6	5	6	6	6	7	6	5
DIDCOT 13	4618	1898	5	6	7	8		8	7	6
DIDCOT 14	4583	1848	6	5	6	6	6	8	7	6
DINNINGTON 4	4528	3861	39	37	35	32	46	26	16	17
DONAGHADEE 1			4	4						
DONCASTER 19	4591	4043	19	19						
DONCASTER 23	4571	4028	8							
DONCASTER 27	4577	4030	14							
DONCASTER 28	4552	4028	27	25						
DONCASTER 29	4623	4051	51	35	19	18	18	18		
DONCASTER 31	4626	4047	30	18					12	
DONCASTER 32	4613	3983	50							
DONCASTER 33	4532	4075	35	35	23	22	17	13	11	
DONCASTER 34	4614	4065							14	4
DUNMURRY 2	93289	93679								23
DURHAM 3	4266	5423						18	5	
DURHAM,BRANDON 1	4237	5396	40	31	29	31	21	21	8	6
DURHAM SHERBURN 1	4320	5425						53	30	8
EALING 3	5175	1807	17	21						
EALING 7	5174	1807			17	13	18	17	13	12
EASINGTON 1	4420	5435	78	71	52	25	23			
EAST BARNET 2	5277	1945	8							
EASTBOURNE 4	5608	992	8							
EASTBOURNE 5	5607	988		7	7	7	7	7	4	4
EASTHAM (WIRRAL) 1	3363	3815	9							
ECCLES 6	3776	3989	15	13	28	15	12	17	13	10
EDINBURGH 12	3230	6765	8	7	6	10	11	6		
EDINBURGH 14	3254	6734	8	10	5	10	12	13	10	10
EDINBURGH 24	3230	6751						9	6	6
EDLINGTON 1	4537	3990	26	28						
EGREMONT 1	3009	5107	21	17						
ELLAND 2	4109	4209	17	14	12	31	22	15	16	15
ELLAND 14	4086	4214	11	11						
ELLESMERE PORT 2	3384	3775	12							
ELLESMERE PORT 9	3441	3759	12	12	9					

SITE NAME & NUMBER	GRID EAST	GRID NORTH	1986/7	1987/8	1988/9	1989/90	1990/1	1991/2	1992/3	1993/4
				Annual Mean		($\mu g/m^3$)				
ELLESMERE PORT 12	3398	3759	11	10	9	9	10	9	8	7
ENFIELD 14	5338	1958	10	12	6	10	12	6	5	5
ESKDALEMUIR 1	3235	6026	2							
ESTON 9	4535	5206	13	9	7	6	8	9	7	9
ETTON 1	4980	4445		4	7	6	5			
FALKIRK 5	2883	6802	17	22	19	5				
FALKIRK 6	2888	6821	12	7						
FALKIRK 7	2882	6802				15	7	8	4	
FALKIRK 8	2880	6803							7	8
FARNWORTH 8	3739	4061	17	16	15	13	14	14	18	14
FEATHERSTONE 1	4429	4195	36	48	41	28	22	19	8	8
FERRYHILL 1	4294	5324	16							
FERRYHILL 2	4293	5326		18	16					
FIDDLERS FERRY 3	3606	3926	16	18						
FIDDLERS FERRY 5	3600	3851	12							
FRASERBURGH 1	3987	8663			3	3	3	3	2	2
FYVIE 1	3768	8377			3	3	4	4	2	2
GARFORTH 1	4402	4324	18	16						
GATESHEAD 8	4254	5615	36							
GATESHEAD 10	4256	3619		31	17	9	10	11	7	7
GLASGOW 20	2595	6653	22	28	28	30	28	24	22	21
GLASGOW 42	2572	6681	14	12	9					
GLASGOW 47	2638	6638	13	6						
GLASGOW 51	2533	6641	15	15	13	15	15	13	10	10
GLASGOW 52	2594	6643	16	20	15					
GLASGOW 66	2520	6712	17	25	21	23	18	11		
GLASGOW 68	2613	6673	14	14						
GLASGOW 69	2568	6663	11							
GLASGOW 73	2612	6627	14	14	11	15	15	14	10	9
GLASGOW 80	2651	6621	14	7						
GLASGOW 86	2593	6679	7	10	15					
GLASGOW 87	2617	6654	15	8						
GLASGOW 91	2600	6643	12	7						
GLASGOW 92	2620	6639	15	17	14					
GLASGOW 93	2585	6617	26	27						
GLASGOW 95	2679	6642	20	22	11	12	14		10	9
GLASGOW 96	2574	6659	15	16	13	19	17	16	12	12
GLASGOW 98	2611	6678			16	22	18	17	15	15
GLOSSOP 3	4035	3941	12							
GLOUCESTER 4	3832	2179	11	6	7	6	8	6	9	9
GLOUCESTER 6	3854	2189	13	9						
GLYNNEATH 1	2880	2066						8	5	4
GOLDTHORPE 1	4462	4043	31	27	28	30	28	3	23	17
GRANGEMOUTH 2	2929	6815	13	14	8					
GRANGEMOUTH 4	2923	6805	11	6						
GRANGEMOUTH 8	2947	6830	12	6						
GREENWICH 9	5382	1773	13	11	14	18	20	12	11	11
GRIMETHORPE 2	4414	4091	46	43	33	27	27	30	24	20
GRIMETHORPE 3	4406	4080	26	31	23	23	28	24	14	10
GRIMSBY 4	5245	4099			6	6	7	9	7	7
HACKNEY 4	5356	1853	19	17	21	14	14			
HACKNEY 11	5359	1862	11							
HADDINGTON 2	3513	6738					10	3		
HADDINGTON 3	3514	6738						11	5	5
HALIFAX 9	4091	4240	9							
HALIFAX 10	4081	4246	8							

SITE NAME & NUMBER	GRID EAST	GRID NORTH	1986/7	1987/8	1988/9	1989/90	1990/1	1991/2	1992/3	1993/4
				Annual Mean		(µg/m³)				
HALIFAX 16	4093	4254	12	13	21	45	39	30	32	29
HAMILTON 5	2720	6550	16	11	11	15	13	5	6	7
HAMMERSMITH 6	5227	1785	17	19						
HAMPSTEAD 6	5271	1874	10	9						
HARLINGTON, YORKS 1	4484	4023	28	28						
HARROW 7	5160	1904	7	7						
HARROW 8	5150	1900			8	6	6	4		
HARROW 9	5143	1911						11	9	10
HARTHILL (S.YORKS) 1	4489	3807	20	19						
HARTLEPOOL 12	4505	5326	9	10	10	6	5	5	5	5
HARTLEPOOL 14	4488	5294	7	8						
HARWELL 1	4468	1863	5	4	4	5	6			
HARWORTH (BASSETLAW) 1	4619	3918	100							
HASLAND 1	4397	3697	11							
HASLINGDEN 4	3785	4234	14	14						
HATTON 1	4058	8373	3	3	3	3	3	3	3	2
HEANOR 7	4434	3464	25	24	37					
HEMSWORTH 3	4428	4134	42	40	29	28	27	20	14	11
HETTON-LE-HOLE 3	4355	5469	50	58	52	45	23	21	16	17
HINCKLEY 1	4428	2938	21							
HINCKLEY 5	4472	3093	12							
HOLMFIRTH 5	4144	4085	16	18	15	11	16	14	9	9
HORBURY 4	4292	4184	14	16	12					
HORWICH 1	3637	4118	12	13	11	10	12	13	11	11
HOUGHTON-LE-SPRING 2	4340	5501	42	49	41	35	32	24	19	13
HOUGHTON-LE-SPRING 3	4343	5496								17
HOYLAND NETHER 5	4373	4005	23	27						
HOYLAND NETHER 6	4377	4007				28	27	29	16	11
HUDDERSFIELD 6	4158	4165	23	27						
HUDDERSFIELD 19	4143	4164	16	18	17	24		16	13	13
HUSBORNE CRAWLEY 1	4964	2361	8	7	8	8	8			
ILFORD 6	5440	1864	14	17	20	20	17	15	14	15
ILKESTON 7	4466	3418	19							
ILKESTON 8	4468	3425	25	22						
IMMINGHAM 3	5191	4150			10	5	5	4	4	4
IMMINGHAM 5	5175	4150	14	6						
INCE-IN-MAKERFIELD 1	3594	4048	27	19						
INVERKIP 5	2243	6723	3							
INVERKIP 6	2200	6609	3							
INVERKIP 7	2210	6739	4	3						
INVERKIP 9	2202	6674	3							
INVERKIP 11	2296	6714	3							
IPSWICH 14	6160	2447	13	10	5	12	7	5		
ISLINGTON 7	5305	1860	18	20	39					
ISLINGTON 9	5316	1842	16	16	17	17	12	9	9	8
KEIGHLEY 11	4061	4412	15	16	12	9	12	13	12	12
KENSINGTON 8	5267	1791	15	14	15	18	13			
KENSINGTON 11	5254	1797	16	19						
KENSINGTON 12	5243	1813	35	34						
KENSINGTON 13	5267	1791						17	13	13
KETTERING 5	4869	2782	7	9						
KIDSGROVE 1	3836	3541	20	16	16	16	12	12		
KILBIRNIE 2	2317	6545	19	18	15					
KILMARNOCK 2	2427	6380	19	15	14	13	14	16	8	9
KILPAISON BURROWS 1	1894	2008	3							
KILSYTH 1	2722	6780	28	15	19					

SITE NAME & NUMBER	GRID	GRID	1986/7	1987/8	1988/9	1989/90	1990/1	1991/2	1992/3	1993/4
	EAST	NORTH		Annual Mean ($\mu g/m^3$)						
KIMBERLEY 3	4502	3450	18	20	23					
KINGSTON-UPON-HULL 12	5078	4281	9							
KINGSTON-UPON-HULL 19	5082	4284	24	17	22	15	13	15	12	10
KINGSTON-UPON-THAMES 14	5181	1685	11							
KINROSS 1	3117	7025	15					8	6	7
KIPPAX 1	4416	4303	30	26	28					
KIRKBY UNDERWOOD 1	5056	3271	5							
KIRKCALDY 5	3263	6932		41	30	29	30			
KIRKCALDY 6	3265	6933								15
KIRKHEATON 1	4181	4181	21	24						
KIRKHEATON 2	4177	4185	13	13	12	13	13	11	6	7
KIRKINTILLOCH 5	2659	6739	23	25	17	18	11	13	9	8
KIRKINTILLOCH 8	2670	6741	28	26	21	21	16	15	10	10
KIRKINTILLOCH 9	2654	6732		36	16	18	15	13	10	11
KNOTTINGLEY 1	4493	4233	35	30	25	29	16	20	14	12
KNOTTINGLEY 3	4497	4239								8
LAMBETH 7	5304	1758	14	15	21	18	14	25	16	15
LAMBETH 14	5306	1798	15	16						
LANGOLD (BASSETLAW) 1	4586	3873	59	54	60	18	26	20	12	12
LEEDS 4	4304	4335	19	19						
LEEDS 24	4282	4342	19	16						
LEEDS 26	4321	4348	16	14	16	14	15	15	13	13
LEEDS 28	4269	4369	12	11	11	9	7			
LEEDS 34	4271	4335	25	27						
LEEDS 36	4299	4274	16	14						
LEEDS 37	4267	4367					15	10	8	7
LEEK 4	3985	3566	18	17	17	11	10			
LEICESTER 19	4588	3041	18	21	24	20	14	13	15	11
LEIGH 4	3662	3999	18	20	19	17	16	15	11	8
LENNOXTOWN 4	2628	6778	16	15	12					
LENNOXTOWN 7	2653	6769	13	17	13					
LERWICK 2	4462	11432				2	3	2	2	
LERWICK 3	4456	11394	1							
LERWICK 4	4468	11419		5	2	2	3	2	2	
LERWICK 5	4462	11422		2	1	1	2	2	1	1
LERWICK 6	4464	11431		3	2	2				
LERWICK 7	4464	11429							3	1
LEWISHAM 14	5381	1749	18	13	26					
LEYTON 14	5382	1864	8							
LIDLINGTON 2	4991	2390	8							
LINCOLN 5	4974	3714	11	11	12	7	10	8	9	7
LITTLE HORKESLEY 1	5971	2312	6	7	8	6	7			
LITTLE LEVER 3	3756	4070	15	14						
LITTLEBOROUGH 5	3938	4164	24	21						
LIVERPOOL 16	3345	3908	17	15	13	13	14	12	10	10
LIVERPOOL 18	3425	3866	16							
LIVERPOOL 19	3409	3944	11							
LIVERPOOL 21	3371	3875	18							
LIVERPOOL 22	3384	3922	24	15	11	12	18	20	14	
LIVERPOOL 23	3417	3870	12	9	8	7	7	6	6	5
LIVERPOOL 24	3387	3925							9	8
LIVINGSTON 1	2066	6682					14	8	6	7
LLANDISSILIO (Dyfed) 1	2122	2212	3							
LONDON, CITY 16	5324	1814	14	20	16	17	24	22	16	20
LONDON, CITY 17	5325	1818	19	23	18					
LONDONDERRY 8			26	23	30	13				

SITE NAME & NUMBER	GRID EAST	GRID NORTH	1986/7	1987/8	1988/9	1989/90	1990/1	1991/2	1992/3	1993/4
				Annual Mean ($\mu g/m^3$)						
LONDONDERRY 9			28	30	22					
LONDONDERRY 11	92431	94170	35	33	28	28	28	25	22	15
LONDONDERRY 12	92438	94200				11	7	10	10	10
LONDONDERRY 13	92444	94170				16	21	19	13	11
LONG EATON 1	4489	3339	29	28						
LONGSIDE 1	4038	8473	4	5	5	4	4	4	4	2
LOUTH 1	5332	3874			15	12	10	12	10	9
LUNDWOOD (BARNSLEY) 1	4372	4069	69	43	44	38	36	35	24	18
LYNEMOUTH 2	4295	5912	23	18	17	16				
MACCLESFIELD 4	3919	3726	21							
MACCLESFIELD 5	3916	3745	20	17	21	16	17	13	14	
MACCLESFIELD 6	3913	3735								11
MAIDSTONE 7	5754	1555	13	13	14	13	13	10		
MAIDSTONE 8	5754	1554						17	19	22
MALTBY 2	4530	3922	29	27	26	22	31	22	18	18
MANCHESTER 11	3838	3981	22	24	25	21	26	25	23	23
MANCHESTER 13	3836	3925	14	13						
MANCHESTER 15	3875	3985	18	17	16	14	21	20	17	18
MANCHESTER 19	3865	4009	15	14						
MANCHESTER 21	3847	4023	16	15	14	13	17	16	15	15
MANCHESTER 22	3835	3965	15	14	19					
MANCHESTER 24	3852	3962	16	15	12					
MANSFIELD 5	4539	3594	14	13	10	13	17	15	12	11
MANSFIELD 6	4543	3617	10							
MANSFIELD 7	4567	3681	29							
MANSFIELD 8	4566	3604	14	15	13	13	15	15	13	11
MANSFIELD 9	4537	3607	31	29	27					
MANSFIELD 10	4532	3607				28	26	24	21	17
MANSFIELD WOODHOUSE 2	4538	3642	40	36	31	32	30	27	24	20
MARSHFIELD 1	3255	1830	6	6	8	7	7			
MARYPORT 1	3042	5361	27	21	16					
MEXBOROUGH 19	4472	4005	29	29	24	19	20	20	16	9
MIDDLESBROUGH 29	4495	5208	11	13	11	11	8			
MIDDLESBROUGH 34	4496	5212						7	11	9
MIDDLETON 3	3871	4063	21	22	24	23	21	19	14	14
MINWEAR 1	2052	2136	2							
MOODIESBURN 1	2700	6708	18	17	12					
MOODIESBURN 4	2662	6686	22	21	16					
MOODIESBURN 5	2684	6698	18	18	14					
MOORENDS 1	4695	4155	74	72	71	45	18	17	14	12
MORLEY 4	4263	4278	14	13	15	13	14	14	13	12
MOTHERWELL 14	2757	6564	10							
MOTHERWELL 17	2760	6596	24	17	9					
NEW OLLERTON 1	4668	3686	43							
NEW OLLERTON 2	4664	3682	48	29	31	21	8	17	14	20
NEWBIGGIN 1	4309	5879	37	14						
NEWBURN 2	4199	5671	9	12	9	9	10	8	7	7
NEWCASTLE-UNDER-LYME 10	3835	3489	23	18	15	15	17	25		
NEWCASTLE-UNDER-LYME 11	3822	3466	23	20						
NEWCASTLE-UNDER-LYME 13	3848	3462	22	21						
NEWCASTLE-UNDER-LYME 19	3851	3489	24	19						
NEWCASTLE UPON TYNE 17	4248	5652	17	23	17					
NEWCASTLE UPON TYNE 24	4285	5650	50				11	7	7	9
NEWCASTLE UPON TYNE 27	4251	5645	16	20	17	18	19	18	16	16
NEWCASTLE UPON TYNE 31	4214	5636	11							
NEWCASTLE UPON TYNE 32	4286	5645	17	21	16	14	7			

SITE NAME & NUMBER	GRID EAST	GRID NORTH	1986/7	1987/8	1988/9	1989/90	1990/1	1991/2	1992/3	1993/4
				Annual Mean		($\mu g/m^3$)				
NEWPORT (Gwent) 22	3310	1880	10	7						
NEWPORT (Gwent) 26	3313	1878		14	13	11	12	8	8	9
NEWRY 3	93078	93268	34	13	12	44	39	24	24	18
NEWRY 4			40	24						
NEYLAND 1	1964	2052	8	7	8	6	7	7	6	6
NORMANTON 3	4385	4224	39	42	39	35				
NORMANTON 4	4388	4228				19	16	16	11	10
NORTHAMPTON 9	4752	2610	16	15	16	13	18	18	12	10
NORTON CANES 2	4023	3090				17				
NORWICH 7	6233	3099	12	12	12	10	12	12	8	8
NOTTINGHAM 4	4558	3419	24	18						
NOTTINGHAM 9	4591	3416	17	10						
NOTTINGHAM 18	4557	3401	18	17						
NOTTINGHAM 19	4538	3452	27	22	19	20				
NOTTINGHAM 20	4575	3403	23	19	11	16	13	15	13	9
OLDBURY 5	3990	2896							8	
OLDHAM 3	3929	4054	9							
OLDHAM 13	3920	4057	11	15	14	10	13	13	11	10
OLDHAM 17	3944	4058	10	11	10					
ORMISTON 2	3412	6691					29	23	19	17
ORRELL 1	3538	4049	19	20						
OTLEY 3	4203	4457	17							
OXFORD 18	4510	2060	11	9		10				
OXFORD 20	4513	2061						15	15	9
PELTON 1	4251	5532	49	47	34	31	25	24	16	10
PEMBROKE 7	1956	2034	2							
PEMBROKE 10	1893	2053	3							
PEMBROKE 13	1955	1990	1							
PEMBROKE 18	1823	2051	2							
PEMBROKE 20	2114	1994	2							
PENICUIK 1	3240	6606							8	9
PENISTONE 2	4246	4030	19	17						
PERTH 1	3102	7244					26	11	9	10
PETERBOROUGH 10	5192	2985		17	12	10	8			
PETERBOROUGH 11	5193	2981							8	
PETERHEAD 1	4136	8461	5	5	6	5	5	5	4	3
PETERHEAD 2	4113	8465	3	3	3	3	3	2	2	2
PETERHEAD 3	4125	8448	2	3	3	3	3	3	2	2
PILSLEY 7	4425	3622	24	15	15	13	13			
PLYMOUTH 11	2475	547	11	7	6	7	12	9	12	6
PONTEFRACT 9	4455	4220	25	25	23	21	21	20	11	10
PONTYPOOL 7	3282	2009	11	7	7	5	4	13	13	10
PORT TALBOT 14	2780	1883	8	8	8	8	8	8	7	4
PORTADOWN 4	93012	93538	21	11	9	15		8	5	8
PORTADOWN 5							14			
PORTSMOUTH 10	4652	1019	10	10	7	9	9	7	6	5
PRESTONPANS 1	3389	6741					27	15	12	12
RATCLIFFE 13	4408	3278	11	10	11	11	11			
RAWMARSH 8	4438	3955	18	20						
RAWTENSTALL 7	3812	4229	14	14	13	12	14	12	12	13
RENISHAW 1	4446	3779	19	16	15	10	9			
RETFORD 3	4707	3811	24	23	21	13	33	23	15	12
RHYDARGAEAU 1	2456	2261	4							
RIPLEY 6	4399	3500	27	23	25	23	20	21	15	13
ROCHDALE 7	3899	4124	18							
ROCKBOURNE 1	4116	1181		3	4	3	5			

SITE NAME & NUMBER	GRID EAST	GRID NORTH	1986/7	1987/8	1988/9	1989/90	1990/1	1991/2	1992/3	1993/4
				Annual	Mean	($\mu g/m^3$)				
ROSSINGTON 1	4615	4983			20	15	16	17	9	9
ROTHERHAM 14	4429	3931	26	22						
RUGELEY 21	4043	3173		50	54	46	44	37	22	14
RUNCORN 9	3519	3821	11							
RUNCORN 10	3511	3833	11	15	15	15	7	12	11	12
SACRISTON 1	4239	5471	47	39						
SACRISTON 2	4240	5473	30	46	31	23	29	21	12	12
ST ALBANS 3	5153	2073	15	16						
ST ALBANS 4	5153	2073			11	9	10	12	10	7
ST AUSTELL 1	1999	518	3	2						
ST HELENS 29	3519	3977	15							
ST HELENS 36	3534	3936	21	16	23	15	16	14	14	14
ST HELENS 38	3513	3955	20	20	25	18	22	15	16	18
ST HELENS 41	3510	3943	14							
ST HELENS 42	3510	3950	18	11						
ST MARYLEBONE 6	5277	1819	19	17						
ST MARYLEBONE 9	5289	1812	19	16						
SALE (TRAFFORD) 7	3783	3913	15							
SALFORD 20	3829	3988	14							
SALFORD 21	3823	3990	12							
SALFORD 22	3784	3989	10							
SALFORD 24	3832	4008	13	11						
SCARBOROUGH 1	5036	4885	20	22	22	15	21	18	16	14
SCUNTHORPE 15	4891	4113	13	13	9	12	12	13	11	11
SEAHAM 2	4417	5492	78	64	51	21	18	7		
SEATON DELAVAL 1	4308	5753	29	31	24	21	22			
SEDGLEY 5	3919	2934	21	28	25	17	14	21	20	17
SELBY 3	4612	4321	14	10						
SELBY 4	4616	4324		13	12	10	11	11	6	
SELBY 5	4612	4322							19	7
SHEFFIELD 40	4364	3888	16	17	15	15	12	5		
SHEFFIELD 82	4355	3871	21	20	19	17	8	11	13	12
SHEFFIELD 83	4352	3854	43	47						
SHEFFIELD 86	4361	3890							10	8
SHILDON 1	4237	5263	21	13						
SHOREDITCH 2	5333	1826	16	20	23	17				15
SHOTTON 1	4395	5409			81	56	46	47	28	10
SKELMANTHORPE 1	4232	4106	29	31						
SLOUGH 16	4962	1819	19	15	17	14	11	6	6	4
SMETHWICK 9	4017	2871	12	12	14	12				
SOUTH KILLINGHOLME 1	5149	4161	15	13						
SOUTH KIRKBY 1	4456	4112	35	34	27	27	25	25	19	10
SOUTH NORMANTON 2	4442	3564	67	46	39	24	19	18	15	13
SOUTH SHIELDS 4	4365	5658	14							
SOUTH SHIELDS 8	4365	5658	28	18	16	14	15	8		
SOUTHAMPTON 37	4418	1122	10	12	13	9	11	11		
SOUTHEND-ON-SEA 2	5873	1862	11	11	11	9	11	9	8	
SOUTHWARK 3	5322	1786	17							
SOUTHWARK 11	5318	1800	34	35						
SPENNYMOOR 2	4247	5329	36	16	10					
STAINFORTH 1	4246	4117		89	43	50	54	44	19	14
STALLINGBOROUGH 2	5200	4133			8	4	4	3	4	4
STALYBRIDGE 7	3963	3987	22	17	17					
STANFORD-LE-HOPE 2	5692	1823						9	8	6
STAVELEY 11	4434	3749	18	8						
STEPNEY 5	5361	1824	8	12	12	8	8	8	7	7

SITE NAME & NUMBER	GRID EAST	GRID NORTH	1986/7	1987/8	1988/9	1989/90	1990/1	1991/2	1992/3	1993/4
				Annual Mean		($\mu g/m^3$)				
STIRLING (BURGH) 4	2795	6934	10	12	8					
STIRLING (BURGH) 5	2797	6946	16	21	13	17	11	13	9	9
STOCKTON-ON-TEES 8	4436	5207	6	6	4	4	6	6	5	
STOCKTON-ON-TEES 11	4446	5193	15	8	6					
STOCKTON-ON-TEES 12	4437	5207							6	4
STOKE NEWINGTON 5	5330	1865	28	30						
STOKE-ON-TRENT 3	3861	3505	20	19						
STOKE-ON-TRENT 11	3866	3447	16	17						
STOKE-ON-TRENT 20	3888	3475	28	23	26	21	24	19	17	16
STOKE-ON-TRENT 21	3875	3450	20	20						
STOKE-ON-TRENT 22	3858	3515	28	24						
STONEBROOM 1	4410	3595	21	13						
STORNOWAY 4	1464	9332	3							
STRATFORD 2	5388	1841	15	21						
STRETFORD (TRAFFORD) 12	3801	3966	15	16						
SUNDERLAND 6	4366	5563	25	19	13					
SUNDERLAND 7	4407	5558	20	17	12					
SUNDERLAND 8	4391	5585	56	52	25	27	23	26	19	17
SUNDERLAND 12	4398	5570	17	16	11	20	22	21	16	15
SUNDERLAND 14	4382	5572	25	27	18	14	10	16	11	7
SUNDERLAND 15	4350	5590	31	42	32	32	35	27	15	14
SUNDERLAND 16	4404	5584	38	37	21	18	17	8		
SUNDERLAND 17	4406	5587						27	16	15
SUTTON COLDFIELD 5	4108	2942	11	16	15	13	10	9	6	7
SWADLINCOTE 6	4297	3196	16							
SWILLINGTON 1	4384	4304	26	21						
SWINDON 2	4147	1858	10	10	12	8	9	9	8	9
SWINTON (YORKS) 7	4460	3992	22	23	21	17	12			
TADCASTER 1	4486	4434	11	10	12	12	12			
TEDDINGTON 3	5159	1710	12	10						
THORNE 2	4689	4130			26	18	11	13	8	
THORNTON CURTIS 2	5121	4196			10	7	7	8	7	6
THURROCK 7	5623	1785	17	17						
THURROCK 12	5614	1778		11	12	12	14	12	12	8
THURROCK 13	5622	1791								11
TOTTENHAM 6	5337	1894	12	16						
TRAFFORD 1	3810	3958	16	14	17	11	14	14	12	10
TRANENT 2	3404	6726					30	18	13	12
TREETON 3	4432	3878	23	23	21	21				
TROWELL 1	4487	3398	19							
URMSTON (TRAFFORD) 9	3766	3949	19							
URMSTON (TRAFFORD) 10	3746	3944	17							
URMSTON (TRAFFORD) 15	3733	3924	14	13						
URMSTON (TRAFFORD) 16	3778	3975	17	19	15					
WAKEFIELD 24	4352	4132	11	15	16	12	13			
WAKEFIELD 26	4331	4208	21	21	14	16	15	17	11	11
WALLASEY 9	3316	3909	11	10	12	5	3	3	5	10
WALLSEND 7	4304	5664	13	12						
WALSALL 13	3995	3005	19	20						
WALSALL 15	4009	2973	16							
WALSALL 18	4014	2987	19	20	16	13	12	6	8	13
WALSALL 19	4002	2982	21	24						
WALTHAMSTOW 8	5374	1887	10							
WARRINGTON 17	3607	3890	17	16	14	16	18	14	14	15
WARSOP (MANSFIELD) 1	4568	3680	46	30	36	26				
WARSOP (MANSFIELD) 2	4569	3675					35	29	23	18

SITE NAME & NUMBER	GRID	GRID	1986/7	1987/8	1988/9	1989/90	1990/1	1991/2	1992/3	1993/4
	EAST	NORTH		Annual Mean ($\mu g/m^3$)						
WATH-UPON-DEARNE 6	4433	4009	20	24	13	15	15	22	11	14
WAUNFAWR 1	2533	3607		3	2	2	3			
WEDNESFIELD 2	3946	3002	14	14	13	12	14	12	10	11
WELSHPOOL 1	3228	3073	11	6	8	6	11	8	9	9
WEMBLEY 7	5188	1853	21	17					18	17
WEMBLEY 8	5189	1854			28	8	12	16	14	
WEST BRIDGFORD 4	4587	3377	8	8						
WEST BROMWICH 16	4007	2933	13	13						
WEST CALDER 1	3022	6634	13	10						
WEST HAGBOURNE 1	4504	1875	7							
WESTHOUGHTON 1	3656	4059	20							
WESTMINSTER 17	5298	1789	15	13			9	12	14	13
WHITBURN 3	2948	6650					44	22	17	16
WHITBY 4	4903	5106	7	9						
WHITEHAVEN 2	2974	5181	34	18	20	17	15	9		
WHITEHAVEN 4	2984	5156	36	26						
WHITEHAVEN 5	2974	5178							9	7
WHITEHEAD 2			6	5	6					
WHITWELL (BOLSOVER) 1	4529	3767	43	47	32					
WIDNES 8	3513	3854	13	15						
WIDNES 9	3528	3866	8							
WIGAN 6	3584	4075	16							
WIGAN 7	3589	4057	22	22	20	14				
WIGAN 8	3592	4056				32	16	19	14	14
WILLENHALL 15	3965	2983	23							
WIMBLEDON 5	5257	1705	13	13						
WINGATE 1	4381	5402			35	37	16			
WOLVERHAMPTON 7	3898	2958	11							
WOMBWELL 2	4401	4030	40	38	37	28	26	24	18	15
WOOLWICH 9	5441	1769	9	9	11	9	11	9	7	7
WORKINGTON 3	2999	5287			9	10	11	9	3	2
WORKINGTON 4	3003	5287	17	14						
WORKSOP 10	4581	3803								13
WORKSOP 11	4579	3796								11
WORSBROUGH BRIDGE 1	4353	4037	24	25						
WORSBROUGH BRIDGE 2	4356	4040		34	27	29	29	30	20	14
WREXHAM 7	3337	3505	18	19	17	15	18	13	11	10
WREXHAM 9	3292	3464	33	32						
YORK 6	4606	4514	13	13	13					
YORK 7	4573	4507	10	9	7					
YORK 8	4607	4536	16	21	13	11	7	13	8	7
YORK 9	4601	4521	19	16	12	8	7	10	8	8

Source: DoE (1992)

Note: Sites in Northern Ireland are listed under the Irish grid system.

Chemical formula	:	Na
Alternative names	:	Particulate sodium
Type of pollutant	:	Suspended particulate matter, trace element
Air quality data summary	:	

Rural Concentrations

Location	Average Annual Concentrations, ng/m^3			
	Mean	Trend	Mean	Trend
	1972-1981	%/yr	1982-1991	%/yr
Harwell, Oxfordshire.	818	-3.3	660	5.8
Styrrup, Nottinghamshire.	1029	-3.5	973	nst
Trebanos, Glamorgan.	1190	-	-	-
Wraymires, Cumbria.	992	nst	877	nst

Source: Cawse et al. (1994)

nst=no significant trend

Location	Nature of site	Measurement period	Mean concentration ng/m^3
Altrincham	Residential	1978-1989	1310
Brent	Residential	1975-1989	1223
Chilton	Rural	1971-1989	730
Flixton	Residential	1975-1989	1398
Lambeth	Residential	1976-1982	1381
Manchester City North	Industrial/ Residential	1975-1988	1360
Manchester City South	Residential	1975-1989	1240
Swansea	Urban	1972-1981	2429
Walsall	Industrial	1976-1989	1447
Wraymires	Rural	1970-1989	928

Source: Lee et al. (1994), Pattenden (1974).

Chemical formula	:	Na
Alternative names	:	Precipitation sodium
Type of pollutant	:	Trace contaminant of rain, trace element

Air quality data summary :

Rural Concentrations

Location	Average Annual Rainfall Concentrations, μg per litre	
	1972 - 1981	1982-1991*
Harwell, Oxfordshire	3582	3220
Styrrup, Nottinghamshire	3621	2530
Wraymires, Cumbria	2278	3080

Source: Cawse et al. (1994)

Note: total deposition expressed as apparent rainfall concentration
* based on soluble fraction only

Site	Precipitation-weighted Annual Mean Sodium Concentration, 1986-93, (μ eql^{-1})								
	OS Grid ref	1986	1987	1988	1989	1990	1991	1992	1993
Achanarras	ND 151550	231	145	217	277	212	235	186	224
Balquhidder	NN 521206	122	45	59	110	100	89	61	145
Bannisdale	NY 515043	122	62	133	116	161	182	91	106
Barcombe Mills	TQ 437149	186	255	153	204	359	137	128	98
Beddgelert	SH 556518	126	75	122	134	193	162	95	111
Bottesford	SK 797376	82	35	59	47	62	54	35	35
Compton	SU 512804	54	67	70	84	129	71	40	55
Cow Green Reservoir	NY 817298	74	40	69	76	90	84	74	72
Driby	TF 386744	95	53	64	98	91	103	67	70
Eskdalemuir	NT 235028	86	37	62	81	86	102	53	63
Flatford Mill	TM 077333	99	60	54	79	79	70	57	54
Glen Dye	NO 642864	-	52	73	83	81	78	65	86
Goonhilly	SW 723214	264	206	212	276	506	327	238	227
High Muffles	SE 776939	61	63	67	95	83	103	78	111
Hillsborough Forest	J 243577	-	-	-	89	140	107	72	87
Jenny Hurn	SK 816986	97	47	80	68	104	55	37	47
Llyn Brianne	SN 822507	94	68	83	112	152	111	72	97
Loch Dee	NX 468779	116	54	136	132	147	123	86	79
Lough Navar	H 065545	248	102	317	139	261	192	133	187

Site	Precipitation-weighted Annual Mean Sodium Concentration, 1986-93, (μ eql^{-1})								
	OS Grid ref	1986	1987	1988	1989	1990	1991	1992	1993
Plynlimon	SN 823854	-	-	-	104	141	102	72	69
Polloch	NM 792689	-	-	-	-	-	213	118	204
Preston Montford	SJ 432143	86	38	86	39	100	164	38	66
Redesdale	NY 833954	114	44	66	91	67	80	59	73
River Mharcaidh	NH 876052	90	37	45	88	62	46	57	143
Stoke Ferry	TL 700988	74	49	50	58	84	75	57	53
Strathvaich Dam	NH 347750	-	83	109	126	174	147	121	212
Thorganby	SE 676428	74	50	52	69	90	96	50	51
Tycanol Wood	SN 093364	116	90	104	232	232	163	120	119
Wardlow Hay Cop	SK 177739	71	52	90	57	140	131	57	95
Whiteadder	NT 664633	112	53	83	92	78	59	79	103
Woburn	SP 964361	71	65	50	60	87	54	28	41
Yarner Wood	SX 867890	98	125	150	166	245	140	104	101

Source: Campbell et al. (1994a)

Location	1992 Monthly Weighted Mean Concentration in Precipitation, mg/l											
	Jan	Feb	Mar	Apr	May	Jun	Jul	Aug	Sep	Oct	Nov	Dec
Eskdalemuir	2.7	1.4	1.4	1.5	1.4	0.7	1.1	0.8	1.1	0.8	2.0	0.9
High Muffles	1.5	2.0	2.0	2.2	0.4	1.8	0.9	0.5	0.2	1.9	0.6	0.5
Lough Navar	1.2	4.0	6.5	2.9	3.7	0.2	1.0	1.7	2.9	3.8	4.3	2.2
Strath Vaich	3.9	4.3	1.9	2.4	1.4	0.5	1.7	0.3	1.1	3.8	3.3	1.1
Yarner Wood	1.5	1.5	3.0	1.9	1.3	0.2	0.6	2.0	1.2	7.8	2.3	2.1

Source: Schaug et al. (1994)

Chemical formula : C_8H_8

Alternative names : Phenyl ethylene, Vinyl benzene, Ethenyl benzene

Type of pollutant : (Volatile) organic compound (VOC), hydrocarbon

Structure :

$HC{=}CH_2$

Air quality data summary :

Urban Concentrations

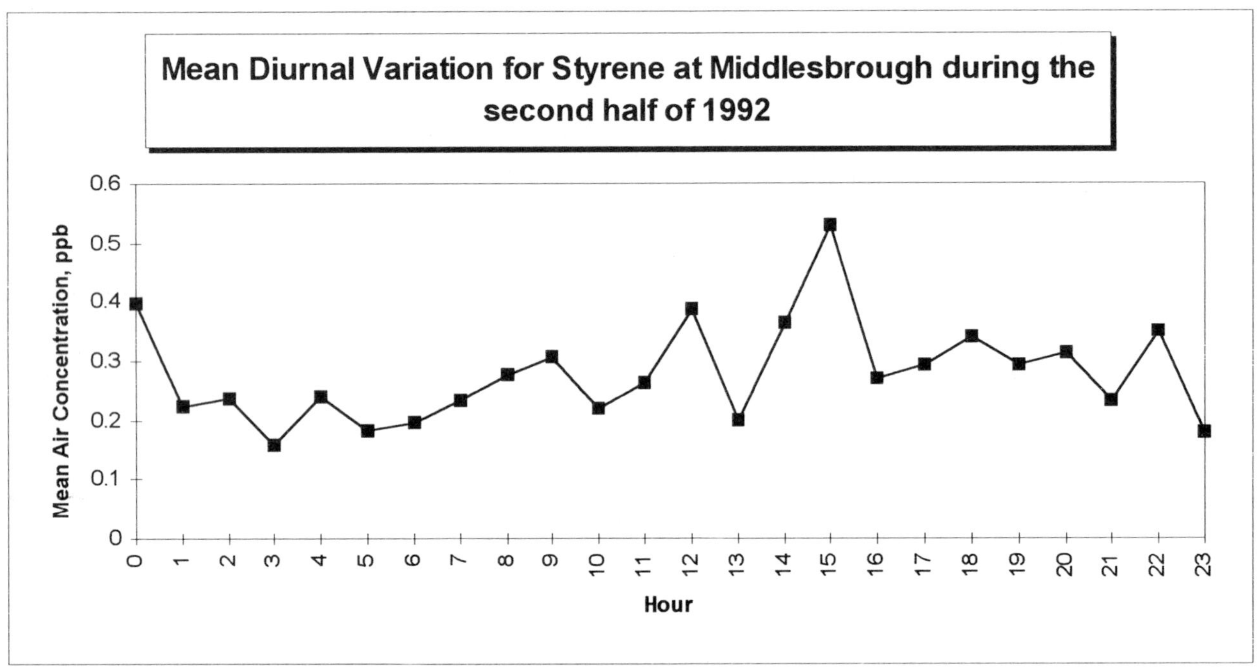

Mean for whole period : 0.29 ppb
Maximum recorded hourly mean : 1.59 ppb

Source: Derwent et al. (1994)

Mean Air Concentration in Leeds, 19/8/94 to 8/9/94	
Location	21 day mean, µg/m^3
Albion Street	0.071
Cliff Lane	0.038
EUN monitoring site	0.042
Kerbside site	0.053
Kirkstall Road	0.057
Park site	0.034
Queen Street	0.040
Vicar Lane	0.156

Source: Bartle et al. (1995)

Chemical formula	:	SO_4
Alternative names	:	Particulate sulphate
Type of pollutant	:	Suspended particulate matter

Air quality data summary :

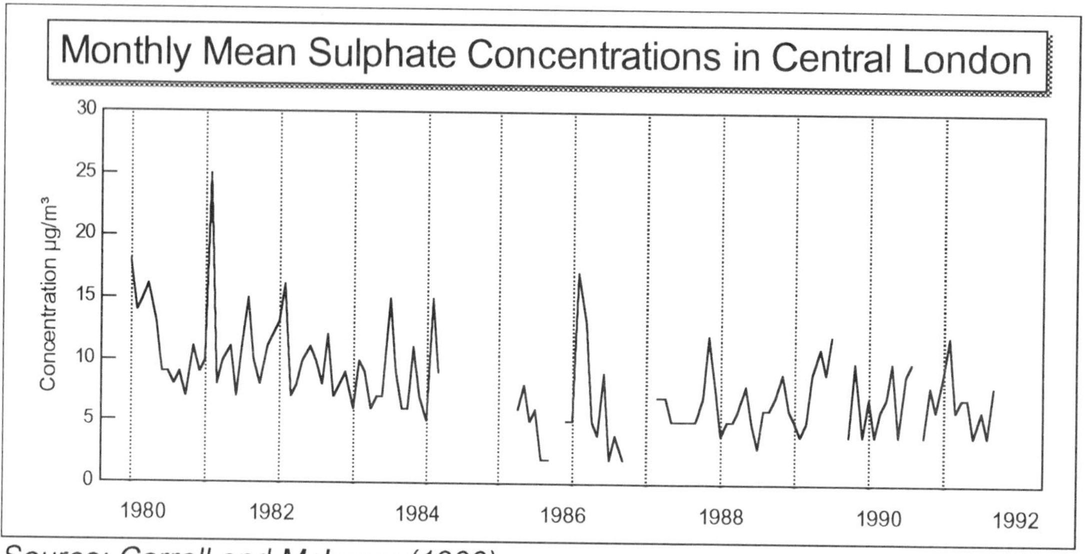

Source: Carroll and McInnes (1988)

Rural Concentrations

Location	1992 Monthly Mean Concentration in Air, µg/m³											
	Jan	Feb	Mar	Apr	May	Jun	Jul	Aug	Sep	Oct	Nov	Dec
Barcombe Mills	-	1.61	1.10	1.92	1.59	1.89	1.11	1.01	0.73	0.92	0.76	1.38
Eskdalemuir	-	0.80	0.71	0.87	1.16	1.45	0.49	0.37	0.77	0.36	0.30	0.63
Glen Dye	0.70	0.62	0.52	0.61	1.11	1.00	0.50	0.34	0.57	0.24	0.23	0.55
High Muffles	1.22	1.03	0.92	1.07	1.75	1.66	0.95	0.82	1.31	0.99	0.88	0.69
Lough Navar	-	0.42	0.51	0.66	1.25	1.12	0.39	0.26	0.34	0.34	0.26	0.75
Stoke Ferry	-	1.78	1.81	3.54	1.56	2.34	1.45	0.69	0.98	0.92	0.60	1.27
Strath Vaich	0.47	0.46	0.40	0.50	1.52	1.74	-	0.19	0.47	0.21	0.12	0.21
Yarner Wood	-	1.19	0.63	1.15	1.37	1.85	0.87	0.46	0.61	0.61	0.33	0.89

Source: Schaug et al. (1994)

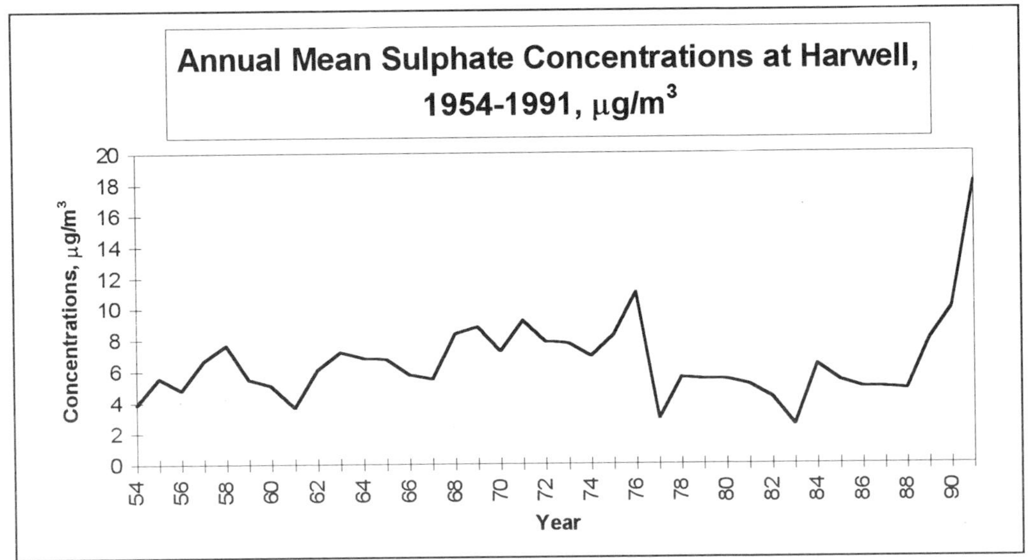

Source: United Kingdom Review Group on Acid Rain (1990)

Chemical formula	:	SO_4
Alternative names	:	Precipitation sulphate
Type of pollutant	:	Trace contaminant of rain

Air quality data summary :

Rural Concentrations

Location	Average Annual Rainfall Concentrations, µg per litre	
	1973 - 1981	1982-1991*
Harwell, Oxfordshire	2139	5420
Styrrup, Nottinghamshire	3161	6110
Wraymires, Cumbria	1074	3140

Source: Cawse et al. (1994)

Note: total deposition expressed as apparent rainfall concentration
* based on soluble fraction only

Site	Precipitation-weighted Annual Mean Non-Marine Sulphate Concentration, 1986-93, (μ eql^{-1})								
	OS Grid ref	1986	1987	1988	1989	1990	1991	1992	1993
Achanarras	ND 151550	24	33	31	29	22	24	25	20
Balquhidder	NN 521206	26	33	28	24	22	27	23	26
Bannisdale	NY 515043	41	38	45	40	41	38	42	45
Barcombe Mills	TQ 437149	46	50	40	44	38	52	43	33
Beddgelert	SH 556518	53	33	24	22	19	23	22	24
Bottesford	SK 797376	90	93	109	83	66	75	73	57
Compton	SU 512804	78	104	64	60	58	63	63	48
Cow Green Reservoir	NY 817298	35	39	44	35	33	34	38	40
Driby	TF 386744	69	74	77	79	80	78	65	49
Eskdalemuir	NT 235028	31	30	33	28	31	30	28	29
Flatford Mill	TM 077333	90	71	67	80	58	71	53	41
Glen Dye	NO 642864	-	48	49	41	39	45	43	38
Goonhilly	SW 823214	30	34	21	29	24	36	22	29
High Muffles	SE 776939	63	74	82	73	67	75	71	56
Hillsborough Forest	J 243577	-	-	-	52	36	42	41	40
Jenny Hurn	SK 816986	110	106	121	98	89	83	77	60
Llyn Brianne	SN 822507	24	29	26	27	27	30	28	26
Loch Dee	NX 468779	32	35	36	24	26	28	27	28

Site	Precipitation-weighted Annual Mean Non-Marine Sulphate Concentration, 1986-93, (μ eql^{-1})								
	OS Grid ref	1986	1987	1988	1989	1990	1991	1992	1993
Lough Navar	H 065545	19	16	14	18	14	18	17	18
Plynlimon	SN 823854	-	-	-	19	19	24	24	23
Polloch	NM 792689	-	-	-	-	-	17	17	14
Preston Montford	SJ 432143	45	60	56	60	37	66	64	48
Redesdale	NY 833954	58	46	62	47	36	43	46	35
River Mharcaidh	NH 876052	24	24	20	19	15	16	16	16
Stoke Ferry	TL 700988	80	76	66	84	81	77	67	54
Strathvaich Dam	NH 347750	-	16	14	12	10	13	18	11
Thorganby	SE 676428	85	80	88	87	82	119	88	79
Tycanol Wood	SN 093364	27	26	23	26	22	31	27	22
Wardlow Hay Cop	SK 177739	71	92	83	80	73	85	73	71
Whiteadder	NT 664633	53	48	61	46	33	45	50	37
Woburn	SP 964361	73	80	85	73	66	63	57	44
Yarner Wood	SX 867890	27	37	22	27	19	28	25	28

Source: Campbell et al. (1994a)

Location	1992 Monthly Weighted Mean Concentration in Precipitation, mg/l, corrected for seaspray											
	Jan	Feb	Mar	Apr	May	Jun	Jul	Aug	Sep	Oct	Nov	Dec
Eskdalemuir	0.60	0.55	0.55	0.45	0.58	4.36	0.81	0.37	0.40	0.33	0.31	0.33
High Muffles	0.74	0.95	0.93	0.83	1.70	1.61	1.05	0.87	0.87	0.78	0.86	0.70
Lough Navar	0.19	0.20	0.22	0.17	0.46	1.35	0.39	0.14	0.18	0.14	0.15	0.13
Strath Vaich	0.35	0.18	0.22	0.15	1.17	1.78	0.34	0.23	0.27	0.18	0.10	0.08
Yarner Wood	0.31	0.31	0.43	0.26	1.30	0.93	0.59	0.29	0.66	0.46	0.27	0.28

Source: Schaug et al. (1994)

Chemical formula : SO_2

Alternative names :

Type of pollutant : Trace gas

Structure :

SO_2

Air quality data summary :

Sulphur Dioxide Annual Mean Concentrations (ppb) 1986 to 1994

SITE NAME & NUMBER	GRID EAST	GRID NORTH	1986/7	1987/8	1988/9	1989/90	1990/1	1991/2	1992/3	1993/4
			Annual Mean, ppb							
ABERDEEN 2	3929	8057	9.7	9.0	7.1	10.9	15.7	12.0		
ABERDEEN 3	3931	8062						9.0	7.5	8.6
ACCRINGTON 5	3758	4285	13.9	19.1	19.5	18.0	18.4	16.9	16.5	17.2
ACKWORTH 1	4440	4167	31.9	27.4	30.8	19.1	18.4	19.5	12.0	11.2
ACTON 13	5208	1824	15.4							
ACTON 14	5206	1822	8.6	7.5						
ACTON 15	5209	1825	6.7	7.5	4.8			5.6	6.7	5.6
ADDLESTONE 1	5052	1646	10.5	11.6	10.5	9.0	9.0	8.3	7.9	7.5
ALFRETON 4	4417	3555	27.0	22.5	24.4	30.8	30.8	26.3	19.9	16.9
ALLERTON BYWATER 1	4417	4279	16.5	15.0	17.2	13.9	13.1			
ALLERTON BYWATER 2	4404	4293	14.6	10.5	9.7					
ALLOA 6	2885	6930	8.6	6.7						
ALNWICK 1	4187	6136	8.2							
ALNWICK 2	4187	6132	14.6	12.4						
ALSAGER 1	3797	3555	9.0							
ALTON 2	4726	1401	10.9	12.7						
ALVA 3	2880	6970	12.0	10.9	10.9					
AMROTH (Dyfed) 1	2163	2079	3.3							
APPLEBY 1	3687	5208	9.7	9.3						
ARMADALE 2	2945	6681	16.9					22.1	24.0	21.7
ARMADALE 3	2938	6685	7.1					6.7	8.6	8.2
ARMAGH 1	92877	93450						6.7	6.0	5.6
ASHINGTON 4	4284	5871	18.4	20.3	10.5	9.7	7.1	6.0	7.5	9.7
ASHTON-IN-MAKERFIELD 1	3576	3991	18.7	24.0				11.2	13.1	9.7
ASHTON-UNDER-LYNE 8	3939	3992	15.4	17.2	14.2	14.6	21.0	6.4	4.9	3.0
ASKERN 6	4557	4136	11.6	13.9	9.0	14.6		15.7		
ASKERN 8	4561	4131	26.6							
ATHERTON 5	3678	4034	17.6	17.2						
AWSWORTH 1	4482	3438	22.1							
BACUP 4	3870	4228	13.9	12.7	12.4	9.7	8.2	7.1	6.0	6.4
BALLINGRY 2	3178	6978	5.2	11.6	7.5	7.5		9.0	7.5	5.6
BALMEDIE 1	3956	8186	4.1	4.5	4.5			5.6	6.0	4.1
BANFF 1	3690	8639	4.1	4.8	4.5	5.6	6.0	7.9	7.5	6.4
BANGOR (CO DOWN) 4			7.5	6.7						
BARKING 15	5460	1831	11.2							
BARLASTON 1	3894	3385	8.2							

SITE NAME & NUMBER	GRID	GRID	1986/7	1987/8	1988/9	1989/90	1990/1	1991/2	1992/3	1993/4
	EAST	NORTH		Annual Mean, ppb						
BARNSLEY 8	4348	4094	22.1	26.6	22.9	27.8	27.8	25.9	26.2	25.9
BARNSLEY 9	4370	4055	21.8	24.0	28.9	24.4	21.0	18.7	21.0	19.1
BARNSLEY 12	4342	4067	17.6	17.6	19.1	21.4	17.6	17.6	16.1	17.2
BARROW-IN-FURNESS 3	3197	4697	11.6	12.4	9.0	8.6				
BARROW-IN-FURNESS 4	3214	4692						9.4	6.7	6.4
BATH 6	3754	1656	13.9	13.1	9.7	13.9	18.4	8.2	9.7	10.5
BATLEY 2	4243	4242	14.6	21.0						
BEDFORD 10	5056	2486	12.7	10.5	25.1	12.0	12.7	10.5	6.0	6.7
BEDLINGTON 7	4266	5821	7.5	9.0	7.1	9.3	7.1			
BEESTON & STAPLEFORD 1	4526	3370	27.8	21.8	22.9	26.3	20.3	17.6	12.4	12.0
BEESTON & STAPLEFORD 2	4490	3368	20.3	16.1						
BELFAST 11	93337	93742	20.6	25.9	15.7	18.0	17.6	9.7	12.4	16.5
BELFAST 12	93324	93737	18.7	22.5	19.1	22.5	26.6	17.6	15.0	22.5
BELFAST 13	93357	93740	35.3	35.3	20.6	23.6	23.6	22.1	18.7	19.5
BELFAST 14			19.5	20.6	12.7					
BELFAST 15	93317	93708	26.3	28.9	15.4	14.2	13.5	12.4	9.0	11.2
BELFAST 17			25.5	36.8						
BELFAST 18			21.4	25.9	16.5					
BELFAST 33	93346	93755	23.6	26.6	17.2	14.2	15.0	14.2	10.9	11.2
BELFAST 39			34.2	31.5	22.5	19.9				
BELFAST 40			20.3	23.3	15.4					
BELFAST 41	93336	93765	39.8	19.9	16.1	18.0		15.4	11.2	10.9
BELFAST 42	93322	93748	25.1	28.1				27.0	24.0	25.1
BIDDULPH 2	3884	3577	16.5	15.7	15.7	16.9	17.2	16.9	13.9	13.1
BILSTON 19	3965	2943	15.7	14.6						
BIRCOTES 1	4627	3920	28.1	12.4	20.3	15.0		11.6	14.6	8.6
BIRKENHEAD 2	3315	3882	12.7	12.7						
BIRMINGHAM 26	4115	2889	12.0	12.4	18.4	15.0	13.5	12.7	12.0	9.4
BISHOPBRIGGS 1	2612	6713	12.7	10.5	8.2					
BLACKBURN 16	3678	4281	17.2							
BLACKBURN 21	3702	4270	7.5	6.3						
BLACKPOOL 6	3317	4367	2.6	3.3	5.6	7.5	6.3	5.6	5.6	6.7
BLACKROD 1	3613	4109	13.5	11.6						
BLETCHLEY 2	4857	2337	15.0	13.5	22.1	12.7	11.2	7.9	6.7	6.0
BLYTH 15	4314	5817	13.5	15.7	12.4					
BLYTH 16	4307	5818	18.7	20.6	14.6					
BOLSOVER 5	4475	3706	24.4	22.9	21.8	20.6	21.4	21.4	16.1	14.2
BOLTON 24	3715	4092	14.2	13.1	14.6	15.0	15.7	13.5	12.7	12.0
BOLTON 27	3690	4078	16.5	15.0						
BOLTON 28	3713	4117	13.5							
BOLTON 29	3741	4096	15.4	11.2						
BO'NESS 2	2989	6808	13.1	8.2	9.0	13.9	13.9	9.7	9.7	12.0
BONNYRIGG 1	3309	6651	12.4	7.1	9.0			10.1	6.4	6.4
BOOTLE 6	3345	3948	23.6	16.1	16.1					
BRADFORD 6	4163	4329	18.0	17.6	10.9	12.4	12.7	15.0	16.5	8.2
BRADFORD 17	4154	4273	14.6	16.1						
BRADFORD 19	4133	4334	15.0	15.0	12.7					
BRADFORD 20	4151	4351	14.2	16.1						
BRADFORD 22	4158	4320	17.6	25.6						
BRADFORD 23	4186	4331	17.6	18.7	16.1					
BRAINTREE 8	5757	2235	9.7	8.6	9.7	7.5	6.3	4.1		
BRAMPTON 1	4414	4019	25.1	23.6				21.7	22.5	21.0
BRIDGWATER 2	3296	1369	7.8	9.3	10.1	12.7	11.6	10.1		
BRIDGWATER 3	3298	1373						7.1	12.4	11.6
BRIERLEY HILL 15	3918	2874	12.0							
BRIMINGTON 1	4405	3736	10.9							

SITE NAME & NUMBER	GRID	GRID	1986/7	1987/8	1988/9	1989/90	1990/1	1991/2	1992/3	1993/4
	EAST	NORTH		Annual Mean, ppb						
BRISTOL 28	3634	1763	14.6	10.9	6.3	9.0	7.5			
BRISTOL 26	3590	1732	14.6					7.5	7.5	6.7
BROCKHILL 1	4002	2702	4.8	3.0	1.5	1.1				
BROXBURN 2	3080	6723	9.0	10.9						
BUNGAY 1	6340	2895	5.2	4.1						
BURHAM 1	5730	1619	9.7	7.1	6.0	4.8	4.1			
BURNLEY 12	3841	4324							9.7	7.9
BURNTWOOD 1	4047	3087	10.9	12.7						
BURTON-UPON-TRENT 12	4240	3235	23.3	16.9	15.4	21.0	15.0	12.0	10.5	9.7
BURTON-UPON-TRENT 13	4242	3233								7.1
BURY 8	3811	4125	13.9	12.7						
BURY 9	3819	4116	8.2	9.0	7.8	7.8	6.7	8.2	7.5	11.6
CAENBY, LINCS 1	4993	3900	7.1	5.6	4.8	4.5	4.1			
CAMBERWELL 4	5343	1735	12.7	13.9	12.7	18.7		13.1		
CAMBORNE 1	1628	407	2.6	0.7	1.1	1.1	0.7			
CAMPHILL 1	2278	6543	1.5	1.8	1.8					
CANNOCK 18	3989	3117	16.5	13.9	13.5	13.9	15.7	16.5	16.5	13.1
CARDIFF 12	3193	1773	9.7	9.7	10.9	10.1	10.5	10.9	9.0	7.5
CARDINGTON 2	5079	2468	14.6	12.4	9.3	6.7	8.2			
CARLISLE 12	3407	5555	3.3							
CARLISLE 13	3398	5550	9.3	9.0	5.6	5.6	6.3	5.6	3.7	5.2
CARRICKFERGUS 2			22.5	3.7	3.0	4.1				
CASTLEFORD 9	4434	4255	27.0	25.9	22.5	18.4	18.0			
CASTLEFORD 10	4437	4257	12.4					13.1	12.4	8.6
CHADDERTON 4	3909	4053	16.9	15.4						
CHAPELTOWN 3	4356	3962	10.5							
CHEADLE 3	4010	3437	15.7	14.2	11.6	14.2	16.5	13.1	12.4	12.7
CHEADLE & GATLEY 6	3859	3886	12.7	12.0	15.7	13.9	20.6	22.1	6.4	7.1
CHELSEA 6	5271	1781	14.6	13.5						
CHESTERFIELD 18	4372	3709	12.4	10.9	10.5	9.7	9.3	9.0	13.5	18.7
CHESTER-LE-STREET 4	4273	5507	18.0	17.2	12.4	10.9	13.5	13.1	12.0	10.5
CHORLEY 6	3585	4178	13.5	15.0	15.4	12.0	9.7	7.4	9.4	10.9
CLIPSTONE 1	4588	3632	19.1	19.1	21.0					
COALVILLE 5	4428	3142	21.4	25.1	19.9	14.2	16.9	17.2	13.5	11.2
COATBRIDGE 5	2712	6638	20.3	15.7	11.2	5.6	2.6	2.2	3.0	6.4
COATBRIDGE 9	2717	6669	13.9	12.7	8.2					
COATBRIDGE 11	2738	6652	26.3	18.7	15.7	15.0	11.6	16.5	13.1	13.1
CONGLETON 2	3860	3629	8.6							
CONISBROUGH 7	4513	3987	17.2	15.4						
CONISBROUGH 8	4501	3996	21.4	19.5	23.6					
CORPACH 1	2055	7780	0.3	0.3	0.3	0.7				
COTTAM 20	4708	3822	13.5	13.1						
COVENTRY 13	4337	2788	15.7	14.6	12.7	13.9	11.6	10.9	10.5	
COWDENBEATH 1	3165	6912	6.3	7.8	7.1	10.5		10.9	8.2	7.1
COWPEN 1	4297	5814	17.2							
CRAWLEY 3	5269	1362	10.1	8.6	13.1	9.7	11.2	10.1	8.2	8.6
CRESSELLY (Dyfed) 1	2064	2062	3.0	1.5	1.5	1.8	1.5			
CREWE 9	3703	3550	15.0	15.7	21.0	7.8	9.0	11.6	21.4	18.4
CREWE 17	3710	3567	18.0	16.1	19.1	7.5	8.6	13.1	20.2	15.7
CREWE 18	3696	3568	13.1	12.4						
CROOK 1	4167	5356	9.3							
CROSBY 3	3321	3990	24.8	16.9	14.2	13.9	15.0	16.1	15.0	13.9
CROWDEN 1	4069	3995	20.6	12.7						
CROYDON 15	5325	1653	15.4	12.0	14.6	11.6	9.7	6.7	4.9	6.4
CUDWORTH 1	4388	4092	19.9	21.0	23.3	22.5	21.0	16.1		
CUDWORTH 2	4387	4091						25.9	23.2	23.2

SITE NAME & NUMBER	GRID	GRID	1986/7	1987/8	1988/9	1989/90	1990/1	1991/2	1992/3	1993/4
	EAST	NORTH	Annual Mean, ppb							
CWMGWRACH 1	2868	2053	24.4					16.5	13.9	12.7
DALKEITH 1	3341	6670	16.9	13.1	12.7			13.5	10.5	11.2
DALRY 1	2293	6492	12.4	10.1	9.0					
DALRY 2	2288	6492	8.6	7.1	5.6					
DARLASTON 3	3986	2991	14.2							
DARLINGTON 10	4289	5149	8.6	6.3						
DARLINGTON 11	4290	5149	6.7	6.7	7.1			4.9		
DARLINGTON 12	4292	5145						7.1	4.5	5.6
DARTFORD 9	5543	1744	13.1	10.5	10.1	10.5	11.2	10.5	7.9	8.6
DARTON 1	4309	4099	20.6	20.3						
DEPTFORD 1	5353	1773	12.7							
DEPTFORD 3	5376	1775	13.9	13.1						
DERBY 17	4353	3342	17.6							
DERBY 18	4345	3333	20.6	16.9						
DERBY 23	4355	3363	25.5	36.8	31.5			20.2	12.7	10.5
DEWSBURY 10	4224	4203	31.2	22.5						
DEWSBURY 12	4235	4212	13.9	10.9	10.9			12.0	10.1	10.9
DIBDEN PURLIEU 1	4411	1068	15.4	14.6						
DIDCOT 1	4493	1808	2.2	6.3	5.6	4.5	5.6	4.9	4.5	3.4
DIDCOT 4	4462	1927	2.2	6.0	6.0	6.0	6.7	5.2	4.9	3.4
DIDCOT 6	4423	1995	3.3	6.0	6.0	4.8	5.2	6.0	5.2	3.4
DIDCOT 9	4562	2010	3.7	6.3	7.1	6.7	6.7	6.7	6.0	3.7
DIDCOT 13	4618	1898	1.8	6.0	5.6	6.7		6.7	6.4	4.1
DIDCOT 14	4583	1848	2.6	5.6	7.1	4.8	7.1	5.2	4.9	3.7
DINNINGTON 4	4528	3861	21.4	21.0	18.7	19.5	19.5	18.7	18.4	15.4
DONAGHADEE 1			6.0	5.6						
DONCASTER 19	4591	4043	13.9	10.5						
DONCASTER 23	4571	4028	19.1							
DONCASTER 27	4577	4030	23.3							
DONCASTER 28	4552	4028	13.1	15.4						
DONCASTER 29	4623	4051	28.9	23.3	16.9	19.1	16.5	19.5		
DONCASTER 31	4626	4047	18.4	12.4					10.9	
DONCASTER 32	4613	3983	31.2							
DONCASTER 33	4532	4075	20.6	16.5	15.7	16.5	14.6	13.9	12.4	
DONCASTER 34	4614	4065							11.6	7.9
DUNMURRY 2	93289	93679								16.1
DURHAM 3	4266	5423						7.5	6.0	
DURHAM, BRANDON 1	4237	5396	16.1	11.6	11.2	9.7	6.0	7.9	4.9	2.6
DURHAM, SHERBURN 1	4320	5425						13.1	7.5	3.7
EALING 3	5175	1807	9.7	6.0						
EALING 7	5174	1807	7.5	7.5	7.5			7.9	8.2	6.7
EASINGTON 1	4420	5435	22.9	19.9	17.2	21.0	14.6			
EAST BARNET 2	5277	1945	33.4							
EASTBOURNE 4	5608	992	8.2							
EASTBOURNE 5	5607	988	4.8	4.5	9.3	15.0		18.0	10.5	3.7
EASTHAM (WIRRAL) 1	3363	3815	4.8							
ECCLES 6	3776	3989	18.7	16.1	22.9	9.3	11.6	16.1	17.2	13.1
EDINBURGH 12	3230	6765	14.6	14.6	13.9	9.7	9.7	13.9		
EDINBURGH 14	3254	6734	17.2	14.6	14.2	10.9	11.2	13.1	13.9	13.9
EDINBURGH 24	3230	6751						8.6	8.6	14.2
EDLINGTON 1	4537	3990	24.0	21.0						
EGREMONT 1	3009	5107	6.7	6.7						
ELLAND 2	4109	4209	32.7	39.8	15.7	10.1	6.0	9.7	13.9	11.6
ELLAND 14	4086	4214	34.9	38.7						
ELLESMERE PORT 2	3384	3775	9.0							
ELLESMERE PORT 9	3441	3759	22.1	14.6	12.4					

SITE NAME & NUMBER	GRID	GRID	1986/7	1987/8	1988/9	1989/90	1990/1	1991/2	1992/3	1993/4
	EAST	NORTH		Annual Mean, ppb						
ELLESMERE PORT 12	3398	3759	10.5	12.0	7.8	8.2	9.3	10.5	9.4	7.9
ENFIELD 14	5338	1958	16.5	17.6	12.7	12.4	11.6	7.1	7.5	8.2
ESTON 9	4535	5206	10.5	12.4	12.0	10.9	9.3	10.1	10.9	9.7
ETTON 1	4980	4445	3.7	3.7	3.3	1.5				
FALKIRK 5	2883	6802	17.2	19.1	19.1	18.4				
FALKIRK 6	2888	6821	10.1	7.8						
FALKIRK 7	2882	6802	4.8	5.6				6.0	8.6	
FALKIRK 8	2880	6803							7.1	8.6
FARNWORTH 8	3739	4061	14.2	12.4	13.1	12.7	13.5	12.0	9.4	11.2
FEATHERSTONE 1	4429	4195	34.2	30.0	30.0	23.3	22.5	19.1	10.5	10.1
FERRYHILL 1	4294	5324	11.2							
FERRYHILL 2	4293	5326	24.4	12.7						
FIDDLERS FERRY 3	3606	3926	14.6	19.1						
FIDDLERS FERRY 5	3600	3851	9.7							
FRASERBURGH 1	3987	8663	4.5	4.8	4.8			7.1	7.5	6.4
FYVIE 1	3768	8377	3.7	4.8	4.5			6.0	6.7	5.6
GARFORTH 1	4402	4324	12.7	12.7						
GATESHEAD 8	4254	5615	14.6							
GATESHEAD 10	4256	3619	15.0	7.8	5.6	7.5		7.1	4.5	5.6
GLASGOW 20	2595	6653	11.6	12.0	13.5	10.9	13.9	14.6	12.4	12.0
GLASGOW 42	2572	6681	12.4	9.0	7.1					
GLASGOW 47	2638	6638	9.3	9.3						
GLASGOW 51	2533	6641	13.9	11.2	11.6	10.9	12.0	9.4	8.2	7.1
GLASGOW 52	2594	6643	12.7	12.4	12.7					
GLASGOW 66	2520	6712	15.0	14.6	13.9	13.5	13.1	12.4		
GLASGOW 68	2613	6673	7.1	7.5						
GLASGOW 69	2568	6663	11.6							
GLASGOW 73	2612	6627	12.0	12.0	11.2	11.6	12.4	11.2	7.9	7.9
GLASGOW 80	2651	6621	11.6	10.5						
GLASGOW 86	2593	6679	12.7	15.7	11.2					
GLASGOW 87	2617	6654	10.5	9.3						
GLASGOW 91	2600	6643	12.4	10.5						
GLASGOW 92	2620	6639	14.6	10.9	13.1					
GLASGOW 93	2585	6617	14.6	15.7						
GLASGOW 95	2679	6642	14.6	13.9	12.7	11.6	12.0	9.7	8.2	8.2
GLASGOW 96	2574	6659	12.0	12	12.7	12.4	13.1	13.1	11.6	11.2
GLASGOW 98	2611	6678	11.2	11.2	14.2			13.9	7.9	7.9
GLOSSOP 3	4035	3941	18.0							
GLOUCESTER 4	3832	2179	16.5	9.3	7.1	7.5	6.0	7.1	9.7	9.0
GLOUCESTER 6	3854	2189	12.0	8.6						
GLYNNEATH 1	2880	2066						19.9	17.2	15.4
GOLDTHORPE 1	4462	4043	23.6	19.9	25.1	27.4	24.4	22.9	21.0	18.0
GRANGEMOUTH 2	2929	6815	10.5	7.5	8.6					
GRANGEMOUTH 4	2923	6805	9.7	9.0						
GRANGEMOUTH 8	2947	6830	9.7	9.0						
GREENWICH 9	5382	1773	18.7	16.9	21.8	21.8	16.5	20.2	12.4	9.4
GRIMETHORPE 2	4414	4091	24.8	24.4	24.0	27.8	19.1	24.0	24.7	23.2
GRIMETHORPE 3	4406	4080	22.9	26.6	20.6	17.2	24.4	32.6	54.4	25.1
GRIMSBY 4	5245	4099	13.1	11.2	10.5			9.4	8.2	8.6
HACKNEY 4	5356	1853	15.4	16.5	12.4	9.7	13.9			
HACKNEY 11	5359	1862	14.2							
HADDINGTON 2	3513	6738	4.1					4.5		
HADDINGTON 3	3514	6738						4.9	3.4	3.0
HALIFAX 9	4091	4240	14.6							
HALIFAX 10	4081	4246	13.5							
HALIFAX 16	4093	4254	14.6	14.2	10.9	11.6	10.5	10.9	14.2	13.5

SITE NAME & NUMBER	GRID	GRID	1986/7	1987/8	1988/9	1989/90	1990/1	1991/2	1992/3	1993/4
	EAST	NORTH		Annual Mean, ppb						
HAMILTON 5	2720	6550	6.0	5.6	6.3	9.7	14.2	19.1	9.0	10.1
HAMMERSMITH 6	5227	1785	12.4	13.9						
HAMPSTEAD 6	5271	1874	10.9	9.0						
HARLINGTON (YORKS) 1	4484	4023	16.1	13.9						
HARROW 7	5160	1904	13.5	13.9						
HARROW 8	5150	1900	13.9	12.4	14.2			12.7		
HARROW 9	5143	1911						15.0	16.5	15.7
HARTHILL (S.YORKS) 1	4489	3807	17.6	19.5						
HARTLEPOOL 12	4505	5326	6.7	5.6	4.1	4.5	6.0	5.6	4.5	4.5
HARTLEPOOL 14	4488	5294	5.6	5.2						
HARWELL 1	4468	1863	5.2	2.6	3.0	3.7	4.1			
HARWORTH (BASSETLAW) 1	4619	3918	54.5							
HASLAND 1	4397	3697	8.6							
HASLINGDEN 4	3785	4234	15.0	13.1						
HATTON 1	4058	8373	4.8	4.8	5.2	4.1	4.8	6.7	6.4	4.5
HEANOR 7	4434	3464	25.5	24.4	27.4					
HEMSWORTH 3	4428	4134	33.8	29.3	25.9	19.1	18.0	19.1	14.6	11.2
HETTON-LE-HOLE 3	4355	5469	21.4	17.2	17.2	15.0	16.1	12.4	11.2	9.7
HINCKLEY 1	4428	2938	17.6							
HINCKLEY 5	4472	3093	15.7							
HOLMFIRTH 5	4144	4085	12.7	17.6	21.4	16.1	15.4	16.9	15.0	13.5
HORBURY 4	4292	4184	16.9	13.1	10.1					
HORWICH 1	3637	4118	14.2	11.6	10.5	13.5	13.9	12.0	10.9	9.4
HOUGHTON-LE-SPRING 2	4340	5501	16.5	11.2	14.2	15.4	14.6	10.9	9.4	4.9
HOUGHTON-LE-SPRING 3	4343	5496								7.5
HOYLAND NETHER 5	4373	4005	18.4	19.1						
HOYLAND NETHER 6	4377	4007	27.4	22.1				19.9	18.7	16.5
HUDDERSFIELD 6	4158	4165	13.9	13.9						
HUDDERSFIELD 19	4143	4164	21.4	21.0	20.6	27.8		23.2	21.4	20.6
HUSBORNE CRAWLEY 1	4964	2361	7.8	5.2	5.2	4.5	4.1			
ILFORD 6	5440	1864	18.4	17.6	15.4	15.0	14.2	12.4	12.4	10.5
ILKESTON 7	4466	3418	19.5							
ILKESTON 8	4468	3425	20.6	17.6						
IMMINGHAM 3	5191	4150	14.6	13.1	14.2			13.9	13.1	11.2
IMMINGHAM 5	5175	4150	13.5	15.4						
INCE-IN-MAKERFIELD 1	3594	4048	19.9	22.9						
INVERKIP 5	2243	6723	2.6							
INVERKIP 6	2200	6609	4.1							
INVERKIP 7	2210	6739	3.7	1.5						
INVERKIP 9	2202	6674	4.1							
INVERKIP 11	2296	6714	2.6							
IPSWICH 14	6160	2447	12.4	10.5	7.8	12.0	8.2	7.5		
ISLINGTON 7	5305	1860	15.0	12.4	15.0					
ISLINGTON 9	5316	1842	15.4	10.9	13.5	18.7	17.2	15.0	13.1	11.2
KEIGHLEY 11	4061	4412	14.2	13.5	12.4	15.0	10.1	9.7	13.5	13.1
KENSINGTON 8	5267	1791	22.1	17.2	17.6	12.7	20.6			
KENSINGTON 11	5254	1797	14.2	15.4						
KENSINGTON 12	5243	1813	16.1	12.4						
KENSINGTON 13	5267	1791						21.0	16.9	17.2
KETTERING 5	4869	2782	9.3	9.0						
KIDSGROVE 1	3836	3541	19.1	15.4	12.4	18.0	11.6	9.4		
KILBIRNIE 2	2317	6545	9.7	9.0	8.6					
KILMARNOCK 2	2427	6380	7.1	6.3	4.8	4.8	4.8	5.6	4.5	3.7
KILPAISON BURROWS 1	1894	2008	3.0							
KILSYTH 1	2722	6780	9.0	8.6	10.1					
KIMBERLEY 3	4502	3450	21.4	16.9	16.5					

SITE NAME & NUMBER	GRID EAST	GRID NORTH	1986/7	1987/8	1988/9	1989/90	1990/1	1991/2	1992/3	1993/4
				Annual Mean, ppb						
KINGSTON-UPON-HULL 12	5078	4281	9.0							
KINGSTON-UPON-HULL 19	5082	4284	9.7	10.9	9.7	14.6	13.1	16.5	12.7	12.4
KINGSTON-UPON-THAMES 14	5181	1685	11.2							
KINROSS 1	3117	7025	6.0					6.0	4.5	3.7
KIPPAX 1	4416	4303	15.4	19.5	16.9					
KIRKBY UNDERWOOD 1	5056	3271	13.1							
KIRKCALDY 5	3263	6932	13.5	12.0	11.6	12.0				
KIRKCALDY 6	3265	6933								9.7
KIRKHEATON 1	4181	4181	13.1	19.1						
KIRKHEATON 2	4177	4185	15.7	14.6	11.2	19.9	15.7	17.6	13.5	11.6
KIRKINTILLOCH 5	2659	6739	15.7	12.4	9.7	9.7	10.5	9.0	8.6	9.4
KIRKINTILLOCH 8	2670	6741	13.9	10.9	9.7	8.6	8.2	7.1	6.4	8.6
KIRKINTILLOCH 9	2654	6732	12.7	9.7	9.3	9.3		8.6	8.6	8.2
KNOTTINGLEY 1	4493	4233	15.4	12.0	8.6	7.5	9.0	11.2	7.5	5.2
KNOTTINGLEY 3	4497	4239								10.1
LAMBETH 7	5304	1758	12.7	13.5	13.5	16.1	22.5	16.5	19.5	12.0
LAMBETH 14	5306	1798	14.2	14.6						
LANGOLD (BASSETLAW) 1	4586	3873	40.2	31.2	11.2	16.5	15.0	15.0	8.6	6.7
LEEDS 4	4304	4335	14.2	11.6						
LEEDS 24	4282	4342	12.7	10.1						
LEEDS 26	4321	4348	12.4	10.9	11.2	10.9	10.1	10.5	9.4	10.9
LEEDS 28	4269	4369	13.9	15.7	15.0	13.5	15.0			
LEEDS 34	4271	4335	13.9	12.0						
LEEDS 36	4299	4274	12.7	12.0						
LEEDS 37	4267	4367	12.4					9.0	9.0	9.7
LEEK 4	3985	3566	12.7	11.6	10.9	12.4	13.5			
LEICESTER 19	4588	3041	12.7	8.6	10.5	12.0	12.4	10.9	6.0	8.2
LEIGH 4	3662	3999	18.4	19.1	18.0	16.1	14.6	13.9	14.6	12.4
LENNOXTOWN 4	2628	6778	12.7	9.3	9.0					
LENNOXTOWN 7	2653	6769	13.9	11.2	10.5					
LERWICK 2	4462	11432	2.2	1.1				0.4		
LERWICK 4	4468	11419	5.2	3.7	5.2	3.0		2.2	2.6	
LERWICK 5	4462	11422	5.2	4.5	5.6	4.8		5.2	4.1	6.4
LERWICK 6	4464	11431	8.2	5.6	6.7					
LERWICK 7	4464	11429							4.1	4.1
LERWICK 8	4468	11422								
LEWISHAM 14	5381	1749	23.3	21.8	16.1					
LEYTON 14	5382	1864	9.3							
LIDLINGTON 2	4991	2390	2.2							
LINCOLN 5	4974	3714	12.0	11.6	15.0	14.6	13.9	12.7	10.5	9.4
LITTLE HORKESLEY 1	5971	2312	6.3	4.1	3.7	3.0	2.6			
LITTLE LEVER 3	3756	4070	13.9	11.6						
LITTLEBOROUGH 5	3938	4164	14.2	17.6						
LIVERPOOL 16	3345	3908	17.6	16.1	16.9	16.9	18.0	13.5	13.5	14.6
LIVERPOOL 18	3425	3866	13.9							
LIVERPOOL 19	3409	3944	13.1							
LIVERPOOL 21	3371	3875	16.1							
LIVERPOOL 22	3384	3922	17.6	13.1	12.0	12.7	16.5	15.7	15.4	
LIVERPOOL 23	3417	3870	21.8	15.0	15.0	16.1	17.6	12.7	13.1	12.4
LIVERPOOL 24	3387	3925							15.7	13.9
LIVINGSTON 1	2066	6682	7.5					6.4	6.4	3.7
LLANDISSILIO (Dyfed) 1	2122	2212	3.7							
LONDON, CITY 16	5324	1814	15.7	12.0	10.9	9.3	7.5	8.2	7.5	8.6
LONDON, CITY 17	5325	1818	16.9	12.7	11.2					
LONDONDERRY 8			12.7	12.7	10.5	12.0				
LONDONDERRY 9			12.4	11.6	10.5					

SITE NAME & NUMBER	GRID	GRID	1986/7	1987/8	1988/9	1989/90	1990/1	1991/2	1992/3	1993/4
	EAST	NORTH		Annual Mean, ppb						
LONDONDERRY 11	92431	94170	20.6	18.7	15.4	18.0	20.3	18.7	16.5	17.6
LONDONDERRY 12	92438	94200	21.8	9.0				10.5	12.4	13.5
LONDONDERRY 13	92444	94170	8.6	11.2				11.2	12.0	14.2
LONG EATON 1	4489	3339	21.8	20.3						
LONGSIDE 1	4038	8473	4.8	5.2	5.6	5.2	4.8	6.7	7.1	6.0
LOUTH 1	5332	3874	14.6	12.0	12.7			13.1	13.5	11.2
LUNDWOOD (BARNSLEY) 1	4372	4069	27.0	22.5	23.6	23.6	21.4	20.2	19.9	19.1
LYNEMOUTH 2	4295	5912	5.2	11.2	10.1	3.7				
MACCLESFIELD 4	3919	3726	13.1							
MACCLESFIELD 5	3916	3745	13.5	17.2	16.1	12.4	13.9	9.4	11.6	
MACCLESFIELD 6	3913	3735								11.2
MAIDSTONE 7	5754	1555	18.4	14.2	12.4	14.2	18.0	19.9		
MAIDSTONE 8	5754	1554						19.1	19.5	19.9
MALTBY 2	4530	3922	24.8	27.0	23.3	21.8	25.1	21.0	21.0	16.9
MANCHESTER 11	3838	3981	16.9	22.1	22.9	21.0	18.0	15.7	15.7	12.7
MANCHESTER 13	3836	3925	17.6	21.4						
MANCHESTER 15	3875	3985	16.9	17.6	16.5	17.6	15.7	14.6	14.2	10.5
MANCHESTER 19	3865	4009	16.9	16.9						
MANCHESTER 21	3847	4023	23.3	26.6	16.1	16.5	14.2	24.0	18.0	9.7
MANCHESTER 22	3835	3965	23.3	25.5	16.5					
MANCHESTER 24	3852	3962	21.8	23.3	17.2					
MANSFIELD 5	4539	3594	19.5	17.2	14.6	14.6	16.1	16.1	13.5	14.2
MANSFIELD 6	4543	3617	21.0							
MANSFIELD 7	4567	3681	24.8							
MANSFIELD 8	4566	3604	24.0	21.4	17.2	16.9	18.0	17.2	15.7	14.6
MANSFIELD 9	4537	3607	25.5	23.6	19.1					
MANSFIELD 10	4532	3607	19.9	21.0				20.2	17.6	16.5
MANSFIELD WOODHOUSE 2	4538	3642	30.0	27.8	25.1	23.6	24.4	24.4	20.6	20.2
MARSHFIELD 1	3255	1830	4.8	3.3	3.3	3.0	4.1			
MARYPORT 1	3042	5361	7.8	5.2	3.7					
MEXBOROUGH 19	4472	4005	23.3	21.4	14.6	16.5	19.1	17.2	14.2	18.4
MIDDLESBROUGH 29	4495	5208	7.8	7.5	6.7	6.7	5.2			
MIDDLESBROUGH 34	4496	5212						6.4	7.9	6.7
MIDDLETON 3	3871	4063	13.9	18.0	18.4	16.9	16.9	14.2	16.5	18.0
MINWEAR 1	2052	2136	3.0							
MOODIESBURN 1	2700	6708	15.0	12.0	10.1					
MOODIESBURN 4	2662	6686	15.7	10.1	8.6					
MOODIESBURN 5	2684	6698	15.4	11.6	9.0					
MOORENDS 1	4695	4155	26.3	23.6	19.5	17.2	24.0	18.4	13.5	18.7
MORLEY 4	4263	4278	16.5	14.6	14.6	12.0	11.6	10.9	9.4	11.6
MOTHERWELL 14	2757	6564	9.0							
MOTHERWELL 17	2760	6596	13.9	11.2	6.3					
NEW OLLERTON 1	4668	3686	21.4							
NEW OLLERTON 2	4664	3682	25.9	19.9	18.4	17.6	14.6	18.0	15.0	18.7
NEWBIGGIN 1	4309	5879	9.7	8.6						
NEWBURN 2	4199	5671	12.7	15.0	9.0	10.5	14.6	11.6	9.0	9.0
NEWCASTLE-UNDER-LYME 10	3835	3489	20.3	16.9	15.4	18.7	13.5	14.2		
NEWCASTLE-UNDER-LYME 11	3822	3466	15.7	12.4						
NEWCASTLE-UNDER-LYME 13	3848	3462	18.7	15.4						
NEWCASTLE-UNDER-LYME 19	3851	3489	19.9	15.7						
NEWCASTLE UPON TYNE 17	4248	5652	21.8	17.2	15.0					
NEWCASTLE UPON TYNE 24	4285	5650	9.7					8.6	8.6	9.7
NEWCASTLE UPON TYNE 27	4251	5645	14.2	22.1	13.5	13.5	11.2	11.6	11.6	8.2
NEWCASTLE UPON TYNE 31	4214	5636	15.7							
NEWCASTLE UPON TYNE 32	4286	5645	13.1	19.9	13.5	13.1	13.1			
NEWPORT (Gwent) 22	3310	1880	6.0	7.1						

SITE NAME & NUMBER	GRID	GRID	1986/7	1987/8	1988/9	1989/90	1990/1	1991/2	1992/3	1993/4
	EAST	NORTH		Annual Mean, ppb						
NEWPORT (Gwent) 26	3313	1878	6.7	5.6	5.6	6.0		4.9	4.5	1.9
NEWRY 3	93078	93268	9.7	12.0	15.4	14.6	10.9	7.9	6.0	6.0
NEWRY 4			10.9	10.5						
NEYLAND 1	1964	2052	4.5	4.1	3.7	4.5	4.5	4.5	3.7	4.1
NORMANTON 3	4385	4224	24.8	22.5	20.3	21.0				
NORMANTON 4	4388	4228	15.7	15.7				15.7	13.9	10.5
NORTHAMPTON 9	4752	2610	9.3	10.1	11.6	9.3	10.1	10.1	7.1	4.9
NORTON CANES 2	4023	3090	8.6							
NORWICH 7	6233	3099	10.1	9.0	8.2	6.7	6.3	6.0	6.7	6.0
NOTTINGHAM 4	4558	3419	20.6	25.1						
NOTTINGHAM 9	4591	3416	19.1	23.6						
NOTTINGHAM 18	4557	3401	16.5	22.1						
NOTTINGHAM 19	4538	3452	23.3	24.4	19.5	14.2				
NOTTINGHAM 20	4575	3403	17.6	26.6	20.6	15.0	14.6	12.4	11.2	9.4
OLDBURY 5	3990	2896							10.1	
OLDHAM 3	3929	4054	15.4							
OLDHAM 13	3920	4057	14.6	13.5	17.2	20.6	17.6	12.7	9.7	9.0
OLDHAM 17	3944	4058	16.1	15.0	16.5					
ORMISTON 2	3412	6691	9.7					8.6	6.4	6.7
ORRELL 1	3538	4049	17.6	20.6						
OTLEY 3	4203	4457	10.9							
OXFORD 18	4510	2060	12.4	14.2	13.5					
OXFORD 20	4513	2061						3.7	6.4	6.0
PELTON 1	4251	5532	16.9	15.7	12.4	11.2	13.5	13.5	12.7	9.4
PEMBROKE 7	1956	2034	3.3							
PEMBROKE 10	1893	2053	7.5							
PEMBROKE 13	1955	1990	3.0							
PEMBROKE 18	1823	2051	2.6							
PEMBROKE 20	2114	1994	2.6							
PENICUIK 1	3240	6606						9.4	6.7	7.1
PENISTONE 2	4246	4030	18.0	16.5						
PERTH 1	3102	7244	7.1					6.0	3.4	3.0
PETERBOROUGH 10	5192	2985	13.5	12.7	12.7	10.5				
PETERBOROUGH 11	5193	2981							10.9	
PETERHEAD 1	4136	8461	6.3	7.5	7.5	6.3	6.7	9.4	9.0	7.1
PETERHEAD 2	4113	8465	3.0	3.3	3.0	3.0	3.7	6.0	6.4	4.5
PETERHEAD 3	4125	8448	3.7	3.7	3.3	3.0	4.5	6.4	7.1	5.6
PILSLEY 7	4425	3622	12.4	11.2	12.0	11.2	9.0			
PLYMOUTH 11	2475	547	2.2	5.2	5.6	6.3	7.8	6.0	5.2	5.2
PONTEFRACT 9	4455	4220	21.4	21.0	16.9	15.4	17.2	16.9	12.4	9.7
PONTYPOOL 7	3282	2009	17.2	13.5	6.0	6.0	5.2	5.2	3.3	4.5
PORT TALBOT 14	2780	1883	10.9	9.7	11.2	10.9	13.9	12.0	9.7	9.0
PORTADOWN 4	93012	93538	14.6	14.6	10.5	6.0		12.0	6.7	7.5
PORTADOWN 5			7.1							
PORTSMOUTH 10	4652	1019	8.2	7.5	7.5	14.6	10.5	11.2	9.7	8.6
PRESTONPANS 1	3389	6741	8.6					7.1	5.2	4.9
RATCLIFFE 13	4408	3278	12.4	10.1	9.7	9.0	9.7			
RAWMARSH 8	4438	3755	16.5	15.7						
RAWTENSTALL 7	3812	4229	15.7	13.5	11.6	10.5	8.6	7.9	6.0	7.1
RENISHAW 1	4446	3779	15.0	15.0	16.9	17.6	13.5			
RETFORD 3	4707	3811	23.6	21.0	12.7	9.3	13.5	12.0	7.1	9.4
RHYDARGAEAU 1	2456	2261	10.1							
RIPLEY 6	4399	3500	24.8	23.3	23.3	27.4	24.0	24.7	20.6	17.2
ROCHDALE 7	3899	4124	14.6							
ROCKBOURNE 1	4116	1181	1.8	1.5	1.5	2.2				
ROSSINGTON 1	4615	4983	16.1	16.9	18.0			17.2	9.4	13.5

SITE NAME & NUMBER	GRID EAST	GRID NORTH	1986/7	1987/8	1988/9	1989/90	1990/1	1991/2	1992/3	1993/4
			Annual Mean, ppb							
ROTHERHAM 14	4429	3931	21.0	16.9						
RUGELEY 21	4043	3173	30.4	21.0	18.0	26.3		30.4	24.0	17.6
RUNCORN 9	3519	3821	12.7							
RUNCORN 10	3511	3833	16.5	12.0	13.5	17.2	16.9	12.0	9.0	9.4
SACRISTON 1	4239	5471	19.5	18.4						
SACRISTON 2	4240	5473	22.9	25.1	18.7	16.9	23.3	18.0	15.4	11.2
ST ALBANS 3	5153	2073	12.4	11.6						
ST ALBANS 4	5153	2073	9.0	12.0	10.9			7.1	7.5	5.2
ST AUSTELL 1	1999	518	9.3	6.7						
ST HELENS 29	3519	3977	12.7							
ST HELENS 36	3534	3936	11.2	13.9	11.6	12.7	13.5	11.2	7.9	10.5
ST HELENS 38	3513	3955	16.1	11.2	10.5	9.0	10.5	9.0	7.9	13.5
ST HELENS 41	3510	3943	14.6							
ST HELENS 42	3510	3950	17.6	14.6						
ST MARYLEBONE 6	5277	1819	15.4	14.6						
ST MARYLEBONE 9	5289	1812	18.7	14.6						
SALE (TRAFFORD) 7	3783	3913	16.5							
SALFORD 20	3829	3988	12.7							
SALFORD 21	3823	3990	17.2							
SALFORD 22	3784	3989	12.4							
SALFORD 24	3832	4008	19.1	17.2						
SCARBOROUGH 1	5036	4885	7.1	7.1	5.6	10.1	8.6	8.2	9.0	8.2
SCUNTHORPE 15	4891	4113	13.9	15.4	17.6	9.3	15.0	11.6	12.0	10.1
SEAHAM 2	4417	5492	18.0	12.7	7.5	11.2	6.0	4.5		
SEATON DELAVAL 1	4308	5753	14.6	12.7	10.9	10.1	10.1			
SEDGLEY 5	3919	2934	12.7	11.2	11.2	12.7	12.0	10.9	10.5	9.7
SELBY 3	4612	4321	16.5	15.4						
SELBY 4	4616	4324	14.6	11.2	9.7	10.9		7.5	6.0	
SELBY 5	4612	4322							10.1	5.6
SHEFFIELD 40	4364	3888	21.8	16.5	15.7	16.1	14.2	16.5		
SHEFFIELD 82	4355	3871	14.2	18.7	18.7	15.4	17.6	15.7	16.5	14.2
SHEFFIELD 83	4352	3854	19.9	16.9						
SHEFFIELD 86	4361	3890							13.9	16.9
SHILDON 1	4237	5263	12.7	12.7						
SHOREDITCH 2	5333	1826	14.2	15.4	14.6	16.9				9.4
SHOTTON 1	4395	5409	20.6	19.5	16.1			10.1	6.4	7.9
SKELMANTHORPE 1	4232	4106	13.9	18.0						
SLOUGH 16	4962	1819	20.3	20.6	15.4	15.7	17.2	15.0	10.1	9.7
SMETHWICK 9	4017	2871	12.4	10.1	10.5	9.0				
SOUTH KILLINGHOLME 1	5149	4161	9.3	9.7						
SOUTH KIRKBY 1	4456	4112	35.3	28.9	29.6	19.9	18.0	20.2	16.9	10.1
SOUTH NORMANTON 2	4442	3564	27.0	18.7	19.5	17.2	18.7	16.9	13.1	11.6
SOUTH SHIELDS 4	4365	5658	13.1							
SOUTH SHIELDS 8	4365	5658	22.9	17.6	16.5	14.2	10.5	7.1		
SOUTHAMPTON 37	4418	1122	7.5	5.6	6.3	8.6	14.6	16.5		
SOUTHEND-ON-SEA 2	5873	1862	13.9	14.6	14.6	13.1	15.4	10.9	10.9	
SOUTHWARK 3	5322	1786	12.0							
SPENNYMOOR 2	4247	5329	15.7	12.4	10.1					
STAINFORTH 1	4246	4117	28.1	15.4	21.8	24.4		21.7	15.7	23.2
STALLINGBOROUGH 2	5200	4133	10.9	10.9	12.4			10.5	9.7	9.7
STALYBRIDGE 7	3963	3987	19.1	19.1	19.1					
STANFORD-LE-HOPE 2	5692	1823						11.6	11.2	13.1
STAVELEY 11	4434	3749	7.8	10.9						
STEPNEY 5	5361	1824	36.0	28.5	16.9	15.0	15.7	15.7	16.9	12.0
STIRLING (BURGH) 4	2795	6934	8.2	9.0	7.1					
STIRLING (BURGH) 5	2797	6946	7.5	7.5	6.0	6.0	7.5	4.5	4.9	4.1

SITE NAME & NUMBER	GRID EAST	GRID NORTH	1986/7	1987/8	1988/9	1989/90	1990/1	1991/2	1992/3	1993/4
				Annual Mean, ppb						
STOCKTON-ON-TEES 8	4436	5207	8.6	8.6	5.2	6.7	5.2	6.7	10.1	
STOCKTON-ON-TEES 11	4446	5193	9.0	9.3	9.0					
STOCKTON-ON-TEES 12	4437	5207							6.4	9.0
STOKE NEWINGTON 5	5330	1865	20.6	19.1						
STOKE-ON-TRENT 3	3861	3505	15.0	13.5						
STOKE-ON-TRENT 11	3866	3447	17.2	14.6						
STOKE-ON-TRENT 20	3888	3475	22.5	17.6	16.5	18.4	19.9	17.6	19.9	19.5
STOKE-ON-TRENT 21	3875	3450	18.4	13.5						
STOKE-ON-TRENT 22	3858	3515	16.9	13.5						
STONEBROOM 1	4410	3595	13.9	13.5						
STRATFORD 2	5388	1841	19.5	18.0						
STRETFORD (TRAFFORD) 12	3801	3966	19.5	22.9						
SUNDERLAND 6	4366	5563	17.2	13.1	10.9					
SUNDERLAND 7	4407	5558	15.0	10.1	8.6					
SUNDERLAND 8	4391	5585	24.0	28.5	20.6	19.1	21.0	14.6	15.0	9.4
SUNDERLAND 12	4398	5570	18.4	23.6	26.6	18.0	15.0	11.2	9.4	6.0
SUNDERLAND 14	4382	5572	20.6	15.7	12.7	22.9	30.8	11.6	9.4	6.7
SUNDERLAND 15	4350	5590	22.9	23.6	18.0	17.2	22.1	14.6	13.9	7.1
SUNDERLAND 16	4404	5584	15.7	13.9	11.2	11.2	11.6	7.1		
SUNDERLAND 17	4406	5587						11.6	9.0	6.7
SUTTON COLDFIELD 5	4108	2942	14.6	15.0	13.9	15.0	13.5	12.4	10.9	9.0
SWADLINCOTE 6	4297	3196	15.7							
SWILLINGTON 1	4384	4304	15.0	14.6						
SWINDON 2	4147	1858	10.5	9.0	9.0	7.8	7.5	6.7	5.2	4.5
SWINTON (YORKS) 7	4460	3992	22.5	24.0	19.5	18.4	16.9			
TADCASTER 1	4486	4434	21.0	14.2	15.0	13.9	15.0			
TEDDINGTON 3	5159	1710	11.2	13.5						
THORNE 2	4689	4130	13.1	12.7	10.9			9.0	6.4	
THORNTON CURTIS 2	5121	4196	9.3	10.5	7.5			6.7	6.0	6.4
THURROCK 7	5623	1785	21.4	19.9						
THURROCK 12	5614	1778	18.4	12.0	10.9	13.5		16.1	15.0	15.0
THURROCK 13	5622	1791								15.4
TOTTENHAM 6	5337	1894	18.0	12.4						
TRAFFORD 1	3810	3958	20.6	21.0	19.1	16.1	22.9	26.6	27.4	23.2
TRANENT 2	3404	6726	11.6					8.2	6.0	3.0
TREETON 3	4432	3878	18.4	18.4	15.7	15.4				
TROWELL 1	4487	3398	20.3							
URMSTON (TRAFFORD) 9	3766	3949	21.4							
URMSTON (TRAFFORD) 10	3746	3944	9.0							
URMSTON (TRAFFORD) 15	3733	3924	18.0	19.1						
URMSTON (TRAFFORD) 16	3778	3975	22.5	26.3	23.3					
WAKEFIELD 24	4352	4132	9.7	7.5	7.5	6.0	6.7			
WAKEFIELD 26	4331	4208	18.0	18.7	15.4	14.2	17.2	18.0	14.6	11.2
WALLASEY 9	3316	3909	12.4	10.9	16.5	9.7	11.2	10.1	7.9	10.9
WALLSEND 7	4304	5664	12.0	12.4						
WALSALL 13	3995	3005	12.4	12.4						
WALSALL 15	4009	2973	12.7							
WALSALL 18	4014	2987	13.5	15.7	12.4	10.9	9.0	7.1	6.4	7.5
WALSALL 19	4002	2982	19.5	18.4						
WALTHAMSTOW 8	5374	1887	10.5							
WARRINGTON 17	3607	3890	11.2	15.4	13.9	10.9	11.2	12.7	12.4	11.2
WARSOP (MANSFIELD) 1	4568	3680	27.8	20.6	22.1	18.7				
WARSOP (MANSFIELD) 2	4569	3675	25.1					23.6	20.6	18.7
WATH-UPON-DEARNE 6	4433	4009	19.1	22.9	15.7	15.7	15.7	19.9	16.1	12.7
WAUNFAWR 1	2533	3607	1.8	1.1	1.1	1.5				
WEDNESFIELD 2	3946	3002	14.6	19.1	11.2	12.0	10.5	12.4	12.7	11.6

SITE NAME & NUMBER	GRID	GRID	1986/7	1987/8	1988/9	1989/90	1990/1	1991/2	1992/3	1993/4
	EAST	NORTH		Annual Mean, ppb						
WELSHPOOL 1	3228	3073	7.8	5.6	6.3	6.0	6.7	5.2	4.9	6.7
WEMBLEY 7	5188	1853	12.0	12.4					12.4	12.7
WEMBLEY 8	5189	1854	15.7	12.0	12.0			11.6	9.4	
WEST BRIDGFORD 4	4587	3377	13.9	13.9						
WEST BROMWICH 16	4007	2933	12.4	10.5						
WEST CALDER 1	3022	6634	11.2	9.3						
WEST HAGBOURNE 1	4504	1875	6.0							
WESTHOUGHTON 1	3656	4059	13.9							
WESTMINSTER 17	5298	1789	14.2	13.1	8.6			7.5	7.5	9.4
WHITBURN 3	2948	6650	9.0					7.5	7.5	6.7
WHITBY 4	4903	5106	6.0	6.0						
WHITEHAVEN 2	2974	5181	9.3	7.5	7.5	6.0	5.6	3.7		
WHITEHAVEN 4	2984	5156	8.6	5.6						
WHITEHAVEN 5	2974	5178							7.1	6.7
WHITEHEAD 2			10.9	7.8	11.2					
WHITWELL (BOLSOVER) 1	4529	3767	22.5	21.4	16.1					
WIDNES 8	3513	3854	15.7	12.0						
WIDNES 9	3528	3866	14.6							
WIGAN 6	3584	4075	12.0							
WIGAN 7	3589	4057	16.9	22.5	20.3	19.5				
WIGAN 8	3592	4056	24.0	14.2				13.1	9.0	7.9
WILLENHALL 15	3965	2983	12.4							
WIMBLEDON 5	5257	1705	15.7	8.6						
WINGATE 1	4381	5402	13.9	16.5	6.7					
WOLVERHAMPTON 7	3898	2958	17.2							
WOMBWELL 2	4401	4030	21.4	22.5	24.8	25.5	20.3	20.2	32.6	18.4
WOOLWICH 9	5441	1769	17.6	20.6	22.5	15.0	18.0	18.7	12.4	10.1
WORKINGTON 3	2999	5287	5.2	5.2	6.0			3.7	3.0	2.6
WORKINGTON 4	3003	5287	11.6	8.2						
WORKSOP 10	4581	3803								14.2
WORKSOP 11	4579	3796								9.7
WORSBROUGH BRIDGE 1	4353	4037	16.9	19.1						
WORSBROUGH BRIDGE 2	4356	4040	19.1	27.4	30.0	21.8		17.2	18.4	19.1
WREXHAM 7	3337	3505	11.2	12.4	10.1	12.0	8.6	9.4	11.2	10.5
WREXHAM 9	3292	3464	9.3	9.7						
YORK 6	4606	4514	14.6	14.2	13.9					
YORK 7	4573	4507	14.2	14.2	12.7					
YORK 8	4607	4536	15.4	19.5	17.2	15.0	13.1	15.0	12.7	10.5
YORK 9	4601	4521	12.4	12.7	10.9	12.0	14.2	12.0	11.6	8.6

Source: DoE (1992)

Note: Sites in Northern Ireland are listed under the Irish grid system.

Sulphur Dioxide Calendar Year Statistics							
Site	Year	Annual mean (ppb)	Max run 8 hour (ppb)	Site	Year	Annual mean (ppb)	Max run 8 hour (ppb)
Barnsley	91	20	158	Bristol B	93	8	62
	92	22	193		94	7	53
	93	26	253				
	94	10	86	Cardiff A	92	7	84
					93	6	65
Belfast A	89	45	467		94	5	37
	90	27	451				
	91	29	432	Central London	73	101	418
	92	26	338		74	59	265
	93	25	289		75	86	652
	94	19	255		76	66	379
					77	62	422
Belfast B	89	45	-		78	70	403
	90	27	-		79	71	504
	91	29	-		80	34	336
	92	15	237		81	26	249
	93	18	219		82	27	256
	94	17	279		83	24	147
					84	19	210
Bexley	94	7	152		85	11	131
					86	16	227
Birmingham A	92	11	104		87	11	186
	93	10	97		88	10	70
	94	7	68		89	12	163
					90	9	68
Birmingham B	94	6	50				
				Cromwell Road	74	12	92
Bircotes	89	21	181		75	65	533
	90	16	218		76	85	548
					77	61	432
Bloomsbury	92	11	114		78	54	297
	93	11	153		79	45	207
	94	10	84		80	44	236
					83	20	113
Bridge Place	90	10	91		84	23	213
	91	10	107		89	20	144
	92	9	175		90	17	145
	93	8	88		91	19	120
	94	6	90		92	15	170
					93	14	99

Sulphur Dioxide Calendar Year Statistics							
Site	Year	Annual mean (ppb)	Max.run. 8 hour (ppb)	Site	Year	Annual mean (ppb)	Max.run. 8 hour (ppb)
Cromwell Road	94	12	90	Newcastle A	92	7	109
(cont.)					93	8	83
Edinburgh B	93	8	106		94	6	98
	94	8	68				
				Rugeley	91	15	170
Featherstone	89	27	186		92	15	298
	90	15	129				
				Sibton	88	7	40
Glasgow B	78	25	108		89	5	29
	79	29	261				
	80	28	271	Southampton	94	5	30
	81	22	100				
				Stevenage	80	15	64
Harrow	80	13	74		81	14	120
					82	10	130
Hull	94	9	62		83	8	61
					84	8	70
Ladybower	88	8	115		85	15	262
	89	8	113		86	20	161
	90	7	127		87	10	121
	91	10	134		88	8	76
	92	8	125		89	8	62
	93	7	77		90	7	59
	94	5	88		91	7	61
					92	5	55
Leeds	93	10	100		93	6	71
	94	10	251		94	6	47
Leicester	94	7	73	Strath Vaich	91	0.7	21
					92	0.3	10
Liverpool	93	15	141		93	0.4	8
	94	12	138		94	0.4	12
Lullington Heath	88	5	68	Sunderland	93	6	92
	89	4	24		94	4	67
	92	3	33				
	93	2	29				
	94	2	20				

Source: Bower et al. (1994)

Data displayed for data captures ≥ 25 %

Location	1992 Monthly Mean Concentration in Air, µg/m^3											
	Jan	Feb	Mar	Apr	May	Jun	Jul	Aug	Sep	Oct	Nov	Dec
Barcombe Mills	1.1	0.9	0.7	2.1	3.5	3.3	1.9	1.2	1.0	3.9	1.9	4.0
Eskdalemuir	2.1	1.1	0.8	0.9	1.4	1.4	0.8	0.7	1.5	0.7	1.0	1.6
Glen Dye	2.7	1.2	0.9	1.0	1.3	0.9	1.0	0.7	1.2	0.6	0.8	1.6
High Muffles	13.2	8.0	4.4	3.9	3.0	3.0	4.5	3.0	4.8	3.5	3.8	8.7
Lough Navar	1.0	0.4	0.5	0.6	1.1	1.0	0.9	0.4	0.4	0.3	0.8	0.6
Stoke Ferry	6.6	5.0	3.6	5.0	4.0	3.4	3.7	2.3	2.7	4.0	3.1	3.9
Strath Vaich	0.4	0.3	0.2	0.3	0.7	0.6	-	0.3	0.4	0.3	0.2	0.3
Yarner Wood	5.4	1.0	0.5	1.0	2.0	2.3	1.6	0.6	0.4	1.9	0.3	1.7

Source: Schaug et al. (1994)

Sulphur Dioxide Annual Mean Concentrations, ppb, in Rural Areas				
Site	East	North	1992	1993
Barcombe Mills	5437	1149	1.54	2.93
Bentra	1587	5459	2.7	2.59
Brockhill 1	4002	2702	3.15	4.03
Burham 1	5730	1619	2.28	2.1
Bush	3246	6638	1.82	2.92
Caenby 1	4993	3900	5.91	5.34
Cam Forest	1070	5785	0.99	1.07
Cambourne 1	1628	407	0.84	0.86
Camphill 1	2274	6546	1.39	1.61
Cardington 2	5082	2464	7.07	5.25
Corpach 1	2054	7782	0.83	0.6
Cresselly 1	2064	2062	0.82	1.8
Cwmystwyth	2774	2745	1.72	2.24
Eskdalemuir	3235	6030	0.88	1.25
Etton 1	4980	4445	3.54	3.23
Faiseat	5622	1615	-	3.41
Forsinard	2890	9425	-	0.5
Fort Augustus 2	2366	8091	0.58	0.61
Glen Dye	3642	7864	0.87	1.07
Great Dun Fell	3711	5322	1.55	2.12
Hebden Bridge	4011	4327	5.93	3.63
High Muffles	4776	4939	4.04	4.34
Husbourne Crawley 1	4964	2361	2.26	2.08
Ladybower Reservoir	4164	3892	8.34	7.88
Little Horkesley 1	5971	2312	2.04	1.7
Loch Leven 2	3159	6990	2.41	2.71
Lough Navar	192	5212	0.5	0.72
Lullington Heath	5538	1016	2.55	2.25
Marshfield 1	3255	1830	3.15	3.57
Pitlochry	2918	7599	0.59	0.65
Preston Montford 2	3432	3143	1.84	2.28
Ratcliffe 13	4408	3278	8.37	7.29
Redesdale 2	3833	5961	1.06	1.32

Site	East	North	1992	1993
Rockbourne 1	4116	1181	1.39	-
Rosemaund	3564	2476	2.53	2.65
Stoke Ferry	5700	2988	2.92	2.48
Strathvaich Dam	2347	8750	0.29	0.66
Wakefield 24	4352	4132	6.33	5.48
Waunfawr 1	2533	3607	1.1	1.36
Wharleycroft	3697	5246	2.73	3.11
Yarner Wood	2786	789	1.05	1.64

Source: DoE (1992)

Chemical formula : $C_{12}H_6Cl_4$

Alternative names : PCB-44

Type of pollutant : (PCB) polychlorinated biphenyl, air toxic

Structure :

Cl Cl Cl Cl

Air quality data summary :

Location	Annual Mean pg/m³		
	1991	1992	1993
Bowland	*	*	14.49
Cardiff C	114.50	89.94	*
London	*	*	*
Manchester B	122.50	113.24	43.03
Middlesbrough	*	*	*
WSL	*	*	*

Source: Davis (1993)

Notes: * signifies no data available

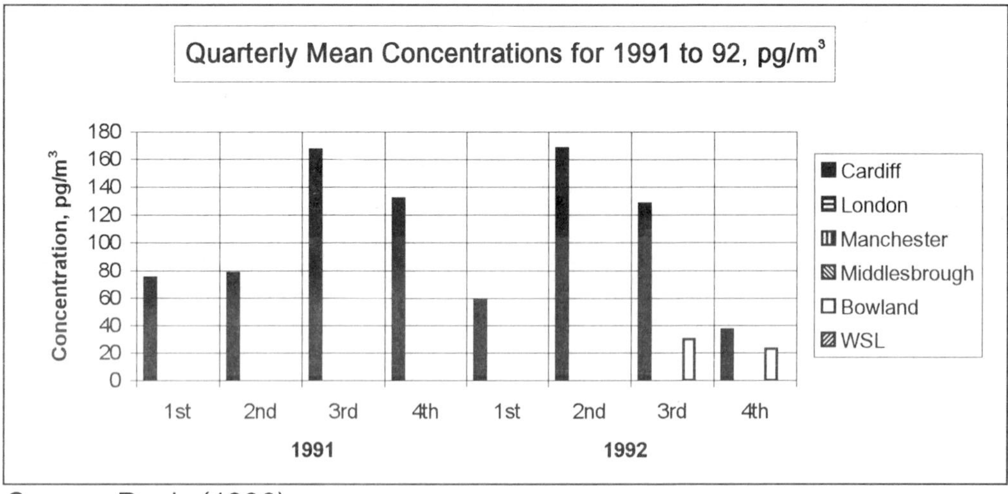

Source: Davis (1993)

2,2',3,5'-Tetrachlorobiphenyl in deposition

Chemical formula : $C_{12}H_6Cl_4$

Alternative names : PCB-44

Type of pollutant : (PCB) polychlorinated biphenyl, air toxic

Structure :

Air quality data summary :

Location	Annual Mean ng/m²/day		
	1991	1992	1993
Bowland	*	*	8.90
Cardiff C	224.40	181.35	*
London	*	*	*
Manchester B	59.96	49.95	*
Middlesbrough	*	*	*
WSL	*	*	*

Source: Davis (1993)

Notes: * signifies no data available

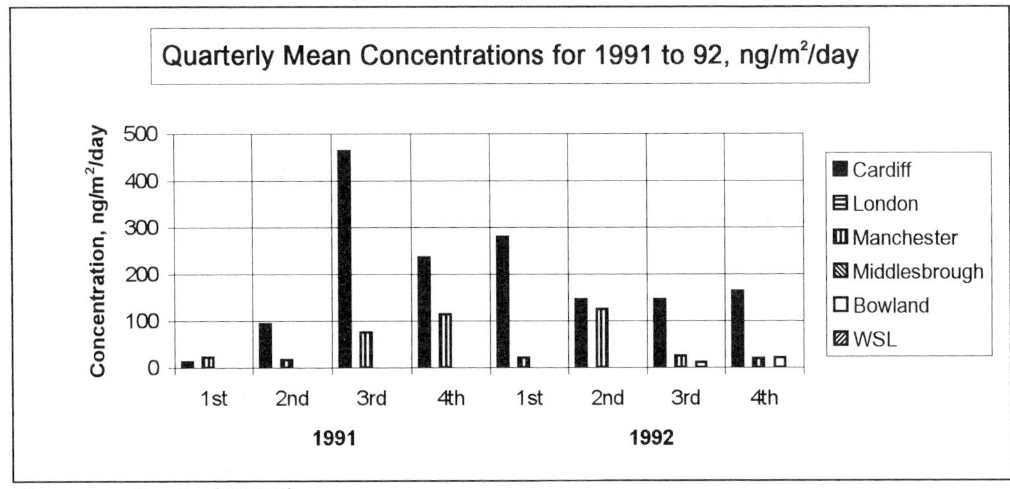

Source: Davis (1993)

Chemical formula : $C_{12}H_6Cl_4$

Alternative names : PCB-52

Type of pollutant : (PCB) polychlorinated biphenyl, air toxic

Structure :

Air quality data summary :

Location	Annual Mean pg/m^3		
	1991	1992	1993
Bowland	*	*	16.79
Cardiff C	131.14	123.10	*
London	603.65	444.42	436.44
Manchester B	113.02	87.36	129.74
Middlesbrough	*	*	58.31
WSL	104.70	*	*

Source: Davis (1993)

Notes: * signifies no data available

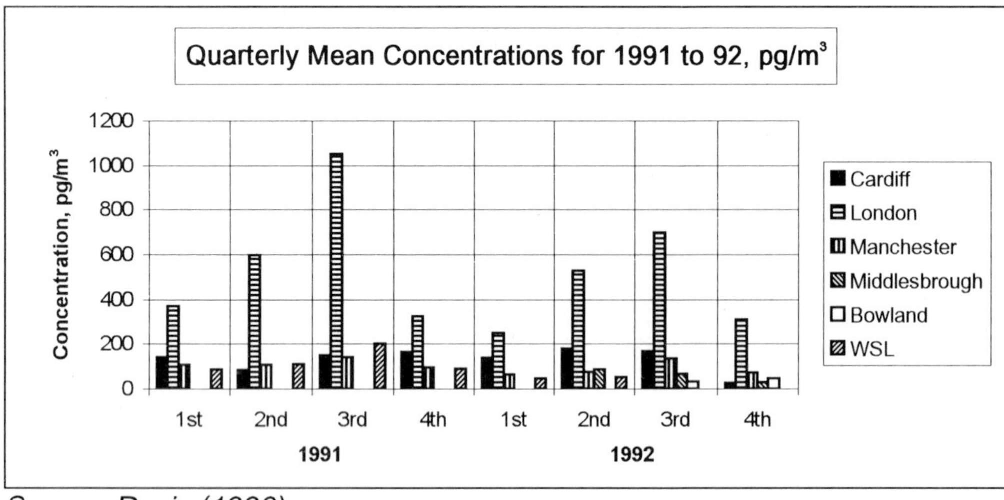

Source: Davis (1993)

Chemical formula : $C_{12}H_6Cl_4$

Alternative names : PCB-52

Type of pollutant : (PCB) polychlorinated biphenyl, air toxic

Structure :

Cl Cl

Cl Cl

Air quality data summary :

Location	Annual Mean ng/m²/day		
	1991	1992	1993
Bowland	*	*	29.63
Cardiff C	403.09	367.93	*
London	135.00	15.39	*
Manchester B	56.79	99.00	*
Middlesbrough	*	*	*
WSL	103.73	*	*

Source: Davis (1993)

Notes: * signifies no data available

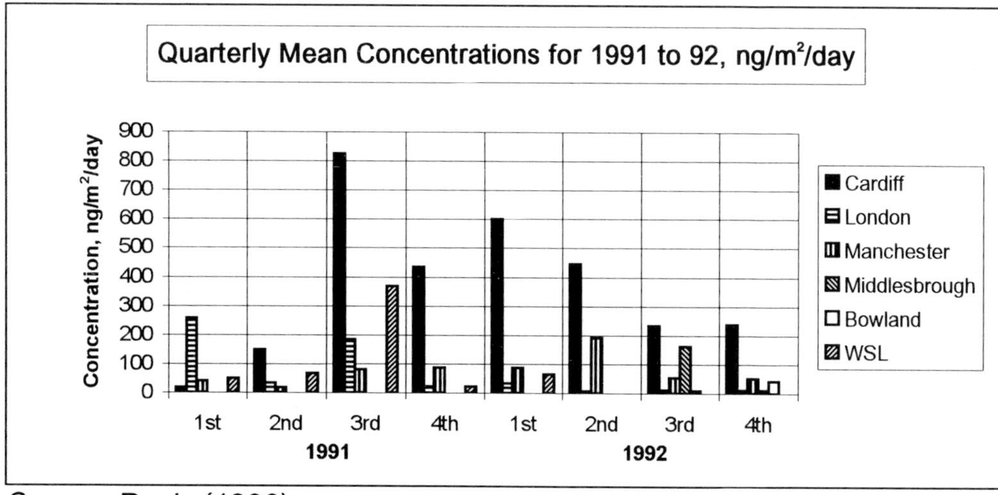

Source: Davis (1993)

Chemical formula : $C_{12}H_6Cl_4$

Alternative names : PCB-61

Type of pollutant : (PCB) polychlorinated biphenyl, air toxic

Structure :

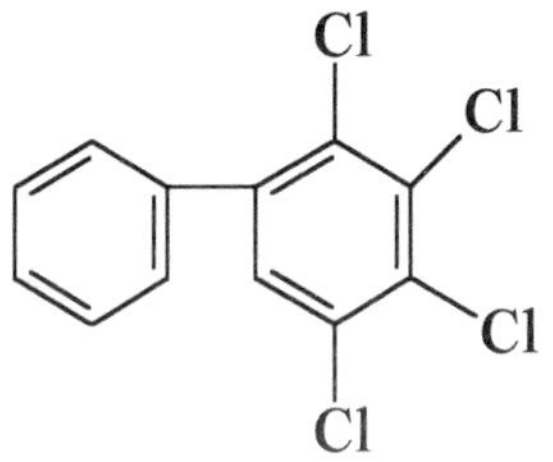

Air quality data summary :

Location	Annual Mean pg/m^3		
	1991	1992	1993
Bowland	*	*	9.70
Cardiff C	18.83	33.57	*
London	*	*	*
Manchester B	19.91	24.47	24.42
Middlesbrough	*	*	*
WSL	*	*	*

Source: Davis (1993)

Notes: * signifies no data available

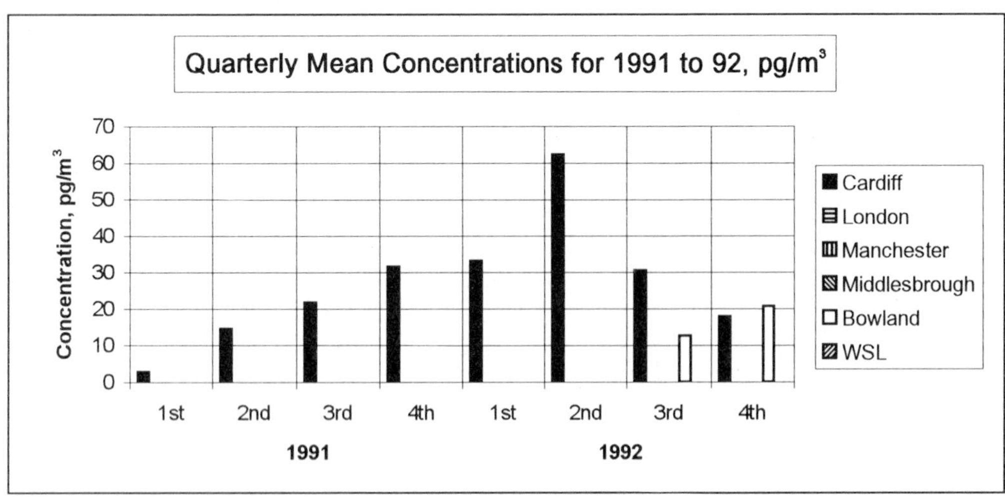

Source: Davis (1993)

Chemical formula : $C_{12}H_6Cl_4$

Alternative names : PCB-61

Type of pollutant : (PCB) polychlorinated biphenyl, air toxic

Structure :

Air quality data summary :

Location	Annual Mean ng/m²/day		
	1991	1992	1993
Bowland	*	*	5.23
Cardiff C	71.63	63.75	*
London	*	*	*
Manchester B	103.03	22.86	*
Middlesbrough	*	*	*
WSL	*	*	*

Source: Davis (1993)

Notes: * signifies no data available

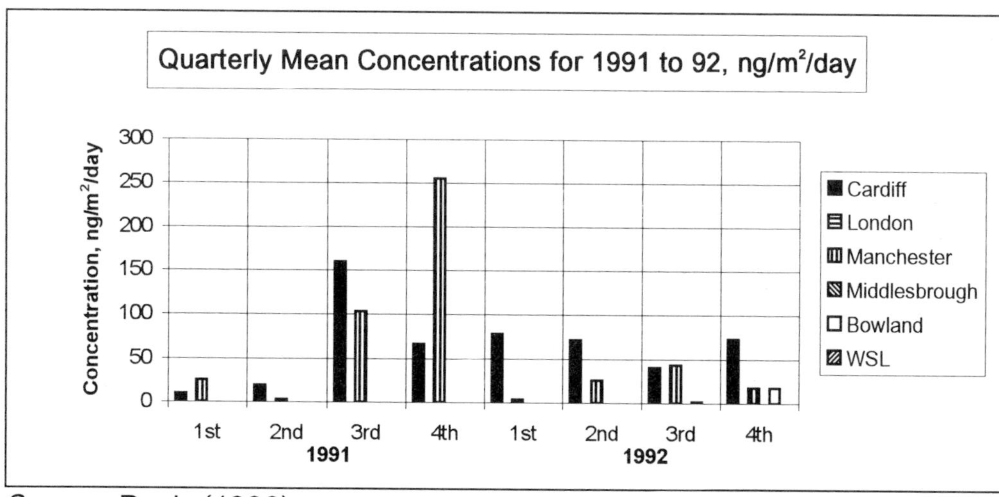

Source: Davis (1993)

2,3',4,4'-Tetrachlorobiphenyl in air

Chemical formula : $C_{12}H_6Cl_4$

Alternative names : PCB-66

Type of pollutant : (PCB) polychlorinated biphenyl, air toxic

Structure :

Air quality data summary :

Location	Annual Mean pg/m^3		
	1991	1992	1993
Bowland	*	*	23.72
Cardiff C	111.78	81.44	*
London	*	*	*
Manchester B	108.94	82.25	*
Middlesbrough	*	*	*
WSL	*	*	*

Source: Davis (1993)

Notes: * signifies no data available

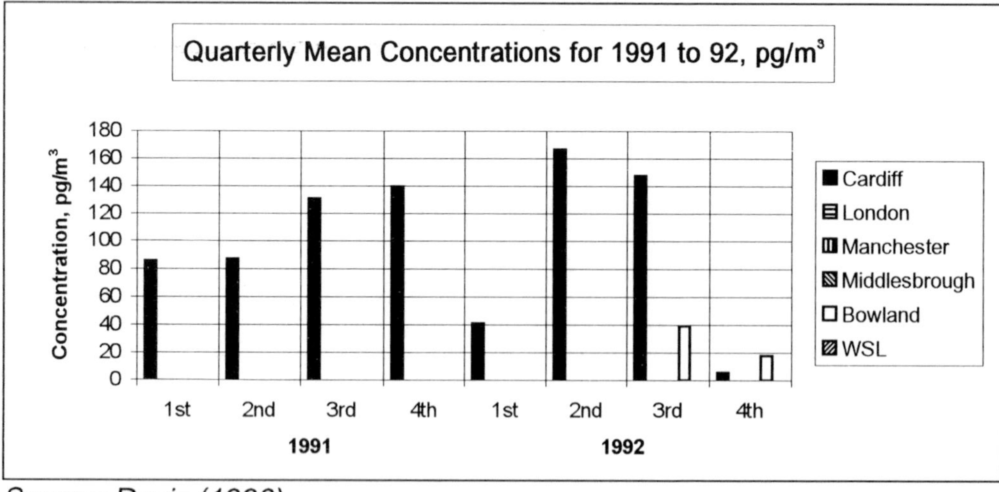

Source: Davis (1993)

Chemical formula	:	$C_{12}H_6Cl_4$
Alternative names	:	PCB-66
Type of pollutant	:	(PCB) polychlorinated biphenyl, air toxic
Structure	:	

Air quality data summary :

Location	Annual Mean ng/m²/day		
	1991	1992	1993
Bowland	*	*	9.36
Cardiff C	243.36	130.58	*
London	*	*	*
Manchester B	47.85	79.38	*
Middlesbrough	*	*	*
WSL	*	*	*

Source: Davis (1993)

Notes: * signifies no data available

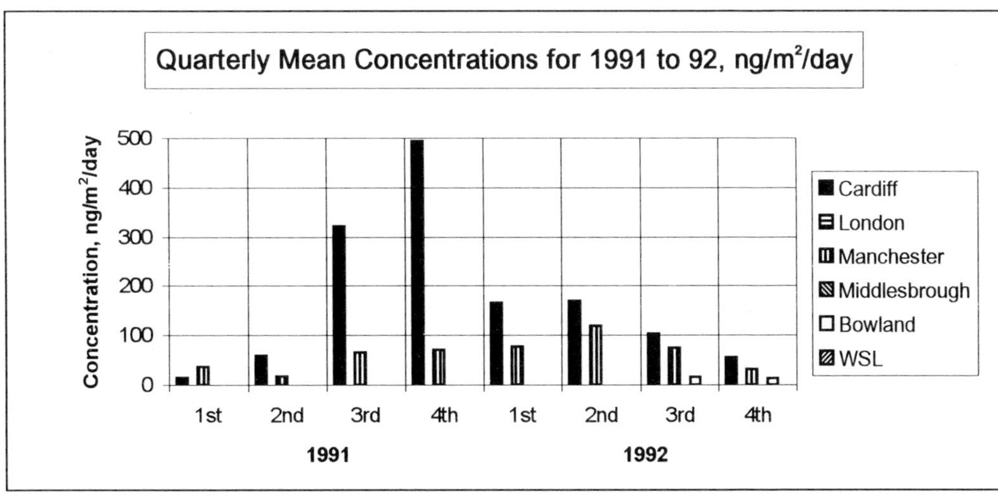

Source: Davis (1993)

Chemical formula : $C_{12}H_6Cl_4$

Alternative names : PCB-77

Type of pollutant : (PCB) polychlorinated biphenyl, air toxic

Structure :

Cl Cl Cl Cl

Air quality data summary :

Location	Annual Mean pg/m^3		
	1991	1992	1993
Bowland	*	*	7.86
Cardiff C	70.71	118.28	*
London	18.36	13.89	14.30
Manchester B	84.39	71.23	58.52
Middlesbrough	*	*	5.82
WSL	3.10	*	*

Source: Davis (1993)

Notes: * signifies no data available. These data represent results for a mixture of PCB-77 and PCB-110 since the separate peaks are not normally resolvable.

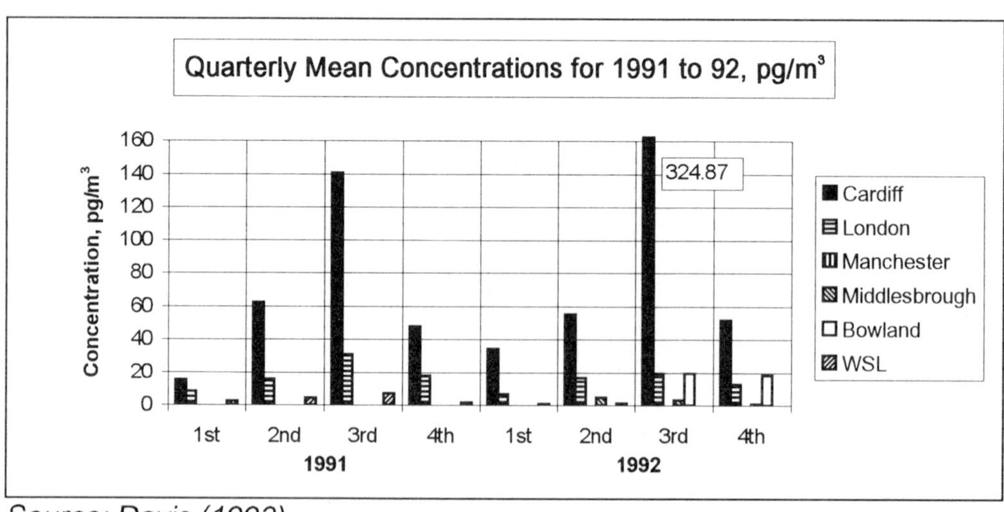

Source: Davis (1993)

Chemical formula : $C_{12}H_6Cl_4$

Alternative names : PCB-77

Type of pollutant : (PCB) polychlorinated biphenyl, air toxic

Structure :

Cl Cl Cl Cl

Air quality data summary :

Location	Annual Mean ng/m²/day		
	1991	1992	1993
Bowland	*	*	15.02
Cardiff C	191.97	101.20	*
London	16.34	2.88	*
Manchester B	24.72	32.47	*
Middlesbrough	*	*	*
WSL	5.33	*	*

Source: Davis (1993)

Notes: * signifies no data available. These data represent results for a mixture of PCB-77 and PCB-110 since the separate peaks are not normally resolvable.

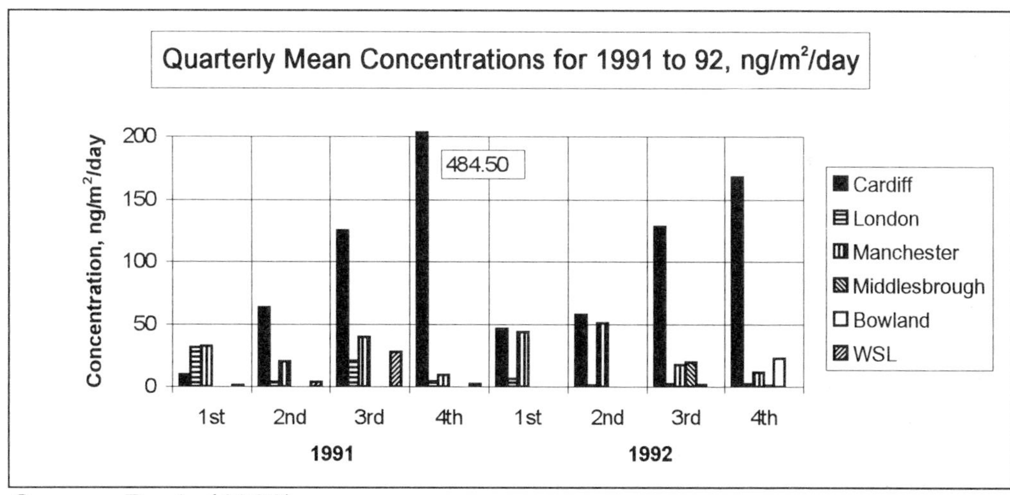

Source: Davis (1993)

Chemical formula : $C_{12}H_4Cl_4O$

Alternative names : 2,3,7,8-TCDF

Type of pollutant : Furan, air toxic

Structure :

Air quality data summary :

Location	Annual Mean pg/m^3		
	1991	1992	1993
Bowland	*	*	0.00
Cardiff C	0.17	0.21	*
London	0.07	0.02	0.00
Manchester B	0.38	0.43	0.36
Middlesbrough	*	*	0.03
WSL	0.01	*	*

Source: Davis (1993)

Note: * signifies no data available

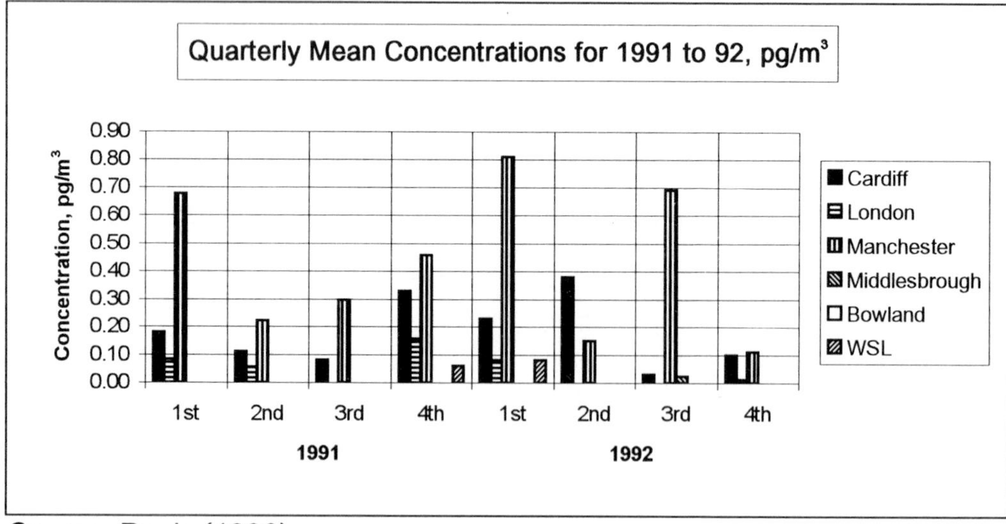

Source: Davis (1993)

2,3,7,8-Tetrachlorodibenzofuran in deposition

Chemical formula : $C_{12}H_4Cl_4O$

Alternative names : 2,3,7,8-TCDF

Type of pollutant : Furan, air toxic

Structure :

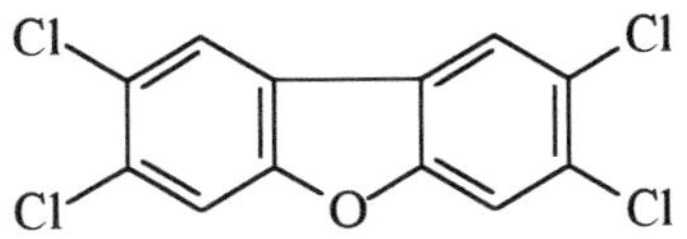

Air quality data summary :

Location	Annual Mean pg/m²/day		
	1991	1992	1993
Bowland	*	*	*
Cardiff C	190.60	128.37	*
London	11.82	0.00	*
Manchester B	86.61	841.82	*
Middlesbrough	*	*	*
WSL	14.57	*	*

Source: Davis (1993)

Note: * signifies no data available

Chemical formula : $C_{12}H_4Cl_4O_2$

Alternative names : 2,3,7,8 - TCDD

Type of pollutant : Dioxin, air toxic

Structure :

Air quality data summary :

Location	Annual Mean pg/m³		
	1991	1992	1993
Bowland	*	*	0.00
Cardiff C	0.03	0.01	*
London	0.00	0.00	0.00
Manchester B	0.06	0.05	0.01
Middlesbrough	*	*	0.00
WSL	0.00	*	*

Source: Davis (1993)

Note: * signifies no data available

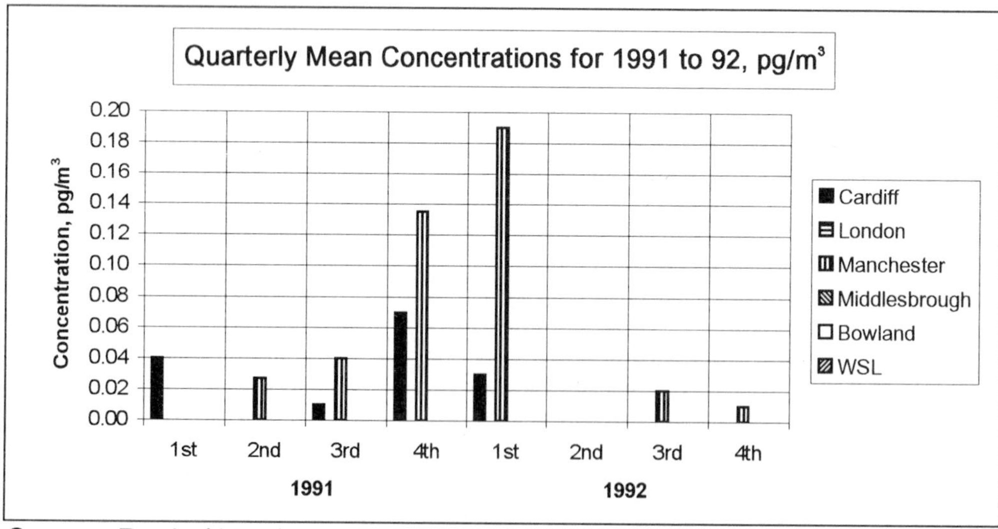

Source: Davis (1993)

Chemical formula : $C_{12}H_4Cl_4O_2$

Alternative names : 2,3,7,8 - TCDD

Type of pollutant : Dioxin, air toxic

Structure :

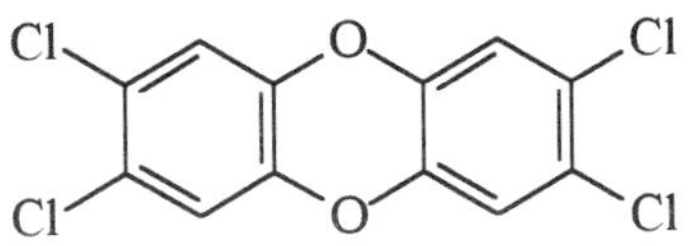

Air quality data summary :

Location	Annual Mean $pg/m^2/day$		
	1991	1992	1993
Bowland	*	*	*
Cardiff C	45.67	18.95	*
London	0.00	0.00	*
Manchester B	57.51	101.82	*
Middlesbrough	*	*	*
WSL	0.00	*	*

Source: Davis (1993)

Note: * signifies no data available

Chemical formula : $C_{10}H_{14}$

Alternative names : Isodurene

Type of pollutant : (Volatile) organic compound (VOC), hydrocarbon

Structure :

$$\text{1,2,3,5-tetramethylbenzene: benzene ring with } CH_3 \text{ groups at positions 1, 2, 3 and 5 } (H_3C)$$

Air quality data summary :

Mean Air Concentration in Leeds, 19/8/94 to 8/9/94	
Location	21 day mean, $\mu g/m^3$
Albion Street	0.056
Cliff Lane	0.036
EUN monitoring site	0.062
Kerbside site	0.106
Kirkstall Road	0.107
Park site	0.040
Queen Street	0.084
Vicar Lane	0.289

Source: Bartle et al. (1995)

1,2,4,5-Tetramethylbenzene

Chemical formula : $C_{10}H_{14}$

Alternative names : Durene

Type of pollutant : (Volatile) organic compound (VOC), hydrocarbon

Structure :

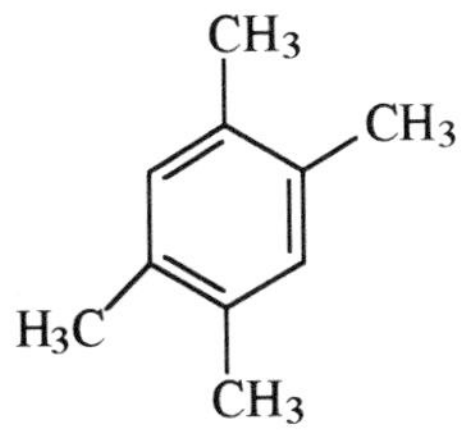

Air quality data summary :

Mean Air Concentration in Leeds, 19/8/94 to 8/9/94	
Location	21 day mean, µg/m^3
Albion Street	0.032
Cliff Lane	0.035
EUN monitoring site	0.034
Kerbside site	0.058
Kirkstall Road	0.059
Park site	0.030
Queen Street	0.047
Vicar Lane	0.161

Source: Bartle et al. (1995)

Chemical formula : Th

Alternative names : Particulate thorium

Type of pollutant : Suspended particulate matter, trace element

Air quality data summary :

Location	Average Annual Concentrations, ng/m^3
	1972-1981
Harwell, Oxfordshire.	0.06
Styrrup, Nottinghamshire.	0.10
Swansea	0.09
Trebanos, Glamorgan.	<0.07
Wraymires, Cumbria.	0.03

Source: Cawse et al. (1994), Pattenden (1974).

Thorium in rain

Chemical formula : Th

Alternative names : Precipitation thorium

Type of pollutant : Trace contaminant of rain, trace element

Air quality data summary :

Rural Concentrations

Location	Average Annual Rainfall Concentration µg per litre	
	1972-1981	1982-1991 *
Harwell, Oxfordshire. A	<0.08	<0.01
Styrrup, Nottinghamshire. A	0.19	<0.01
Wraymires, Cumbria. A	<0.03	<0.01

Source: Cawse et al. (1994)

Note: total deposition expressed as apparent rainfall concentration.
* based on soluble fraction only

Titanium aerosol

Chemical formula : Ti

Alternative names : Particulate titanium

Type of pollutant : Suspended particulate matter, trace element

Air quality data summary :

Rural Concentrations

Location	Average Annual Concentrations, ng/m^3	
	1975-1981	1982-1991
Harwell, Oxfordshire.	<18	<20
Styrrup, Nottinghamshire.	<33	<34
Trebanos, Glamorgan.	<23	-
Wraymires, Cumbria.	<16	<16

Source: Cawse et al. (1994)

Titanium in rain

Chemical formula : Ti

Alternative names : Precipitation titanium

Type of pollutant : Trace contaminant of rain, trace element

Air quality data summary :

Rural Concentrations

Location	Average Annual Rainfall Concentration µg per litre	
	1972-1981	1982-1991 *
Harwell, Oxfordshire.	<60	<21
Styrrup, Nottinghamshire.	<90	<23
Wraymires, Cumbria.	<40	<25

Source: Cawse et al. (1994)

Note: total deposition expressed as apparent rainfall concentration.
* based on soluble fraction only.

Chemical formula : C_7H_8

Alternative names : Methylbenzene

Type of pollutant : (Volatile) organic compound (VOC), hydrocarbon

Structure :

CH_3 (benzene ring structure)

Air quality data summary :

Remote rural concentrations

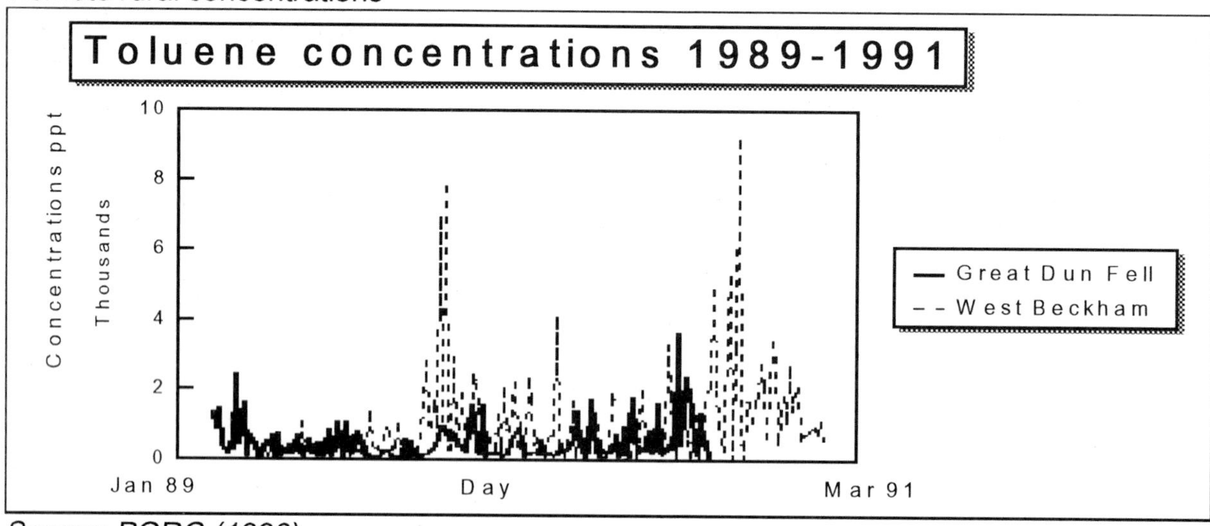

Source: PORG (1993)

Rural concentrations

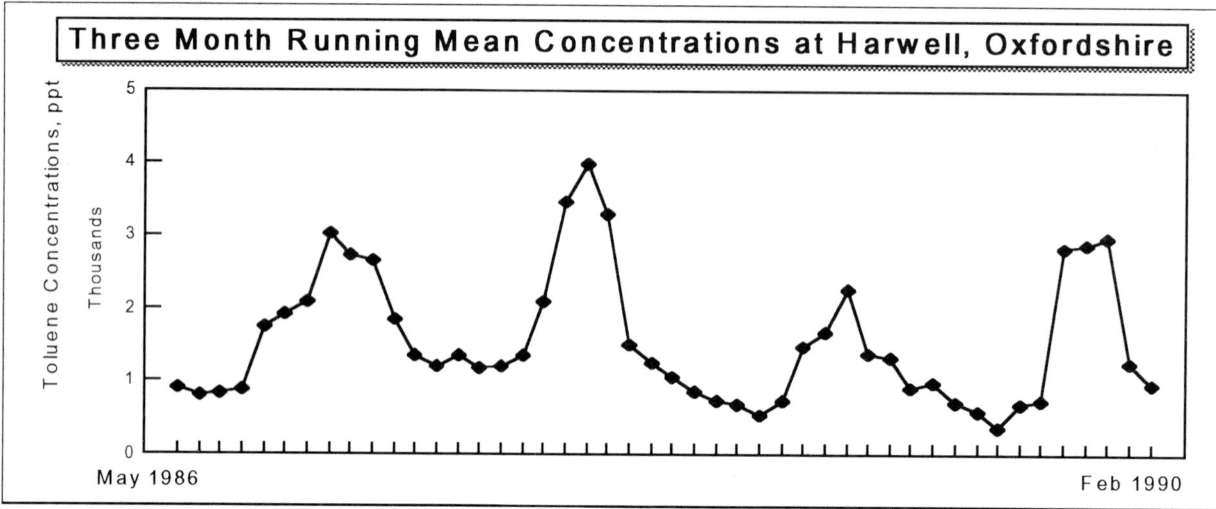

Source: PORG (1993)

Urban Concentrations

Mean Air Concentration in Leeds, 19/8/94 to 8/9/94	
Location	21 day mean, µg/m³
Albion Street	1.620
Cliff Lane	1.080
EUN monitoring site	1.702
Kerbside site	2.462
Kirkstall Road	2.687
Park site	0.835
Queen Street	1.876
Vicar Lane	5.960

Source: Bartle et al. (1995)

	1994-95 Monthly Means, ppb								
	Belfast C	Birmingham B	Bristol A	Cardiff B	Edinburgh A	Eltham	Harwell	Middlesbrough	UCL
Jan 94	2.39	3.88	-	3.37	0.09	1.57	-	2.66	2.80
Feb 94	3.16	4.13	-	3.83	1.91	1.75	-	1.82	4.82
Mar 94	1.35	1.93	-	1.57	1.21	0.91	-	1.40	1.93
Apr 94	1.53	1.91	0.21	1.54	1.61	1.15	-	0.40	2.05
May 94	2.00	3.33	1.24	2.01	1.60	1.15	-	0.65	3.23
Jun 94	1.42	1.79	1.01	1.41	1.29	1.07	-	0.73	2.57
Jul 94	1.54	2.70	1.41	1.73	1.92	1.40	-	2.59	3.04
Aug 94	1.72	2.24	1.76	1.83	1.82	1.33	-	2.06	2.72
Sep 94	2.77	2.36	1.98	2.07	1.94	1.57	-	9.75	3.22
Oct 94	3.57	4.20	4.03	3.81	2.51	2.35	-	4.22	2.69
Nov 94	3.01	3.79	2.86	4.31	2.49	2.89	-	3.75	1.90
Dec 94	3.15	3.58	2.86	3.52	2.44	3.44	-	1.47	2.47
Jan 95	2.03	1.62	2.13	2.49	1.50	2.38	0.51	1.55	2.58
Feb 95	1.57	1.74	1.97	2.05	1.20	1.85	0.43	1.29	1.96

Source: Dollard (1995)

Six monthly mean concentrations for toluene form July to December 1992, (ppb):

Location	Mean Concentration, ppb	Location	Mean Concentration, ppb
ADDLESTONE 1	3.8	BRISTOL 26	4.2
BARKING 15	4.7	BURHAM 1	1.4
BATH 6	3.4	CAMPHILL 11	1.9
BELFAST 13	2.7	CARLISLE 13	2.6
BIRMINGHAM 26	2.3	CRAWLEY 3	1.6
BRADFORD 22	3.5	DARTFORD 9	2.9

Location	Mean Concentration, ppb	Location	Mean Concentration, ppb
DIBDEN PURLIEU 1	2.2	MANCHESTER 15	4.6
EALING 3	3.6	MANCHESTER AIRPORT	1.5
EDINBURGH 14	1.5	MIDDLESBROUGH 35	2.5
ELLESMERE PORT 9	10.5	NORWICH 7	2.4
ESTON 9	2.3	NOTTINGHAM 20	2.9
GLASGOW 86	3.4	PETERHEAD 2	1.2
GLASGOW 92	3.1	PLYMOUTH 11	1.9
GLASGOW 96	3.4	PONTYPOOL 7	5.0
GRANGEMOUTH 2	2.7	SELBY 4	1.9
HAMMERSMITH 6	9.5	SHEFFIELD 86	2.9
ILFORD 6	7.6	ST ALBANS 3	3.6
ILKESTON 8	2.8	STAINFORTH 1	2.7
IMMINGHAM 5	2.3	STEPNEY 5	2.3
IPSWICH 14	2.2	STEVENAGE 4	1.6
ISLINGTON 9	3.7	ST HELENS 29	2.1
KENSINGTON 11	3.3	SUNDERLAND 8	3.5
KENSINGTON 14	7.1	TEDDINGTON 3	2.8
KNOTTINGLEY 1	3.6	WALSALL 15	3.2
LEEDS 37	3.2	WALTHAMSTOW 8	4.0
LIVERPOOL 16	3.3	WIDNES 9	2.4
LIVERPOOL 19	3.1	WOLVERHAMPTON 7	1.0
LONDONDERRY 11	2.1	WREXHAM 7	3.1
MAIDSTONE 7	5.7	YORK 7	3.0
MANCHESTER 11	3.5		

Source: Downing et al. (1994)

Total suspended particulates

Chemical formula :

Alternative names : Thoracic particles

Type of pollutant : Suspended particulate matter

Air quality data summary :

Rural Concentrations

Location	Concentrations, ng/m^3			
	Mean	Trend	Mean	Trend
	1972-1981	%/yr	1982-1991	%/yr
Harwell, Oxfordshire.	26970	-5.1	26970	nst
Styrrup, Nottinghamshire.	44140	-5.1	40460	-7.2
Trebanos, Glamorgan.	31880	-	28110	-
Wraymires, Cumbria.	22070	nst	20840	-15.4

Source: Cawse et al. (1994)

nst=no significant trend

Chemical formula : C_4H_8

Alternative names : trans but-2-ene

Type of pollutant : (Volatile) organic compound (VOC), hydrocarbon

Structure :

$$\begin{array}{ccc} H_3C & & H \\ & C{=}C & \\ H & & CH_3 \end{array}$$

Air quality data summary :

Urban concentrations

1994-95 Monthly Means, ppb									
	Belfast C	Birmingham B	Bristol A	Cardiff B	Edinburgh A	Eltham	Harwell	Middlesbrough	UCL
Jan 94	0.19	0.59	-	1.61	-	0.11	-	0.30	0.39
Feb 94	0.24	0.31	-	0.96	0.18	0.11	-	0.59	0.43
Mar 94	0.18	0.38	-	0.54	0.13	0.24	-	1.56	0.28
Apr 94	0.23	0.40	0.25	0.54	0.17	0.45	-	1.55	0.48
May 94	0.28	0.35	0.16	0.72	0.16	0.35	-	0.34	0.65
Jun 94	0.28	0.29	0.15	0.15	0.17	0.12	-	0.18	0.27
Jul 94	0.25	0.18	0.23	0.90	0.26	0.27	-	0.64	0.29
Aug 94	0.21	0.44	0.29	0.54	0.24	0.16	-	0.43	0.33
Sep 94	0.25	0.36	0.20	0.38	0.24	0.21	-	0.99	0.40
Oct 94	0.27	0.38	0.53	0.23	0.21	0.28	-	0.92	0.49
Nov 94	0.21	0.57	0.24	0.09	0.15	0.29	-	0.69	0.48
Dec 94	0.22	0.66	0.24	0.26	0.16	0.37	-	0.31	0.46
Jan 95	0.16	0.32	0.22	0.24	0.09	0.25	0.06	0.29	0.29
Feb 95	0.11	0.33	0.27	0.22	0.08	0.20	0.06	0.32	0.27

Source: Dollard (1995)

Remote rural concentrations

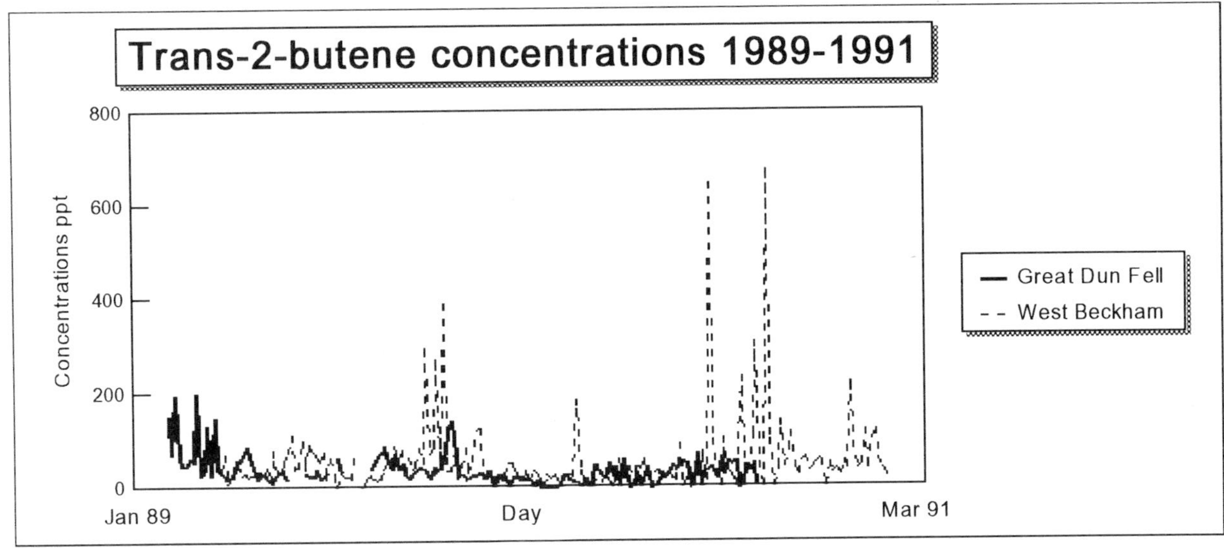

Source: PORG (1993)

Trans-1,3-dimethylcyclopentane

Chemical formula : C_7H_{14}

Alternative names :

Type of pollutant : (Volatile) organic compound (VOC), hydrocarbon

Structure :

H_3C—CH—CH_2—CH(CH_3)—CH_2—CH_2— (ring)

Air quality data summary :

Mean Air Concentration in Leeds, 19/8/94 to 8/9/94	
Location	21 day mean, µg/m^3
Albion Street	0.045
Cliff Lane	0.032
EUN monitoring site	0.045
Kerbside site	0.052
Kirkstall Road	0.066
Park site	0.035
Queen Street	0.063
Vicar Lane	0.143

Source: Bartle et al. (1995)

Chemical formula : C_5H_{10}

Alternative names : trans pent-2-ene

Type of pollutant : (Volatile) organic compound (VOC), hydrocarbon

Structure :

$$\begin{array}{ccc} H_3C & & H \\ & C{=}C & \\ H & & CH_2CH_3 \end{array}$$

Air quality data summary :

Urban concentrations

	1994-95 Monthly Means, ppb								
	Belfast C	Birmingham B	Bristol A	Cardiff B	Edinburgh A	Eltham	Harwell	Middlesbrough	UCL
Jan 94	0.13	0.90	-	0.44	-	0.09	-	0.50	0.42
Feb 94	0.17	0.27	-	0.37	0.14	0.10	-	0.68	0.60
Mar 94	0.08	0.10	-	0.53	0.15	0.28	-	0.65	0.43
Apr 94	0.10	0.11	0.08	0.14	0.19	0.17	-	2.05	0.73
May 94	0.10	0.13	0.25	0.19	0.23	0.12	-	0.93	0.62
Jun 94	0.10	0.13	0.12	0.15	0.08	0.21	-	0.13	0.29
Jul 94	0.10	0.19	0.23	0.21	0.13	0.11	-	0.63	0.33
Aug 94	0.12	0.40	0.26	0.38	0.14	0.11	-	0.38	0.38
Sep 94	0.18	0.18	0.18	0.17	0.13	0.15	-	1.52	0.32
Oct 94	0.23	0.36	0.99	0.38	0.17	0.23	-	0.93	0.53
Nov 94	0.20	0.35	0.22	0.24	0.16	0.25	-	0.55	0.46
Dec 94	0.17	0.37	0.20	0.17	0.13	0.22	-	0.15	0.32
Jan 95	0.11	0.16	0.19	0.15	0.09	0.31	-	0.16	0.20
Feb 95	0.08	0.14	0.17	0.15	0.07	0.14	0.02	0.12	0.17

Source: Dollard (1995)

Chemical formula : $C_{12}H_7Cl_3$

Alternative names : PCB-18

Type of pollutant : (PCB) polychlorinated biphenyl, air toxic

Structure :

Air quality data summary :

Location	Annual Mean pg/m³		
	1991	1992	1993
Bowland	*	*	148.16
Cardiff C	321.41	461.94	*
London	*	*	*
Manchester B	236.31	160.56	252.61
Middlesbrough	*	*	*
WSL	*	*	*

Source: Davis (1993)

Notes: * signifies no data available

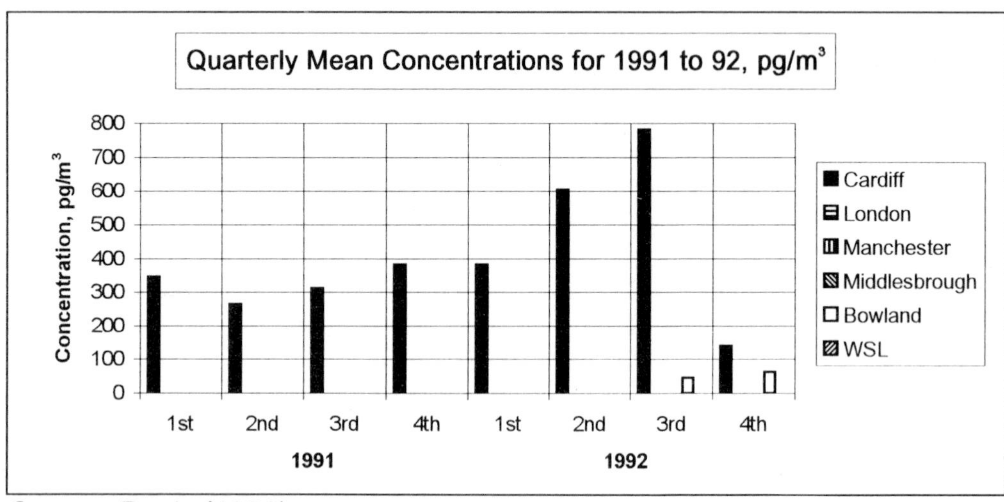

Source: Davis (1993)

Chemical formula : $C_{12}H_7Cl_3$

Alternative names : PCB-18

Type of pollutant : (PCB) polychlorinated biphenyl, air toxic

Structure :

Cl Cl

Cl

Air quality data summary :

Location	Annual Mean ng/m²/day		
	1991	1992	1993
Bowland	*	*	66.16
Cardiff C	1332.23	842.95	*
London	*	*	*
Manchester B	82.09	153.03	*
Middlesbrough	*	*	*
WSL	*	*	*

Source: Davis (1993)

Notes: * signifies no data available

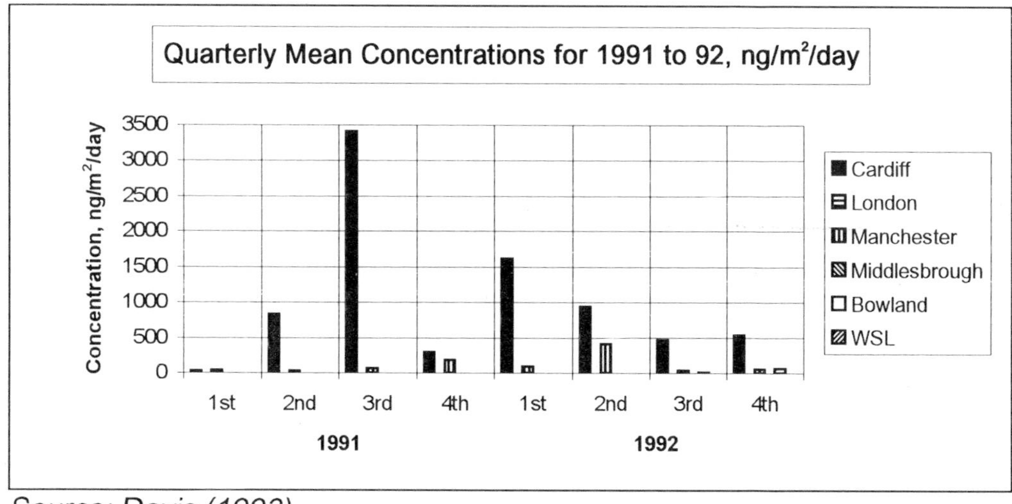

Source: Davis (1993)

2,4,4'-Trichlorobiphenyl in air

Chemical formula : $C_{12}H_7Cl_3$

Alternative names : PCB-28

Type of pollutant : (PCB) polychlorinated biphenyl, air toxic

Structure :

Cl
Cl
Cl

Air quality data summary :

Location	Annual Mean pg/m³		
	1991	1992	1993
Bowland	*	*	38.34
Cardiff C	191.37	202.14	*
London	607.30	496.25	475.10
Manchester B	139.14	128.83	156.79
Middlesbrough	*	*	125.06
WSL	188.22	*	*

Source: Davis (1993)

Notes: * signifies no data available

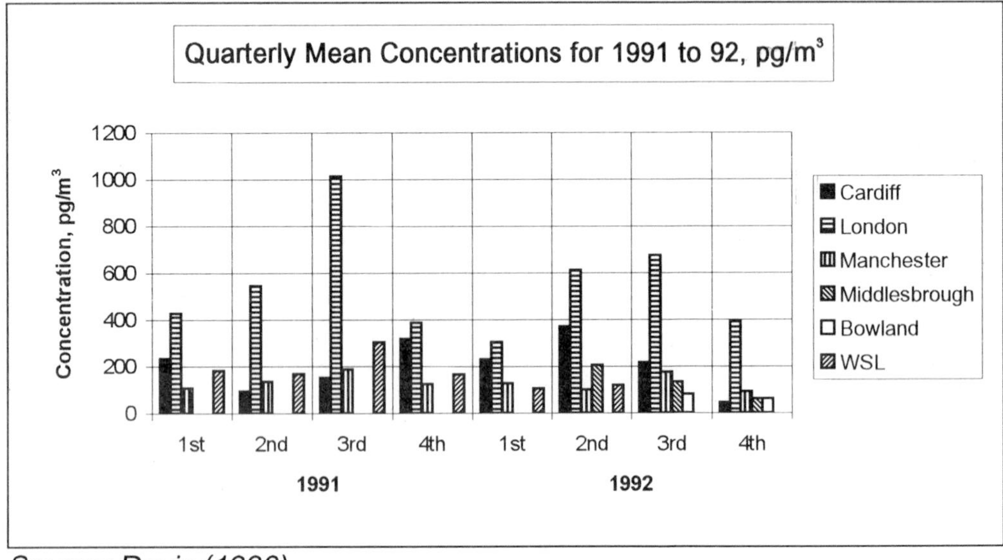

Source: Davis (1993)

2,4,4'-Trichlorobiphenyl in deposition

Chemical formula : $C_{12}H_7Cl_3$

Alternative names : PCB-28

Type of pollutant : (PCB) polychlorinated biphenyl, air toxic

Structure :

Air quality data summary :

Location	Annual Mean ng/m²/day		
	1991	1992	1993
Bowland	*	*	76.19
Cardiff C	1063.88	1716.46	*
London	353.00	22.95	*
Manchester B	163.76	264.15	*
Middlesbrough	*	*	*
WSL	234.67	*	*

Source: Davis (1993)

Notes: * signifies no data available

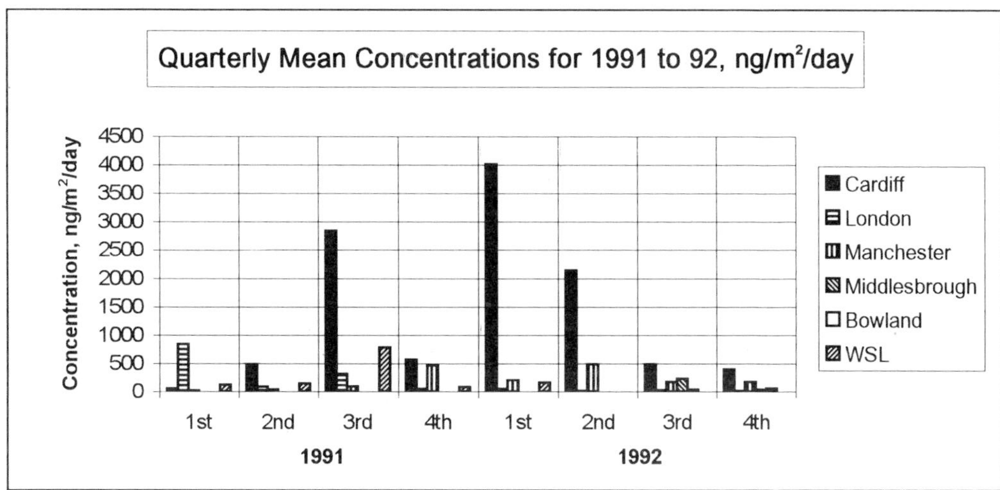

Source: Davis (1993)

2,4,6-Trichlorobiphenyl in air

Chemical formula : $C_{12}H_7Cl_3$

Alternative names : PCB-30

Type of pollutant : (PCB) polychlorinated biphenyl, air toxic

Structure :

Cl
Cl Cl

Air quality data summary :

Location	Annual Mean pg/m^3		
	1991	1992	1993
Bowland	*	*	5.42
Cardiff C	15.50	18.99	*
London	*	*	*
Manchester B	8.05	24.61	17.96
Middlesbrough	*	*	*
WSL	*	*	*

Source: Davis (1993)

Notes: * signifies no data available

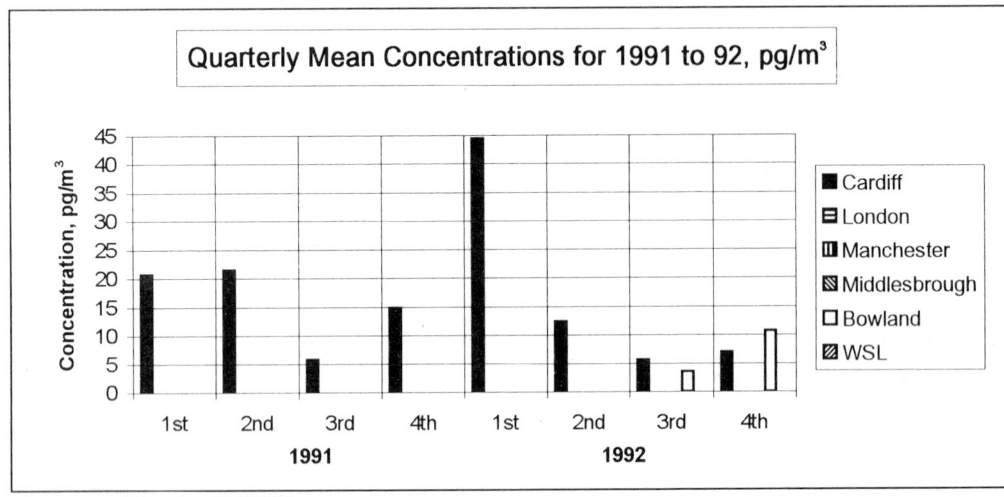

Source: Davis (1993)

2,4,6-Trichlorobiphenyl in deposition

Chemical formula : $C_{12}H_7Cl_3$

Alternative names : PCB-30

Type of pollutant : (PCB) polychlorinated biphenyl, air toxic

Structure :

Cl Cl Cl

Air quality data summary :

Location	Annual Mean ng/m²/day		
	1991	1992	1993
Bowland	*	*	10.49
Cardiff C	9.27	43.68	*
London	*	*	*
Manchester B	7.80	34.50	*
Middlesbrough	*	*	*
WSL	*	*	*

Source: Davis (1993)

Notes: * signifies no data available

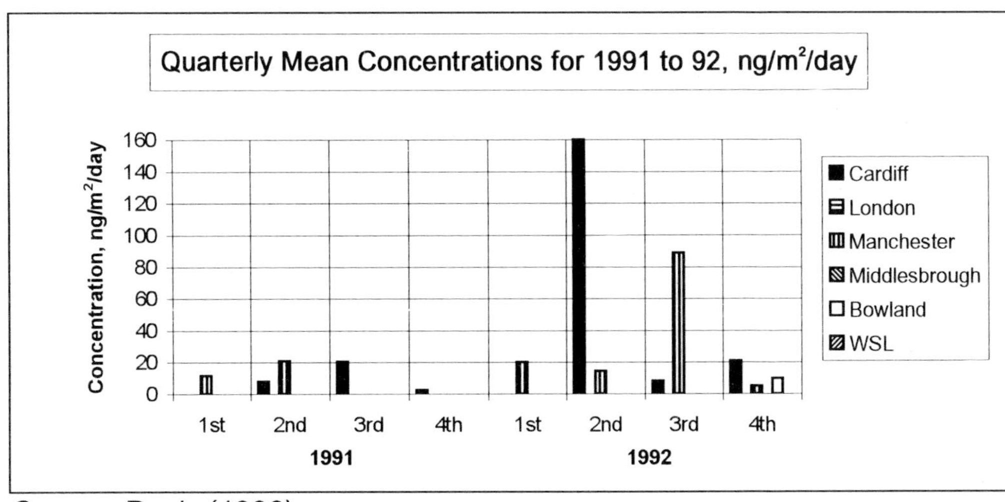

Source: Davis (1993)

Chemical formula	:	$C_2H_3Cl_3$
Alternative names	:	Methylchloroform, genklene
Type of pollutant	:	Ozone depleting halocarbon, (volatile) organic compound (VOC)
Structure	:	CCl_3CH_3
Air quality data summary	:	

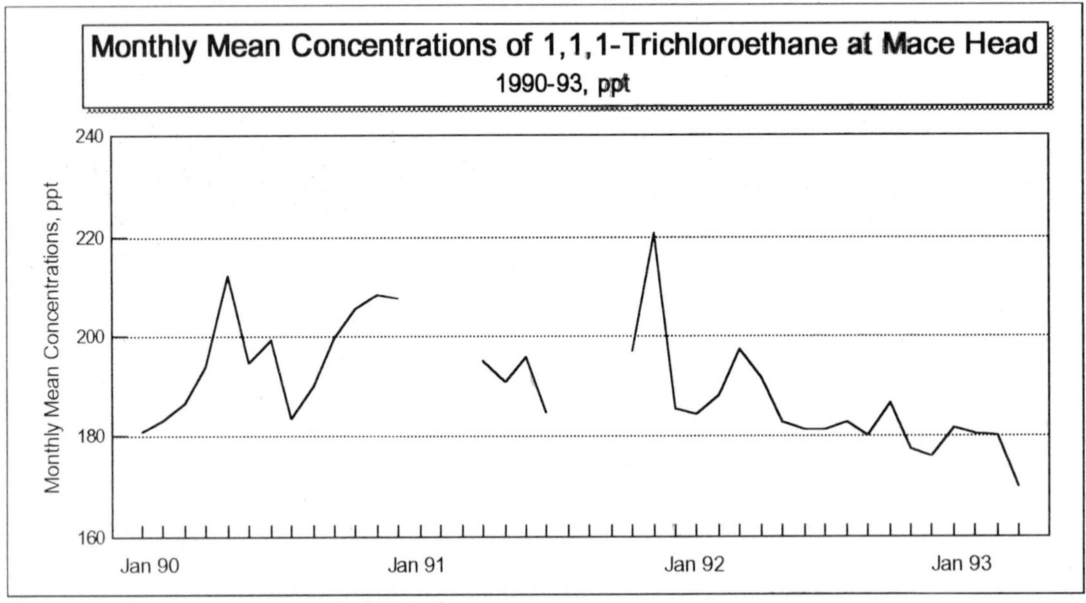

Source: Simmonds et al. (1994)

1,2,3-Trimethylbenzene

Chemical formula : C_9H_{12}

Alternative names : Hemimellitene

Type of pollutant : (Volatile) organic compound (VOC), hydrocarbon

Structure :

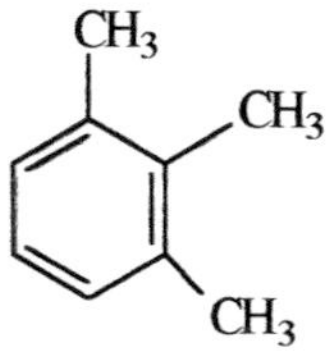

Air quality data summary :

Mean Air Concentration in Leeds, 19/8/94 to 8/9/94	
Location	21 day mean, $\mu g/m^3$
Albion Street	0.145
Cliff Lane	0.081
EUN monitoring site	0.132
Kerbside site	0.226
Kirkstall Road	0.336
Park site	0.116
Queen Street	0.173
Vicar Lane	0.522

Source: Bartle et al. (1995)

Chemical formula	:	C_9H_{12}
Alternative names	:	Pseudocumene
Type of pollutant	:	(Volatile) organic compound (VOC), hydrocarbon
Structure	:	

Air quality data summary :

Mean Air Concentration in Leeds, 19/8/94 to 8/9/94	
Location	21 day mean, µg/m^3
Albion Street	0.603
Cliff Lane	0.388
EUN monitoring site	0.641
Kerbside site	1.079
Kirkstall Road	1.594
Park site	0.472
Queen Street	0.841
Vicar Lane	2.608

Source: Bartle et al. (1995)

Chemical formula : C_9H_{12}

Alternative names : Mesitylene

Type of pollutant : (Volatile) organic compound (VOC), hydrocarbon

Structure :

Air quality data summary :

Mean Air Concentration in Leeds, 19/8/94 to 8/9/94	
Location	21 day mean, μg/m³
Albion Street	0.234
Cliff Lane	0.162
EUN monitoring site	0.245
Kerbside site	0.428
Kirkstall Road	0.609
Park site	0.230
Queen Street	0.338
Vicar Lane	0.951

Source: Bartle et al. (1995)

Note: These data represent concentrations of a 1,3,5-trimethylbenzene and 4-methyl nonane mixture.

Chemical formula	:	C_9H_{20}
Alternative names	:	
Type of pollutant	:	(Volatile) organic compound (VOC), hydrocarbon
Structure	:	

$$\begin{array}{l} \quad\;\; CH_3 \\ \quad\;\; | \\ CH_3-C-CH_2-CH_2-CH-CH_3 \\ \quad\;\; | \qquad\qquad\qquad\;\; | \\ \quad\;\; CH_3 \qquad\qquad\quad CH_3 \end{array}$$

Air quality data summary :

Mean Air Concentration in Leeds, 19/8/94 to 8/9/94	
Location	21 day mean, $\mu g/m^3$
Albion Street	0.035
Cliff Lane	0.040
EUN monitoring site	0.032
Kerbside site	0.047
Kirkstall Road	0.041
Park site	0.045
Queen Street	0.041
Vicar Lane	0.119

Source: Bartle et al. (1995)

2,2,4-Trimethylpentane

Chemical formula : C_8H_{18}

Alternative names : Isooctane

Type of pollutant : (Volatile) organic compound (VOC), hydrocarbon

Structure :

$$CH_3-\overset{\displaystyle CH_3}{\underset{\displaystyle CH_3}{\overset{|}{\underset{|}{C}}}}-CH_2-\underset{\displaystyle CH_3}{\underset{|}{CH}}-CH_3$$

Air quality data summary :

Mean Air Concentration in Leeds, 19/8/94 to 8/9/94	
Location	21 day mean, $\mu g/m^3$
Albion Street	0.510
Cliff Lane	0.287
EUN monitoring site	0.455
Kerbside site	0.589
Kirkstall Road	0.724
Park site	0.229
Queen Street	0.606
Vicar Lane	1.744

Source: Bartle et al. (1995)

Note: These data represent concentrations of a 2,2,4-trimethylpentane and 1,1,1-trichloroethane mixture.

Chemical formula	:	C_8H_{18}
Alternative names	:	
Type of pollutant	:	(Volatile) organic compound (VOC), hydrocarbon
Structure	:	

$$\mathrm{CH_3{-}\underset{\displaystyle CH_3}{\underset{|}{C}H}{-}\overset{\displaystyle CH_3}{\overset{|}{\underset{\displaystyle CH_3}{\underset{|}{C}}}}{-}CH_2{-}CH_3}$$

Air quality data summary :

Mean Air Concentration in Leeds, 19/8/94 to 8/9/94	
Location	21 day mean, µg/m³
Albion Street	0.088
Cliff Lane	0.057
EUN monitoring site	0.089
Kerbside site	0.119
Kirkstall Road	0.119
Park site	0.034
Queen Street	0.131
Vicar Lane	0.393

Source: Bartle et al. (1995)

2,3,4-Trimethylpentane

Chemical formula : C_8H_{18}

Alternative names :

Type of pollutant : (Volatile) organic compound (VOC), hydrocarbon

Structure :

$$CH_3-\underset{\displaystyle CH_3}{\underset{|}{CH}}-\underset{\displaystyle CH_3}{\underset{|}{CH}}-\underset{\displaystyle CH_3}{\underset{|}{CH}}-CH_3$$

Air quality data summary :

Mean Air Concentration in Leeds, 19/8/94 to 8/9/94	
Location	21 day mean, μg/m^3
Albion Street	0.208
Cliff Lane	0.133
EUN monitoring site	0.187
Kerbside site	0.285
Kirkstall Road	0.290
Park site	0.082
Queen Street	0.287
Vicar Lane	0.889

Source: Bartle et al. (1995)

Tungsten aerosol

Chemical formula : W

Alternative names : Particulate tungsten

Type of pollutant : Suspended particulate matter, trace element

Air quality data summary :

Rural Concentrations

Location	Average Annual Concentrations, ng/m^3	
	1972-1981	1982-1991
Harwell, Oxfordshire.	<0.6	<0.4
Styrrup, Nottinghamshire.	<1	<0.6
Trebanos, Glamorgan.	<0.6	
Wraymires, Cumbria.	<0.5	<0.4

Source: Cawse et al. (1994)

Tungsten in rain

Chemical formula : W

Alternative names : Precipitation tungsten

Type of pollutant : Trace contaminant of rain, trace element

Air quality data summary :

Rural Concentrations

Location	Average Annual Rainfall Concentration µg per litre	
	1972-1981	1982-1991 *
Harwell, Oxfordshire.	<1	<0.8
Styrrup, Nottinghamshire.	<1	<0.7
Wraymires, Cumbria.	<0.6	<1

Source: Cawse et al. (1994)

Note: total deposition expressed as apparent rainfall concentration.
* based on soluble fraction only.

Undecane

Chemical formula : $C_{11}H_{24}$

Alternative names : Hendecane

Type of pollutant : (Volatile) organic compound (VOC), hydrocarbon

Structure :

$CH_3—(CH_2)_9—CH_3$

Air quality data summary :

Mean Air Concentration in Leeds, 19/8/94 to 8/9/94	
Location	21 day mean, $\mu g/m^3$
Albion Street	0.169
Cliff Lane	0.106
EUN monitoring site	0.149
Kerbside site	0.190
Kirkstall Road	0.313
Park site	0.224
Queen Street	0.168
Vicar Lane	0.298

Source: Bartle et al. (1995)

Chemical formula : V

Alternative names : Particulate vanadium

Type of pollutant : Suspended particulate matter, trace element

Air quality data summary :

Rural Concentrations

Location	Average Annual Concentrations, ng/m^3			
	Mean	Trend	Mean	Trend
	1972-1981	%/yr	1982-1991	%/yr
Harwell, Oxfordshire.	11.2	-12.0	6.1	nst
Styrrup, Nottinghamshire.	14.9	-12.0	8.1	-8.1
Trebanos, Glamorgan.	11.7	-8.0	9.2	-
Wraymires, Cumbria.	7.7	-8.3	3.3	-9.2

Source: Cawse et al. (1994)

nst=no significant trend

Urban Concentrations

Location	Mean Annual Concentrations ng/m^3						
	1972-1981	1985	1986	1987	1988	1989	1990
Swansea	26.0						
Central London		14.3	13.5	14.3	16.1	15.2	19.7

Source: Pattenden(1974) , DoE (1992)

Location	Nature of site	Measurement period	Mean concentration ng/m^3
Altrincham	Residential	1978-1989	15.4
Brent	Residential	1975-1989	26.5
Chilton	Rural	1971-1989	9.0
Flixton	Residential	1975-1989	20.9
Lambeth	Residential	1976-1982	31.3
Manchester City North	Industrial/ Residential	1975-1988	26.7
Manchester City South	Residential	1975-1989	32.2
Walsall	Industrial	1976-1989	21.2
Wraymires	Rural	1970-1989	5.5

Source: Lee et al. (1995)

Chemical formula : V

Alternative names : Precipitation vanadium

Type of pollutant : Trace contaminant of rain, trace element

Air quality data summary :

Rural Concentrations

Location	Average Annual Rainfall Concentration µg per litre	
	1972-1981	1982-1991 *
Harwell, Oxfordshire.	7.5	2.6
Styrrup, Nottinghamshire.	13	2.3
Wraymires, Cumbria.	3.3	0.96

Source: Cawse et al. (1994)

Note: total deposition expressed as apparent rainfall concentration.
* based on soluble fraction only.

Chemical formula : C_8H_{10}

Alternative names : 1,3-dimethylbenzene, meta-xylene

Type of pollutant : (Volatile) organic compound (VOC), hydrocarbon

Structures :

Air quality data summary :

Remote rural concentrations

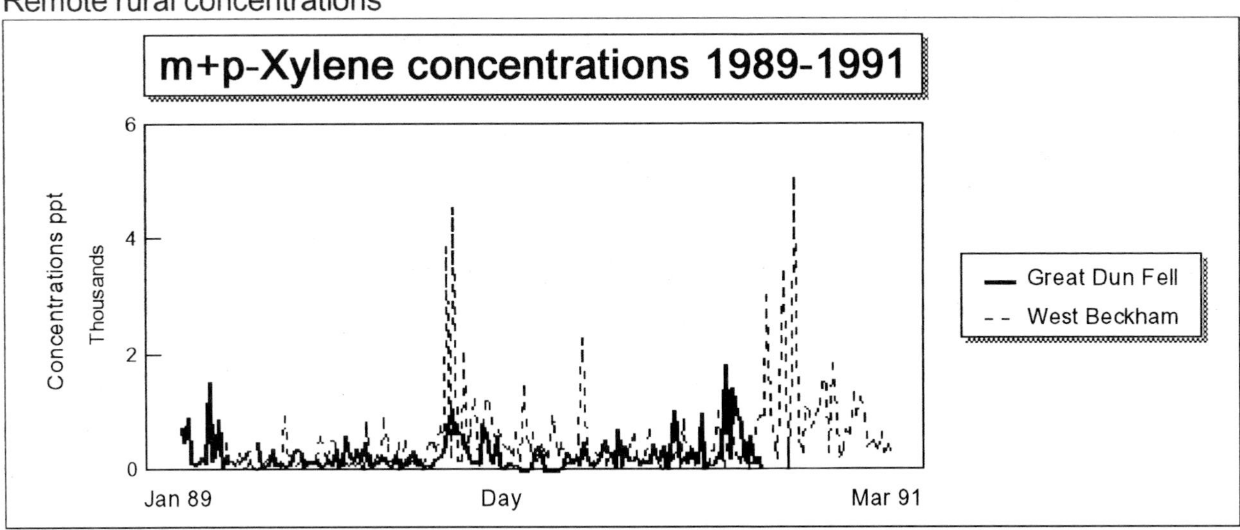

Source: PORG (1993)

Rural concentrations

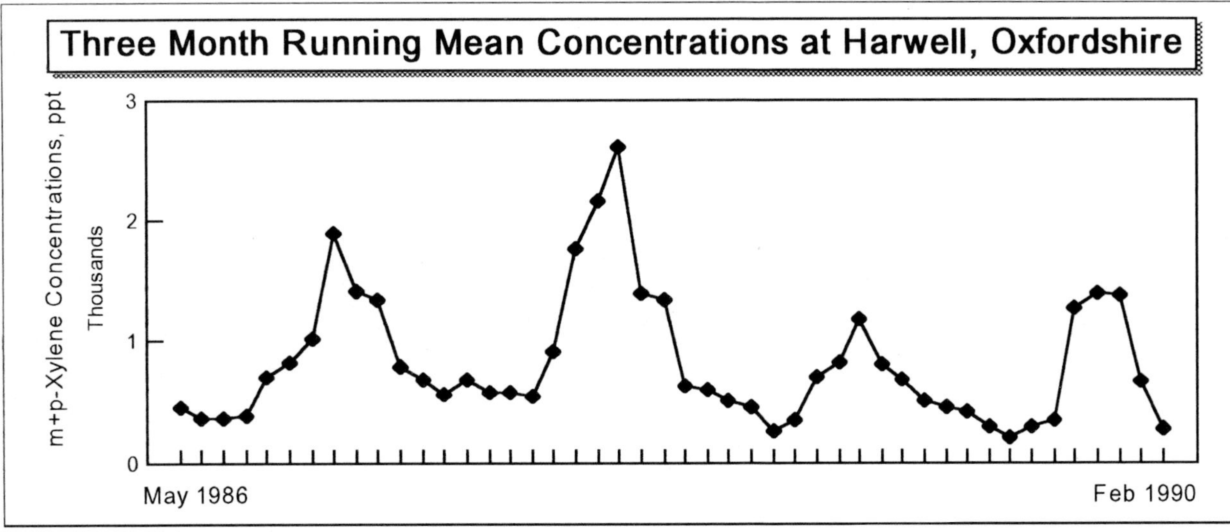

Source: PORG (1993)

Urban concentrations

	1994-95 Monthly Means, ppb (m+p-xylenes)								
	Belfast C	Birmingham B	Bristol A	Cardiff B	Edinburgh A	Eltham	Harwell	Middlesbrough	UCL
Jan 94	1.28	2.20	-	1.76	0.08	0.29	-	1.43	0.36
Feb 94	1.72	2.00	-	2.25	1.17	0.52	-	1.61	2.98
Mar 94	0.79	2.68	-	0.79	0.61	0.63	-	1.05	1.39
Apr 94	1.00	1.76	0.18	0.71	0.98	0.50	-	1.65	1.72
May 94	1.23	1.47	1.50	0.30	1.58	0.59	-	0.36	2.64
Jun 94	0.92	2.15	2.36	0.64	0.62	0.63	-	1.12	1.35
Jul 94	0.90	1.64	1.45	0.73	0.65	0.78	-	1.55	1.97
Aug 94	1.16	1.22	1.58	0.84	0.70	0.71	-	0.52	1.16
Sep 94	1.84	1.14	1.71	0.81	0.87	0.82	-	4.95	1.79
Oct 94	2.40	0.90	2.76	1.62	1.37	1.10	-	1.56	2.92
Nov 94	2.05	2.34	2.95	1.63	1.16	0.38	-	2.15	3.03
Dec 94	1.96	2.32	2.46	1.18	1.45	0.86	-	1.02	2.41
Jan 95	1.39	1.42	2.58	1.35	1.08	1.37	0.21	0.71	1.50
Feb 95	1.04	1.23	1.15	1.01	0.60	1.05	0.16	0.62	1.46

Source: Dollard (1995)

Mean Air Concentration in Leeds, 19/8/94 to 8/9/94	
Location	21 day mean, ppb
Albion Street	4.95
Cliff Lane	3.37
EUN monitoring site	5.38
Kerbside site	8.09
Kirkstall Road	9.20
Park site	3.59
Queen Street	6.72
Vicar Lane	20.47

Source: Bartle et al. (1995)

Note: These data represent values for a m-xylene and p-xylene mixture.

Six monthly mean concentrations of m- and p-xylene from July to December 1992, (ppb):

Location	Mean Concentration, ppb	Location	Mean Concentration, ppb
ADDLESTONE 1	1.3	BURHAM 1	0.3
BARKING 15	1.5	CAMPHILL 11	0.0
BATH 6	1.5	CARLISLE 13	0.5
BELFAST 13	1.5	CRAWLEY 3	0.8

Location	Mean Concentration, ppb	Location	Mean Concentration, ppb
BIRMINGHAM 26	2.6	MAIDSTONE 7	3.2
BRADFORD 22	1.3	MANCHESTER 11	1.5
BRISTOL 26	0.8	MANCHESTER 15	1.5
DARTFORD 9	1.1	MANCHESTER AIRPORT	0.2
DIBDEN PURLIEU 1	1.6	MIDDLESBROUGH 35	0.8
EALING 3	1.8	NORWICH 7	0.7
EDINBURGH 14	0.7	NOTTINGHAM 20	1.4
ELLESMERE PORT 9	7.2	PETERHEAD 2	0.2
ESTON 9	0.8	PLYMOUTH 11	0.9
GLASGOW 86	1.5	PONTYPOOL 7	1.6
GLASGOW 92	1.5	SELBY 4	0.5
GLASGOW 96	1.8	SHEFFIELD 86	0.5
GRANGEMOUTH 2	1.0	ST ALBANS 3	1.2
HAMMERSMITH 6	0.1	STAINFORTH 1	0.2
ILFORD 6	3.4	STEPNEY 5	1.0
ILKESTON 8	1.1	STEVENAGE 4	0.7
IMMINGHAM 5	0.4	ST HELENS 29	4.0
IPSWICH 14	0.9	SUNDERLAND 8	1.3
ISLINGTON 9	1.3	TEDDINGTON 3	1.3
KENSINGTON 11	1.2	WALSALL 15	1.1
KENSINGTON 14	2.9	WALTHAMSTOW 8	1.5
KNOTTINGLEY 1	0.9	WIDNES 9	0.6
LEEDS 37	0.9	WOLVERHAMPTON 7	0.3
LIVERPOOL 16	0.9	WREXHAM 7	1.1
LIVERPOOL 19	0.7	YORK 7	0.7
LONDONDERRY 11	1.3		

Source: Downing et al. (1994)

Notes: It is currently not possible to separate the two isomers (m+p)xylene in these data.

Chemical formula : C_8H_{10}

Alternative names : 1,2-dimethylbenzene, ortho-xylene

Type of pollutant : (Volatile) organic compound (VOC), hydrocarbon

Structure :

CH3 CH3

Air quality data summary :

Remote rural concentrations

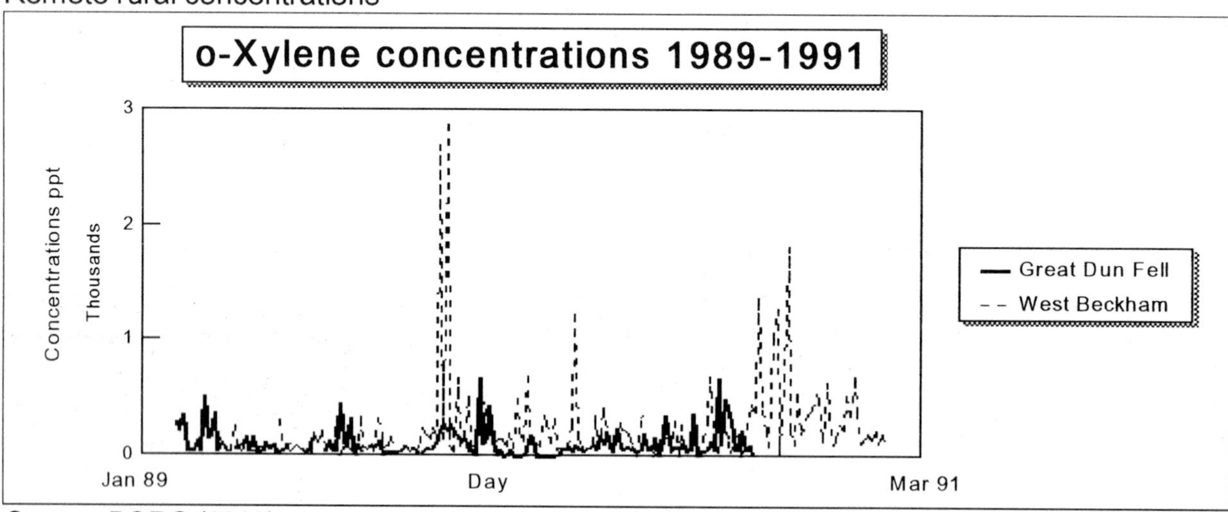

Source: PORG (1993)

Rural concentrations

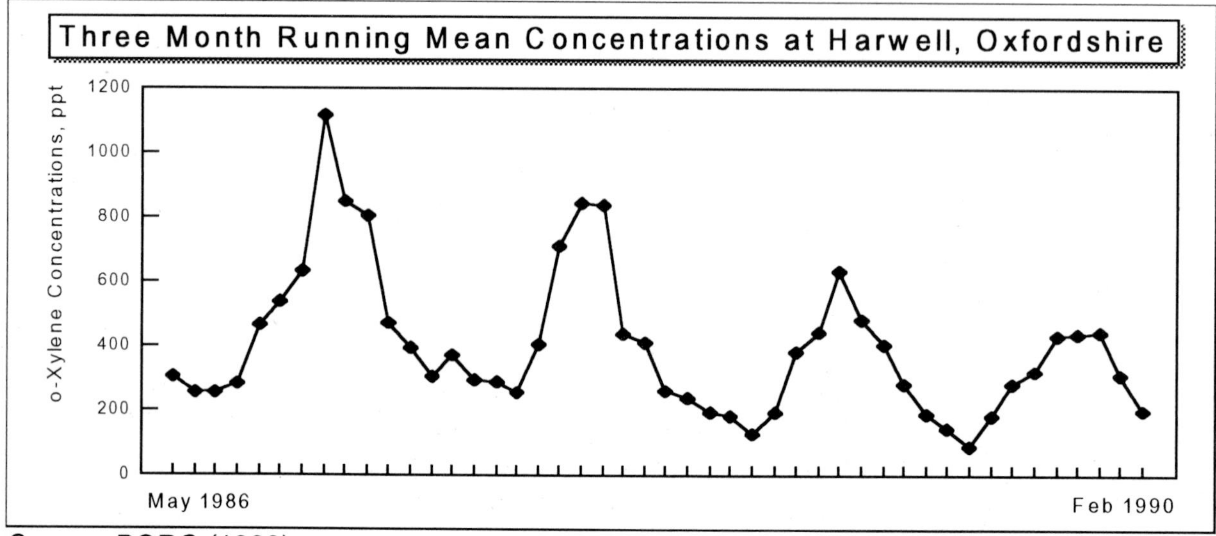

Source: PORG (1993)

Urban concentrations

	1994-95 Monthly Means, ppb								
	Belfast C	Birmingham B	Bristol A	Cardiff B	Edinburgh A	Eltham	Harwell	Middlesbrough	UCL
Jan 94	0.53	1.07	-	0.62	0.98	0.47	-	0.58	0.83
Feb 94	0.64	1.23	-	0.77	0.67	0.61	-	0.87	1.26
Mar 94	0.30	1.06	-	0.55	0.32	0.37	-	0.66	0.56
Apr 94	0.33	0.93	0.18	0.49	0.58	0.21	-	2.11	0.68
May 94	0.40	1.02	0.43	1.06	0.34	0.26	-	0.46	1.02
Jun 94	0.35	1.12	0.50	0.37	0.44	0.25	-	1.29	0.94
Jul 94	0.59	1.60	0.44	0.34	0.24	0.35	-	0.86	1.12
Aug 94	0.66	0.73	0.54	0.33	0.28	0.47	-	0.49	0.22
Sep 94	0.87	0.63	0.82	0.45	0.27	0.38	-	4.13	0.90
Oct 94	0.93	0.95	1.08	0.83	0.44	0.58	-	0.84	1.17
Nov 94	0.75	0.95	1.18	0.84	0.40	0.81	-	0.86	1.22
Dec 94	0.77	1.10	1.23	0.87	0.48	1.25	-	0.39	1.10
Jan 95	0.56	0.50	1.00	1.17	0.45	0.87	0.12	0.30	0.59
Feb 95	0.42	0.61	0.47	0.63	0.36	0.66	-	0.30	0.59

Source: Dollard (1995)

Six monthly mean concentrations of o-xylene from July to December 1992 (ppb):

Location	Mean Concentration, ppb	Location	Mean Concentration, ppb
ADDLESTONE 1	0.4	GRANGEMOUTH 2	0.2
BARKING 15	0.5	HAMMERSMITH 6	0.1
BATH 6	0.6	ILFORD 6	1.1
BELFAST 13	0.5	ILKESTON 8	0.4
BIRMINGHAM 26	0.6	IMMINGHAM 5	0.1
BRADFORD 22	0.5	IPSWICH 14	0.2
BRISTOL 26	0.2	ISLINGTON 9	0.4
BURHAM 1	0.1	KENSINGTON 11	0.4
CAMPHILL 11	0.1	KENSINGTON 14	1.1
CARLISLE 13	0.3	KNOTTINGLEY 1	0.7
CRAWLEY 3	0.3	LEEDS 37	0.2
DARTFORD 9	0.6	LIVERPOOL 16	0.3
DIBDEN PURLIEU 1	0.3	LIVERPOOL 19	0.3
EALING 3	0.7	LONDONDERRY 11	0.4
EDINBURGH 14	0.3	MAIDSTONE 7	1.3
ELLESMERE PORT 9	2.3	MANCHESTER 11	0.3
ESTON 9	0.4	MANCHESTER 15	0.5
GLASGOW 86	0.3	MANCHESTER AIRPORT	0.1
GLASGOW 92	0.3	MIDDLESBROUGH 35	0.3
GLASGOW 96	0.4	NORWICH 7	0.3

Location	Mean Concentration, ppb	Location	Mean Concentration, ppb
NOTTINGHAM 20	0.6	ST HELENS 29	0.9
PETERHEAD 2	0.1	SUNDERLAND 8	0.4
PLYMOUTH 11	0.3	TEDDINGTON 3	0.5
PONTYPOOL 7	0.6	WALSALL 15	0.5
SELBY 4	0.3	WALTHAMSTOW 8	0.6
SHEFFIELD 86	0.3	WIDNES 9	0.1
ST ALBANS 3	0.3	WOLVERHAMPTON 7	0.4
STAINFORTH 1	0.2	WREXHAM 7	0.4
STEPNEY 5	0.2	YORK 7	0.3
STEVENAGE 4	0.5		

Source: Downing et al. (1994)

Mean Air Concentration in Leeds, 19/8/94 to 8/9/94	
Location	21 day mean, ppb
Albion Street	2.33
Cliff Lane	1.56
EUN monitoring site	2.28
Kerbside site	3.80
Kirkstall Road	3.75
Park site	1.56
Queen Street	3.15
Vicar Lane	9.20

Source: Bartle et al. (1995)

p-Xylene

Chemical formula : C_8H_{10}

Alternative names : 1,4-dimethylbenzene

Type of pollutant : (Volatile) organic compound (VOC), hydrocarbon

Structure :

CH_3–C_6H_4–CH_3

Air quality data summary :

Remote rural concentrations

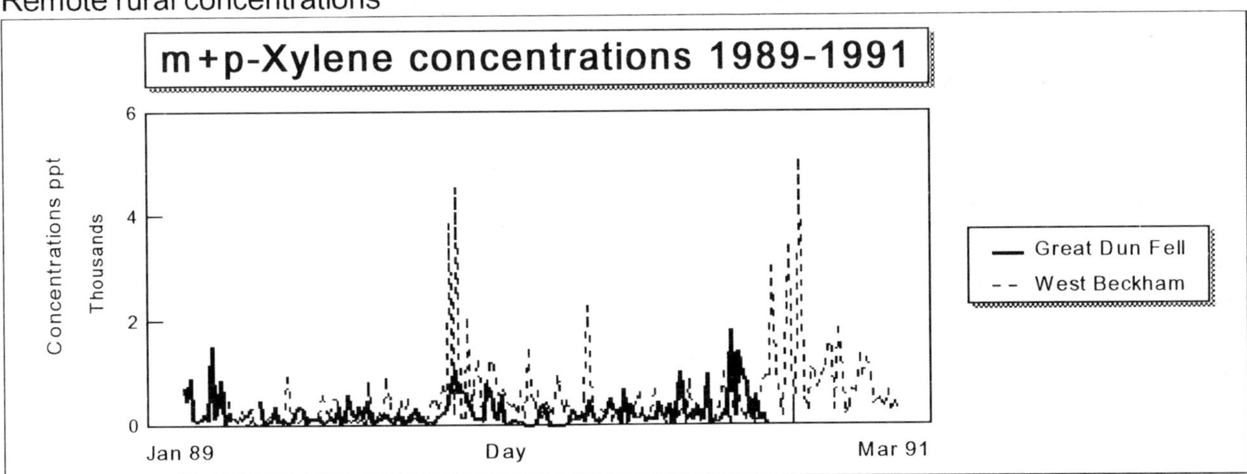

Source: PORG (1993)

Rural concentrations

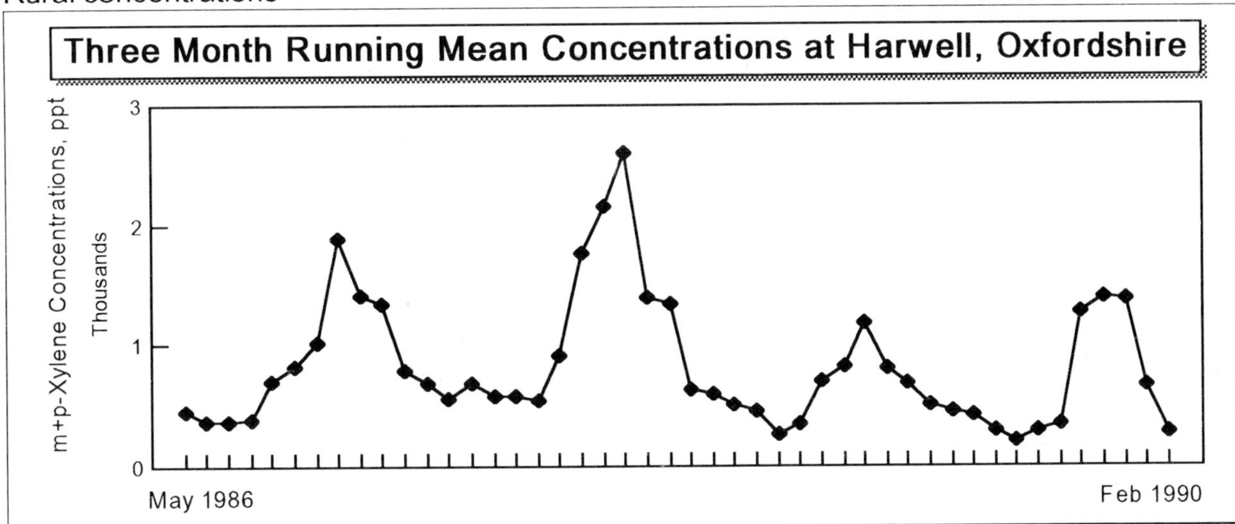

Source: PORG (1993)

Urban concentrations

1994-95 Monthly Means, ppb (m+p-xylenes)									
	Belfast C	Birmingham B	Bristol A	Cardiff B	Edinburgh A	Eltham	Harwell	Middlesbrough	UCL
Jan 94	1.28	2.20	-	1.76	0.08	0.29	-	1.43	0.36
Feb 94	1.72	2.00	-	2.25	1.17	0.52	-	1.61	2.98
Mar 94	0.79	2.68	-	0.79	0.61	0.63	-	1.05	1.39
Apr 94	1.00	1.76	0.18	0.71	0.98	0.50	-	1.65	1.72
May 94	1.23	1.47	1.50	0.30	1.58	0.59	-	0.36	2.64
Jun 94	0.92	2.15	2.36	0.64	0.62	0.63	-	1.12	1.35
Jul 94	0.90	1.64	1.45	0.73	0.65	0.78	-	1.55	1.97
Aug 94	1.16	1.22	1.58	0.84	0.70	0.71	-	0.52	1.16
Sep 94	1.84	1.14	1.71	0.81	0.87	0.82	-	4.95	1.79
Oct 94	2.40	0.90	2.76	1.62	1.37	1.10	-	1.56	2.92
Nov 94	2.05	2.34	2.95	1.63	1.16	0.38	-	2.15	3.03
Dec 94	1.96	2.32	2.46	1.18	1.45	0.86	-	1.02	2.41
Jan 95	1.39	1.42	2.58	1.35	1.08	1.37	0.21	0.71	1.50
Feb 95	1.04	1.23	1.15	1.01	0.60	1.05	0.16	0.62	1.46

Source: Dollard (1995)

Mean Air Concentration in Leeds, 19/8/94 to 8/9/94	
Location	21 day mean, ppb
Albion Street	4.95
Cliff Lane	3.37
EUN monitoring site	5.38
Kerbside site	8.09
Kirkstall Road	9.20
Park site	3.59
Queen Street	6.72
Vicar Lane	20.47

Source: Bartle et al. (1995)

Note: These data represent results for a m-xylene and p-xylene mixture.

Six monthly mean concentrations of m- and p-xylenes from July to December 1992 (ppb):

Location	Mean Concentration, ppb	Location	Mean Concentration, ppb
ADDLESTONE 1	1.3	BRADFORD 22	1.3
BARKING 15	1.5	BRISTOL 26	0.8
BATH 6	1.5	BURHAM 1	0.3
BELFAST 13	1.5	CAMPHILL 11	0.0
BIRMINGHAM 26	2.6	CARLISLE 13	0.5

Location	Mean Concentration, ppb	Location	Mean Concentration, ppb
CRAWLEY 3	0.8	MANCHESTER 11	1.5
DARTFORD 9	1.1	MANCHESTER 15	1.5
DIBDEN PURLIEU 1	1.6	MANCHESTER AIRPORT	0.2
EALING 3	1.8	MIDDLESBROUGH 35	0.8
EDINBURGH 14	0.7	NORWICH 7	0.7
ELLESMERE PORT 9	7.2	NOTTINGHAM 20	1.4
ESTON 9	0.8	PETERHEAD 2	0.2
GLASGOW 86	1.5	PLYMOUTH 11	0.9
GLASGOW 92	1.5	PONTYPOOL 7	1.6
GLASGOW 96	1.8	SELBY 4	0.5
GRANGEMOUTH 2	1.0	SHEFFIELD 86	0.5
HAMMERSMITH 6	0.1	ST ALBANS 3	1.2
ILFORD 6	3.4	STAINFORTH 1	0.2
ILKESTON 8	1.1	STEPNEY 5	1.0
IMMINGHAM 5	0.4	STEVENAGE 4	0.7
IPSWICH 14	0.9	ST HELENS 29	4.0
ISLINGTON 9	1.3	SUNDERLAND 8	1.3
KENSINGTON 11	1.2	TEDDINGTON 3	1.3
KENSINGTON 14	2.9	WALSALL 15	1.1
KNOTTINGLEY 1	0.9	WALTHAMSTOW 8	1.5
LEEDS 37	0.9	WIDNES 9	0.6
LIVERPOOL 16	0.9	WOLVERHAMPTON 7	0.3
LIVERPOOL 19	0.7	WREXHAM 7	1.1
LONDONDERRY 11	1.3	YORK 7	0.7
MAIDSTONE 7	3.2		

Source: Downing et al. (1994)

Notes: It is currently not possible to separate the two isomers (m+p)xylene in these data.

Zinc aerosol

Chemical formula : Zn

Alternative names : Particulate zinc

Type of pollutant : Suspended particulate matter, trace element

Air quality data summary :

Rural Concentrations

Location	Annual Concentrations, ng/m^3			
	Mean	Trend	Mean	Trend
	1972-1981	%/yr	1982-1991	%/yr
Harwell, Oxfordshire.	99	-13.0	38	nst
Styrrup, Nottinghamshire.	229	-15.0	125	-7.5
Trebanos, Glamorgan.	130	-19.7	51	-
Wraymires, Cumbria.	59	-12.9	22	nst

Source: Cawse et al. (1994)
nst=no significant trend

Urban Concentrations

Location	Mean Annual Concentrations, ng/m^3						
	1972-1981	1985	1986	1987	1988	1989	1990
Swansea	384.0						
Central London		90.6	93.4	93.9	119.9	111.1	139.1
Brent		71.8	63.7	161.6	125.0	42.9	53.9
Motherwell		240.5	227.8	220.4	359.4	221.4	211.8
Glasgow C		110.3	127.4	156.6	135.6	95.4	95.0
Leeds		106.5	82.3	78.8	89.3	65.0	66.4

Source: Pattenden (1974), DoE (1992)

Location	Nature of site	Measurement period	Mean concentration ng/m^3
Altrincham	Residential	1978-1989	113
Brent	Residential	1975-1989	126
Chilton	Rural	1971-1989	76
Flixton	Residential	1975-1989	115
Lambeth	Residential	1976-1982	177
Manchester City North	Industrial/ Residential	1975-1988	339
Manchester City South	Residential	1975-1989	134
Walsall	Industrial	1976-1989	2634
Wraymires	Rural	1970-1989	39

Source: Lee et al. (1995)

Chemical formula : Zn

Alternative names : Precipitation zinc

Type of pollutant : Trace contaminant of rain, trace element

Air quality data summary :

Rural Concentrations

Location	Average Annual Rainfall Concentration, µg per litre	
	1972-1981	1982-1991 *
Harwell, Oxfordshire.	73	41
Styrrup, Nottinghamshire.	172	48
Wraymires, Cumbria.	27	53

Source: Cawse et al. (1994)

Note: total deposition expressed as apparent rainfall concentration.
* based on soluble fraction only.